The First Cold War

The First Cold War

*The Legacy of Woodrow Wilson
in U.S.-Soviet Relations*

Donald E. Davis *&* Eugene P. Trani

University of Missouri Press
Columbia and London

Copyright © 2002 by
The Curators of the University of Missouri
University of Missouri Press, Columbia, Missouri 65201
Printed and bound in the United States of America
5 4 3   06 05 04 03

Library of Congress Cataloging-in-Publication Data

Davis, Donald E.
    The first Cold War : the legacy of Woodrow Wilson in U.S.-Soviet relations /
    Donald E. Davis and Eugene P. Trani.
        p. cm.
    Includes bibliographical references and index.
    ISBN 0-8262-1388-X (alk. paper)
    1. United States—Foreign relations—Soviet Union. 2. Soviet Union—
Foreign relations—United States. 3. United States—Foreign relations—
1913–1921. 4. Wilson, Woodrow, 1856–1924. 5. Soviet Union—History—
Allied intervention, 1918–1920. 6. United States—Foreign relations—
1945–1989. 7. Cold War. I. Trani, Eugene P. II. Title.

183.8S65 D386 2002
327.7304'09'041—dc21

                                                                    20020224566

⊗™ This paper meets the requirements of the
American National Standard for Permanence of Paper
for Printed Library Materials, Z39.48, 1984.

Designer: Jennifer Cropp
Typesetter: Bookcomp, Inc.
Printer and binder: Thomson-Shore, Inc.
Typefaces: Cochin

To the memory of
Richard D. McKinzie

Contents

Foreword

by Lawrence S. Eagleburger

This book is more than just an "interesting" addition to the voluminous catalog of Cold War studies. Rather, it is a major contribution to our understanding of the roots of a struggle that consumed us for the better part of half a century.

The authors' thesis is that a relatively straight line can be drawn from the attitudes and policies of the Wilson administration toward the Soviet Union (after much fumbling around in search of a policy) to the attitudes and policies of postwar American administrations toward the USSR (after rejection of Franklin D. Roosevelt's more conciliatory approach). In short, the "Cold War"—in its fundamentals of how the Soviets were perceived and to be dealt with—had its genesis some decades earlier than is commonly thought to be the case. The detailed explication of this thesis is thoroughly and compellingly made.

So what? It is here that *The First Cold War* makes a unique contribution. It tells us more about ourselves, how and what we think about our place in the world and how we go about furthering our interests, than simply a recitation of events over some five decades. It describes the factors that affected the thinking (or lack thereof) of policy makers over a significant period of time, and explains the policies they embraced. And in the end we see how U.S. foreign policy is as much a product of the American psyche— rooted in a history of more than two centuries—as it is of any event or series of events.

On a more mundane level, this is an extremely well sourced work. The footnotes not only identify from whence the footnoted items come, but often themselves add clarifying comments that are both interesting and useful. They also are evidence of meticulous research into the vast and often maze-like store of documents, papers, notes, and scholarly (and not so scholarly) works pertaining to the Russian Revolution and its aftermath in the Soviet Union and internationally.

Further, and somewhat to my surprise, the University of Missouri Press has found two academics who write intelligible and interesting prose with style and verve. They should be husbanded for future use.

Lawrence S. Eagleburger
Charlottesville, Virginia
July 2001

Mr. Eagleburger joined the Foreign Service in 1957, was first posted to Honduras, and then served on the Cuban desk. He was assigned to the Belgrade embassy in 1961, returning there as ambassador in 1977. He has been a special assistant to Dean Acheson and Henry Kissinger as well as an assistant secretary, undersecretary, deputy secretary, and finally secretary of state in 1992. His many awards include the Presidential Citizens Medal, the State Department's Distinguished Service Award, and honorary knighthood bestowed by Queen Elizabeth II. He is currently international ambassador-at-large for the American Red Cross.

Foreword to the Russian Edition

by Vyacheslav Nikonov

It is a very rare honor to write the foreword for your teachers' book. I have this honor.

As a graduate student at Moscow State University in 1981, I listened to Professor Eugene Trani's lectures about his interpretation of Wilsonianism. Richard McKinzie, a kind of third coauthor, also taught at Moscow State University, but not so long ago he died prematurely. I knew Donald Davis from Illinois State University well, but rather from his work than personally. All these serious and talented scholars dedicated more than twenty years to this book. It should be regarded as a very serious study on a subject to which the reading part of the Russian public cannot remain indifferent.

Lately, in order to understand ourselves, we have thought a lot about our past to get to the essence of events and phenomena. It is difficult to suppose that the reader is not familiar with 1917, the intervention, and the civil war. However, our perspective is from the inside. Trani and Davis offer the widest view from the outside. Scrupulously studying the archives of America, Russia, and other countries, they re-create the amazingly convex picture that existed in the minds of Western politicians during our revolutionary cataclysms. We have a unique opportunity to glance into the kitchen where the policy relating to Russia was cooked up, to understand the logic that in the final analysis led to almost a century of conflict between the East and the West.

This book is provocative in a good sense of this word. The authors very convincingly prove that the "Cold War" began long before George Kennan addressed the issue of the "containment of communism" in 1947. Woodrow Wilson and his secretaries of state, Lansing and Colby, by the early 1920s had already formulated all the ingredients that at the end of the 1940s Walter Lippmann included in his "Cold War" formula. It is possible to agree with this, taking note of the amazing similarity of the ideas of the Wilsonians and the postwar American politicians of the Truman era. One can argue this proposition by emphasizing the difference in the historical epochs and the absence in the 1920s of the global bipolar rivalry that unfolded in the nuclear and missile age. A beautiful idea and, as with each beautiful and well-proven idea, it deserves applause.

In the book of Davis and Trani, a kaleidoscope of stormy events passes before us from Petrograd and Washington, Archangel and Seattle, Omsk and Paris, Vladivostok and London, Murmansk and Tokyo. Ideology, geopolitics, military interests, allied obligations, internal political events, class contradictions, historical prejudices, human defects, errors, and ignorance whirled about.

The authors clearly show that both the United States and Russia were very badly prepared for the challenges to bilateral relations thrust upon them in 1917. The two countries did not know each other, were not interested in each other, and strongly disliked each other.

If we had even more courage than Davis and Trani, we could have detected the signs of the "Cold War" even before the First World War. American public opinion considered tsarist Russia the citadel of despotism. The American press portrayed our country as disgusting. In the United States, Nicholas II was presented as the symbol of tyranny. In St. Petersburg, Wilson was considered a dangerous radical liberal. Only one percent of Russia's and the United States' trade was with each other. The only issue on the relationship's agenda was the future of a trade treaty signed in 1832. The United States abrogated this treaty in 1912 because of Jewish lobbyists who were unhappy about the discrimination against Jews with American passports when they came to Russia. Here it is easy to make analogies with that time and, say, the 1970s when the Jackson-Vanik amendment (still effective) tied the application of the Soviet Union's status of most favored nation to the freedom of Jewish emigration.

Woodrow Wilson, upon becoming president in 1913, had alternately appointed three ambassadors to Russia. Two never reached St. Petersburg. Only after two years was the fourth try crowned by success—David Francis arrived and to his astonishment discovered that the embassy did not even subscribe to one Russian newspaper.

In the beginning of the First World War, the United States remained neutral. Francis's function amounted to unsuccessful attempts to mediate between the belligerent sides. More fruitful actions were undertaken at the request of Berlin and Vienna on improving the position of German and Austrian prisoners of war. Together with the entire Russian progressive public, the ambassador was shocked by "ministerial leapfrog" and considered tsarist premiers incorrigible reactionaries. He was very surprised by the overthrow of tsarism. That fact one can hardly hold against him since all direct participants in the process, including Lenin, were astonished.

After February 1917, a period of democratic Russophilism began in the United States. Washington, with the assistance of Francis, was the first to recognize the Provisional Government of Prince Lvov. The global picture that the Russian empire had spoiled was now clarified: the completely democratic Entente now opposed the authoritarian Central Powers headed by Germany. America could enter the war for the defense of democratic values with good reason.

In greeting the "democratic Russian people, who had thrown out an autocracy that was alien to it," American leadership was certain that such a people would put all of its forces on the altar of a common victory over Germany. The miscalculation was enormous: the democratic instincts of the people, their desire to wage war, and the ability of the Provisional Government to control the situation in the country were greatly exaggerated. The forces of radicalism, anarchy, and Soviet opposition were grossly underestimated. Instead of helping Lvov and Kerensky, who immediately found themselves to be in a desperate position, the Wilson administration at first got involved in a policy review. Then it created a commission that arrived in Petrograd in June with the formula, "no fight, no loan."

Disorders in the country and an unwillingness to fight were diagnosed as a public relations problem. To solve it, large amounts of money were allotted in the struggle with German propaganda and for the education of Russians in democratic values. The Provisional Government was driven into conditions in which to obtain locomotives, loans, or military deliveries, it was forced to chase unwilling people to the front and to promote liberal ideas that were completely meaningless for the overwhelming majority of the population. In spite of numerous warnings that without Western aid Kerensky could not survive, Wilson did practically nothing for his support. When the Bolsheviks had already made the decision for an armed uprising, Francis attempted to force Kerensky to organize an offensive at the front. It seemed as if the only thing Americans could do to help him was to make available the automobile of the ambassador's assistant for Kerensky's escape from Petrograd. The role of the West in the fall of the Provisional Government was really impressive.

Davis and Trani have vividly depicted these intellectual torments that Wilson and his team in Petrograd experienced after the October coup. Three approaches collided: Judson, chief of the military mission, and the leaders of the Red Cross mission correctly supposed that the Bolsheviks, having taken power, had ceased being German spies and had converted to becoming defenders of Russia, and thus that de facto recognition of Lenin would help restore the front; Consul General Summers, on the contrary, issued a call to unambiguously and publicly refuse recognizing the Soviets. In the end, a third point of view won—that of Ambassador Francis, who proposed doing nothing in the expectation that any day the Bolshevik regime would collapse.

The novelty of the American position was that up to October 1917 the chief motive was the retention of Russia in the war, and afterwards it was the total nonacceptance of the Bolsheviks. Already in December, Secretary of State Lansing drew the conclusion (not changed later) that the Bolsheviks were inhuman, dishonorable, and unprincipled; they had created an authoritarian system relying on force; they wanted to throw out free capitalism and replace it with an extremist form of proletarian despotism. The danger was realized almost reflexively: for the first time in history, a regime had come to power in a powerful state that openly rejected and challenged Western values and lifestyles, and which in this case proposed its own radical alternative, and on a global scale at that. For the overthrow of the Bolshevik regime, Lansing considered it possible to forget (for a time) about democracy and to support the establishment of a military dictatorship with the aid of troops who would ensure stability and Russia's participation in the war.

Any kind of diplomatic contact with Lenin or Trotsky was forbidden. There were ambassadors and embassies, but they did not communicate with the authorities. Moreover, in February 1918 some of them actually moved to Vologda. The West began to consider Russia as a subjectless state with no government, but with separate illegitimate political players. Bolshevik attempts to secure some kind of support from the United States in opposition to the German invasion or to entice countries of the Entente to the peace negotiations at Brest met with no response.

The idea of influencing the Russian problem by the most decisive means lingered in the air and gradually ripened. Obviously, Wilson did not want to interfere. American public opinion, as before, had little interest in Russia, and involvement in the internal affairs of a distant and mysterious country contradicted the president's democratic principles and the isolationist political tradition of the United States.

The following events changed America's position to the side of intervention: Bolshevik dispersal of the Constituent Assembly, Bolshevik conclusion of the Brest peace with the Germans (in many respects forced in the absence of a hint of aid from the West), and the extreme pressure from the governments of England and France, who desperately sought restoration of the eastern front and the overthrow of Lenin. At the end of December 1917, London and Paris had already divided the south of Russia into spheres of influence: England's included the Kuban, the North Caucasus, and Transcaucasia, while France's included Bessarabia, Ukraine, and the Crimea. They began rendering direct aid to Generals Kaledin, Alekseyev, and Kornilov. The Anglo-French projects included, likewise, the landing of the Japanese in the Maritime Provinces and their occupation of the Trans-Siberian railroad, establishment of control over the northern seaports, and a possible direct military intervention into Russia.

Wilson could not openly aid anti-Bolshevik forces since for this, according to American laws, Congress had to declare war on Russia. It clearly did not burn with a desire to do this. The Wilson administration feared a massive presence of mainly Japanese allied forces in Siberia because this might arouse pro-Bolshevik nationalist feelings. In addition, it was not clear just how to get the Japanese out afterwards. However, during April and May 1918, under the influence of both the allies and the decisive men in his own administration, Wilson gave in and agreed to a limited intervention.

The plan was simple and looked effective. Allied troops were put ashore at Murmansk and Archangel to shield military stores and transport communications from the Germans and their Finnish allies. Limited Anglo-Japanese contingents established control over Vladivostok and the Trans-Siberian railroad to Irkutsk from the east. The White Guard was armed and supplied (secretly from the side of the United States) to keep the Germans out of southern Russia, to establish democratic regimes, and to overthrow the Bolsheviks. The Czechoslovaks, whom the Bolshevik government improvidently allowed to evacuate to France through the Maritime Provinces, were to seize the Trans-Siberian railway from the west. The Czechoslovak presence also gave an additional justification for intervention: these "cousins of the Russians" prevented the transformation of Siberia into a "German granary" and were needed "to defend Siberia from the uncontrolled activity of former German and Austrian prisoners of war."

The plan was implemented almost completely. In Archangel and Murmansk, the American expeditionary forces (AEFNR) of about five thousand men were deployed. Following the Japanese and English occupation of Vladivostok, about eighty-five hundred American soldiers of the Twenty-seventh and Thirty-first infantry regiments arrived from the Philippines. Czechoslovaks overthrew the Soviet regime from the Urals to the Pacific Ocean. By the way, the authors of the book, in my view, actually somewhat underestimate the role of the foreign factor in kindling the bonfire of the Russian civil war.

When the German revolution occurred and Berlin capitulated in November 1918, the former anti-German justification for intervention disappeared.

In Russia, two unfinished goals remained: the White armies still had not established democratic authority, and the Bolsheviks had not been overthrown. The question about the future of Russia became one of the central issues at the Paris conference that during the entire first half of 1919 was putting an end to the world war.

A decisive Winston Churchill argued for a war with the Bolsheviks by the forces of the English and French armies with the support of the Poles, Czechs, Finns, and White Guards. The more moderate French Marshal Foch proposed to organize an intervention by Polish troops, which were to be withdrawn from France as a prelude to a subsequent linking of Western allied forces. Wilson and English Premier Lloyd George, clashing with the explicit unwillingness of their own peoples to prolong the "pleasures" of war and not convinced in a full and quick success of the enterprise, rejected the most belligerent projects. They rejected the hand extended by Moscow. Moscow was not represented in Paris, but was prepared to recognize tsarist debts, open doors for foreign investments and concessions, stop revolutionary activity abroad, grant amnesty to the enemies of the Leninist regime, and recognize the independence of Finland, Poland, and Ukraine in exchange for diplomatic recognition and the cessation of intervention. The rationality of such a compromise was confirmed for Wilson by the February 1919 Bullitt Mission. It concluded that Lenin's position was solid and that the victory of Kolchak and Denikin would lead to a still greater bloodbath.

Bullitt's conclusions did not appear in time. Revolution in Hungary and other events, which testified to the rapid propagation of Bolshevism in Germany, Poland, the Baltic states, Austria, and Italy, gave birth to the "red scare" in the West and repulsed Americans from any kind of a desire to associate with the Soviets. Wilson decided that only a victory of the White Movement would return Russia to democracy. Western governments divided responsibilities: the English supplied Denikin, the French, the Czechoslovaks, while the United States took it upon itself to provision Kolchak.

Meanwhile, the American military presence in Russia began to cause perplexing questions in the U.S. Congress. Wilson rushed to remove troops from Archangel and to assure the legislators that the contingent in Siberia was necessary for the protection of American railroad engineers and to aid in the delivery of humanitarian freight. Simultaneously, the president sent to Kolchak a commission headed by Morris and Graves. They gave detailed information about Kolchak's activity, which the reader for the first time can glean from this book. The commission arrived at the conclusion that the personal honesty of Kolchak and the moderately liberal views of the civilian members of the Omsk government could in no way compensate for the total disorganization of his army, wallowing in intrigues and the corruption of the reactionary military. The British war cabinet also came to analogous conclusions in relation to Denikin. The White-Czechoslovaks asked to go home. The beginning of the end of large-scale interference by the West in Russian internal affairs started in August and September of 1919. Namely, at this time, as Davis and Trani show, the "hot" war began to give way to the "cold" war.

After the sharp but successful fight in the Congress over the ratification of the Paris agreement and the League of Nations (where the isolationist mood of Americans needed to be forcefully dragged), Wilson set out on a tour along the western states of the country to try to carry these states. That is when he formulated the basic postulates of the "first Cold War." The League of Nations headed by the United States would erect a barrier to the path of the Bolsheviks, who were "just as ruthless, just as pitiless as the agents of the Czar himself," and who extended "night, chaos, and disorder" and, therefore, must fall.

The final passage to the "first Cold War," in the opinion of the book's authors, was already formulated when Wilson, because of his malady (from October 1919), stopped participating actively in governmental affairs. Lansing by this time had ascertained that the Bolsheviks could not be over-thrown by force, that they would only surrender their position gradually, and that with the advent of new leaders it might be possible to deal. As an irony of fate, it became necessary to deal with Stalin, who was not at all prepared to surrender any positions.

At the end of 1919, the United States began to evacuate its troops from the Maritime Provinces. In February of the following year, the Irkutsk revolutionary committee executed Kolchak, and seventy-two thousand Czech-oslovaks stretched themselves from Vladivostok to their native land. It remained for Moscow to cope with the Japanese, the troops of Pilsudski, who was dissatisfied with the eastern borders of Poland along the "Curzon Line" and consequently captured Kiev, and the remainders of the White Guards under Wrangel's banner.

The document that the authors argue formulated the "first Cold War" was the note that on August 9, 1920, was issued under Bainbridge Colby's authorship. He had replaced Lansing as secretary of state. The United States itself declared the guarantee of the territorial integrity and independence of Poland, officially took up the nonrecognition of the Soviet regime, and laid on itself the mission of opposition to the extension of world revolution. However, the American government was prepared to close its eyes to private trade with Russian companies.

Such a policy also was continued by subsequent Republican administrations, who little understood Russia but stood on even more rigid anti-communist positions. This gave Stalin numerous occasions to talk about hostile imperialist encirclement. To oppose imperialist encirclement, it was necessary to turn the screws within the country. The upper chronological boundary of the "first Cold War" Davis and Trani define as 1933, when Franklin Roosevelt extended diplomatic recognition to the Soviet Union. He was the last Western leader to do so.

The authors of the book treat Wilson's policy in relation to Russia rather critically, considering that the president missed a chance to direct Russia along a democratic path because of the incorrect counsels of his advisers, the embassy, and his own indecision. He hardly deserves this criticism. First, Wilson's policy was not and could not be independent and carefully thought out. America still did not have the experience of interaction with Russia, and the world had encountered a new phenomenon—communism. The U.S. president in many respects followed his English and French allies and frequently acted under their influence in order that they would leave him alone. Second, I do not believe that a chance to democratize Russia then, in general, existed, considering the inertia of the Russian political tradition, the concrete situation, and the balance of political forces in the country in 1917. That is all the more so because Davis and Trani themselves introduce a formula that deserves to enter into the annals of political thought: "Perhaps it is not in the realm of possibility for one state to save another from its destiny, if destiny it be." Wilson attempted to refute this formula; it did not materialize.

The famous Russian historian Vasilii Klyuchevksy noted the surprising repetition of Russian history. However, it is obvious that repetition or, more precisely, stereotyping, is characteristic not only for our country but also for all of world history. Once developed, clichés and behavioral models emerge time after time and in similar conditions. The stereotypes that emerged after the First World War were easily reproduced after the Second World War and prevailed to the last decade of the twentieth century.

Humankind grows only slightly wiser. But now there is hope that in the future Russia and the United States will no longer reach the level of hostility and mutual misapprehension that arose in the years of the "first Cold War."

Well, so much for the foreword.

Read a very professional and well-written history.

Vyacheslav Nikonov
President, Polity Foundation
Doctor of History, July 25, 2001

Dr. Nikonov, Molotov's grandson, is the founder and president of the Polity Foundation. He holds a Ph.D. in history from Moscow State University and is the author of numerous articles and five books. He served in the Russian State Duma from 1994–1996 and chaired the Subcommittee for International Security and Arms Control. Polity is involved in numerous projects and works closely with such organizations as the World Bank and the Carnegie Endowment.

Preface

In this book we contend that President Woodrow Wilson's administration initiated a "cold war" that lasted from 1917 to 1933. This set a precedent for the Cold War, 1946 to 1991. Wilson reached this stance during a period of policy experimentation with Soviet Russia from November 7, 1917, to August 9, 1920. He first publicly enunciated his version of a cold war doctrine during a speaking tour of the western United States in the fall of 1919. He made that doctrine official policy in the Colby Note, issued August 9, 1920, by Secretary of State Bainbridge Colby. The Colby Note, with some amendments introduced during the administration of President Warren G. Harding, remained the basis of American relations with Soviet Russia until November 16, 1933. At that time, President Franklin D. Roosevelt normalized relations by recognizing Soviet Russia.

We analyze our thesis, what we call the "first cold war, 1917–1933," in a chronological narrative. The Introduction discusses America's unpreparedness for dealing with Russia in 1913 when Woodrow Wilson became president. Chapters 1 and 2 show the tentative steps President Wilson took in appointing a permanent ambassador to Imperial Russia. He lacked faith in his third and final appointment, David R. Francis. Wilson's uncertainty about Russia and Ambassador Francis, further complicated by the overthrow of Tsar Nicholas II on March 15, 1917, led him to policy-making by committee: appointing the Root Mission and the Stevens Railway Commission in the spring of 1917, after America entered World War I, to solve the Russian riddle. Wilson lost an opportunity to save Russian democracy because of his committees' and ambassador's confusing advice and his own tentativeness.

Chapters 3 through 5 examine various alternative policies, clandestine or public, confronting President Wilson in his effort to deal with the Bolshevik Revolution of November 7, 1917. He first selected a watch-and-wait policy, hoping that Soviet power would be quickly overthrown and that the Provisional Government would prevail. He steadfastly refused to recognize Lenin's government, which threatened to take Russia out of World War I. Instead, he adopted a propaganda initiative aimed at convincing Lenin to stay in the war. Failing this, he hoped that counterrevolutionaries would either seize power or establish rival governments that maintained the Eastern Front. Watching and waiting failed because Lenin stayed in power and the Soviet government signed the Treaty of Brest-Litovsk on March 3, 1918, with Germany and its allies. This occurred in spite of Wilson's Fourteen Points address of January 8, 1918, his message to the Fourth All-Russian Congress of Soviets of March 11, 1918, and various unofficial efforts at accommodation with Lenin and Trotsky.

In Chapter 6, we demonstrate that British and French pressure forced Wilson to intervene militarily in northern Russia and Siberia. The intervention aimed to resurrect the Eastern Front, protect Allied supplies stored in Russia, help stabilize democracy where it existed, and support the exodus of the Czechoslovak Legion—soldiers recruited into the tsar's army. Intervention failed in all but the last goal. Chapter 7 deals with the president's efforts during the Paris Peace Conference in the spring of 1919 to salvage his Russian policy by inviting belligerents in Russia's civil war to the bargaining table at Prinkipo; only the Bolsheviks accepted that offer. Wilson's trusted adviser, Edward M. House, then sent William C. Bullitt to Moscow to reach an accommodation with Lenin. Bad publicity spoiled this opportunity. Wilson explored the possibility of feeding starving Russia. However, the Bolsheviks sought recognition before accepting the food relief offered by Norwegian explorer Fridtjof Nansen. Chapter 8 details Wilson's frustrations with the Bolsheviks and with the failure of Admiral Alexander Kolchak's Siberian movement to offer sanctuary for the reconstitution of a democratic Russia. At that point, Wilson issued the Colby Note.

We conclude by comparing President Wilson's Russian policy to President Harry S. Truman's Cold War. We believe that Wilson's policy closely resembles the Cold War with the exception of an arms race. Therefore, we call the Wilson administration's policy "the first cold war."

We wish to thank our colleagues, Elaine Jones, Susan E. Kennedy, Melvin I. Urofsky, and George E. Munro at Virginia Commonwealth University, as well as John Milton Cooper, Jr., and Wayne A. Wiegand at the University of Wisconsin, and Tony Badger of Cambridge University, for their careful reading of the manuscript and their many helpful suggestions. Alla Porshakova, associate professor at Moscow State Linguistic University, advised us on all of the significant Russian archives cited in this manuscript and assisted in all aspects of the Russian publication by OLMA-Press of Moscow. A special thanks goes to Robert H. Ferrell, our mentor, friend, and master teacher from graduate school days at Indiana University. His continuing interest and help made this book possible.

To our spouses, Lois E. Trani and Mary L. Davis, who have shared our friendship since the early 1960s and graduate school at Indiana University, we express our deep devotion and profound thanks for allowing us to finish this odyssey. In particular, we wish to thank Mary for straightening out the format of our endnotes and typing them, as well as the drafts of many of the chapters. The authors bear sole responsibility for whatever shortcomings and errors remain.

We mourn the loss of Dick McKinzie, who drafted the first chapters, and with affection dedicate this book to his memory.

The First Cold War

Introduction

1913
Russo-American Relations

At noon, March 4, 1913, Woodrow Wilson, recently New Jersey's governor and before that president of Princeton University, took the oath that made him America's twenty-eighth president. Wilson inherited the collapse of America's Russian policy as it had existed from 1832 to 1912. The Taft administration abrogated America's commercial treaty with Russia at the end of 1912. Furthermore, this effort succeeded because of a determined effort by American Jewish organizations to assert the passport rights of American Jews in Russia. These two factors operated against a background of U.S. commercial ambiguities toward Russia and a low level of American diplomatic professionalism in Russia. Add to this Wilson's lack of knowledge of Russia. The future of Russo-American relations did not look promising in March 1913 when Wilson took office.

Wilson looked forward to his new tasks. Addressing the honored guests seated on the stands facing the Capitol and the thousands of spectators in the surrounding park, he exhorted them to make the most of this, the happiest era in the 132-year history of the Republic. In one of the shortest inaugural addresses, he said the country had entered a robust phase of its life. Abundant resources, self-government, and hard work, he believed, had made the nation "incomparably great in its material aspects" and great, "very great" in its moral force.

The government, he said, was close to perfection. America possessed a system that "stood through a long age as in many respects a model for those who seek to set liberty upon foundations that will endure against fortuitous change, against storm and accident."[1] He did not explain this belief in detail, as he well could, having studied American government at Johns Hopkins University and published a book entitled *Congressional Government* (1885) in which he criticized the dominance of the legislative branch over the judicial and, especially, the executive. As president he now was about to right this error of post–Civil War administrations by which the presidency had lost

1

its power. For the rest of his term, Wilson's guides would be the British writers whose precepts he had taught. Here, he had relied on the British historian J. R. Green, who had written about a league of states, such as the United States, and the British statesman Edmund Burke, who had put forth the notion of a nation behaving as a person.

In foreign relations he was less well read, possessed fewer guides, and in actual fact had not thought much about how such relations should be arranged. He had his opinions, however. He approved, as did most Americans, of the Spanish-American War, although he did not agree with the idea of taking the Philippines. His principal guide in foreign relations was perhaps George Washington's Farewell Address, as he had reinterpreted it in light of the Spanish-American War. He had decided that President Washington's guide to foreign affairs—his counsel against "ordinary combinations and collisions"—held only so long as the American nation was immature. When it came of age in 1898, the new era demanded amendment of the advice of a century before. He had given the subject little further thought. Typical was his well-known comment to a correspondent, shortly before he reached the presidency, that it would be "the irony of fate" if his administration should have to deal mainly with foreign affairs.

Wilson had no special interest in or knowledge of Russia. In the years before his presidency Wilson made a few remarks about Russia. As early as 1880 he wrote that European despotisms were being abandoned or limited as in Russia. In 1887 he elaborated on this theme by noting that even in Russia public opinion must someday rule. That year he referred to Russia's autocratic government as abnormal. He took pains to indicate that while ties of amity might exist between such countries as America and Britain, there were few if any between such dissimilar nations as America and Russia. In 1904 he responded to news of a possible peace between Russia and Japan as an "ambrosia." In lecture notes of the period he marked for "topical analysis" the question of "absolutism—The Government of Russia." In 1911 he jotted down notes for a speech at Carnegie Hall, "The case versus Russia," in which he made a point of defending American Jews seeking to be treated as other Americans when applying for visas to travel in Russia without being discriminated against by the government of Tsar Nicholas II. Wilson simply had no special interest in or knowledge of Russia up to this time.

The president's friend, the wealthy Texan Colonel Edward M. House, was briefed concerning Russia. The only matter, House confided to his diary, was to find someone to replace Ambassador Curtis Guild. House advised offering William Jennings Bryan, the three-time presidential candidate who had helped Wilson obtain the nomination in 1912, the secretaryship of state and "afterwards to suggest that it would be of great service if he would go to Russia at this critical time." It was perhaps a way to get Bryan, an enthusiast for causes that embarrassed Wilson, out of sight. For the ambassadorship House ended up recommending a not very prominent envoy to Argentina, Charles H. Sherrill.[2]

The morning after his inauguration, the new president started his day at nine o'clock. One of the topics that he did not take up that day, and perhaps should have, concerned the government and people of a faraway nation — Imperial Russia, a nation that the nineteenth-century French commentator Alexis de Tocqueville had compared in its achievements and promise to the United States. It did not occur to the president, and doubtless could not have, that over the next decades until the very end of the twentieth century and into the twenty-first century, Russia, with its myriad of peoples, its medieval traditions, and little practice in self-government, would lie at the center of American foreign relations. For Wilson the problem was that the place was so distant. His immediate concerns were those of domestic politics.

American relations with Russia had been partial, undeveloped. Historically, Russia and the United States had had only sporadic contact, and much of this had been in the form of ceremonial trips by leaders. For many years they had had only cursory contact. America's first diplomatic agent to St. Petersburg, Francis Dana, had received de facto recognition in 1783. The young John Quincy Adams, who accompanied Dana, was cautious about Russia. Another illustrious American in 1849 described Russia as "the barbaric citadel of despotism." That year Americans welcomed the Hungarian patriot Louis Kossuth, who had fled the Russian occupation of Budapest. The visit of the Russian fleet to San Francisco and New York City during the Civil War, and the sale of Alaska in 1867, helped relieve Americans of their gloomy views. Grand Duke Alexis Alexandrovich, son of the tsar, visited the United States in 1871 as part of an around-the-world tour and was well received, as was in turn General Ulysses S. Grant in Russia in 1878. In 1891–1892, during the great Russian famine, Americans sent grain. President Theodore Roosevelt supported a pro-Japanese policy, initiating the Russo-Japanese Peace Conference of 1905 in Portsmouth, New Hampshire, for which he received the Nobel Peace Prize. Then Secretary of War William Taft made an extensive trip to Russia in 1907 while he, like Grant, was touring the world.

Economic contacts had been promising. American engineers built a locomotive for Tsar Nicholas I in 1842. The artist James Whistler's father designed the Moscow–St. Petersburg railway at the same time that Whistler's mother posed for his famous painting. Hubbard reapers and mowers from Cleveland were sold in Russia, as well as Carnegie steel rails and rolling stock for the Chinese Eastern Railway. Americans constructed icebreakers to clear Baltic ports and dredges for rivers. Perry Collins in the 1860s sought to lay a telegraph line across the Bering Strait. By the 1890s, there seemed a virtual Americanizing of Russia. It really was not that—for Russia was just entering the industrial age, and modernity, American or European, had hardly touched vast portions of the country. Thus, economic relations with the United States, not to mention diplomatic ties, were of minor importance.

In Russia affairs seemed peaceful enough. On March 6, 1913, in St. Petersburg, twenty-one guns of the fortress of St. Peter and St. Paul fired a salute to the three-hundredth anniversary of the House of Romanov. Tsar Nicholas, his wife, their four daughters, and their eight-year-old son prepared for days of ceremony. Later they would make a jubilee tour of cities important in their family history. President Wilson sent a cable to mark the occasion: "On this three hundredth anniversary of the accession of Michael Feodorovitch Romanoff to the Imperial throne of Russia, I extend to Your Majesty cordial felicitations and the earnest hope of the Government of the United States that the bond of friendship which now unites the two nations may ever continue and strengthen." Assistant Secretary of State Alvey A. Adee, who was the composer of such routine congratulations, probably wrote it in the State Department. There is no evidence that the president saw it.

As for perceptions of the later Romanov tour, much depended on the perspective of the reporter. Everywhere it was the same, said an intimate who traveled with the tsarina: crowds pressing against police lines, peasants dropping to the ground to kiss the shadow of the tsar, cheers, acclamations, prayers, choruses singing the national anthem—"demonstrations of love and fealty it seemed that no time or circumstance could ever alter." Watching the same events, the chairman of the council of ministers, Count Vladimir N. Kokovtsov, considered them "attractively arranged, but somehow empty." He saw more curiosity than enthusiasm and considered the turnout "comparatively small."[3]

In 1913 neither Americans nor Russians cared much about the other's ceremonies, whether they were inaugurations or tercentenaries. The peoples did not know each other. There was almost nothing to indicate that the otherwise calm surface of relations between the United States and Russia might change and alter the course of history. In 1913 two issues dominated American-Russian relations: negotiations regarding a commercial treaty and treatment of Jews by Russia.

1.

The Russian-American Treaty of Navigation and Commerce had defined and guaranteed the terms of trading since 1832. It expired on January 1,

1913. In 1911 there was an outburst of anti-Russian feeling in the United States, in the form of anger against the tsar's failure to honor American passports held by Jews and conviction that Russia's policy toward Jews created an international problem of human rights. President Taft was left little alternative but to abrogate the treaty.

The demonstration against Russia by revoking the commercial treaty in 1911 was the achievement of an American Jewish Committee, an organization that considered Jewish-American émigrés from Russia its constituents. Their memories were painful and humiliating, and they hoped to persuade the government of their adopted country to retaliate, to do something for those left behind. The committee wanted the United States to take the first step toward forcing the tsar to abolish the Pale of Settlement and antisemitic laws. It dared hope that democracy around the world, and Jews in Britain, France, and Germany, could convince their governments to follow the lead of the United States.[4] Although it failed in the larger objective, the committee proved able to obtain a political outcome for its cause.

The prejudices in Russia that impelled Jews to emigrate were as real as they were unfair. Nearly a thousand pages of laws, executive orders, and judicial interpretations restricted occupations, education, and residence of Jews, who could not sign deeds, mortgages, or rental agreements in rural areas nor, because they might be smugglers, live within forty miles of a border. Not only in the Pale did the tsarist government limit Jews in schools to 10 percent, but also in Moscow and St. Petersburg. No Jews could serve as officers in the army. Russian peasants, aware of these restrictions, became known around the world for instigating pogroms, burning houses, rape, and murder.[5]

The émigrés made two issues into a cause célèbre: the religious test by Russian consuls when American citizens applied for visas, and failure to treat holders of passports equally once they entered Russia. There was no disputing that consuls rejected Jews who asked for visas, except, depending on the time and consul, Jews "of the better class" or those "useful to the internal development of the country." And the Department of State had documented cases of former Russian Jews, naturalized and traveling on passports, who had been fined, imprisoned, or sent to the Pale once they entered Russia.[6]

To the American Jewish Committee it seemed that the way to arouse opinion against the tsar's treatment of Jews was to call attention to this discrimination by forcing America to cancel its commercial treaty; Russia would then feel pressure to change. Manhattan lawyer Louis Marshall announced that the era of "the cringing ghetto spirit" had passed. He took as his first premise that the Treaty of Navigation and Commerce, as well as treaties Russia had concluded with other nations, guaranteed foreigners who visited Russia, Jews and non-Jews alike, the same privileges. Rights to a visa would apply equally to every citizen of a nation possessing a treaty. The committee set out to publicize Russian duplicity and to persuade Americans to demand cancellation if Russian behavior did not change. "The moment Russia is compelled to live up to its treaties and admit the foreign Jew into its dominion on the basis of equality with other citizens of foreign countries," banker Jacob Schiff reasoned, "the Russian government will not be able to maintain the Pale of Settlement against its own Jews." And if the United States abrogated its treaty, Marshall added, Britons, French, and Germans would take note and Russia "would eventually yield to the opinion of the civilized nations of the earth."[7]

Article I of the Treaty of 1832 provided that citizens of each country were "at liberty to sojourn and reside in all parts whatsoever . . . in order to attend to their affairs." Americans and Russians were to enjoy "the same security and protection as natives of the country wherein they reside, on condition of their submitting to the laws and ordinances there prevailing." According to the Russian interpretation, this meant that Jews from America would be treated according to ordinances prevailing for Russian Jews. The United States had long insisted that the operative phrase was "the same security and protection as natives," meaning nonrestricted Russians.[8]

The campaign worked. When the committee had accumulated four thousand press clippings in favor of abrogation, it arranged a meeting in Carnegie Hall to hear advocates of the cause. Reporters noted that in speaking to the audience, newspaper tycoon William Randolph Hearst whipped the crowd to "intense patriotism." Governor Woodrow Wilson, "repeatedly hailed from the galleries as the next President," assured the crowd that Americans were "not willing to have prosperity" that came from trading with Russia if some Americans had to "suffer contempt for it." This led George P. Bakhmetev, Russian ambassador, to believe that Wilson was a dangerous radical with fantastic ideas. He also felt a presidential victory for Theodore Roosevelt might create a dictatorship; therefore, he wrote Russian Foreign Minister Sergei D. Sazonov that Taft was the preferable candidate. A resolution in the House of Representatives declared that "the United States will not . . . be a party to any treaty that discriminated . . . between American citizens on the grounds of religious belief" and ordered the president to declare the Russian-American Treaty terminated.[9]

When abrogation came to a vote on December 13, 1911, only one congressman voted against it. Fearing the Senate might pass a more strident resolution, President Taft cabled Ambassador Curtis Guild his reluctant acceptance. Guild reported that "The scene was very painful." When he met with Sazonov to communicate Taft's message, he recalled that because the treaty was "no longer fully responsive" to needs of the signers, the United States would regard it as inoperative two years later, on January 1, 1913. Sazonov found the decision to risk losing millions in trade "incomprehensible." Guild afterward noted that Russia would never admit every Jew who carried a passport, but Sazonov was "prepared to consider an arrangement by which the United States might cooperate for the transfer of all Jews from Russia to the United States." Ambassador Bakhmetev summarized a meeting with then Secretary of State Philander C. Knox, as well as with Taft, that both were against the anti-Russian campaign in the press. Knox recommended renegotiating the treaty. Bakhmetev told Jewish organizations their campaign had led to deterioration of the Jewish position in Russia, but to no avail.

Absence of a treaty did not affect Russian-American business. Quasi-official arrangements filled the void. In 1913 the Russian government chartered the Russian-American Chamber of Commerce. It assigned a commercial attaché to its Washington embassy to encourage traders. By the end of the year the American Association of Manufacturers had opened a branch in Russia.[10] Nor did abrogation prevent other kinds of travelers from making the long trek to Russia.

2.

When Wilson took office, contacts between Russians and Americans were mainly through journalists posted abroad, traders who dealt in the items each country offered the other, and a scattered and remarkably unimportant official representation—the ambassador, of course, and several consuls.

Of this group, journalists misinformed Americans by reinforcing stereotypes. No newspaper in either country kept a regular correspondent in the other, save a reporter for the Associated Press in St. Petersburg. When events required it, dailies in America cited British journalists. Typically these British correspondents were men of birth, education, interest in Russia, and "sufficiency of means." Usually they had fallen in with the Russian aristocracy and never quite got the whole story. Ambassador Guild insisted that such Britons were responsible for "many of our erroneous ideas." Moreover, foreign journalists amounted to a handful that wrote features for magazines. They could be depended on to romanticize peasants, castigate the tsar, and draw comparisons between progress in the United States and lack of it in Russia.[11]

No one contributed more to the image of Russia in America than George

Kennan did. Distantly related to the later diplomat-historian, a self-taught expert who first traveled through Russia as part of an effort by Western Union to string a telegraph line across Eurasia, he became immensely popular as author of a book about Siberia, the government's destination for political wrongdoers. It was he who made Siberia synonymous with deprivation. He had been known to hobble onto the lecture stage barefooted, in prison pajamas and irons. A Jew-hating tsar and the Jew-hating oligarchy had so long perpetuated atrocities among the peasants that he gave people to understand if Christ turned up in a Russian village He would be arrested within hours and sent to the Pale. If Christ continued to teach, He would be exiled to the mines. The Russian government had no right to exist; furthermore, as he said, "it is the duty of the Russian people to overthrow it."[12]

In Kennan's mind, almost everything about Russian officialdom stood in the way of history's "inexorable movement toward liberal democracy." The good people in the drama were peasants, "naturally liberal and tolerant," Marseillaise-singing champions of democracy. He offered vignettes to promote this view. He told of political prisoners in a St. Petersburg jail passing bits of red flannel underdrawers and white-and-blue kerchiefs through toilet pipes that connected the cells, so inmates could defy authorities on the Fourth of July by waving American flags through windows.[13]

Although other travelers discovered ignorance or religious fervor, humor or hospitality more interesting, they accepted Kennan's conclusions. They seldom found themselves corrected. In those years the Library of Congress contained six hundred books in Russian and only at Harvard was the language taught. Harvard and the University of Chicago were the only universities that offered courses on Russia. America's Russian experts could be counted on one hand.[14]

Economic relations offered no remedy to lack of knowledge. Neither country obtained anything important from the other. Boots reusable for their rubber, animal or human hair, and licorice root ranked among Russia's top ten exports to the United States. Rosin and twine were among the ten sent in return.[15] That no one knew what or how many goods passed between the two countries also bespoke the character of the exchange. According to Russian statistics, customers bought twice the American copper and four times the cotton that, according to American statistics, went to Russia. In all, the tsar's officers said, Russians paid $42 million a year for American products; in all, officials of the Department of Commerce said, U.S. annual purchases were $25 million. Russians calculated sales to the United States at $7 million; Americans calculated sales to Russia at $21 million.[16] U.S. firms had plants or offices in Russia—Singer, International Harvester, New York Life Insurance—but they did not change the picture.

Consignment of trade to German and British middlemen explained some of the disparity in figures. Only one shipping line made runs between Russian and American ports. Trade tended to become lost in the commerce with Germans and Britons. Products loaded at Portsmouth were consolidated with orders for Riga or Odessa; products loaded at Boston or New Orleans had a way of becoming German or British products. Government reports showed that Americans bought German furs years after Germany had been trapped out and that Russia bought thousands of bales of German cotton, a crop Germans did not grow. Outlets for the Gramophone Company and Eastman Kodak were managed from London, with British markings. The same was true for Parke, Davis in pharmaceuticals.

Nevertheless, no matter whose figures one used or what trends seemed to be emerging, Russians bought 1 percent of products Americans sold overseas, and American purchases accounted for the same. Carelessness in statistics showed Americans and Russians had little interest in correcting the data. Russia and the United States qualified as debtor nations: they could not have paid their debts by selling. The United States fell short by $7 billion, a large part of which it owed to Britons who financed railroads. The French claimed most of Russia's $1 billion debt, although German syndicates had begun to acquire a share. Against these figures the $1 million or less invested by Russians in the United States, and $50 million invested by American business in Russia, counted for little. [17]

Observers who expected Russians to experience their own upward spiral of production and consumption predicted profits for firms that could adjust to the Russian market. Businesses large enough to open foreign operations, however, declined the challenge. They made profit at home and in the markets of Latin America. They would have had to modify products and find ways to compensate for the head start enjoyed by others. Singer and International Harvester built factories in Russia primarily to avoid taxes on imports. Germans had a much greater foothold in Russia, carrying samples and catalogs that described their products in Russian and listed prices in rubles. [18]

One of America's five consul generals and a civil servant that believed it his task to increase Russian-American trade, Alfred L. M. Gottschalk, lamented his country's lost opportunities. "Why we do not sell more," he wrote, "seems to depend entirely upon . . . our peculiarly American way of looking at international trade." He contrasted the possible ifs that might improve trade. If America had better equipment, if more commission houses existed in Moscow, if Americans had branch banks there, if direct steamship lines went between Russia and America, if heads of export houses learned Russia's needs, then trade would improve.[19]

America had another problem in trade. Even if American firms could convince themselves to give twelve or eighteen months of credit instead of demanding cash, selling in Russia bore no resemblance to drumming windmills or crockery along the Atchison, Topeka, and Santa Fe. Russians conducted a great deal of business at fairs or bazaars. Each summer four hundred thousand traders and hangers-on crowded into the shops and stalls of Nizhni-Novgorod, attending the largest fair. They spent $150 million at forty-five hundred outlets, many on such streets and lanes as Striped Linen Row, Soft Goods Row, Spoon Row, Soap Row, and Bell Row. American merchants desired to advance trade with methods that marked their domestic market, rather than Russian ways. They were impossibly narrow in their grasp of what Russians desired, how it might be possible to confront the admittedly vast Russian market.[20]

3.

All the while, diplomats handled relations between the United States and Russia. Unfortunately, the U.S. diplomatic corps lacked competence. Its public servants were too few to handle matters. There were 213 people employed in Washington, D.C., from men whose cutaway coats were badges of office to messengers and the secretary's chauffeur. Less than 450 individuals were on foreign posts.[21]

The front-line representatives in Russia offered an equally strange American mosaic. There was, in fact, nothing interesting to say in 1913 about the embassy in St. Petersburg. Ambassador Guild, who upon his arrival found that the embassy did not subscribe to a Russian newspaper, was not only pained over abrogation of the commercial treaty but also disappointed that President Wilson had not asked him to continue as ambassador. A skeleton staff under Chargé d'Affaires Charles Wilson took in and processed only the essential diplomatic laundry.[22]

Election of presidents and abrogation of treaties had no effect on the consular service. Gottschalk did visit Warsaw, Riga, St. Petersburg, Moscow, Odessa, and Batum, while another inspector went to Vladivostok.[23] The consul general was a finicky, self-assured, and intelligent person, and he took his duties seriously. His task was to move around and observe and if possible improve America's representatives, and he made sure he saw as much as possible and when necessary recommended changes.

Inspector Gottschalk thought that Leslie Davis, a former guide to tourists who held the consul's post in Batum, was too "awkward, rough and shy" ever to serve "in any but a remote, uncivilized and unexciting place." Gottschalk believed that instead of going three hundred miles to climb Mount Ararat, Davis should have been monitoring ports on the Black Sea and gathering statistics on the flow of products in and out of Persia. The inspector faulted him for his "plain" manner and for habits "not quite those of better society at home."[24]

From Odessa, Gottschalk reported that people found Consul John Grout unattractive because of a "pronouncedly nervous manner, which at times amounts to undignified excitability. . . . He is troubled, moreover, with a sort of eruption (not constant) over the forehead and nose, which would suggest to some people, when allied to his generally nervous manner, that he overindulged in intoxicants." Because of neurasthenia, as the inspector put it, Grout was inclined to stay at his desk "instead of mingling as much with business men, during business hours, as some consuls might."[25]

When Gottschalk arrived in Riga, through which passed a third of Russia's trade with the United States, he found the consulate run by Laurance Hill, a British subject whose family had lived three generations in Russia. After a week's stay Gottschalk rated him sixteen on a scale of one hundred, "one of the worst specimens of polite, denationalized persons I have ever known — and I have a life's experience among Creoles and Levantines of all sorts." Hill was a lazy hypochondriac who felt no loyalty to the Department of State. The only good thing was that he would retire soon and be replaced by Douglas Jenkins.[26]

In St. Petersburg Chargé Wilson told Gottschalk that Jacob Conner was "not completely normal." The man had "neurotic conditions, which closely resemble insanity," so the inspector opined. As an official he was "at present mentally unfit." Conner's worst sin was against the service. He had allowed the consulate's shield, its outside sign, to become so weathered and shabby that the landlord had ordered the janitor to tear it down and deposit it at Conner's office door. Conner informed his superior in Moscow, Consul General John Snodgrass, with whom he had picked fights, that he would be signing no more letters as "Your obedient servant" because he was no one's servant. He belittled instructions from Washington as "damned foolishness" composed by "insignificant clerks." Gottschalk wrote him off as "wholly and completely disloyal and insubordinate."[27]

Although "something of an old beau," the consul in Warsaw, Thomas Heenan, could no longer remember the month or year he had entered the service, not to mention points of any international issue. Heenan walked the streets every afternoon, but the sixty-five-year-old never left the city, never studied the Poles, and was seldom seen socially or in business circles. He had no future "except in a small post where it was understood that his clerk was to do all the work."[28]

Only in Moscow and Vladivostok did taxpayers receive competence. Because Consul General Snodgrass was on leave, it fell to Vice Consul Alfred W. Smith to stand Gottschalk's inspection. Smith would "never see a chance until it is very plainly before him," the report read, for the reason that he lacked brilliance. Gottschalk liked him; he was the only person in charge of an American facility in all of Russia who spoke Russian. He had married "a gentlewoman" and was managing an office in the country's commercial center, burdened with correspondence. The office furnished information on trade in Russian, Polish, German, French, and English. It pleased the inspector to note that "business relations are carefully preserved, and seem excellent."[29]

In Vladivostok, where the Trans-Siberian railway ended, another less caustic inspector visited Consul John Jewell. Here was a man of "excellent appearance, quiet and dignified," who supervised "all details of the work of his office." No physical impairments, no mental quirks; he was absolutely suited, according to the report, to this seaport office "with hardly any seaport or other business."[30]

Dismissing the dead wood and hiring good wood was easier said than done. Since 1906 the civil service had protected diplomatic tenure. Regardless of local living costs, salaries had been tied to the class of the facility and there were nine classes. Consuls made $2,500 or $3,500 a year. Gottschalk reckoned necessities and amenities costing $1,000 in the United States cost $2,500. Davis lived a "rather shabby" life in Batum. Although Conner in St. Petersburg shared the expense of a flat with a businessman, $3,500 did not permit him to dress, entertain, or travel "as an official of a foreign government is expected to, in Russia." Another bachelor, Jewell in Vladivostok, lived with the British and French consuls. Grout in Odessa, his wife, and two boys used $2,000 a year from real estate and investments to pay for their expenses. Vice Consul Smith spent $1,200, derived from a block of family-owned buildings in Odessa, to sustain him in Moscow in a manner that Gottschalk thought "modest verging on—not exactly shabby, but nearly that."[31]

America's well-born families considered the diplomatic corps an honorable, even intellectually and culturally broadening, place for college-graduated sons to begin, and they could afford to cover the differences. But the corps comprised two services, the one diplomatic, the other consular. The latter dealt with trade matters, not pourparlers in the salons, and that did not suit the tastes of well-off Americans; their sons did not enter into it.

The consular service was for cast-offs or men who liked to adorn the smaller cities of a largely unknown nation. The lack of quality as Gottschalk beheld it was sad evidence, if such were needed, that the government, representing its people, was making little effort to discover what was going on.

If Wilson thought about Russia at all in the first few days and weeks of his administration, he might well have reflected on the tenuous nature of what he had inherited from the previous administration: absence of a treaty defining commercial relations and no prospects of getting one as long as the Jewish passport question remained unresolved; an amateur diplomatic and counsellor service in Russia; no permanent ambassador to St. Petersburg for more than a year. This unpromising start became hopelessly confused with the onset of the Great War in Europe and, then, revolution in Russia.

One

1914–1916
Three Ambassadors for St. Petersburg

In the years of peace and into the years of war, up until April 1917, when the United States entered World War I as a belligerent, President Wilson did not give much time or thought to the subject of relations with the government of Russia. But even though he was not much interested in Russia, he had to appoint an ambassador. This did not prove to be an easy task. The will perhaps was there, but Wilson's mind is not easy to fathom. He may have been busy, although all accounts of the president's activity in his first term in the White House testify to a short workday. The president might not have believed that his country's relations with Russia justified much time and thought. He preferred to turn his attention elsewhere; he worked on reforming the mechanisms of the government. In foreign relations the problems of Mexico and, then, beginning in August 1914, those of the European war appeared more important. The latter had largely to do with American neutrality. His efforts failed to force the belligerents, Germany in particular, to respect American neutral commerce on the high seas.

The president's first order of business concerning Russia was to replace Republican ambassador Curtis Guild with a Democratic appointee. His leading candidate refused after much delay. His second choice immediately stepped down after his nomination due to unfavorable publicity. His third selection failed to live up to expectations after fifteen months of tenure. His fourth choice, David R. Francis, held the ambassadorship for the re-mainder of Wilson's presidency. Ambassador Francis got President Wilson to recognize the democratic Provisional Government in April 1917. This decision fit nicely into the president's declaration of war message that upheld democracy over autocracy. Afterwards, Wilson lost confidence in Francis and appointed committees to formulate his Russian policy. This dilution of decision making detracted from the Wilson administration's ability to create a strong and consistent policy. It left a vacuum in America's Russian policy that allowed ad hoc voices to spin alternative policies. This confused

15

situation completely broke down with the increasing inability of the Provisional Government to rule successfully. At the moment of the ambassador's greatest triumph, the recognition of the Provisional Government, missions of experts superseded him.

With this virtual void of leadership in the making of Russian foreign policy, the State Department and ambassador might have been factors in bringing the United States into a better relationship with Russia. The department itself under President Wilson's first secretary of state, his political ally and the Democratic wheelhorse William Jennings Bryan, unfortunately did not prove very helpful.

Without presidential leadership in this area, at least while Bryan was secretary, the only possible source of change in relations would have been the St. Petersburg embassy. Everything came down to the talents of the American ambassadors in St. Petersburg. Guild could do little; Henry M. Pindell and George C. Marye, the first two selections of the State Department and President Wilson, were failures. Finally, the president settled as a final resort on David R. Francis, who took hold of the office. He was smart enough and more active, yet unprepared for Russia, and ignorant, more a spectator than a mover. There was more concern over a commercial treaty than over the bettering of relations to shore up a weak regime.

Francis, formerly the governor of Missouri, represented the heartland of the American Middle West. An individual with considerable political experience, which was essential for the Russian post, he lacked understanding of Russia. He was unaware of how perilous the situation was, especially after the European war broke out and Russia's weaknesses were exposed.

1.

Before the war's outbreak, upon the takeover of the government in Washington by the Wilsonians, Ambassador Guild wrote a friend that he would not fail to state matters as they stood. He wrote that as a former ambassador he would remain silent on relations with Russia except that "the misunderstanding in the United States of problems here is so serious and the conditions here so delicate."[1] He thought it his duty to inform the president-elect; he was not looking for favors. He cited examples of American misunderstanding: negotiations for a treaty had been taking place in St. Petersburg when they were supposed to be in Washington; American Jews were not the only ones singled out for poor treatment but, rather, all foreign Jews were treated alike and every other nation acquiesced; Americans thought that Russia bought a trifling number of goods in the United States. He mentioned how painful the scene in St. Petersburg was over abrogation of the 1832 treaty. He had avoided a breach between America and Russia. Guild was able to appeal to the Council of Ministers for favorable treatment of American Jews on an individual basis and he put the embassy in order, started subscription to Russian newspapers, found an efficient chief clerk, hired a reliable translator, and came twice to Washington with information, stating, "I do wish to lay what I have learned here at the disposition of the new President before he takes any positive action."[2]

Guild wrote a confidential report regarding what appeared as a change on the passport question. Premier Ivan Goremykin had said that a bill was being prepared to simplify passports. Guild recommended awaiting developments. In March 1913 he had saved the administration embarrassment by reminding Bryan to have the president send a cable recognizing the tercentenary of the Romanov dynasty.[3] The promise of more consultations ended after Guild's return in mid-1913.

The president saw a report in the *New York Times* in August 1914 referring to an editorial by Guild in the *Boston Commercial Bulletin*. Guild had maintained that the president told friends he foresaw a boom for American business in selling to both sides during the war. The former ambassador labeled this a heartless utterance by a hardened cynic. "No, Mr. President, not even on the sordid lines of material and selfish gain are the awful facts of today's history to be viewed with exultation, still less with gaiety." The *Boston Herald* wrote that the president's secretary, Joseph P. Tumulty, denied any reference by the president to prosperity as a result of the war. The *Boston Globe* reported a Tumulty telegram to Guild that the statement was "unqualifiedly false." Guild responded that he had quoted from a dispatch in the *Boston Herald* and was glad the president repudiated it. He tried to straighten out the affair by telling Tumulty he had only quoted the *Herald*. He had not made the statement himself, he said, and they were both "victims of some very yellow journalism."[4]

By this time there was no possibility of Guild's return. Wilson offered Charles R. Crane the ambassadorship and soon the president was begging the Chicago plumbing magnate not to decline: "I simply cannot adjust my mind to giving up the idea of having you represent us at the Court of Russia." Crane's father, who had built the family business, had died in 1912. The family expected its eldest son to attend to the business.[5] Crane had displayed an interest in Russia and often traveled there.

Meanwhile, Ambassador George P. Bakhmetev called at the State Department to say the tsar believed America and Russia ought to have a commercial treaty and that an American ambassador would facilitate negotiation. "I suppose there is no hurry about it," Bryan remarked. The president replied that he would rather argue with the Russians over the rights of Jews "when we have got some of our pressing business off our hands."[6]

Crane was the only appropriate candidate. For months neither the president nor the secretary considered anyone else. Intermediaries gave the impression that Crane might take the post in a year or so. Bryan suggested the idea of a temporary appointment. At this point the name of a newspaper publisher in Peoria, Henry M. Pindell, arose. Senator J. Hamilton Lewis of Illinois put forward Pindell's name. Because Pindell had been a Wilson supporter in the recent election, Lewis promised him a soft berth in St. Petersburg until Crane was ready. Bryan reminded the president that Pindell, an original Wilson man, would "enable us to recognize Illinois again when his successor is ready to be appointed." Wilson sent Pindell's name to the Senate in November 1913 in an effort to accommodate "Ham" Lewis. Watching from the Department of State, Counselor John Bassett Moore saw a risky game in which the president hoped to dupe the Senate. The Senate gave its consent to Pindell's ambassadorship early in 1914. Pindell declined.[7]

By this time Wilson was sixteen months into his term. Bryan had once considered William G. Sharp of Ohio, but as a former member of the House Foreign Affairs Committee, Sharp had recommended abrogation of the commercial treaty. He was persona non grata in St. Petersburg, according to Bakhmetev, although he became ambassador to France. Wilson now gave the name of a California banker, George C. Marye, to the Senate. Marye was confirmed on July 9.[8]

The first secretary of the embassy in Berlin, Joseph C. Grew, joked that Marye must have exclaimed, "Ambassador, Ambassador!" before a mirror in amazement over his appointment.[9] From the time of Guild's resignation until the appointment of Marye, the embassy was under the guidance of its first secretary, Charles Wilson. When Marye took his post the administration's aims in Russia were still limited to a trade treaty that would resolve the passport issue. There was little other concern about the relations between the two countries.

Marye corresponded with Guild as well as with Guild's predecessor, Charlemagne Tower, to find out about his tasks. Guild, he confessed, had been "one of the most popular men in official life in the Russian capital." No doubt he read Guild's article in the *Yale Review* that stated how Americans had many "erroneous ideas of Russia."[10]

On July 3, 1914, the *New York Times* reported Marye's selection under the heading, "Hope for Russian Treaty: Administration Expects Marye to Reopen Negotiations." The article noted that when the White House announced Marye's appointment, it suggested that he "might take up that subject."[11]

Colonel House's account of Marye's appointment displayed the shallowness of the administration's policy: "It was thought he would make a campaign contribution and [Thomas J.] Pence, [Joseph P.] Tumulty and several Senators were led to urge his appointment on that account. Marye's secretary was filling them full of what Marye would do for the party, and then Marye left without giving the campaign committee a dollar."[12]

Marye did not reach St. Petersburg, now renamed Petrograd to give it a Slavic sound, until October 1914, a delay of four months. By then, World War I had begun and Russia had lost the battle of Tannenberg in late August.

At this time the president asked the embassy to make known his wish to mediate the great conflict. The United States was a signatory of the Second Hague Peace Conference of 1907. Wilson would welcome an opportunity to act in the interest of peace under one of the conventions of that conference. The tsar responded by thanking Wilson but noting that the war was imposed on Russia. It was, he continued, "premature to contemplate the possibility of peace."[13]

Bakhmetev had told Marye in Washington that it was too dangerous for him to proceed to Petrograd. The Russian ambassador pointed out that the position of American ambassador had been vacant for two years. Marye had to represent German and Austrian interests since they had requested and received American protection of their embassies, prisoners of war, and all other matters. Would it not look as if the United States was hurrying for the sake of the Central Powers? Official circles in Petrograd, Bakhmetev continued, had been hostile to the United States since abrogation of the treaty. Anyway, the war would be over in a few months, and then it would be safe for Marye to set forth.[14]

Bryan informed Wilson of Bakhmetev's opinions and stressed his feeling that a bad impression would be made if, after a two-year delay, an ambassador appeared just as the Germans and Austrians asked the United States to represent their interests. "With regard to Marye," Wilson replied, "I think the course you propose is the right one to pursue. I think I would, through Wilson, the Chargé, obtain the views of the Russian Government." Marye spoke to Tumulty, to Senator Ollie M. James of Kentucky, twice with Bryan, and again to Bakhmetev. A cable from Chargé Wilson confirmed that although the tsar believed that Marye's presence was not necessary, he would cordially receive him. That changed Bakhmetev's mind, and Marye departed for his new post. Before leaving, he had conversations with the president, Schiff, Marshall, and Herman Bernstein. He arrived in London, then proceeded to Petrograd via Berlin.[15]

Parenthetically, Count Sergei Witte of Treaty of Portsmouth fame had met with Chargé Wilson and "in strictest confidence" told him that the Russian government wanted Witte to go to America and help to arrange a large loan. He said that he would not go unless Russia revised its passport restrictions. He assured the chargé that the loan would be spent for American goods. The State Department deemed this information so important that its counselor, Robert Lansing, sent it to the president with the comment, "It would be most gratifying if a treaty such as is proposed could be negotiated . . . as it would be accomplishing the seemingly impossible." The response was that the first of Witte's conditions was essential if he were to be a special envoy. Lansing cautioned as to the second, that the United States could not take any part in loans to belligerents. It should be noted that Lansing had become counselor in 1914 and was appointed secretary of state in 1915 with Bryan's resignation in the midst of the German sinking of the *Lusitania* and the resulting diplomatic crisis.[16]

Meanwhile Bakhmetev proposed a system of promissory notes to pay for supplies purchased in the United States. Lansing believed that this was different from a war loan. The ambassador suggested short-term obligations where amounts and interest were to be determined by the American government. The initial amount desired was $5 million.[17]

Shortly after his arrival, Marye visited the embassy at 34 Furshtatskaya, off Liteiny Prospekt. The following day he saw Foreign Minister Sazonov, who arranged for the tsar to receive him and accept his letters of credence. Marye was impressed by the tsar and, after a series of conversations with Sazonov, prepared a report on commercial relations. The *New York Herald* wondered at the delay of the treaty and maintained that Russia was eager to increase its imports tenfold. On reading this report, Lansing concluded that Russia would "discuss that passport question because of the desire manifested by Count Witte and by M. Sazonoff . . . to negotiate a commercial treaty."[18] Unfortunately, Witte died before he could undertake the mission.

The tardiness of Marye's negotiation of a treaty led House to tell the president he, the colonel, would be willing to go to Petrograd and make the treaty. Wilson responded, according to House, that "He hated to ask me to go to Russia in winter, but he thought it would be of great advantage, and he expressed a lack of confidence in the ability of Marye to do such work." House was more emphatic about Marye and in a letter to the president wrote: "I do not believe that Marye is equal to the job. I do not hear good things of him."[19]

Chargé Wilson had cautioned the secretary of state against accepting the German and Austrian request to look after their interests. He pointed out that America had done service for Japan during the Russo-Japanese War, with a most unfortunate effect. The German Foreign Ministry approached the American ambassador in Berlin, James W. Gerard, with the request: "Formally asked by Foreign Minister if United States will take over German embassies in France and Russia and any other countries with which Germany may be at war." On August 3, 1914, the State Department granted permission to the embassy to act for Germany and Austria-Hungary.[20]

At this point the plight of German and Austro-Hungarian prisoners (POWs) in Russia then reached such extremes that the Austrian ambassador in Washington, Constantin Dumba, asked the president to make a personal appeal to the tsar. Charles B. Smith, a congressman from Buffalo and member of the committee on foreign affairs, offered to go to Petrograd to help with prisoners and assist with the commercial treaty. The president declined the offer, fearing to confuse American interests. The German government cabled the principles to be followed for prisoners, which included inspection of camps, freedom to converse, ascertaining needs, and sending of mail and food. The American YMCA and Red Cross would also play important roles in prisoner relief.[21]

The president consulted with Charles P. Anderson, a member of the State Department who, together with Lansing, was handling the prisoner question. Both officials cautioned the president to include a paragraph to the effect that because the United States did not represent Russian interests in Germany or Austria, America could not help with Russia's prisoners. Wilson made it the fourth paragraph of a letter asking that "this Government might be able to supply or vouch for, the right to distribute to the prisoners in Siberia, either military or civil, money, medicines, and supplies." Marye cabled that Sazonov and the tsar were eager to grant the request but wanted assurance that "the same thing would be done for my people in Germany." Marye told the tsar that the president would see to its fairness. The tsar referred the matter to Sazonov, whose note to Marye used such language as "perfect mutuality," "in the same amounts," and "extend the same kindnesses."[22]

When Bryan resigned in 1915 the issue was unresolved. The new secretary, Robert Lansing, reported to Marye that America had arranged with Spain to extend to Russian prisoners in Germany and Austria-Hungary the relief and assistance American agencies gave to German and Austrian prisoners in Russia. He suggested that supplies sent to Siberia might go through China. Spain gave its consent for its representatives in Vienna and

Berlin to "render all possible assistance to representatives [of the] American Red Cross and other American philanthropic societies." The Russian government gave its approval for the American Red Cross to help in this enterprise.[23]

Looking after German and Austrian interests meant that the embassy staff, in cooperation with the Red Cross and YMCA, had to check conditions in Russia's prisoner camps and make sure that Germans and Austrians were fairly treated, as well as care for German and Austrian nationals in the Russian and Russo-Polish war zones. According to a Russian-German agreement, nationals in the war zone who were under the age of seventeen or over forty-five, as well as women and children and all people otherwise incapable of military service, were to return to their countries.

It was Marye's duty to report to Sazonov the complaints he was receiving. One complaint came from the German envoy in Stockholm, Helmuth von Stödten. Hearing that Americans had been traveling in a private railroad car, he asked if the money came from German funds for use in aiding Germans. Marye took this accusation as an insult and decided to discuss it with Stödten. He noted that if Stödten or any other officials complained about embassy conduct, they should lay the charges before the German foreign office, which would take up the matter with the State Department. Further, Marye stated, the United States billed transportation conducted during inspections to the Russian government. Marye sent American dispatches through the German embassy in Stockholm for speed, not comment by Stödten.[24]

The problem with passports was as bothersome as that of representing governments, if in a different way. Schiff reminded the president of his obligation to see that this issue was settled.[25] The president selected a commission to send to Russia to aid in the endeavor. It was composed of Crane; the president of the University of Virginia, Edwin Alderman; perhaps the Slavic expert at Harvard, Archibald Cary Coolidge; and the presidents of two other universities. The war prevented the commission from becoming active even though Lansing wrote Crane that it was provided for in Bryan's "cooling off" treaty between the United States and Russia of 1914. Lansing sent Marye a confidential memorandum: "Make informal and direct inquiries at Foreign Office as to how Russian Government would view proposal to enter into preliminary negotiations for new commercial treaty between Russia and the United States. . . . The passport question to be discussed in the negotiations with a view to settling it in a way which will be satisfactory to both parties."[26]

Ambassador Marye and Chargé Wilson reported changes in regulations to the department. American passport regulations required that in cases of naturalization the date and previous allegiance be listed. In contrast, a U.S. passport described the holder as a citizen of the United States and stated age and description as well as the object of the visit, but not whether a citizen was naturalized. The United States contended that once persons became naturalized, they were equal to native-born, and Lansing said it would not be practical to change passports to include such information. The State Department agreed to attach to passports the application that did show the type of citizenship that applicants had previously held.[27]

Marye received a message saying that the State Department was ready for him to take up the question of a commercial treaty. He spoke to Sazonov, who said he would consider a proposal. Marye told Sazonov that a treaty should follow the lines of the treaty of 1832 and that they could reserve the passport problem for later resolution.[28]

Lansing's intent was to arrange a treaty with Russia while ironing out other difficulties. Marye reported that possibilities for such a treaty were good. Lansing cabled Marye: "Your dispatch No. 184 June 23 relative to new treaty received with gratification. A project is being drafted which will be forwarded to you as soon as possible." The president remained skeptical of Marye, telling Lansing: "I do not feel that I have any means of estimating Marye's ability or his aptitude for an important task of this kind. Perhaps you know him and can judge how carefully and minutely he will have to be instructed and guided. My intimate thought is that the whole matter had better be most carefully formulated from this side of the water so far as the proposals of the government are concerned." Lansing replied that he had no idea of Marye's ability but negotiations would have to be in Petrograd. "My idea," he said, "is that we can instruct Marye very definitely in regard to the negotiations as it progresses."[29]

What followed was the case of a missing draft treaty. When Marye's secretary, Raymond T. Baker, returned to the United States for a visit, Lansing prepared a draft, which Baker was to take with him when he returned to Russia. He left without the draft. It was expected that the draft would come in the diplomatic pouch. But, as of Marye's resignation in January 1916, no draft appeared.[30]

Probably the president had lost faith in Marye, partly because of complaints by the German government to Colonel House. These confirmed the longstanding source of trouble for Marye, raised by House in a letter to Wilson:

> Another thing I will bring to your attention when I return is our Embassy at Petrograd. The German Government is seriously thinking of taking their affairs out of our hands. They claim that more German and Austrian prisoners

are dying in Russia from bad treatment than are now being lost on the battle-fields, and they attribute it largely to the lack of interest our representatives are giving the matter. From what I can learn from disinterested sources like Gerard and Renfield, Mayre [*sic*] seems totally unfit.[31]

Marye had been prompted to take up the treaty because there was interest in the Duma in changing or eliminating Jewish laws. He felt the passport issue might disappear before any treaty was brought before Sazonov. One indication of this was that the tsar had already issued a rescript that out-standing proceedings against Jews carrying on business outside the Pale would be dismissed.[32]

However, Marye submitted his resignation in January 1916: "The sever-ity of the winter in Petrograd I find trying to my health." His wife claimed life in Petrograd was "dull beyond the power of language to convey." Wil-son accepted Marye's resignation. House thought it was essential to rid the service of Marye, whom he felt was unfit and an embarrassment to the gov-ernment. Herbert H. D. Pierce, former minister to Norway, was dispatched to Russia, and until a new ambassador could be chosen, negotiations were tabled.[33]

2.

Many suggestions for a new ambassador were made. House believed a former minister to Argentina, John Garrett, might be suitable. Wilson remembered Brand Whitlock, then working on Belgian relief, but Whitlock refused. The president asked Lansing about a "gentleman in St. Louis," and Lansing thought he "would be a good one." Even Crane's name came up again. Edward O. Wood suggested a lawyer from the Midwest, Alfred Lucking. Crane promoted the New York lawyer George Rublee.[34]

In the end, Wilson asked David R. Francis of St. Louis, and Francis accepted. As Assistant Secretary of State William Phillips wrote, "It seems utterly hopeless to try to do anything in Russia, and I am counting the hours until you can get there and straighten out this very bad and complicated mess."[35] Phillips' comments spoke volumes about Marye's tenure.

Francis, former mayor of St. Louis, governor of Missouri, and secre-tary of the interior, had developed several ideas about American-Russian relations. American Jews were needlessly anti-Russian and should make fewer complaints; abrogation of the 1832 treaty benefited no one and accom-plished nothing; J. P. Morgan and Company was pro-British and additional American creditors had to be found; the British government had conspired with Morgan to keep the United States away from Russian markets by censoring information about Russia; the United States had to get its own cable to Russia and to take over German commercial trade.[36]

Upon arriving at his post, Francis saw that there was no system or discipline at the embassy, that it was demoralized and far behind in its work. He visited Sazonov and to his astonishment found that the foreign minister would not negotiate a treaty. The minister mentioned that at a forthcoming Allied economic conference Russia would agree to no new arrangements. Russia harbored no resentment over abrogation of the treaty. According to Francis, "I told Sazonoff, who speaks very good English, that I was greatly disappointed, and in fact decidedly so, because to negotiate such a treaty had been the main object I had had in view when accepting the appointment as Ambassador."[37]

President Wilson's ambassador believed that the delay over the treaty was due to British influence, a factor to which he had given thought while on shipboard. He had his own banking connections in New York, and cabled friends and the president that he found J. P. Morgan pro-British to the extent that he wanted to replace German dominance in the Russian trade with the British. American cables often went through Britain, and during the war the British acted as an intermediary by not relaying messages or editing them. Francis wanted direct connections because of what he foresaw as America's unlimited commercial possibilities.

Whether or not Sazonov was aware of the advantages of a treaty, he was the only individual in the government who Francis felt could aid his cause. The new State Department counselor, Frank L. Polk, believed Sazonov did not want a treaty; the "only explanation in my mind is that they are unwilling to make a treaty with us during the war as they wish to keep friendly with Japan; or the other theory would be that they have some understanding with Japan as to their relations in China and want to be independent of us in every way." Francis commented on Polk's observation: "This is unquestionably the case. Sazonoff said as much to me." The president wrote to Francis: "I have been very much concerned by your report of the present disinclination of the Russian Government to negotiate a new commercial treaty with us. I hope that you will watch very narrowly, and with as much curiosity as you can venture to exercise, the relations growing up between Russia and Japan."[38]

Francis wrote Senator William J. Stone of Missouri that "It is absolutely impossible to negotiate a commercial treaty in [which] the Jews are mentioned therein—there is no use making the effort." To Lansing he opined, "M. Sazonoff remarked to me that Russia has some Japanese subjects, and that she likes the Japanese, but that they are objectionable to America; that Russia, however, had not asked us to permit the Japanese to come into our country—and the same thing, said he applies to China." Sazonov thought that Russian Jews were pro-German and disloyal and that nearly every spy in Russia was a Jew.[39]

The Allied conference in Paris from June 14 to 17, 1916, confirmed Sazonov's position on renewal, as he had told Francis: "In effect they propose an offensive and defensive commercial alliance between the allied powers, not only during the war but throughout the reconstruction period following, and recommend such an alliance to continue through the period of permanent peace." Francis reported that the Russo-Japanese Treaty of January 3 of that year was strictly a military alliance and not commercial, as Sazonov had assured him. He continued to wish for a treaty if only the Jews would not "vent their spleen."[40]

Russians believed that because the oceans provided America with safe borders, America focused on commerce and not preparedness. It was more profitable, said the Russian consul general in Seattle, N. Bogoyavlensky, for rich America to develop trade and seek alliances against competitors, especially Japan. Though the war was seen to make Americans rich, it could bring involvement in the fighting. The consul believed that Wilson's desire to stop the European conflict was based on fear of involvements. L. Alurievsky of the *Stock Exchange Courier* in Petrograd was writing Bakhmetev that trade had to increase, but Russians had little practical experience in accomplishing that objective. The correspondent in New York City for publications of the Russian ministry of finance, A. G. Sack, was able to get a five-page supplement into the *New York Evening Post* and asked for data from the ministry to encourage the "vast interest in USA to Russian [commercial] values [and the] . . . publishing of official data of financial positions."[41]

Suddenly Sazonov resigned as foreign minister. Francis cabled: "Resignation attributed to ill health."[42] As Francis discovered, the tsar had demanded Sazonov's resignation because of pressure by Empress Alexandra and Minister of Interior Baron Boris V. Stürmer, president of the Council of Ministers, who replaced Sazonov as foreign minister.

Francis estimated Stürmer to be in his seventies. He spoke English "very indifferently." He "does not seem to have the respect of any of the prominent Russians whom I have met. His appointment is decidedly a reactionary victory." Francis quoted a Russian banker: " 'It is just as appropriate as would be the appointment of a tailor to the place I occupy.' " In a candid message Francis revealed that Stürmer was a reactionary and an opportunist with no convictions or intellect: "I have had two conferences with him and must say that he did not impress me as a man with a breadth of view or as imbued with high ideals." Stürmer showed Francis the customary courtesies and appeared interested in a treaty, but refused to act. By the end of August, the ambassador thought that getting a treaty with all the privileges of a most-favored nation would be impossible. He blamed the Jews.[43]

Ambassador Francis encouraged the vice president of the National City Bank of New York, Samuel McRoberts, to come to Russia. With the help of a syndicate of New York banks, McRoberts negotiated a credit in America of $50 million against 150 million rubles deposited in the Imperial Russian Bank. American banks would receive 6.5 percent per annum and a commission of one-quarter of 1 percent every three months, plus a favorable purchase of rubles and bonds. Francis had gotten government agreement to pay half the cost of $6 million to lay a cable between America and Russia. "The $50,000,000 loan to the Russian government, which was under negotiation for several months without being consummated, was not finally affected until McRoberts, accompanied by Rich, came to Petrograd."[44]

The State Department complained that Francis violated propriety by establishing direct relations with ministries of the government instead of going through the foreign office. To this he replied, "Baron Stürmer is in my judgment always pleased when he can 'pass the buck' to any other Department." The procedure was, he insisted, advantageous because he enjoyed relations with the minister of finance, Peter Bark. Yet when he took up the commercial treaty, Bark could only consent to details and insisted that the principles would have to be agreed upon by Stürmer. "I took up the matter with the Foreign Office and was advised by Assistant Minister Neuratoff [Neratov] that the time was not propitious for agreeing upon general principles. You can see therefore that if my diplomatic relations were strictly confined to the Foreign Office, I would make very little progress." Bark sent the ambassador back to Stürmer. At the foreign ministry Neratov believed that the times were unpropitious for general principles. It was obvious that a treaty would be impossible while the war continued.[45]

The embassy kept watch on political events. When the Fourth Duma reopened in November, Francis paid attention to speeches of the ministers of war and marine pledging army and navy support for the war and thanking the Duma and people for their cooperation. He told Lansing that "Stürmer's removal would produce pacifying effect and restore confidence. Emperor at front and inaccessible except to his staff and Empress who thought to favor Stürmer." He wrote a friend that some people thought Russia was on the eve of revolution. There was talk of removing Stürmer as well as other ministers: "if the Emperor should insist upon retaining Stürmer and should prorogue or dissolve the Duma, a revolution is likely to follow." Stürmer ultimately was removed. Francis cabled Lansing that this action eased the situation, though his successor, Alexander F. Trepov, might prove equally bad because he was not the choice of the Duma and "he is a much more dangerous man in that position than Stürmer was because he is a man with deep convictions and with a nerve of iron."[46]

The drama quickly played itself out. In December 1916 Francis wrote his son about unsettled conditions. He told his daughter-in-law that things were depressed and there were no dances, receptions, ballets, operas, or theater. The nobility feared a revolution if popular concessions were granted. He mentioned the assassination of Gregory Rasputin, the tsarina's faith healer and confidant, in a letter to the granddaughter of President Ulysses S. Grant, Princess Julia Cantacuzene-Speransky, but reserved details for his son: "the killing of a professed priest named Rasputin, whose influence over the Empress and through her the Emperor has been deplored by this country . . . he was shot and at about 6 a.m. Dec. 17th . . . the body was placed in an automobile and was taken to a bridge over the 'island,' a hole was cut in the ice and his body thrown therein. . . . and yesterday afternoon Dec. 19th, your January 1st, the body was found. One side of the face was badly mutilated." In a cable he said the killing "produced great tension" and, as a result, Premier A. F. Trepov was replaced with the aged Prince Nikolai Golitsyn; the minister of justice, A. A. Makarov, was sacked, as was the minister of education, Count Paul Ignatiev; and the minister of agriculture, Count Vladimir Bobrinsky, resigned. Alexander D. Protopopov, whom all despised as Rasputin's ally, stayed on as minister of the interior. Only Nikolai N. Pokrovsky, minister of foreign affairs, appeared "candid, courageous and sincere."[47]

Within a few months the 304-year-old Romanov dynasty collapsed. The March Revolution surprised the ambassador. The first inkling he had was on March 8, 1917, considered by many the first day: "Internal conditions in Russia are so far from being satisfactory that they are almost threatening." The Petrograd commandant, General Sergei S. Khabalov, ordered workers not to strike on threat of being shot. "Reported troubles in the streets between people and police. Streetcars stopped account strike operators." To Lansing he cabled, "several demonstrations on the streets and dissatisfaction by the laboring classes and especially by the women, who find great difficulty in getting food."[48] Efforts were made "to produce strike and lawless demonstrations." He wrote his wife, "it is now reported that there will be a general strike among the laboring people and hostile demonstrations by the women and the populace generally tomorrow and Tuesday, when the Duma will open." Cossacks had been successful in dispersing the crowds. On March 11 he scribbled in his date book, "Street troubles Riots Police using machine guns on Nevsky. Fifty people reported killed."

The ambassador recorded the storm's intensity: "Regiment soldiers mutinied killed Col commanding Joined people against police. Other regiments mutinying Many fights between soldiers and police all over city Jails opened by Army." That same day conservative Octobrist Party member Vasilii V. Shulgin told his Duma colleagues to seize power before factory workers did. Although the Duma's committee accepted the recommendation, the Provisional Government was not proclaimed until March 15. Francis recognized the reality of events: "Fierce fighting in streets and all around Embassy on Fourstaskina Serquiskaia Liteiny and Znaminskaia especially Police have machine guns on house tops. Many generals and commanding officers killed. Looks like a real revolution."[49]

In a cable Francis felt this was the "best managed revolution that had ever taken place," noting that a new government was in charge with Mikhail V. Rodzianko, president of the Duma, at its head. But he had not yet heard that Rodzianko had been pushed aside in favor of Prince George E. Lvov, a moderate Kadet Party member, and that Rodzianko's efforts to persuade the Duma committee to have the tsar form a responsible ministry had failed. The committee instead opted for the tsar's abdication. The Kadet Party, liberals directed by Paul N. Miliukov, a history professor, formed a government without Rodzianko. Francis continued to think Rodzianko was in charge. On March 16, he learned who ruled Russia: "Situation apparently under control of Duma which named Ministry with Lvov, Minister of the Interior and President of Ministers."[50]

House suggested to President Wilson that the United States recognize the government "as soon as England and France do." But Francis was one step ahead. He knew that at a British War Cabinet meeting, the secretary for foreign affairs had been authorized "to give the British Ambassador at Petrograd full discretion to recognise the de facto government, if and when he considered this to be advisable."[51]

It was the perspicacity of Francis that gave the United States the opportunity to first recognize the Provisional Government. The French ambassador, pressed by Miliukov, played a game, as did the British, to wait for a commitment to the war by the new government: "I'm not yet in a position," said Maurice Paléologue, "to tell you that the Government of the Republic recognizes the government you have set up; but I'm certain I'm only anticipating my instructions in promising you active and sympathetic assistance on my part." Francis cabled for permission to recognize because, as he put it, the old government had ceased to exist, the new was democratic, and it was prepared to prosecute the war. These were not necessary conditions for America to recognize the government. They were judgments based on conversations with Miliukov. Francis seemed more worried that if the Russians did not persist in the war and the Central Powers were victorious, the empire would be restored. As he wrote: "I have impressed this on Rodzianko and Foreign Minister Miliukoff [Miliukov] and they both expressed agreement." When Lansing discussed recognition with the president, the secretary of state noted that the Central Powers represented autocracy and the Allies democracy: "for the welfare of mankind and for the establishment of peace in the world. . . . Democracy should succeed." America's entering the war "would strengthen the new democratic government of Russia, which we ought to encourage and with whom we ought to sympathize. If we delay, conditions may change and the opportune moment when our friendship would be useful may be lost." Lansing cabled Francis: "See Miliukoff [Miliukov] for apt. with head of Provisional Gov't to tell him US desires 'to open relations with the new government of Russia.' "[52]

At a cabinet meeting on March 20, 1917, American neutrality was abandoned and the question of including Russia in the president's forthcoming war message to Congress was brought up. Lansing reported, "The President said that he did not see how he could speak of a war for Democracy or of Russia's revolution in addressing congress. I replied that I did not perceive any objection but in any event I was sure that he could do so indirectly by attacking the character of the autocratic government of Germany. . . . To this the president answered, 'Possibly.' "[53] After the cabinet met, Wilson asked Lansing and Postmaster General Albert S. Burleson how long it would take to prepare war legislation for Congress, and they replied one week. The following day he announced the calling of Congress for April 2.

In his war message to a joint session of the Congress that evening, the president referred to Russia by echoing Lansing's note of a partnership of democratic nations against autocracies, which could not be trusted to observe covenants. The Russian people were democratic and had overthrown an alien aristocracy. The "great, generous Russian people have been added in all their naïve majesty and might to the forces that are fighting for freedom in the world, for justice, and for peace. Here is a fit partner for a League of Honor."[54] The Senate acted on the war resolution on April 4, and the House approved it on Good Friday, April 6, 1917. Meanwhile, Francis had enjoyed his greatest triumph when he presented the following message to Prince Lvov on March 22, 1917:

> I have the honor as American Ambassador, and as representative of the Government of the United States accredited to Russia to hereby make formal recognition of the Provisional Government of all the Russias and to state that it gives me pleasure officially and personally to continue intercourse with Russia through the medium of the new Government. May the cordial relations existing between the two countries continue to obtain and may they prove mutually satisfactory and beneficial.[55]

The results were immediate. K. M. Onu at the Russian embassy in Washington informed the Associated Press that the ministry of foreign affairs gave "extraordinary significance at the present time to an economic rapprochement of Russia and the United States." It ordered B. E. Shatsky to work with the American-Russian Chamber of Commerce to organize a bureau in New York and Chicago. Shatsky spoke at a luncheon of the Chamber at the Biltmore Hotel. He told businessmen that this was Russia's 1776. American capital would be necessary in reconstruction, especially for railroads: "The conclusion of a Commercial Treaty between Russia and the United States is now a question of but a short time. Everybody and everything in Russia will welcome a rapprochement between Russia and the United States." The next day, the Provisional Government placed an "urgent" order for two thousand railway engines and forty thousand cars of rolling stock and planned to send an authorized person with specifications for more orders.[56]

Americans were added to the London Inter-Allied Supply Office at a meeting of the Inter-Allied Conference to gain cooperation in procurement, transport, and financing. The head of the Russian procurement committee in America, General Zaliubovsky, cabled the need to cooperate with Washington on procurement by giving information, trying for requisitions from plants receiving orders, helping in every way to bring prices down. Zaliubovsky realized how important assistance would be.[57]

Francis was critical of his staff's attitude during his recent success. They viewed all political appointments with resentment: "Their constant effort is to demonstrate to the appointee who has not been trained in the service not only their superior knowledge of the forms but his want of knowledge and utter helplessness without their assistance and guidance." By recognizing the Provisional Government he meant to convince his staff "not only that I am the Ambassador (which they had no doubt of before) but that my taking them into conference doesn't mean that they can control my action in any particular."[58]

The head of the American Federation of Labor, Samuel Gompers, sent his greetings to the Russian workers. There were suggestions about what the American government should do in regards to the Provisional Government. General G. J. Sosnowsky of the Polish Committee asked Wilson to send war matériel over the Trans-Siberian railway, along with American troops and a unit of Polish Falcons with an American general at their head. Secretary of War Newton D. Baker thought the idea worth considering. Lansing threw in a suggestion that the president say something to assure the Provisional Government of his personal support for the establishment of democratic institutions.[59]

The First Cold War Cabinet, the White House, Summer 1917. Front row, left to right: Secretary of Commerce William Redfield, Secretary of State Robert Lansing, Secretary of Agriculture David Houston, President Woodrow Wilson, Secretary of the Treasury William McAdoo, Postmaster General Albert Burleson. Back row: Secretary of the Navy Josephus Daniels, Secretary of Labor William B. Wilson, Secretary of War Newton Baker, Attorney General Thomas W. Gregory, Secretary of the Interior Franklin K. Lane. Courtesy of the Prints and Photographs Division of the Library of Congress.

The most important suggestion, as it turned out, was made independently of the administration. Oscar Straus, who had been a leader in the struggle for abrogation of the commercial treaty, wrote Lansing, "we could send over to Russia a selected number of men of international experience who might be highly welcomed and most useful in enlightening the masses in Russia, presenting to them from America's concrete experiences the blessings and opportunities free government affords."[60] The idea had occurred to other persons, each with his own ideas about goals. House and Wilson endorsed the suggestion.

The First Cold War Cabinet plus one, Summer White House in Cornish, New Hampshire, Summer 1917. Colonel Edward Mandell House with President Woodrow Wilson. Courtesy of the Still Picture Unit, National Archives.

What if America at this critical moment had poured whatever material, money, and troops it could spare into support for the Provisional Government? Could Wilson have saved the government? Some individuals thought so and gave of their wisdom, actions, and largesse to prevent the government's collapse. Perhaps it is not in the realm of possibility for one state to save another from its destiny, if destiny it be. Wilson's efforts unfortunately were so small as to beg the question. In fairness, the ardor and optimism of Ambassador Francis, advice of his military attaché Brigadier General William V. Judson, efforts of American Red Cross official Raymond Robins, a million dollars paid out of his own pocket by the chief of the U.S. Red Cross Mission, William B. Thompson, all aimed at preserving the Eastern Front, were to no avail. No one sensed Russia's profound social, economic, and political distress.[61]

It was encouraging that President Wilson recognized the Provisional Government, whatever his motives. It was a bright light in an otherwise dismal record for the Wilson administration's Russian policy of interminable delays in appointing an ambassador and failing to renegotiate a commercial treaty. Now the president had to act swiftly to support his new Russian ally at history's turning point by adopting and acting upon a policy of substance.

Two

1917
The Root Mission and Stevens Railway Commission

Through March 1917 the United States focused primarily upon reviving the 1832 treaty of commerce with Russia. These negotiations proved difficult, owing to professional incompetence, bureaucratic impediments, and misunderstandings between the two countries. The March Revolution in Russia and the rise of the Provisional Government completely altered the situation, especially since the Wilson administration immediately recognized the new government. Now President Wilson needed to follow up this recognition with a vigorous policy, to be carried out by Ambassador Francis, that aimed at securing the new Russian democracy from internal and external foes. Instead, the president opted for delay and further ambiguity: he selected two "committees," the Root Mission and the Stevens Railway Commission, to study the situation in Russia. While he awaited their expert advice, he cautiously extended credits. This watch-and-wait policy further reflected Wilson's and his administration's lack of understanding of Russian affairs at the very moment when the most profound understanding was necessary. The time from March to November 1917 represented a lost opportunity of gargantuan proportions. Russian democracy was irretrievably lost to Bolshevism and a stalwart ally sacrificed to German militarism.

1.

The head of the mission, Elihu Root, appeared well suited to such a task. His background seemed impeccable. The chief officer of New York City's most important law firm, he was a former secretary of war (under Presidents McKinley and Roosevelt), secretary of state (Roosevelt), and senator from New York. Secretary of State Lansing's description of the Root Mission, approved by Wilson, was to "cooperate and aid Russia in the accomplishment of the task," that is, the war. They eventually advanced a credit of slightly more than $300 million to propagandize Russian soldiers and improve the Trans-Siberian railway in order to get war matériel to the Eastern Front. When Root got to Petrograd, he put the purpose of his mission bluntly: "No fight, no loan." He later complained that the mission was "a grand-stand play," in which the president "wanted to show his sympathy for the Russian Revolution. When we delivered his message and made our speeches, he was satisfied: that's all he wanted."[1] The Root Mission sought to dissuade Russia from signing a quick peace agreement with Germany and its allies. Wilson and Lansing would have perceived an armistice and peace treaty with the Central Powers as a terrible blow for democracy. Indeed, the new Russian government would have violated the London Treaty of September 1914 that forbade a separate peace to be made by one of the Allied powers.

Root's mission was designed to confirm friendship, encourage Russian democracy, and look to "the best ways and means to bring about effective cooperation between the two Governments in the prosecution of the war against German autocracy."[2] However, Russia had to be prevented from dropping out of the war. In this way, the mission failed utterly.

Russian Foreign Minister Paul Miliukov promised Wilson that the Provisional Government would continue to fight the Germans, and the president accepted the pledge at face value.[3] To Wilson it seemed logical to accept Miliukov's commitment. Nevertheless, Wilson wanted to greet the new democracy. Therefore, when Assistant Secretary of State William Phillips spoke with the adopted son of the Russian writer Maxim Gorky, Zinovi Peshkov, the Russian suggested a "commission of three men to speak with the Russian people" to create an atmosphere of friendship that would be helpful in negotiation. As Lansing noted, "we must prepare the way to negotiate a new treaty with Russia which will secure satisfactory commercial relations after the war is over." The secretary asked Wilson to consider the suggestion in light of a long-term relationship with the new democracy.[4]

Oscar Straus had suggested sending a select few who might enlighten Russia on democracy. The idea gained currency when Colonel House reported that he had promised Straus to take up the matter. Straus thought that House ought to be chairman of such a commission and that former President Taft and the writer George Kennan should be included on it. House declined. Straus suggested putting Taft's name forward as well as the propaganda value of such a commission.[5]

House indicated that a commission would show "goodwill and financial support" if the Russians could "compose their internal differences and not make a separate peace at this time." The British ambassador to the United States and House's close friend Cecil Spring Rice commented that Americans were "very anxious about the Russian Revolution."[6]

Lansing made the first move after receiving a note from Ambassador Francis that Russian naval defenses were precarious, its military not wholly satisfactory, and that socialist circles were urging peace. He forwarded the cable to Wilson, adding his concern about socialism and asking the president to proceed with a commission of three persons, including Samuel Gompers, head of the A.F. of L. [American Federation of Labor], to influence the socialists. Josephus Daniels, secretary of the navy, worried that German socialists were trying to influence Russian socialists to support a separate peace.[7]

The president liked the idea of a commission. He desired men of "large vision, tested discretion, and a sympathetic appreciation of just what it is they have been sent over for." He mentioned Straus, Willard Straight, Gompers, Benjamin Wheeler, and the University of Chicago scholar Samuel Harper. Charles Crane might join the commission. It should include the "right men," enthusiastic for the revolution's success. Lansing backed Gompers, but not Straus, Straight, or Wheeler, and suggested the head of the YMCA, John R. Mott; the businessman Cyrus McCormick; two financiers, Howard Elliott and S. R. Bertron; and Crane. Harper, Lansing noted, was not as well liked as he had thought. Wilson jotted at the bottom of Lansing's memorandum his first and second lists: Gompers, Crane, Bertron, McCormick, Root; and as seconds, Mott, Gompers, Crane, New York lawyer Bainbridge Colby, McCormick, and Bertron.[8] The tedious process of naming the mission's members thus played out with much disagreement over its composition, particularly over finding a representative diversity that was also favorable to the Wilson administration.

House asked Wilson to consider the president's son-in-law, Secretary of the Treasury William G. McAdoo, to head the mission. He recommended appointing Henry Morgenthau, the wealthy New Yorker, or Straus as a Jewish representative. At a cabinet meeting following a conference with Counselor Polk, Lansing also suggested McAdoo. Root's name was considered.[9] McAdoo spoke to Lansing concerning Root and obtained his backing. He wrote the president about how the country would support Root. It was McAdoo who had suggested Root at the cabinet meeting. Only Daniels opposed Root due to his conservatism, offering the names of former Secretary of State Bryan and Theodore Roosevelt because Russians considered them liberals. Lansing and McAdoo criticized these choices, as did Wilson. The president asked Lansing to find out if Root was a friend of Russia; after a talk with Root, Lansing said that he was.[10]

Secretary Lansing cabled Francis to ask Miliukov if the mission would be acceptable and if a "prominent Hebrew" could be on it.[11] Meanwhile, McAdoo discussed it with Lansing and wrote Wilson, "I feel certain that

Mr. Root is the right man to head this Commission. . . . Messers. Charles R. Crane, Cyrus McCormick and S. R. Bertron would make excellent members." He added Eugene Meyer, Jr., a prominent Jewish businessman; Associate Justice Louis D. Brandeis of the Supreme Court; and A. H. Smith, president of the New York Central Railroad, and also suggested representatives of the army and navy. At last, the president wrote Lansing that he had given much thought to the mission:

> I hope that in your conference with him today you will find Mr. Root a real friend of the revolution. If you do, the Commission that has framed itself in my mind would be as follows:
>   Elihu Root, New York
>   John R. Mott, New York
>   Charles R. Crane
>   Cyrus H. McCormick, Chicago
>   Eugene Meyer, Jr., New York
>   S. R. Bertron, New York
>   John F. Stevens, New York

He feared to send Gompers, who was no socialist, but he felt that a pro-socialist labor representative would have to be sent.[12] The president added Stevens because of his reputation as an engineer.

The reasons that Wilson agreed to Root had almost nothing to do with Russia. He thought Root was an example of American unity during wartime. Wilson was a Democrat, Root a Republican, and it was a good opportunity to demonstrate that Wilson could place the needs of the nation ahead of party. Root had encouraged Republicans to work with the administration and not to demand cabinet positions in Wilson's wartime government. The *New York Times* ran a story, "Root Opposes Coalition Plan, Such a Cabinet Not Needed When We Are All Behind the President" and "Must Support Democrats," describing how Root had delivered his endorsement as keynote speaker at a Republican dinner. Root also added dignity to the delegation. As he admitted to former President Taft, he detested the journey: "You have no idea how I hate it, but it's just like our boys going into the war: there can be no question in doing it."[13] He felt trapped not only by his sense of duty to his country but also by his words at the dinner.

Lansing recorded in his desk diary: "Root agreed to head Com. to Russia." Thomas W. Brahany, a member of the White House staff, attending a reception at the Pan American Union Building, overheard the New Yorker speaking with the president: "The President was very cordial. I understand the President wishes Root to go to Russia as a member of a special American Commission and I think Root advised the President last night of his willingness to go."[14]

Of course there were individuals who disagreed with the appointment. Rabbi Stephen S. Wise of New York wrote Wilson that Root represented a style of government opposed to that of Wilson. Meyer London, congressman from New York, begged the president to revoke the appointment of Root, the "last man in the world to command the confidence of that awakened country." Senator Hiram W. Johnson of California said much the same thing. Straus and Francis were wary of the appointment.[15]

But Root had his boosters, especially Taft, who wrote him: "I had no idea that Wilson would be wise enough to select the best man in the United States to go to Russia." The *New York Times* echoed this sentiment by endorsement of the idea of a commission and support for Root: "We give the highest possible proof of the depth and sincerity of our interest in the welfare of the new Government of Russia by sending to Petrograd a mission having at its head a statesman of the eminence of Elihu Root."[16]

Lansing informed Francis of the mission and clarified the mistaken Russian idea that British and French missions then in America were holding conferences on the war and ignoring the Russian government. Their missions wished to give Americans information to help avoid problems in military cooperation and expressed gratification over America's entry into the war. The Italian government was planning to do likewise. As Lansing told Francis, the "primary purpose of this commission" was to "convey to the Russian Government the friendship and good will of this nation and to express the confident hope that the Russian people, having developed a political system founded on the principle of democracy," would continue in the war. The commission would seek the most efficient means of cooperating. It was at this moment that Lansing learned of the Russian government's intention to send a mission to America to be chaired by Boris A. Bakhmetev, assistant minister of trade and industry and intended ambassador to replace George P. Bakhmetev.[17] (The two Bakhmetevs were not related.)

The president reported to his friend and former Princeton classmate Cyrus McCormick that a government ship would be ready in a week for the voyage to Vladivostok. Arrangements were being made to assemble a staff. Root wanted Colonel T. Bentley Mott as his secretary and suggested Count Tolstoy, son of the Russian writer, to accompany the mission. He also nominated pro-Ally socialist William E. Walling, who spoke Russian. Secretary of War Baker had a chance to chat with Root about the mission and suggested the well-known war correspondent Stanley Washburn.[18]

While Root's appointment continued to raise criticism from liberals, Postmaster General Burleson asked that Colonel William V. Judson be placed on the staff. After all, Burleson reasoned, Judson had been detailed by the War Department as an observer during the Russo-Japanese War and was, like Washburn, in touch with Minister of Defense Alexander Guchkov. But Baker also wanted Walling. Wilson agreed: "Mr. Walling," he wrote Lansing, "is the man we want."[19]

The mission needed additional representatives from the military, and for this purpose Wilson selected Major General Hugh L. Scott, recently retired as chief of staff and succeeded by General Peyton C. March; Wilson also appointed as ordnance expert Rear Admiral James H. Glennon. Baker noted that Scott was selected because he was to show Russians the importance America attached to the mission. Reluctant to serve, Scott said that he would accept the president's wishes cheerfully, although the country might need him for conduct of the war. He doubted the possibility of the mission's success: he thought that whatever encouragement it might offer would be too little, too late.[20]

Lansing continued to weigh the value of having a Jew on the mission. He worried over its appropriateness, thinking that it might look as if America was more interested in the passport issue than a commercial treaty. Bertron and Harper asked that Jews should not be on the mission, but House wanted Straus. Lansing hoped Gompers would represent Jews, but Gompers declined. Lansing learned from the foreign ministry, via Francis, that there were no Russian objections to a Jew. Wilson settled on Eugene Meyer. Even so, Francis reported that members of the Provisional Government had cautioned against a Jew as either chairman or vice-chairman. Thus Wilson asked Lansing to get Meyer to withdraw. Lansing had Justice Brandeis explain the situation to Meyer and reported that the latter agreed to step aside. However, Prince Lvov denied his government ever made such a request.[21]

The president sought to find an acceptable socialist. Secretary of Labor William B. Wilson backed Walling. Lansing had read Walling's book, *The Socialist and the War*, and had seen an essay in it by Charles Edward Russell. Root again suggested Walling. However, Walling told Polk that another socialist might be more effective because he himself had differed with most of them over the war issue. Socialists such as Russell, Upton Sinclair, and William J. Ghent had condemned the antiwar resolution adopted by the socialist national executive committee. On Lansing's advice, the president asked the secretary of labor to invite Russell.[22]

Staff for the mission included General Judson, Colonel Mott, and Stanley Washburn. Basil Miles of the State Department went as secretary, with Washburn his assistant. Eugene Prince, privately employed in Petrograd, acted as translator.[23]

During the process of composing the mission, Lansing persuaded Wilson to clarify America's war aims. Francis received a note, prepared by Lansing with Wilson's approval, calling for Germany's defeat, a peace of no annexations or indemnities, and a "common covenant" for securing peace. But important socialist elements of the Petrograd Soviet wanted an immediate peace.

M. I. Tereshchenko, Paul Miliukov's replacement after the riots created by the May 1 promise of Foreign Minister Miliukov that Russia would fight to victory instead of seeking an immediate peace, received Wilson's note. Wilson should have been aware that this very point, fighting rather than an armistice, incited the riots. Lvov's Council of Ministers declared their government's adherence to its military obligations. Tereshchenko nevertheless requested that the phrases "The war has begun to go against Germany" or "The day has come to conquer or submit" be eliminated. The first case might be interpreted as suggesting that no further efforts were necessary. In the second, he believed that any peace, German or Allied, would be dictated and annexationist, qualities to which the Petrograd Soviet would object. Lansing told Francis, however, that Wilson's note was "not subject to any change." Wilson was impressed with the new coalition government's pledge to live up to its obligations. "I have read the attached paper," he wrote Lansing, "with the profoundest interest. I hope with all my heart that the new forces in Russia may be guided by the principles and objects it sets forth!" It was at this time that Wilson's message, summarizing America's war aims and peace program and containing none of the changes urged by Tereshchenko, went to Francis for publication. Wilson's message was published on May 28, leaving Root's mission little else to do but congratulate the new Russian government. The president was only prepared to advance large sums of money, supplies, and troops on the condition that Russia stay in the war. Francis and Tereshchenko thought that the president's message was a response to the May riots caused by the "Miliukov Affair," but Lansing stressed that it was for the Russian people.[24]

The mission prepared to take leave of Washington on May 14, two months after the tsar's abdication. At a luncheon hosted by Lansing, Root remarked that Secretary of the Navy Daniels had banned liquor from all ships, although Root's wife had placed two cases of Scotch on board the ship taking the mission from Seattle to Vladivostok. When Russell joked about the secretary's righteousness, Mott interjected that American mothers would thank him for his temperance measure with the navy.[25] With such light-hearted banter, the mission began its perilous journey.

The trip across the country to Seattle was enlivened by a stopover in Chicago, where Professor Harper spoke about stability in Russia (Harper later joined Root in Russia).[26] "Soviet Sam," as his students came to call him in the 1920s, was wide of the mark. The mission reached Seattle and departed on the cruiser USS *Buffalo,* arriving in Russia on June 3. Ten days later it reached Petrograd. Three critical months had now passed since the March Revolution. The honeymoon was over.

While the mission was being assembled, Francis had publicized Wilson's war message and Gompers's greetings to the people of Russia. He reported on his efforts to support the Provisional Government. The ambassador emphasized his insistence on Russia's staying in the war, especially during the year that it might take America to mobilize. He recommended sending railway experts and an immediate $100 million credit. Negotiations were carried on for five hundred locomotives and ten thousand freight cars; McAdoo cabled Francis that Root would delve more fully into Russia's financial needs. Nevertheless, by November, $325 million in credits were extended to the Provisional Government, but only $187,729,750 was spent. Another $125 million had been authorized.[27]

In a cable Francis explained that in the Russian capital power was shared between the liberal Provisional Government and the socialist Petrograd Soviet. This forced the former to move cautiously, as it wanted to pursue the war while the Soviet was reluctant to keep Russia in the war. Even so, the Soviet initially endorsed the Provisional Government's war policy. A delegation of British and French socialists had advised it on this matter. As to the worry of the American government over the Jewish issue, Francis indicated restrictions were being removed even if prejudices persisted. He sent the secretary of state a pessimistic report from Consul General Maddin Summers in Moscow that the Russian army had ceased to exist and that returning soldiers were a source of chaos. He noted Bolshevik leader V. I. Lenin's violent speeches. The U.S. consul in Petrograd, North Winship, warned the State Department that the Petrograd Soviet showed little support for the war, calling it "distasteful and irksome." He predicted a coalition government: "The masses want not a separate peace, but an end of the war. A cessation of hostilities on the front now exists, and this state will continue. A Russian offensive should not be hoped for." He continued, "The Consulate can not forbear to mention here what it considers the gravest menace to Russia at the present time; namely, the narrow partisanship, the bigotry and fanaticism of the socialist press." Francis cabled, "Guchkov, Minister of War, resigned ostensibly on account of illness, but really because objected to workmen's committee, demanding right to approve orders. Excellent man, resignation deplorable." Guchkov's resignation had followed Miliukov's. Francis recommended support "to sustain new Ministry as it is most potential influence in representing and preventing lawlessness."[28] The resignations of Miliukov and Guchkov proved a further blow to the Root Mission, for they indicated a swing to the socialist left in the Provisional

Government's first coalition with some members of the Petrograd Soviet following the "Miliukov Affair."

Francis met the mission on June 14 when it arrived in Petrograd from Vladivostok and escorted it to the Winter Palace, the mission's residence. The following day it was introduced to Tereshchenko and the Council of Ministers at the Mariinsky Palace. Root's speeches emphasized the mission's purpose: welcoming Russian democracy and continuing the war. Losing the war to Germany's "military autocracy" meant exchanging freedom for servitude, according to Root. As Root came to understand the primitive nature of Russian democracy, he realized that Russia was not willing to make the utmost sacrifices to preserve what Russians could not comprehend. Indeed, as Root gained a greater appreciation for Russia's recently won freedom, its situation became more perilous to him. From the beginning, this Yankee statesman harbored a doubt as to whether Russia had the will to protect itself against a "malign and sinister control of German autocracy." Shortly after his return to the states, he told a gathering chaired by Straus that Russians had never been taught to govern themselves, had no institutions of national self-government, and were wholly ignorant of how to sustain a popularly elected government.[29]

In addressing Petrograd's Russian-American Chamber of Commerce, Root had stated the mission's purpose: "We came to Russia to bring assurances of the spiritual brotherhood of the two great democracies, and we came, moreover, to learn how we could best do our part as allies of the Russian democracy by material as well as spiritual aid, in the great fight for the freedom of both our nations."[30] Initially, this meant expediting a previous order of 375 locomotives, 10,000 rolling stock, and adding a new order of 500 locomotives and another 10,000 freight cars. Root advanced a $1 million credit and promised more along this line. The expected arrival of American railway experts would double railroad efficiency. However, the United States extended little in the way of specific help, and Root's emphasis continued to be on the "certainty of a permanent and persistent and effective ally" for winning the war. Notwithstanding his timidity about U.S. credits while in Russia, when he addressed the Union League Club of New York in August, Root's attitude was far from the parsimonious stance he took in Russia. Here he recommended "rendering the full measure of help to Russia. . . . Material, substantial, practical aid is needed that Russia shall go on with the war. That we must give if we are true to our assurances, and if we are true to our principles."[31] Yet his own belated grandstanding got him nowhere with Wilson.

Root came to explain the threatened collapse of Russia by a conspiracy theory, no doubt influenced by the view of Ambassador Francis: Russian will to fight was seriously eroded by German propagandists in collusion with extreme socialists, anarchists, internationalists, and the old tsarist secret police and bureaucrats. Germans swarmed across Russia's borders, bribing sympathizers. Here was a clear reason why Russia now needed more material help than ever before. Otherwise, these "sinister influences" would destroy free Russia and then offer Germany a separate peace. Root lamented, "it was the eleventh hour that we came into the vineyard. . . . The great opportunity of the American people was slipping away before they could grasp it."[32]

Even while he was still in Russia, Root reported, "German Government's intrigues in Russia have made President Wilson anxious to try the scheme as soon as possible."[33] The scheme here referred to was thought up by the British intelligence officer in Washington, Sir William Wiseman. House and Polk had asked Wiseman about employing an agent in Russia to counter German propaganda. Wiseman inquired of Sir Eric Drummond, secretary to Sir Edward Grey, the British foreign secretary, "House understood that you would put the proposal before the proper person in London and advise him through me of the result." Wiseman mentioned that Washington had made seventy-five thousand dollars available for the project and had asked an equal amount from the British government. "I will," he said, "arrange to submit reports regarding Russian scheme to House." He ended, "I shall of course not report to House or any one here as to methods explored, but only as to results."[34]

The British foreign office cabled that it was entirely in favor of the idea of an Anglo-American agent. It thought the United States should handle the matter. "Dual control is difficult, and we feel it would be better that we should not in any way appear even unofficially."[35] Wiseman recommended that House explain the scheme to Wilson, "who has become particularly interested since receiving messages from Mr. Root." He did not think that the Americans would go along unless the British did and, most significantly, "It is possible that by acting practically as a confidential agent for the United States Government I might strengthen understanding with House that in future he will keep us informed of steps taken by the United States Government in their foreign affairs, which would not ordinarily be a matter of common knowledge to governments of the two countries." The question of control, in Wiseman's opinion, was not difficult because "they will leave everything to me. You may be sure that great discretion will be used and that H.M. [His Majesty's] Government will not even unofficially appear."[36]

Nothing sufficient came of this scheme to counter German intrigue and propaganda. All the while, the mission continued gathering observations about the situation in Russia. Four days after his arrival, General Scott grasped the extent of the chaos in the Russian army. He sent a grim message to Secretary of War Baker: "We find things in pretty bad shape; there are several million soldiers away from the front and but little discipline, among those that are there every organization is said to be run by a town meeting affair—with but little regard for the officers." He conferred with Alexander Kerensky, Guchkov's socialist replacement as minister of war and navy, and reported that the latter was not sanguine about carrying on the war. Scott found that the military needs of Russia were largely dependent on an immediate supply of locomotives and freight cars. He mentioned stirring up war enthusiasm but felt the generals would not appreciate such a suggestion. Why should substantial material help be given, Scott believed, if Russia was to make peace? Root agreed.[37]

Yet Root thought an American informational campaign could counter German and socialist propaganda. He requested one hundred thousand dollars as start-up money for an effort requiring $5 million to produce leaflets, posters, newspapers, pamphlets, and films to be distributed at the front. If Russia was to be saved, it would have to be saved on the cheap. Root suggested YMCA canteens to build morale behind the lines. He pointed out the immaturity of Russian democracy, which required "kindergarten" materials to remove confusion.

Lansing cabled Root that his recommendations for creating an agency for publicity were getting prompt consideration in Washington. McAdoo offered an initial thirty thousand dollars and promised the remainder after a plan was developed. Root again cabled concerning the mission's view that an "extensive educational publicity campaign be undertaken" as the "best possible contribution." The president approved McAdoo's thirty thousand dollars and the principle of the idea. The French and British distributed a million copies of Root's speech to the Provisional Government and Tereshchenko's reply. The mission used the thirty thousand dollars to hand out half a million copies of Wilson's "Message to Russia."[38]

The writer George Creel had been appointed to head the Committee on Public Information (COMPUB) in Washington. Creel agreed to the Root Mission's recommendation of the importance of propaganda, but felt the $285,500 immediately asked for should be closer to $810,000 because "What we do in Russia must be done well and done quickly." He proposed dividing propaganda into a news and feature service ($500,000), a film service ($300,000), and a soldiers' newspaper ($10,000). His committee, he indicated, would take charge of the operation by setting up shop in Petrograd.[39] As wartime costs went, this was still a pittance.

Not everyone on the mission agreed with Root about a propaganda campaign to save Russia. The contrast was stark. For instance, General Judson reported to Postmaster General Burleson in late June, on Russian affairs: "The situation here is the most difficult imaginable to estimate." His source was former war minister Guchkov, who felt conditions were nearing a precipice. "As far as concerns men," Judson said, "the Russian Army vastly outnumbers the enemy: probably it is not so well as regards heavy guns and perhaps machine guns. The Russians have the munitions for a great campaign. It is all a question of the state of their minds. This appears to tremble in the balance." He had not disagreed with the diagnosis that propaganda would help resolve Russia's problems, but his views went far beyond mere propaganda: "Meantime the Russians are detaining 126 enemy infantry divisions on their front as against 154 such divisions on the Western front." He concluded, "The present situation is vastly better than it would become if the Russians were to quit." Almost no one else but General Scott hinted at the idea of the Russians quitting the war, and Scott was willing to risk American maintenance of the Russian army even if it meant wasting resources that might better be used elsewhere. Judson recommended that "Aside from affording the Russians moral and financial support it seems to me that our assistance should take the form of 20,000 to 30,000 cars and about 1000 to 3000 locomotives, sent as quickly as possible to Vladivostok; 100 to 300 airplanes in complete organization; & 1 to 3 regiments of R.R. engineers to assemble locomotives at Vladivostok and operate the road as far westward as the Russians [see] fit."[40] At last some suggested real help.

Journeys of the mission to and from Moscow provided a chance for oratory that emphasized faith in democracy. Root's optimism fooled some, but not House, Lansing, Polk, or Baker. Baker complained, "We eagerly await the meager dispatches we get from Russia. We do not hear very much." He continued, "The Russian Mission here has given us a very encouraging view of conditions in Russia."[41]

Washburn agreed to the need for propaganda but focused on other tactics:

My feeling is however that we have a very difficult period ahead of us this summer and especially this winter in Russia . . . the Finns generally so hostile to Russia and so soaked in German propaganda . . . Personally I see no military obstacle to their [Germans] taking Petrograd in from 60 to 90 days. . . . Propaganda has seemed to me from the beginning to be the only solution but apparently this view is not shared in Washington. . . . German propaganda has run riot here for three months. . . . In the fall there is going to be widespread destitution in the big cities here [but] I am of the opinion that we should at once prepare on a large scale an American Russian Relief to be available here when the cold weather comes.[42]

Kerensky became prime minister in July as a result of Lvov's resignation over Ukrainian separatism. He began a crackdown on the Bolsheviks, accusing them of being responsible for the July Days insurrection protesting the war, which followed the unsuccessful "Kerensky" offensive of late June—Russia's last military effort of World War I.[43] Lenin fled to Finland and Trotsky was arrested along with other important Bolsheviks. The new Russian ambassador in America, Boris A. Bakhmetev, when he was not giving propaganda speeches on Russia's supposed stability, sounded a more realistic note. He told House that Vladivostok had eight months' worth of supplies but did not have the rolling stock to get them to the front. Archangel would close in October due to freezing. Financial credits were only extended by $125 million, raising the total to $450 million—still far out of proportion to what America promised the other Allies. "Unless money can be had," said House, "he [Bakhmeteff] believes the Government cannot last." The politics of the Petrograd Soviet edged farther and farther to the left the longer the war continued. House seemed to understand the extremity of this situation. He warned Wilson:

> I am wondering if you cannot say a word to Denman, on the one hand, and McAdoo on the other, and send word to Willard or Felton regarding the necessity for rolling stock. Felton has the matter in direct charge, but is favoring France rather than Russia, I am told. If the war is to end on the field it seems fairly clear that it cannot end on the Western Front. Have you thought of the advisability of sending some of our troops to Russia via the Pacific? They would have open warfare instead of trench warfare, and would be a steadying force to the Russians. I do not think we can devote too much attention to the Russian situation, for if that fails us our troubles will be great and many.[44]

Now, with little accomplished, the Root Mission prepared to return home. Except for Crane, who remained on personal business, and Judson, who was detached to head the military mission with the rank of brigadier general, the mission would go back via the Trans-Siberian to Vladivostok and the cruiser *Buffalo* with only the start of a propaganda campaign to show for its efforts. Members cabled Washington individually. Washburn stated that there was no government; committees changed; the labor situation was bad; cities lacked fuel and food; German agitators moved about freely; only a miracle could change things. Mott echoed Washburn's pessimism. Scott also reported on the approaching collapse, inadequacy of railway stock, and inefficiency of railroad management. He again asked whether assisting the Russians financially would help them stay in the war. There would be an advantage: "[I]t would pay us to lend Russia a billion dollars and send her all the cars and engines we can, if doing so would prevent her from making peace this winter with Germany."[45]

The mission reached Seattle on August 6. A final report, drafted at sea, was submitted to Mott, who gave it to the president. The question of war supplies and an expeditionary force to fight alongside the Russians was subordinated, indeed buried, to that of improving morale, which, it was thought by Wilson, rested on maintaining a free government. Only winning the war would prevent the Germans from reinstalling the tsarist government. The Wilsonians were badly mistaken in their belief that Russians would fight and die to the last man in order to save their newly found democracy, even with a $450 million credit. A supplementary report by Washburn proposed propaganda from America by George Creel with a journalist, Edgar Sisson, heading it in Russia in order to boost the Russian democratic ideal. It would be a very hard sell. A cable service was to be established between Petrograd and Washington as well as a YMCA program and a motion picture service.[46] Such was the help offered to Russia by the Wilson administration.

Lansing read the report and its supplement and spoke with mission members. Like House, he remained skeptical of democracy in Russia and the will to continue the war. He was in a quandary about the views of the mission and could not rely upon them: "I am astounded at their optimism."[47]

Various views on the Russian crisis and the success of the Root Mission began to circulate. Walling gave a harsh judgment: "They sent the Root Commission which was lost in Russia like babes in the woods." At a British War Cabinet meeting, Major-General F. C. Poole expressed the opinion that four-fifths of Russians wanted an immediate peace. House thought that making Russia a virile republic was more important than bringing Germany to its knees. Wiseman saw the situation as hopeless and told House so. Major-General Alfred W. F. Knox, once British observer to the tsar's army, informed the War Cabinet that the situation was desperate and that General L. G. Kornilov, commander in chief of the Provisional Government's army, should have been supported when he tried to overthrow Prime Minister Kerensky's government in early September. Even Cyrus McCormick had thrown up his hands when told of General Kornilov's effort, saying the news was so bad that he simply could not understand it.[48]

Root sought a private conference with the president about a program of assistance. It took place on August 30. According to William Phillips of the State Department,

> Senator Root and Dr. Mott had a conference, this afternoon with the President on subject of the program of assistance for Russia, which calls for the expenditure of several millions, partly in publicity work. The President felt

that the government should not hand out the money, but that the same result should be gained in some round-about way. I do not know how in the world he is going to do it.[49]

The American press feared a takeover by the left, since Kornilov's rightist coup had failed. Henry Morgenthau had written to Lansing that America must "prevent any internal disturbance in Russia at this time." A *New York Times* editorial had said that the mission would offer Russia its wisdom to stop radicalism. Lansing viewed the mission's role as prevention of a seizure of power by socialists.[50] These views were very different from Root's "no fight, no loan" formula. The question had now become the survival of Russian democracy itself instead of simply Russia's continued military participation. Everything now depended on what Phillips correctly characterized as Wilson's "some round-about way" diplomacy.

2.

At this point, with the Root Mission virtually a failure, its members back in Washington or otherwise dispersed to their homes, some account must be offered of the simultaneous mission of the engineer John F. Stevens, formerly chief engineer on the Panama Canal project. His commission was supported by the Wilson administration in the hope that he might be able to make the Trans-Siberian railway more efficient and ease the passage of Allied war supplies from Vladivostok to the front so that the Russians could continue the war with Germany. Such an effort might keep the Provisional Government in the war in support of the Allies and their new associate, the United States. This ended up being the main material support offered to Russia by Wilson.

The British War Cabinet had reported that "Americans were apparently coming to terms as regards the assistance of the latter in reorganizing the Siberian railways." Lansing received an appeal from Petrograd, which he paraphrased: "I would urgently recommend that there be sent to Vladivostok immediately a commission of railroad experts." Maddin Summers, U.S. consul general in Moscow, suggested that railroad men go to Vladivostok to relieve the congestion there. Hugh Moran, a YMCA worker in Irkutsk, told him that the Trans-Siberian was the "alimentary canal" of Russia and that it would require a group of experts, not just a few dozen, to get it working properly.[51]

There was talk that John F. Stevens might head a railway commission. Stevens had earlier accepted service on Root's mission. Root, in response to Lansing's suggestion, asked what sense it made to send a separate railroad commission and risk "three bodies dealing with the Russian Government at the same time—the regular Embassy, the President's Mission & the RR Commission." He therefore suggested that the latter be attached to his mission as advisers. Wilson decided in favor of a separate commission. This turned out to be another error in judgment: the mission and the railroad commission got in each other's way. Lansing drew up two draft instructions for the president's consideration concerning Stevens. In draft "A," Stevens was to let it be known that his commission was "subsidiary" to Root. In draft "B," Stevens was to restrict himself to transportation, the supply of material for railway construction, and the furnishing of men to manage and operate lines. The president rejected draft "A" because "It bears no resemblance to that of the Commission of which Mr. Root is to act as chairman. It is not going to ask what can the United States do for Russia, but only to say we have been sent here to put ourselves at your disposal to do anything we can to assist in the working out of your transportation problem." The Stevens commission was to report nothing to Washington but only serve at the pleasure of the Russian government. It was left to Lansing to explain to Root that his mission was political, while Stevens's was technical.[52] Ultimately, Root's judgment of the Stevens commission proved correct, and Stevens entangled himself in unwarranted promises of American aid.

When addressing a meeting of the Council of National Defense the previous March, Washburn had recommended that America take over the management of the Trans-Siberian railway. Not only might German submarines close the Baltic but also the German army, with Finnish help, could cut the route south of Archangel. This would shut Russia off from most Allied aid, which would mean that Russia's main aid would come virtually alone from America via the poorly managed and ill-equipped Trans-Siberian railway. Baker told Lansing that Daniel Willard, chairman of the Advisory Commission of the National Defense Council, supported Washburn's recommendation. Willard suggested that a small number of competent railway men travel to Russia to study what would be required to avoid war matériel getting stranded in Vladivostok. Willard apprised Francis, who replied that the Russian government reluctantly consented to such an inspection. He maintained that congestion had to be relieved, and the Russian embassy in Washington authorized America to send another commission. On May 1 Lansing made the recommendation to Wilson, and on May 3 Lansing cabled Francis that Stevens would head for Vladivostok within a week. On May 8 the commission conferred with Wilson and departed for Russia.[53]

Members of the Stevens commission included John E. Greiner, consultant for the Baltimore and Ohio Railroad; George Gibbs, mechanical engineer with the Pennsylvania Railroad; W. L. Darling, civil engineer;

and Henry Miller, general manager of the Wabash. Francis assigned Frank Golder of Harvard University and Eugene Prince to act as translators. On May 15 Ambassador Francis reported to Lansing that N. V. Nekrasov, minister of finance, had given Stevens total control of the Vladivostok terminal. Francis hoped control would be extended to the entire Siberian system. He sent Captain E. Francis Riggs, his assistant military attaché, to meet the commission in Vladivostok. Riggs and the commission arrived in Petrograd in June.[54]

Stevens made Vladivostok the center of assembling operations for locomotives and other supplies from America. He was, of course, intent not only on ordering supplies but also on making the rail system efficient. The commissioner cabled Willard that arrangements were made for constructing a large locomotive-assembly plant and that spare equipment at Panama, such as hoists and cranes, were to be sent. He complained of Root's meddling with his work and demanded no outside interference as Wilson promised. Secretary of the Interior Franklin K. Lane told Wilson, "The second greatest matter of help is the improvement of the facilities upon the Siberian railroad. Mr. Willard, who has kept in touch with John F. Stevens, says that he is ready to provide men to go to Vladivostok to set up the locomotives."[55]

Stevens reported to the Russians his recommendations for equipment and introduction of managerial techniques. His goal, he told them, was for another twenty-five hundred locomotives and forty thousand freight cars, which meant a credit by the United States of $375 million. President Wilson, however, did not become aware of this message until August, when Lansing wrote, "I fear Mr. Stevens is assuming an authority and giving the Commission a diplomatic character, which neither possesses. I call your particular attention to the portion of the address marked in red, by which he *pledges* the United States to do certain things, a pledge he had no power to make." Root complained that Stevens was making promises of a diplomatic character. Wilson could not easily repudiate Stevens's promise, and Lansing recommended that he accept it. Wilson suggested that Lansing let Stevens know that he should not create the impression that he represented or spoke for the government. At the same time, the president did not wish to discredit Stevens's assurances.[56]

Prime Minister Kerensky decided to put the railways under military control and to adopt Stevens's recommendations. When the American railroad expert left for Vladivostok in late August, he noticed a distinct improvement in the Trans-Siberian railway. W. M. Black, chief engineer and a brigadier general, informed Secretary Baker that he had made arrangements to send to Russia about two hundred officials for operational and instructional purposes. He increased that number to more than three hundred.[57]

Ambassador Francis cabled for a railway manager. Willard replied that Stevens would be an adviser to the minister of communications and Henry Miller would manage the Trans-Siberian. The State Department informed Francis that mechanics and engineering instructors were being sent. George Emerson of the Great Northern was to be dispatched in three weeks with three hundred specialists.

Washington's seeming interference almost drove the prickly Stevens to quit. Francis cabled Lansing that he had intervened by special request to beg Miller to stay in Vladivostok instead of leaving on November 3 to await Emerson's arrival; he finally left San Francisco on November 18 with his force of 350 men, a week and a half after the Bolshevik Revolution. Exasperated, Stevens cabled Willard, "Any further efforts toward helping railroads absolutely useless. No government. Mutinous laborers and soldiers command the situation making efforts no value. . . . Will shortly leave for the United States." Willard begged Stevens to stay. By November 27, Emerson's force was in Honolulu. It arrived in Vladivostok on December 14, 1917. Three days later, Stevens took these Americans to Japan until the ice floes and politics had cleared. They sat in Japan for two months.[58]

3.

Russian problems besides the Trans-Siberian continued. House had warned the president that Russia might not last in the war until the end of the year. A few days later, he reported a conversation with Bakhmetev. The ambassador recited a litany of problems, including undependable shipping, port congestion at Vladivostok requiring more rolling stock for alleviation, and the need for the greater use of Archangel in summer months. Bakhmetev emphasized finances: "Unless money can be had he believes the Government cannot last. With it, he believes, conditions will steadily improve and a stable democracy will be established." To repeat, House had suggested that the president think about an expeditionary force. Ivan Narodny, chief officer of the Russian-American Society, also advocated an expeditionary corps to Russia. Coincidentally, he seconded House the next day with a memorandum to the president. Wilson referred this to the State Department for an answer, but House did not record what, if anything, Wilson replied to his or Narodny's suggestion. Wilson restricted American help to the Provisional Government to modest credits, propaganda, and transport.[59]

Sir George W. Buchanan, British ambassador to Russia, had sent a memorandum to Foreign Secretary Arthur James Balfour. Balfour had only been appointed after December 1916 when David Lloyd George succeeded Herbert Asquith as prime minister. Buchanan emphasized the importance of transportation and that its solution required foreign assistance. Balfour believed this was a perfect task for the United States and passed the cable to Polk, who sent it to the president. The solution would have, according to Balfour, transcendent importance. Buchanan admitted that he had no precise knowledge concerning the political crisis. Even so, as he observed, "there are such vast difficulties of every kind besetting the Russian Government that it would be in vain to look to them for any help in the military way, in the course of the current year." Buchanan could not see how the Russian army could remain in existence without proper supplies, which is where the United States came in. In a supplementary memorandum, he suggested that the United States undertake the entire task, except along the Murman coast, as that was to be considered at a conference on transportation that was meeting in Paris.[60]

Sir Eric Drummond cabled British Ambassador Buchanan that President Wilson seemed to favor a policy strengthening Russia only if "whatever future eventualities may transpire, he would be in a position to affect Japan's power." If this supposition were true, it would further explain Wilson's reluctance to provide help beyond that needed to balance Japan's power in Asia. Russia could, if Drummond understood Wilson correctly, manage its European affairs pretty much on its own. Drummond went on to say that Wilson had purposely retained his own special envoy in Russia in a position superior to that of Francis. That envoy was Charles Crane, who communicated "directly with the President and not through Secretary Lansing. They have a secret code of their own,"[61] implying that Crane was the source of Wilson's opinion about Japan. If so, no data subsequently surfaced to sustain Drummond's interpretation. Nevertheless, Drummond's remark, like so many others, did not reflect well on Ambassador Francis or, for that matter, President Wilson.

On August 7 the War Cabinet felt it was time to urge the Russian government to "place the affair of the State in order, since disaster would inevitably overtake the Russian nation unless effective steps were taken." The Russians were complaining, according to military attaché General Alfred Knox, of the coldness of the British attitude, to "whose opinion more weight was attached than to that of any other Ally." The War Cabinet went on to say that it questioned "helping a government that delayed to take the necessary steps to restore discipline." The War Cabinet was pessimistic about the survival of the Provisional Government.[62]

Lansing's evaluations were interesting, though ambivalent. He expressed profound reservations about Russia and astonishment at the optimism of

Root's mission. By this time he doubted Root's assessment of Kerensky's "personal force and ability to carry through his plans." Root had assured the secretary that "everything would come out all right."[63] Lansing speculated otherwise. He was skeptical about Kerensky's compromises with the radicals and thought that attempts at harmonizing moderates and radicals would fail. In what he called the normal process of revolution, Russia would go through similar stages as the French Revolution: "First, Moderation. Second, Terrorism. Third, Revolt against the New Tyranny and restoration of order by arbitrary military power. In my judgment the demoralized state of affairs will grow worse and worse until some dominant personality arises to end it all."[64] It remains a question of speculation as to how much of this pessimism Lansing shared with Wilson.

Matters might go otherwise, Lansing confessed, and he prayed that Root was right, "Yet the logic of events in my opinion does not warrant such hopes."[65] While there was the faintest chance that Root was right, the United States should do everything "to strengthen morally and materially the existing government." If Root were wrong, "nothing that we can do will stay the current which is toward a period of disorder and national impotency. All our efforts will amount to nothing; they will simply be chips swept along by the tide to be swallowed up in the calamity which seems to me to be in store for Russia." The secretary sketched out the meaning of this analysis for foreign policy: "I think that our policy should be based on the hypothesis that Russia will go from bad to worse; and we should prepare for the time when Russia will no longer be a military factor in the war. No other course is safe." As to the Root Mission, he remained in a "quandary."[66]

During August the president heard from the remaining members of the Root Mission and contemplated a response. Members seemed to show agreement with Lansing's assessment. The president also shared in all Allied information, according to House, and this information was not very pleasant. It resembled Ambassador Page's comments from London on British opinion: "Russia, as a fighting force, probably will not recover in time."[67] Page's report reflected the opinion of the War Cabinet:

> General Poole pointed out that 80% of the Russian people were anxious for immediate peace and that Mr. Kerensky had only a small minority behind him who were in favor of standing by the Allies, and that this minority depended to a very large degree upon the help and assistance of every kind which the allies, particularly Great Britain and France, could now render them, not merely morally but materially. The Russian Government regarded the continued shipment of guns as the all important symbol of continued assistance. . . . Cessation of the supply of additional guns might prove an important factor in influencing Russia towards a separate peace.[68]

Stanley Washburn's letters to the secretary reached the president in August. Washburn thought that some immediate publicity within the Russian army might help. He later predicted that there would be no fuel or food unless some miracle coming from the Stevens Railway Commission could help relieve the disastrous situation. He remarked that the Root Mission had only great potential value. Washburn commented that although someone might be stationed in the embassy for propaganda purposes, the change of generals and the substitution of new men in the Russian government were bad signs; by winter there would be a crisis leading to "an extraordinarily severe period for Russia and everywhere will be the demand for a restoration of a strong government of some sort."[69] He urged House to establish some kind of propaganda work in Russia. As he told Lord Northcliffe, the British newspaper magnate, "I took up with him [House] a broad program of publicity and other measures, which I believe to be vital for the preservation of the Ally interest in Russia. He stated that he would use all of his influence to get these through. I do not know how much influence he has but I should say it is an important factor with the President."[70]

House continued to believe it was more important to maintain Russian democracy than to try to beat "Germany to its knees."[71] House was lenient to Russia's war commitment if democracy could be preserved. He thought that another Allied statement of war aims by Wilson, stronger and clearer than those of May, would not only bring revolution in Germany but also strengthen the hand of Russian liberals. To further this aim, House encouraged the president to promote democratic propaganda "to meet the German effort in that direction."[72]

The only thing accomplished for Russia that autumn was that Mott's designated five hundred YMCA secretaries were sent to strengthen morale in the Russian army, in spite of Lansing's charge that such an action would appear more American than Russian.[73]

All in all, Root's mission, YMCA secretaries, a few railway experts, some Red Cross workers, a small propaganda effort, and some credits—such were the efforts that constituted Wilson's foreign policy toward Russia during the months of the Provisional Government. The Wilson administration was increasingly aware of the worsening situation, but it failed to act. Everything turned into a morass of detailed negotiation. An initiative came from the French, who were "greatly disturbed over the situation in Russia and proposed to hold an Inter-Allied Conference in Paris . . . to aid Russia and prevent further disintegration." The French ambassador to London, Paul Cambon, suggested that House come as the American representative, though it was impossible for him to go at that time. Instead, at the end of October the assistant secretary of the treasury, Oscar T. Crosby, was selected by Wilson and named president of the Inter-Allied Council. Lansing knew that the conference would be useful but had suggested that someone already in Europe should attend: "The only man of real acuteness who understands the Russian situation among our diplomatic representatives seems to me to be Ira Nelson Morris, our Minister to Sweden." That spoke volumes about the administration's confidence in poor Ambassador Francis. Lansing told Wilson, "I think that this matter should be immediately decided as the situation in Russia is certainly critical and everything should be done that can be done to give stability to the Government there and possibly such a Conference as is suggested would be of material aid." To emphasize how serious the Petrograd situation was, on that same day, October 3, Lansing made notes in his desk diary of a tea at the White House in which he overheard Bakhmetev say something to the effect that "to prevent bloodshed in Petrograd was almost impossible and that the radicals would have to be put down by force."[74]

On October 10 a cable came from the British Embassy in Petrograd to Sir William Wiseman that he shared with House, and House with Wilson. It warned that Kerensky's government was not expected to last more than three weeks; at that time, the Second All-Russian Congress of Soviets would be assembled under the domination of the most extreme socialists, the Bolsheviks: "General Staff expect grave trouble. Workmen and Soldiers' Council [the Petrograd Soviet] now completely under control of extreme left."[75]

On October 21 Bakhmetev told House that if the present government were to maintain itself, it was necessary for the Inter-Allied Council, scheduled to meet in Paris, to "recognize Russia's political as well as her war needs." Yet Francis cabled as late as October 30 suggesting that the secretary of the treasury put off extending a $235 million credit increase until America could be further assured of the reliability of the Russian government. As he noted, the "Provisional Government would be greatly strengthened if, as I believe likely, Bolshevik outbreak occurs and is suppressed." Only then should that credit be extended. On November 2, Polk cabled Francis to tell Kerensky "tactfully" that Russia might not get assistance "unless they intended to do their share of fighting."[76] This had been, after all, Root's formula when he was in Russia: no fight, no loan.

After surveying the Wilson administration's attitude and diplomacy to the Provisional Government at Russia's moment of great crisis, from March to November 1917, one wonders whether Ambassador Francis is so deserving of the ridicule heaped on him. There was more than a share of mendacity in Washington. Indeed, the problem of helping Russia lay squarely on Wilson's shoulders, not on the shoulders of Francis. It was, after all, Wilson's lost opportunity of gargantuan proportions and consequences, not the ambassador's.

The American effort to deal with the myriad problems that beset the Provisional Government was aborted by the Bolshevik Revolution of November 7, 1917. The short-lived regime of Prince George Lvov and Alexander Kerensky could not control the troubles that had afflicted Russia for decades, which had come to a crisis when Russia entered the war in 1914 against Germany and which soon brought near chaos. Perhaps it was too much to have hoped for a democratic change once republicanism came to Russia, and the tsar and his incompetent regime had been replaced by the Provisional Government. American help for Russia required expertise, not the mission of a leader of the Republican Party who in some sense was a rival to the president. It therefore accomplished little to send Elihu Root, who, however intelligent, was no more attuned to Russian problems than was the president, or than was John Stevens, who knew railroads but little else.

The result of the Root Mission and the Stevens Railway Commission was to delay a quick and firm U.S. policy to aid Russia on a grand scale. When each mission finally offered its suggestions, they were either wrong or too paltry to save the Provisional Government. The weak suggestions of the missions exposed Wilson's faulty premise that committees of experts could make a strong Russian policy for him at a critical moment. Instead, the president should have exercised his leadership by directing his policy through his secretary of state and ambassador. Now events overtook weak presidential leadership and contributed to a catastrophe for Russia, America, and their allies.

Three

Wilson and Lansing Face Lenin and Trotsky

The Russian catastrophe occurred on November 7, 1917, when Lenin's Bolshevik Party seized power from the Provisional Government. The Bolsheviks immediately sued for an armistice with the Central Powers by issuing a Declaration of Peace on November 8, 1917. The armistice began on December 17. Soviet Russia and the Central Powers signed a peace treaty at Brest-Litovsk on March 3, 1918. These Bolshevik actions threw President Wilson and his allies into a panic. The stunned Wilson administration clung to a belief that Lenin's government would be overthrown within days or weeks. When that hope did not materialize, other hopes emerged.

By the time that it was necessary to have acted concerning Russia, President Wilson had done little. He had failed to negotiate the treaty. He was not willing to risk anything unless Russia remained in the war, though he was repeatedly warned that Russia might collapse. Ambassador Francis and Secretary of State Robert Lansing had pushed the president to recognize the Provisional Government. The president had bypassed Francis in arranging the Root Mission and Stevens Railway Commission, which accomplished little. When the Bolshevik Party seized power in November, President Wilson watched and waited, hoping for a different result. Francis received virtually no instructions from Washington for a month.

1.

Francis had exercised a cautious optimism about the stability of the Provisional Government. His optimism was not shared by other American officials in Petrograd. General William V. Judson, chief of the American military mission in Russia, for example, was more pessimistic. Judson had originally come to Russia with Elihu Root, and also had been appointed chief military attaché on the day the mission departed for home. Judson reported both to Ambassador Francis as chief military attaché and to the

War Department as head of the American military mission. Such a dual position meant his loyalties were divided. This left his position ambiguous.[1]

Judson had earlier suggested sending American troops to Russia's aid "but was so entirely unsuccessful in securing the adoption of such a recommendation that I said very little about it afterward." His suggestion was met with silence in Washington and Judson ultimately abandoned it. Judson also believed that it was crucial for the Kerensky government to reintroduce some measure of discipline within the newly democratized Russian army. After all, according to Order Number One issued on March 1, 1917, by the Petrograd Soviet, enlisted men elected their own officers and these new "officers" were not allowed to wear epaulets.[2]

The reason for not acting seemed simple, as Wilson told Senator John Sharp Williams of Mississippi: "I entirely agree with your argument about sending troops to Russia. There are many reasons why it would be unwise even if it were practicable."[3] Williams had written that Root was wrong in making such a suggestion because American forces should not be separated but instead should strike at one point. Russians would resent Americans telling them how to fight Germany, especially when supplies were needed; Russia had manpower but could use better transport for munitions.[4] This slide to virtual inaction in Russia by the Wilson administration was vividly chronicled by General Judson.

The chief of the military mission realized that the Russian army's success depended on the reintroduction of discipline, which could be accomplished only if the Allies persuaded Prime Minister Kerensky to work toward this object. Otherwise, "It is at least an even chance that coming event may take Russia out of the war within the next few months. Our larger war plans should be made accordingly." He wrote Scott that the June or "Kerensky" offensive was "a flash in the pan" and had made things more difficult. The British ambassador agreed, and at the same time complained that it would be "vain to look to them for any help in the military way, in the course of the current year." Judson advised that the "Government be pressed by the Allied Ambassadors, one and all, to take at once, the steps it must take sooner or later, if the Russian Army is ever to have its strength restored."[5]

Matters had appeared so desperate in October that Judson had cabled, "We are using every resource but must have immediate support or all efforts may be too late." He renewed his efforts with Francis on the issue of discipline and indicated that its lack meant a drift to anarchy. Because Kerensky appeared unable or unwilling to restore discipline, the Provisional Government could not exist much longer. The War Department made no reply and Francis imagined, "Why, Judson, I can understand how soldiers feel on this subject, but politicians like me understand human nature much better, and

Map 1: Petrograd Area with U.S. Embassy Insert

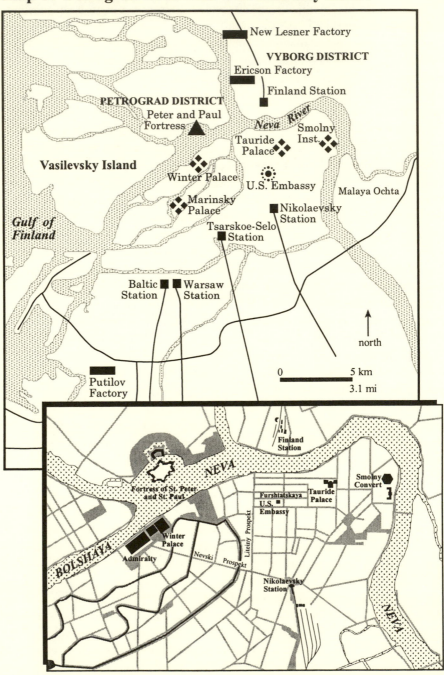

I can assure you that the Russian Army will never quit but will fight like lions, inspired by a sense of freedom newly won." Kerensky promised to restore the death penalty in the army. Francis reported that Foreign Minister M. I. Tereshchenko had left the embassy, confirming that the death penalty was restored in the ranks by the Council of Ministers and would be promulgated soon. This, according to Francis, "showed a firmer policy in regard to army discipline and extreme socialism." The ambassador had had an interview with Kerensky and "endeavored to impress upon him necessity for restoring discipline; to-day he promulgates proclamation appealing for support of officers." Just before the Bolshevik Revolution, Francis also belatedly proposed an intervention by American troops. "What would you think of our sending two or more army divisions via Vladivostok or Sweden to her aid if I could get the consent of Russian Government there for or even induce Government to make such a request?"[6] Francis believed that such a gesture would raise Russian morale.

On the very eve of the Bolshevik Revolution, Judson had sent a message pointing out that reestablishment of discipline meant death for desertion, conspiracy, mutiny, violence, and disobedience; it demanded abolishing the committees created during the March Revolution to run the army in place of officers of the imperial army; it required renewing the officer corps and reestablishing marks of respect, ranks, and authority of officers. "It seems easy to prophesy that unless a rigid discipline is soon restored the country will drift into anarchy, which would eventually be followed by a strong government of the old autocratic type." He advocated "utmost pressure, present, continuous and simultaneous, should be exerted in this matter." The general remarked that "If Russia fails, through a neglect to rediscipline her army (and she can fail in no other way), the war may be lost. And if the war should be lost the pains of defeat would fall principally upon Russia of all the larger powers. . . . Russia would offer Germany the greatest available prizes of territory and commercial and industrial dependence." Judson told Francis that the "corps of professional officers is rapidly losing its morale." Half measures were dangerous. The government could not use force anywhere—railroads, factories, mines—unless it had a disciplined army to do so. He concluded, "one always arrives at a disciplined army as a point of departure."[7]

Judson predicted that the "maximalists" were ready to control an All-Russian Congress of Workmen's and Soldiers' Deputies [Soviets] meeting. If they succeeded, he warned the War Department, they would form a government with the disastrous result of a separate peace. He could not conceive how the United States would fail to act unless it contemplated an early peace.[8]

William Boyce Thompson cosigned Judson's message. Thompson's signature was important because he was head of the American Red Cross Mission and had contributed $1 million out of his own pocket to improve propaganda in lieu of little action by Wilson. A British representative in Washington, Sir William Wiseman, as earlier mentioned, had sent a similar recommendation to House: the general staff expected trouble, as the Petrograd Soviet was under control of the left. House commented in turn to Wilson that he was sending the cable which had come from Petrograd to the president: "interesting *if true,*" said House.[9] Wilson paid no attention to House or the cable.

Judson's cables continued: "Gradual disintegration of power of Government in all directions. Anarchy nearer daily; strikes and threats of strikes everywhere." He warned that most socialists were calling for peace, separately or jointly, especially the Bolsheviks. "Political conditions overshadow everything," the general maintained, "but economic and financial disaster hastening on."[10] The military attaché made another prediction:

> The Government is perhaps politically stronger but lacks the bayonets with which to sustain itself. The opposition of the Bolsheviks, with 30,000 armed workmen and support promised from Cronstadt and Baltic Fleet which apparently does not recognize the Government, is getting nasty. There may soon be an uprising.[11]

Judson foresaw that the Petrograd garrison would be neutral and was so unreliable that it could not be gotten out of Petrograd; if soldiers were sent from the north to defend the government, they would be corrupted. He emphasized that relatively small expenditures on Russia would have a tenfold effect on the war. The left "may possibly have enough vitality to attempt to forcibly seize state. Such a seizure or civil war might upset all hopes."[12]

A headline in the November 2 *Washington Post* read: "Russia quits war." Lansing cabled Francis the same day that the *Post* report was unwarranted; he had told the press that the Provisional Government was attacking its problems energetically so as to "carry the war through to a victorious completion." Francis even reported unsuccessful attempts at demonstrations by the Bolsheviks. Minister of War General A. I. Verkhovsky denied advocating a separate peace or flirting with the Bolsheviks. Francis mentioned that Verkhovsky had resigned, withdrawn his resignation, and then was granted an indefinite leave. The ambassador expressed a cautious optimism, as had Root earlier. This encouraged Russell Leffingwell, assistant secretary of the treasury, to meet with Polk; their topic was American credits and the bottom line was that "they might not get assistance unless they intended to do their share of fighting."[13] Root's formula persisted.

Charles Russell, a former Root Mission member, wrote Wilson that at the moment Russians lacked heart and felt no obligation to the Allies. An educational campaign at $5 million would appeal to their democratic enthusiasm; if it were done during the winter, they would be fighting next spring as hard as anybody. Wilson replied a few days later that this thought ran along the lines of his own thoughts, though work in Russia was extremely difficult because no one channel connected with another. Wilson even wrote George Creel on November 10 that Russell's letter was important and wished that Creel would take it to heart because it went to the center of the Russian subject.[14]

<h2 style="text-align:center">2.</h2>

In his diary Francis shattered this optimism: "Bolshevik uprising; reported 5 regiments Cossacks here to subdue them; bridges blocked; general furore [*sic*]; reported 30 wounded and promiscuous firing." On November 7, Francis cabled the State Department that his aide's car had been commandeered by Kerensky, who was escaping Petrograd to rally Cossacks under General Peter Krasnov. Kerensky asked America not to abandon its optimism in democratic Russia by recognizing Lenin's Soviet government.[15] Francis lamented that the Bolsheviks appeared to have control of everything. They had formed a government and notified the Allies that Russia could not fight further and would offer peace terms to Germany.

Lansing's own desk diary, dated November 8, recorded the epochal event: "telegram (AP) from Petrograd saying Bolsheviks had overthrown govt." Francis, and perhaps Lansing and Wilson, remained assured of the Bolsheviks' swift defeat because "Kerensky reported coming from front with Cossack troops. Ambassador held meeting with British ambassador at British Embassy at 6 p.m." No embassy received guidance, probably because all thought Lenin would be swept away as previous governments had been.[16]

Newspapers first brought word to Washington of the Bolshevik coup. They began publishing the story on November 8; Lansing remained silent although he got Francis's official report on the evening of November 10. Papers filled with events in Petrograd. The president met with the cabinet to discuss Russia. Josephus Daniels reported Wilson's reaction, which now seems stunning in its passivity: "McAdoo: Shall we lend money to Russia? WW thought we could not yet presume R. would fail—must wait."[17]

From Ambassador Morris in Stockholm came a cable explaining that the Bolsheviks had made a successful coup and noting that Lev Trotsky, Lenin's lieutenant, had declared that the Provisional Government no longer existed. Then Lenin, chairman of the council of people's commissars [SOVNARKOM], appointed Trotsky as commissar for foreign affairs. The latter began his work by publishing Russia's secret treaties and dealing with the outside world as the chief agitator of the Bolshevik Revolution. Morris outlined the Bolshevik's program: cessation of hostilities, turning land over to the peasants, settling the country's economic crisis.[18]

President Wilson was remarkably unperturbed about the turmoil that was convulsing Petrograd. He played a round of golf, attended church the next day, and left for Buffalo and the American Federation of Labor convention, returning the following evening. In his speech to the convention he made his first public reference to the new government in Petrograd as composed of "fatuous dreamers" because they believed they could live in the presence of a Germany so powerful that it could "undermine or overthrow them by intrigue or force" at any time.[19]

Wilson wrote a Florida congressman, Frank Clark, that he had not "lost faith in the Russian outcome by any means. Russia, like France in a past century, will no doubt have to go through deep waters but she will come out upon firm land on the other side and her great people, for they are a great people, will in my opinion take their proper place in the world."[20]

Given the news, it seems strange that the president went to Buffalo, referred to Russia's dreamers, and followed with the remark to Clark. These things might be explained by a claim that inaction was an attempt to balance "surface froth" against historic Russia, or by Trotsky's assertion that Wilson only entered the war at the demand of finance capitalists who had persuaded the president that war would create an economic boom.[21]

Francis remained hopeful when he learned that Kerensky was coming from the northern front with troops, but he noted that the Soviet government had cabled Germany, asking for a three-month armistice. Yet Washington appeared to believe Lenin was unimportant, or so it would seem because Polk met with Leffingwell and told him to "go slowly on closing contracts." Crane seemed to be the only person, according to Cyrus McCormick, who was not surprised at events in Russia.[22]

At the State Department William Phillips, assistant secretary of state, and Basil Miles, now chief of the Division on Russian Affairs, oversaw the routine by screening reports as well as visitors to Secretary of State Lansing. Miles had been third secretary of the Petrograd embassy, assistant to Francis in 1916, and accompanied the Root Mission. Both Phillips and Miles kept the bad news from Petrograd within the department as long as possible.[23]

Francis had first admitted, "Kerensky not heard from." But then Lansing was buoyed by the Russian embassy's news that Kerensky was marching on Petrograd with two hundred thousand troops. The ambassador's spirits also lifted; his reports now said that Kerensky was within five miles of Petrograd. There was even talk of a truce between Kerensky and Lenin.[24]

More messages came from Ambassador Ira Morris in Sweden as well as from Ambassador John Garrett at The Hague. From Morris, Lansing knew about the failed effort of Mayor Schreider of Petrograd to form a committee of safety, and that those reports of Kerensky's intervention were wrong. From Garrett came news that Russian diplomatic missions in Western Europe refused to carry out any of Trotsky's instructions once he had been named commissar for foreign affairs. Francis complained that he had received no directions from Washington since November 3: "I have sent you daily cables, some of them through Stockholm, telling you of conditions here." On November 14 he reported Kerensky's defeat.[25]

Though Francis noted a move by the Russian railway union to stop transport if fighting did not end, nothing came of the union's warning. The Congress of Soviets proceeded to name a Bolshevik government in the early morning hours of November 8, and the embassy first received Trotsky's official communication advising the ambassador of its formation. Fighting, Francis reported, continued in Moscow. The socialists, he thought, had agreed on a compromise ministry. By November 14, receiving no instruction from Washington, he sent a message through the Associated Press wire to make sure his information was being received: "Rennick just returned from Gatchina says Kerensky entirely defeated and attempting negotiate with Petrograd." Soviet forces, he remarked, were not all Bolshevik but included some that opposed Kerensky because he "destroyed army discipline and permitted killing of officers." He talked about a compromise ministry with Victor Chernov, head of the Socialist Revolutionary Party, as premier, and ended on another optimistic note: "If Avksentieff [Kerensky's cabinet] accepts this probably means settlement of this revolution."

On the same day Polk wrote in his diary that, temporarily, funds on order of the embassy for the Provisional Government could go ahead.[26] That in itself reflected the Wilson administration's optimism, its watch-and-wait policy fully expecting a prompt return to power of liberal forces. Certainly, it was thought, only the most minimal arrangements, if any, with the Soviet government were necessary.

Consul General Maddin Summers, whose wife was a nobleman's daughter and whose family stood to lose everything, counseled a harder line to Francis, consisting of determined action against the Bolsheviks. However, Judson explained the incapacity of the ambassador: "Mr. Francis, our

Ambassador, seems to me completely exhausted and overwrought by the strain he has recently been under. This circumstance is most distressing. The American Ambassador never required more than now to be able to act with cool and vision."[27]

3.

In the midst of this turmoil, Judson had the unpleasant task of confronting Ambassador Francis about his supposed peccadilloes with his seductive French teacher, Matilda de Cram, an "exceedingly bright and attractive person about forty." Her influence seemed greater than that of the embassy staff and the military mission combined. The ambassador was accused of talking over the public business with her and sharing the contents of many if not most of his cables. According to Judson, the ambassador had met the lady on the ship to Petrograd. Judson received a dossier on her from the Interallied Passport Bureau and French Counter-Espionage in Petrograd. The dossier noted her friendship with a German spy and her evenings at the embassy. When Judson confronted Francis, the ambassador denied everything. Thompson, head of the Red Cross Mission, Raymond Robins, a member of that mission, and J. Butler Wright, counselor of the embassy, were convinced that she was a German spy. Francis received a cable from Lansing "to take immediate steps to sever her connection with the Embassy." Judson related that Wright "expected such a message to arrive." After Wright decoded it, Francis said he would "get the 'blankety blank blank' who had caused it to be sent." Judson appealed to Francis to end his friendship with de Cram: "Doubtless for a month or more thereafter he erroneously attributed to me the submission to Washington of some report on Madame de Cram."[28]

The "de Cram affair" probably made Francis initially less receptive to other points of view concerning the Bolsheviks.[29] And, of course, he awaited official orders from Washington. Judson speculated that the femme fatale reported to Count Wilhelm von Mirbach-Harff, Russian expert in the German foreign office, soon to be named Germany's ambassador to Soviet Russia, and "it is very probable [that he] controlled the activities of Madame de Cram and through her influenced the theories and opinions of our Ambassador from the time we entered the war until Russia retired from the war."[30]

This side show with the ambassador did not prevent Judson from reporting that the capital was in Bolshevik hands, the Winter Palace taken, the ministry, except for Kerensky, arrested, the Council of the Republic dissolved. "As the old Government was relatively powerless there was not much bloodshed," he reported. The Bolsheviks constituted almost half of the Petrograd Soviet and were forming a government and calling for peace. Judson wavered on Kerensky's chances: "It seems probable that anti-Bolshevik forces may regain control, notwithstanding the state of the army and the popularity of peace therewith." By November 9, he realized that "No signs are visible to us that the Bolsheviks will be overcome in a few days. The food supply is the vital and perhaps determining question. Railroads are still functioning, although precariously." There was, Judson said, "Not much stomach for fighting or certainty as to preferences among the troops anywhere. The Red Guard is undisciplined, but knows its own mind, and has determination." Because he was responsible for the security of Americans in Petrograd, Judson cabled, "Trotsky has assured two of my officers that they would protect foreigners."[31]

In mid-November Postmaster General Burleson received a note from Wilson: "Thank you for having let me see the enclosed [Judson] letters." But it is hard to tell what letters of Judson's Wilson saw. Later, on November 23, Baker sent "a telegram which came to the War College in code from General Judson, our military attache at Petrograd. You will observe that he asks that a copy of this be sent to the Postmaster General to be sent to you. Instead of burdening the Postmaster General with it, I am sending it direct." Judson had requested his message be copied "to show the President of the United States." He maintained that there were shocks to be expected as a result of the Bolshevik coup. It might throw Russia into anarchy and that would put the country out of the war. Another of its shocks would intensify the struggle as represented by socialism versus reaction, setting back democracy. The immediate result would be to strengthen autocracy, prolonging the war. There might be a way out: "our President could solve this problem" by offering peace terms that the Allies and the Central Powers could not refuse without appearing unfair.[32]

Raymond Robins, the Red Cross representative, went to see General Judson about the safety of his workers. He agreed with Judson's assessment. He had another conference with Judson and a group of Red Cross workers, commenting, "The game here is played out." Robins remained in charge of a final contingent after Thompson's and the others' departure for home. One Red Cross official observed that the "Embassy people are very bitter on the Bolshevik subject."[33]

Robins had his first interview with Trotsky on November 10. He had gotten Thompson's approval and replaced his anti-Bolshevik translator with Alexander Gumberg, a New York friend of Trotsky. Gumberg proved a significant go-between for the American colony. Robins told Trotsky that "he would be dealing with whoever was in power because he wanted to continue Red Cross activities and keep Russia in the War." Trotsky, he maintained, welcomed the American Red Cross mission, except for Thompson, because of Thompson's cash contribution to anti-Bolshevik propaganda. The Soviet government would work against Germany to the extent justifiable given Russia's predicament and help transport to Petrograd Red Cross condensed milk and medical supplies.[34]

About this time, November 16, Robins saw Judson.[35] However, Judson did not mention Robins in his diary until November 27 when the Red Cross was in close touch with Trotsky: Robins believed the Bolsheviks had to be dealt with because they would be in power for some time. Judson revealed that Robins asked Trotsky why he directed troops at the front to fraternize if he did not favor a separate peace. Trotsky indicated that it was to demoralize German soldiers with revolutionary propaganda.

Judson surmised that this propaganda was "strong evidence that the Bolshevicks [*sic*] are not working under German direction." He concluded:

> The Bolshevicks are beginning to exhibit the only guts visible among all the different contending political elements in Russia. They are the only ones apparently who can do anything with the soldiers and if the latter are to stay in position and ever do any fighting (even defensively) it may be that it must be under the Bolshevicks. As the Bolshevicks remain in power there is evidence that they become more conservative.[36]

The word "guts" was one Judson picked up from Robins when referring to Bolsheviks.[37]

It was up to Robins to keep busy with the Bolsheviks because of Thompson's forced exit from Russia. The Bolsheviks had not forgotten the Wall Street tycoon's contributions to moderate socialists in support of the Provisional Government. On November 27, Thompson turned operations over to Robins and, as the Red Cross used military rank, raised him from major to lieutenant colonel. Thompson said, "I desire that you have full discretion and liberty of action to meet any situation that may arise, subject of course, to the War Council under which we are acting."[38]

Robins, given to hyperbole, had concluded that the Bolshevik Revolution was the "most fundamental hour in the life of the world." Like Judson, he understood Bolshevism's significance earlier than most individuals. "Trotsky and Lenin suffered to be out. Curious Teutonic influences. Nothing to all of the above." The Bolsheviks were not German agents, and if the Germans thought they had bought them "they bought a lemon."[39] He realized that Trotsky's efforts at propaganda among German troops, his cooperation on Red Cross matters, and his efforts to guard military stores showed a willingness to cooperate on a selective basis with the Allies. The Bolsheviks needed leverage in negotiations with Germany to prevent Russia's partition; this might be provided by the Allies, allowing Lenin to avoid Russia's subjugation. If Russia could not be kept in the war and had to make a separate peace, at least the terms of that peace might not allow Germany unlimited use of Russian resources. If Russia were granted recognition and aid, it would turn Germany's triumph into a Pyrrhic victory. An opportunity still existed for America, or so Robins believed.

Robins was responding to Francis's order to Judson to "do nothing or permit no act to be performed by anyone connected with the Embassy or under my control that could be construed as direct or indirect recognition of what is generally known as the 'Bolshevik' Government." Francis emphasized that he was repeating the order, and instructed Judson to "do nothing" by quoting — so he said — a phrase from Judson's memorandum, to refrain from "trivial intercourse" with the Bolshevik government, that is, "telephone, guards, and the like even when emergencies might arise" because, as Francis noted, he was in the embassy and accessible at all hours.[40] In lieu of instruction from Washington, this hiatus seemed the procedure Lansing and Wilson wanted. For better or worse, what else could Francis do but to watch and wait until a policy from Washington emerged?

Judson reported that the Allied missions had received notes from Trotsky informing them that the new government had instructed General Nikolai N. Dukhonin, commander in chief of Russia's armies since General Kornilov's arrest in September, to arrange for a truce. This caused trouble with the United States. Trotsky had taken charge of foreign affairs and, as Judson noted, "T. was handed the keys by an assistant minister who, with most of the other officers, soon departed, leaving Trotski alone with his private secretary, Zalkinde." The latter indicated that foreign missions would be notified of the change of government. The embassy received a communication from the Soviet government, signed by Trotsky as Commissar for Foreign Affairs. It announced formation of the SOVNARKOM by the National Congress of the Councils of the Deputies of the Workmen and Soldiers [Soviet] with Lenin as president. It declared the "formal proposal for an armistice without delay on all fronts and for the opening without delay of negotiations for peace." On November 21, Judson recorded that the "Bolsheviks have directed Dukhonin to propose to the Commander of the opposing army a three month's truce and have resolved to inform the Allied Missions of this order." Robins greeted the news cryptically: "Peace may come! Amen!" The following day he jotted down: "Renstein Trotskii and peace." He wrote: "The Day of Peace in Russia . . . as far as proclamation can [be] brought to pass. Excitement!"[41]

Trotsky now directed military authorities to cease operations with a view to peace negotiations. Francis cabled that Allied chiefs would take no notice of Trotsky's directive. They requested their governments not to reply to the "pretended government established by force and not recognized by Russian people." He directed Lieutenant Colonel Monroe C. Kerth, the U.S. representative at the Russian army's headquarters [*Stavka*] at Mogilev, "to join in protest" and "Judson to authorize Kerth to protest against armistice which at that time was thought and meant to be separate armistice." What Allied military representatives were protesting was the violation of the London Treaty of 1914 that forbade a separate peace. Judson cabled: "I have instructed Kerth to protest against a separate armistice on ground the U.S. and Russia are virtual allies in present war."[42] Francis and Judson were clearly stepping beyond anything authorized by Washington. The general later recounted:

> I learned on the morning of November 25, in a telegram from Lieutenant Colonel Kerth, who was at Stavka, that such a protest had been submitted, but that he naturally had not signed it as we were not parties to the London agreement, to which reference had been made in the note of protest. Kerth asked for instructions. I immediately telegraphed him, on my own judgment and initiative but also in accordance with instructions from the Ambassador, received after I had formulated the telegram, to file a protest against a separate armistice on the ground that America was a virtual ally of Russia.[43]

4.

The policy of watching and waiting, a hiatus to see how things settled before doing anything in the hope that democracy might yet be restored, now passed out of Washington's distant hands. Instead, policy was up to those in the American colony eager to save the Eastern Front. Colonel Durnovo, aide of General V. V. Marushevsky, chief of the general staff in Petrograd, gave Judson a record of a conversation between Dukhonin and himself that quoted a monitored message that the failure of America to protest when others had done so was creating uncertainties which it was of the utmost importance to remove. To underscore Kerth's yet undelivered message, Judson complied with Durnovo's request to issue a statement to the Soviets similar to the intercepted message. Francis approved Judson's statement addressed "To the Chief of the Russian General Staff, Petrograd" and delivered that evening. Marushevsky "expressed great satisfaction with its terms." His sympathies were tsarist and he served the Bolsheviks under duress. Judson's letter quoted the intercepted press message that the United States would institute an embargo: "if the Bolsheviks will remain in power and will put through their program of making peace with Germany, the present embargo on exports to Russia will remain in force." It also indicated that of the $325 million credit to the Provisional Government, $191 million had been appropriated, leaving a balance of $134 million.[44]

Trotsky and his colleagues probably accepted Judson's letter as some kind of official diplomatic statement on the way toward recognition and perhaps as a warning that if the peace program continued the United States would withdraw the remainder of its credits. And though the letter was signed both in Judson's capacity as attaché to the U.S. embassy and as chief of the American military mission, it was a matter-of-fact communication indicating that the press report had no standing even though Judson and Francis might be of the opinion that they would receive a similar communiqué. Judson's letter to Marushevsky simply corrected an impression made by the press. Judson was aware that Lenin sought an armistice by all belligerent nations.[45]

The situation was changing rapidly. So was Judson's attitude. On the morning of November 25, at about the same time Judson's assistant was getting ready to bring the first letter over to Marushevsky, a cable went to the War Department showing his change of attitude toward the Bolsheviks: "In my opinion situation is such that some government and order with promise of benefits to allies could be brought about now through diplomatic intervention." Judson had been stunned by the vehemence of the Soviet reply to the Allied military missions' November 23 note. The Soviet accused the Allies of interfering with Russia's domestic affairs and fomenting a revolution. Kerth's note was lumped together with the communications of the other Allies as was Judson's letter to Marushevsky. The Allied note protested in the "most energetic manner" against any violation of the London Treaty, whereas Kerth said his government "categorically and energetically protests against any separate armistice." These exchanges were exacerbated by Allied efforts to force General Dukhonin to do something to prevent a Soviet peace move. They asked the general to insist that political parties "refrain from all speech and action which will aggravate the very dangerous situation which exists at this time on the front, vis-a-vis the enemy." General Berthelot, chief of the French military mission, related that France would not recognize the Soviets. General Lavergne, French representative at *Stavka*, told Dukhonin: "the 'criminal pourparlers' should be repudiated by the Supreme Command."[46]

Izvestiia, a leading Bolshevik newspaper, commented on the French and American notes: "the United States has declared a kind of boycott against us [that] goes hand and hand with the telegram of General Berthelot. It would seem that the North American plutocrats are ready to trade locomotives for the heads of Russian soldiers."[47] On December 1, Trotsky switched from the threat of Judson's letter to Marushevsky, to Kerth's note of November 27 for Dukhonin in support of the Allied protest. Trotsky accused Kerth of calling on Dukhonin to "carry out a policy directly contrary to the one carried out by the Council of People's Commissaries." He continued, "the Soviet Government, which is responsible for the fate of the country, cannot allow Allied diplomatic and military agents for any purpose to interfere in the internal life of our country and attempt to fan civil wars."[48]

The garrison at *Stavka* now mutinied and arrested General Dukhonin and his staff. N. V. Krylenko, Bolshevik Commissar for War, arrived with sailors who murdered Dukhonin. These actions, along with talks with Robins and Thompson, persuaded Judson to make a quick about-face on November 27 in a second letter to Marushevsky because it had become apparent that "Bolsheviks were in to stay . . . and that the Bolsheviks, whatever we might think of them, were in a position to determine many questions that would perhaps vitally affect the outcome of the war." He noted Trotsky's complaint of the united protest to Dukhonin and the deep concern of British Ambassador Buchanan and his military attaché General Knox to that protest. Buchanan indicated the protest was nothing short of a "veiled threat" and that it was interpreted to mean, "we are about to call on Japan to attack Russia." He went further: "It was an ill-advised step that has done us any amount of harm."[49]

After a period of consternation among American officials in Petrograd following the seizure of power, several views had emerged. First, there was Francis's view that a do-nothing policy, that is, watching and waiting, should follow in which there would be little connection with the Bolsheviks. At that moment, the ambassador was in the dark as to Washington's policy, but as it turned out, he surmised it correctly. As late as November 28 he cabled Lansing, "Have received no instructions concerning recognition. Reported that President Wilson has made emphatic public statement concerning the Russian situation. Is it true?"[50] Second, there was Judson's opinion that contact had to be made with the Bolsheviks to protect Americans and influence the Bolsheviks to stay in the war. In this he reflected the views of Thompson and Robins, the two Red Cross officials in Petrograd. Third, there was the conservative attitude of Consul General Summers, who strongly endorsed a cable sent November 27 to Creel by a freelance journalist in Moscow at that time and a friend of Colonel House, Arthur Bullard: Lansing must "clearly and publicly" state the ground upon which the Wilson administration refused to recognize the Soviets. Bullard meant nonrecognition must be based on the illegal means by which Lenin attained power and his government's undemocratic and violent nature.[51]

Given these three alternatives, which would the president in Washington decide that the country must ultimately follow? At the crucial point in relations between the United States and the new Bolshevik government, there was not the slightest evidence, no indication of the administration's official policy. One can only conclude that there was no policy except that of doing nothing—watching and waiting—in the hope that Lenin's government would be overthrown.

Four

December 1917
The Struggle for a Policy

Although President Wilson apparently preferred to ignore the Bolshevik Revolution, others were pressing the United States to act. Numerous alternatives were proposed. For instance, the British considered aid to Lenin's Russian enemies in order to restore the Eastern Front. The French concurred and talked about intervention by the Allies to restore the Provisional Government. Secretary of State Robert Lansing and the State Department began to argue that some form of aid to those Russians still willing to fight was in order. Colonel House considered reconciliation, not recognition, in order not to force the Russians into the German's hands. Naturally, Americans in Petrograd had their own wide range of ideas about what U.S. policy should be: Ambassador David Francis opined that reconciliation with the Bolsheviks was not possible, while General William Judson supported accommodation with Lenin in order to preserve the Eastern Front as long as possible and to prevent Russia from falling completely into German hands. In the immediate aftermath of the Bolshevik Revolution, all of these points of view were weighed, and a couple were actually tried.

At first, doing nothing, as Ambassador Francis correctly assumed, became President Wilson's principal way of dealing with the Bolsheviks. The president expected that the new government would soon collapse. But selecting that procedure created a sort of policy vacuum in regard to attempts to retain the Eastern Front, whether that meant overthrowing the Bolsheviks with a pro-Allied government, convincing Lenin that it was in his group's interest to fight on, or making the Germans pay a very high price for Russia's neutrality. Finally, in December, alternatives to do-nothing or watch-and-wait policies emerged. The British, with French assistance, strengthened their advocacy of a plan for reconstructing a front in southern Russia, perhaps overthrowing the Bolsheviks, and of another plan for Japanese intervention in Russia's Far East. These propositions required Wilson's participation in order to be effective. Other American nationals in Petrograd and Moscow, as well as advisers in Washington, offered their alternatives to the administration. Colonel House returned from one of his transatlantic trips with his own alternative. Then there was Secretary Lansing and the State Department, where calls could be heard for an anti-Bolshevik policy. Various Bolshevik actions, at one time or another, gave these alternatives plausibility and provided the seedbed for the kind of anti-Communist crusade associated with the Cold War.

1.

It was very important for someone in an official capacity to take the initiative to visit Trotsky to ascertain exactly what might be worked out with the Bolsheviks. That action fell to the Americans. In a speech to the Petrograd Soviet, Trotsky indicated that two unofficial Americans, close to capitalist circles, had been to see him. They had tried to convince him that General Judson's second letter expressing conciliation was America's policy. Trotsky told his audience that relations could be built on Allied expectation of commerce after the war and not "platonic sympathy for the Russian nation of which the American imperialists wish to persuade me." Likewise others, less sympathetic but official, tried their alternatives on Trotsky. For instance, General Henri A. Niessel, head of the French military mission, eventually came haughtily to demand a continuation of the war. Trotsky threw him out. When the French Ambassador, Joseph Noulens, tried to smooth things over, the commissar was all sweetness and light. However, it was General Judson, the first high-ranking American official to visit Trotsky, who succeeded in breaking the Allied boycott and America's pretending that the Bolsheviks did not exist.[1]

Judson's bold visit to Commissar for Foreign Affairs Trotsky was preceded by the meddling of Colonel Raymond Robins of the American Red Cross and his translator Alexander Gumberg. Ambassador Francis played a coy game by cabling Lansing, apparently trying to ascertain the identity of the two unofficial Americans presuming to speak for the United States. In a curious way, he was trying to get Lansing to block any Americans from having conversations with the Bolsheviks, thus removing the onus from him. In actuality, Francis not only realized that the Americans were Robins and Gumberg but also knew what was going on. It was not done behind his back nor was he left guessing, as was later suggested. Francis was testing the waters with Lansing. Further, he understood that the head of the Committee on Public Information [COMPUB], George Creel's representative and a "rank newcomer to Petrograd," Edgar Sisson, could not possibly arrange anything with Trotsky without the help of Robins and Gumberg. This assistance was easy for Gumberg. Lenin's comrade, Felix Dzerzhinsky, had issued him a pass to Smolny Institute, first seat of the Bolshevik government.[2] Gumberg, a Russian emigrant to the United States and a businessman, had been Trotsky's friend when the latter was living in New York. The question of contacts must have come up repeatedly at embassy meetings.

As to further identifying the two Americans visiting Trotsky, Robins's diary makes it obvious. "Get things from Judson. See Gen'l then to BB [Bessie Beatty] and arrange man for front. . . . have cleared for step with Smolny."[3] It was logical that the go-between role of Robins and Gumberg, the two Americans, would be well known to the ambassador. Robins was busy with Red Cross activities and had conferences before he could get over to the Smolny Institute to arrange further Red Cross work. Certainly Sisson went with Gumberg's assistance. Judson recalled that Sisson afterward informed him that he had only been able to set up an interview between Trotsky and Judson. As Judson said, "there was nothing to do, in view of all the circumstances, but to visit Smolny and interview Trotsky at once."[4]

Judson's all-important visit was intended to break the ice and to come to some understanding with the Bolsheviks in order to salvage something of the Eastern Front. This process reveals the utter confusion existing in Allied diplomacy at that time and shows why it was so necessary to do something and do it quickly to prevent a disaster: the collapse of the Eastern Front.

It was agreed at an embassy conference between Francis, Robins, Sisson, embassy counselor J. Butler Wright, Judson, and Captain E. Francis Riggs, Judson's assistant, on the afternoon of November 30, that Sisson would arrange a meeting between Trotsky and one of Judson's subordinates. Time was of the essence: on November 27 the Bolsheviks had arranged for official conversations with Germany and its allies to begin on December 2 at Brest-Litovsk. There was simply no time for Judson to cable the War Department for permission. Judson pressed Francis to allow him to go. When Judson arrived at the embassy, the atmosphere was troubled. Judson wanted to tell Trotsky that it was essential to get a no-troop-transfer clause into the armistice, by which he meant to prevent a drifting of German troops to the front in France. Francis opposed anything that might imply recognition until he had heard from Washington. He was finally aware of Lansing's belated admonition of November 30 to do nothing but watch and wait. The ambassador therefore opposed the proposed meeting of Judson and Trotsky. Judson argued that he alone would be criticized for any proposal. He would not see Trotsky in his role as the embassy's military attaché but as chief of the military mission and, therefore, the responsibility of the War Department. Nevertheless he still wanted the ambassador's approval.

Sisson claimed that the ambassador agreed. Francis had met with other ambassadors, and they had each determined whether or not to send a representative.[5] Failing Francis's approval, Judson felt his initiative would be difficult.

British Ambassador George Buchanan would not send any representative until he had London's approval. Judson dined with him, General Knox, and General Niessel, chief of the French military mission. He planned to see Francis afterward. Knox wished to go with Judson, but Buchanan and Niessel were against it.[6] Judson's car had been seized by Lenin's Red Guards while he dined, and he did not reach the American embassy until midnight. He thought he had convinced Francis, though he recognized the ambassador's misgivings. At midnight, November 30, they compromised: Riggs would go to Trotsky as arranged by Sisson. A rebuff of Riggs would be less embarrassing than if experienced by Judson. Still, "if Riggs were to make no satisfactory progress, or if he were to come to the conclusion that it would be well for me to join him or to visit Trotsky after him, I was to hold myself in readiness and continue the interview myself." The two went over what might come up in a Judson-Trotsky conversation, particularly that Colonel Kerth had acted on his own when directing a protest to Dukhonin, a bald-faced lie unlikely to pass Trotsky's scrutiny. It was at this point that Judson received Francis's final approval: "According to my best recollection, (and the whole matter is deeply impressed upon my memory) you [Francis] then asked 'Well what do you think about it now!' I replied that I thought I should go. And you said 'Then go ahead.'"[7] It was December 1. The armistice would begin the next day. Time was essential.

Both Sisson and Robins afterward supported Judson's claim that the ambassador approved Judson's meeting with Trotsky. Even Francis briefly indicated that Judson's conversation with Trotsky had his backing: "Judson saw Trotsky to-day [December 1] with my approval as at yesterday's meeting of Allied chiefs I advocated unofficial effort to influence armistice terms at conference beginning to-morrow. No objection was offered to each chief's exerting such influence unofficially and not personally."[8]

This was the first meeting between a leading Bolshevik and an important American or Allied official. Trotsky later made a fuss about it. All this activity excited the Allied missions and the press, and it was the end for Judson in Russia.

2.

As Judson prepared to visit Smolny, others advanced alternatives, and a notable project arose in Washington. Ambassador Boris A. Bakhmetev, the Provisional Government's representative to the United States, wrote the State Department cautioning against provocative statements made by the Allies. Russia, he felt, was not with Lenin. Russians wanted peace but not a German-imposed peace. A conciliatory move directly to the Russian people should be made, as Russia was exhausted.[9]

Then Colonel House asked the department to suppress American press criticism of the idea that Russia should be treated as an enemy. That attitude, he believed, would throw Russia into support of Germany.[10] Bakhmetev and House saw the value of conciliation to separate the people from Lenin and prevent Russia from coming under the control of Germany. Both urged conciliating the war-weary people of Russia but not the Bolshevik government, which they saw as a temporary proposition.

Contrary to these views, Lord Robert Cecil, minister of blockade in the British War Cabinet, telegraphed Lord Bertie, British ambassador in Paris, that the moderate socialists in Russia were as useless as the Bolsheviks in negotiating and that only a military government offered any hope. Perhaps one of the counterrevolutionary generals from the old Imperial army would take the lead, reconstitute the Eastern Front, and overthrow the Bolsheviks.[11]

Basil Miles, at the Russian desk of the State Department, saw the convening of the Constituent Assembly on January 5/18, elected just eighteen days after the Bolshevik coup, as the opportunity to speak directly to the Russian people and offer help even if the Bolshevik government ceased fighting. Lansing scribbled at the bottom of Miles's memorandum: "President thinks this would be unwise."[12] That meant doing nothing, more watching and waiting.

Francis advised the president that the Allies should call a conference and state their war aims, thus showing their desire to stop the war, and also that Allied missions in Petrograd should request a conference with a committee of the Constituent Assembly dealing with the state of the nation. The president wrote Lansing, "I take it for granted you will advise Francis not to do what he suggests in the paragraph of this dispatch which I have marked. It would be most unwise to interfere in any way or to have any sort of initiative." Lansing cabled Francis as instructed.[13]

A new and dangerous proposal was emerging, one consonant with Lord Cecil. Lansing inquired of House: "Department would be glad to have a report from you on the general attitude of your colleague on the matter of the recognition of the de facto government of the Trans-Caucasus." House, Prime Minister Lloyd George, and Foreign Secretary Arthur J. Balfour thought that the Russian situation was becoming critical, the Allied military people had made a mess, and, no doubt referring to the notes to General

Dukhonin at *Stavka,* the situation could not be worse. French Ambassador Jean Jules Jusserand agreed when speaking to Frank Polk at the State Department; he called the situation hopeless. Desperation was reflected in Lansing's comment to Wilson that he had heard nothing further about four hundred thousand Russian troops still willing to fight.[14]

The Inter-Allied Conference meeting in Paris with Colonel House representing President Wilson finally took up Ambassador Buchanan's alternative to give Russia back its word of not making a separate peace and let it decide whether to make peace on Germany's terms. House reported that Buchanan's proposal brought violent opposition from Baron Sidney Sonnino, Italy's foreign minister. The group called on the Provisional Government's last ambassador to France, Vasilii Maklakov, who seconded House's proposal: reconsider war aims only with a stable Russian government, not the unstable Bolsheviks. After all, the Allies and the United States declared that they were not waging a war for aggression or indemnity and their sacrifice prevented militarism from overshadowing the world. House's proposal, supported by Maklakov, soon gained the backing of the Inter-Allied Conference. It was decided to allow each power to send an answer to its own ambassador in Petrograd that the Allies were willing to reconsider war aims with a stable Russian government. Simultaneously, Lord Lansdowne, former British foreign secretary, spoke out in the press for an honorable end to the war, submission of disputes to arbitration, and the use of collective security. His message had special pathos because he had lost both his sons in the war.[15] Thus, the Bolshevik peace initiative had forced reluctant statements from each Ally to its ambassador, conciliatory moves by Buchanan and Judson, and Lansdowne's public statement.

The president held out for a victory over Germany while doing nothing with the Bolsheviks in the hope that democratic forces would soon emerge to overthrow Lenin and carry on the struggle with Germany. Russia could not remain free against the German menace. Secretary of the Navy Josephus Daniels reported that some in the cabinet felt that the Bolsheviks might maintain themselves; others thought they would fail. Wilson sided with the latter. "WW said Cossacks and others in S. Russia would not follow T. [Trotsky] but declared for continuance of war, and had asked help and recognition. Too chaotic to act yet."[16]

3.

In this very chaotic atmosphere, Judson took his alternative directly to Trotsky, sensing that something had to be done immediately. No directive had been received from Washington, nor had the other Allied missions been told that their governments were reconsidering war aims if they could deal with a stable Russian government. Almost a month had passed and Allied confusion in Petrograd persisted.

Judson was with Trotsky for forty minutes on December 1, the day before the armistice at Brest-Litovsk was to begin. He spoke to Trotsky through an interpreter and found the commissar for foreign affairs friendly. He pointed out that he was interested in how Russia and America could support each other. Trotsky volunteered that Russia had obligations to its Allies, such as detention of enemy troops along the Eastern Front, and no exchange of prisoners. According to Trotsky these matters were on his mind. After preliminary negotiations at Brest-Litovsk, there would be, according to him, a week's recess and that would give the Allies a chance to join in the negotiations. If they failed or refused to join, an appeal would be made directly to their people. [17]

Judson claimed that his visit made it more certain that the armistice protocol had a provision designed to detain enemy troops on the Russian front and, though eventually violated, some troops were retained that otherwise might have been removed to fight in the west. He persuaded Trotsky to bring in technical experts to avoid German lies and treachery. The general encouraged Trotsky to become more uncompromising, increasing the chance of a break between Germany and the Bolsheviks. Judson considered that he had limited for a time the release of prisoners and the exchange of goods. Finally, he thought that he might have won enough of Trotsky's confidence so that he might be consulted again if a break in the negotiations occurred. [18]

One problem with Judson's negotiations was that Trotsky sought propaganda advantages from them. Trotsky's remarks about the interview, their play in the press, the reaction among the Allies, was sufficient, given Wilson's and Lansing's preference for doing nothing, to get Judson recalled. Francis's renunciation of Judson's trip to Trotsky was painful because Francis had already cabled the department his approval. Judson's discussion of Kerth with Trotsky indicated Francis's prior approval of the visit. Judson's cable to the War Department emphasized the urgency of his visit as well as its unofficial character and the fact that he had the ambassador's consent. Judson thought Trotsky would observe and protect Allied interests only to the extent that the armistice would be of long duration, enemy troops would remain in their positions, and there would be no exchange of prisoners or products. Judson's diary was terse: "I came as an individual; pointed out certain directions in which the interests of Russia and her Allies still run parallel; and secured voluntary recognition that Russia has certain obligations to her Allies." [19]

In his final report months later, Judson added:

> By special direction of the Ambassador, just before my interview was ter-
> minated, I brought up the question of Kerth's protest to explain that the
> Ambassador had given no orders as to whom to address the protest (it had
> been sent to Dukhonin). I had occasion to explain that I referred to protest
> already made and not to any new protest. Trotsky interrupted me to say that
> what was past in this connection had no further interest, and that there was
> no reason to discuss the matter.[20]

This last point was the condition Francis made for his consent to the interview: "You then suggested that it might be explained that Kerth had of
his own accord directed his protest *to Dukhonin;* that such was not by your
instructions." Here was further proof that Francis approved the interview.[21]

Trotsky's reaction to Kerth had bothered Judson to the extent that he
cabled the War College staff: "Trotsky makes statement that Soviet government can not permit such interferences with internal life country which
tend to kindle civil war. Further such steps, he says, will bring heavy consequences for which his government refuses to accept responsibility."[22] Francis needed Judson to correct this damage. When Trotsky reported the interview to the Bolshevik newspaper, *Izvestiia,* he put a favorable spin on it by
omitting references to conditions the Soviets might impose on the Germans
that ran parallel to the Allies and only stated that negotiations would be open
and could be joined by the Allies at any time. Most important, Trotsky put
these words into the mouth of Judson in the *Izvestiia* article: "The time of
protests and threats addressed to the Soviet Government has passed, if that
time ever existed." To that supposed statement, Trotsky reported to *Izvestiia*
that he had replied, "the formal side of the affair was of no interest and might
be considered closed by the statement of the General."[23]

Judson maintained he never made that exact remark. Yet the press picked
up on it, and the Allies and neutrals complained about it. Judson did admit,
"As a matter of fact I did not say this, although from the standpoint of
expediency it was quite true."[24] The day after, Judson remarked:

> Before the interview I well knew that Mr. Trotsky might be tempted in the
> manner common among politicians to distort the circumstance and substance
> of it, and I had determined that whatever the result I would engage in no
> debate as to what happened. His account was less inaccurate than I appre-
> hended it might be. It excited the Ambassador, as I knew it would, but I have
> urged him as insistently as I know how to make no comment to anyone on
> any discrepancy.

Judson later complained that the press reported his interview without regard to the facts.[25]

The heat was on; Francis buckled. The day after Judson's interview Francis cabled Lansing:

> Judson's visit to Trotsky exciting comment, especially among Allied missions who consider it step toward recognition. Judson has insisted for some time that Soviet is *de facto* government and relations therewith should be established. After discussing matter with Allied colleagues as reported in 2050, December 1, 9 p.m.,[26] I consented that Judson should send subordinate to discuss armistice provisions only and was not aware that Judson had gone himself until after visit made.[27]

Trotsky gave a speech for its propaganda effects. He made Judson the butt of a remark claiming the Soviets used a new diplomacy where everything was open and illustrated it with Judson's visit. The Germans, Trotsky claimed, had threatened Russia with ambition for territory if an armistice should take place. Trotsky criticized Allied agents for trying to influence Russia to continue fighting; grave consequences threatened if they should incite a civil war. It was at this time that Judson had called on Trotsky. Trotsky wished to show Judson coming to his office in hope of deferring an armistice. Without directly referring to Judson, he actually was forthright about the issue: "The demand will be made, that during the armistice the Germans do not transfer any troops to the western theatre of war, as Russia could not consent that the armistice should be utilized to crush England and France." He dismissed this possibility, the one Judson warned of and the same one carefully edited out of his *Izvestiia* article, by asserting that Germany would respect Russia because, "Germany will not dare to refuse, as every German soldier will understand that we demand an honest armistice." He referred to Judson's remark about the Germans as crafty negotiators, which was particularly apt in regard to the fate of Courland and Lithuania. Trotsky's curious twists and underlying optimism were not enough to save Judson. Within days his position crumbled. Ambassador Morris reported from Stockholm on the *Izvestiia* article by emphasizing Judson's supposed remark that the time had passed to threaten the Soviet government.[28]

4.

Simultaneously, London moved swiftly against Ambassador Buchanan's recommendation of accommodation by accepting House's request at the Inter-Allied Conference to negotiate only with a stable government. The War Cabinet told Buchanan that "the policy of the British Government was to support any responsible body in Russia that would actively oppose the Maximalist [Bolshevik] movement, and at the same time give money, freely, within reason, to such bodies as they were prepared to help the Allied cause." Such a policy encouraged civil war and implied some kind of intervention on the part of the British to aid their side against Lenin's government. House was jubilant only about supporting a stable government, not the Bolsheviks. He had not bought into any kind of intervention. "After my conference with Balfour last night, he wrote a dispatch to the British Ambassador at Petrograd which goes far in the direction I have been urging." Lansing read that dispatch. Its claims against Russia's armistice were based not on the September 4, 1914, arrangement but on deeper principles: a fair and democratic peace. If Russia had a stable government, democratic and pro-Allied, acceptable to the Russian people, and could deal with an honorable German government, the British would go along. Notwithstanding these virtually impossible conditions for the Bolsheviks, Buchanan was at liberty to point out that no responsible German statesman said anything to agree with the Bolsheviks or the Allies. By substituting argument for action, the only peace obtainable for the Soviet government would be neither democratic, nor lasting, but German and imperialist. Balfour sent this telegram without consulting London.[29] It obviously awaited the success of the forthcoming Russian Constituent Assembly, which had been elected after the Bolshevik coup and was scheduled to meet in early January. Lenin had approved the election, but the Bolsheviks had only won a minority of the delegates. On January 18, 1918, it convened; the following day Lenin dissolved it.

House's policy gained support. Jusserand cabled Pichon, the French foreign minister. He told Pichon that Judson's note referring to the general's second letter, apparently the one "appearing to approve the idea of a general peace, is completely the opposite of Mr. Wilson's idea. I have it from Mr. Polk that it was sent without either authorization or forewarning, that it very much surprised the Department of State, and that explanations have been asked of Mr. Francis." In an important addendum to his cable Jusserand noted, "I have signaled this note to Colonel House who has responded by telegram that it was, without doubt, 'an absurd fable.'" Here was clear indication of the direction affairs were taking in Washington. Wilson told Jusserand, "the attitude should be one of the most absolute caution (reserve), limiting intercourse to current necessary affairs and avoiding everything which could give the appearance of encouragement and abstaining from protests which are a form of recognition of the existence of this group."[30]

Nothing so definitive as this had been received in Petrograd. No position had been arrived at beyond allowing what Judson had described as trivial intercourse and Francis as doing nothing. Phillips told Lansing that the

French would not countenance de facto recognition and considered the armistice a breach of the September 4, 1914, agreement. Phillips realized that the United States was not a signatory and need not take such a harsh alternative. He referred to Bullard's message indicating the necessity to explain why America declined de facto recognition. The United States, in Bullard's opinion, need not go so far as to say it would never recognize an undemocratic government based on violence or fear but, conversely, should show an interest in democratic Russia's welfare.[31] This alternative would at least temporarily close the door to the Bolsheviks while Wilson searched for a democratic alternative. Such an alternative would, of course, have to rid Russia of Lenin's government. Bullard's policy, if adopted, would have had Wilson aid and abet counterrevolution.

Lansing had meanwhile inquired about another alternative—an army forming in the south to counter the Bolsheviks—and been told by Francis of its difficulty. The secretary of state permitted George Creel to start a propaganda barrage by Edgar Sisson in Petrograd and Moscow as a counter to German propaganda. The president rejected sending another fact-finding mission.[32]

As the president prepared to address Congress on the state of the union in December, reports appeared of Judson's visit to Trotsky. By then Francis's first cable approving the visit arrived. Wilson's address to Congress referred to the situation in Russia as one resulting from a lack of education of the Russian public as to the true nature of the war and the extent of the dangers posed to Russia by a German victory. Wilson declared the Russian people had been "poisoned by the very same falsehoods that have kept the German people in the dark, and the poison has been administered by the very same hands." There had been an insufficiency of Allied propaganda while German agents, perhaps Bolsheviks, conducted a campaign of lies among Russians, or so Wilson implied. The remedy to this lack of education and falsehood was an intense application of the truth, which could not be "uttered too plainly or too often."[33] Creel and Sisson administered the truth, according to Wilson, by following Root's earlier suggestion.

Did those parleys have any possibility of success? In the president's view propaganda could sway moderates in the forthcoming Russian Constituent Assembly, justifying the president's do-nothing policy toward the Bolsheviks. Wilson's policy presented to Congress seemed plausible: educate, propagandize, and do nothing until Russians rid themselves of the Bolsheviks; refuse de facto recognition of the Soviet government on the strength of Bullard's argument that Bolshevism's undemocratic character was founded on an "arbitrary and irresponsible authority based solely on physical control over the residents."[34]

Lansing prepared a private memorandum with which Wilson subsequently agreed.[35] The United States "watched with deep concern the overthrow by force of the provisional authority representing the revolution at Petrograd, and the popular election of a Constituent Assembly called to establish a constitutional government based on the principle of democracy." America was willing to help Russia in its transition to democracy, but "the Government has watched with disappointment and amazement the rise of class despotism in Petrograd and the open efforts of the leaders of the Bolsheviki to withdraw from the conflict even at the expense of national honor and the future safety of democracy in Russia." Withdrawal, Lansing contended, was contrary to Russia's true will. The Bolshevik threat that if they were not recognized, they would appeal to peoples of the nations, was annoying. Lansing labeled this threat an arbitrary and irregular foreign policy that again illustrated Bolshevism's despotic nature. He believed in Russia's democratic aspirations and her honoring of her treaty commitments. Bolshevism, according to Lansing, was despotic, dishonorable, reckless, and unprincipled in its methods. Lansing identified it as an authoritarian system, created and sustained by force, dominated by self-appointed representatives of a single class, and dedicated to the overthrow of capitalism and its replacement by an extreme form of socialism.[36] An ideological basis for the first Cold War had now begun to crystallize.

It was clear from Jusserand's comments to Pichon, Balfour's cable to Buchanan, and Lansing's private memo that there would be no recognition of the Soviet government, and there was an expectation that the Russian people would come to their senses and restore democracy by overthrowing the Bolshevik tyranny. In the meantime, the Allies would actively, though surreptitiously, seek alternatives to the Bolsheviks.

Buchanan realized his own difficult position in Petrograd because Trotsky on November 26 threatened the arrest of British nationals if George Chicherin and Pavel Petrov, Bolshevik operatives in Britain, were not released from British jails. These men had been arrested in late August on charges of sedition. This situation was made painful for Buchanan due to his previous cable to London suggesting accommodation. It was not until December 14 that Buchanan told Trotsky that their cases would be reconsidered. Trotsky then revoked his threat.[37]

A unified Allied policy was beginning to fall into place. Buchanan maintained British sympathy for the Russian people without grudges or the contemplation of any "coercive or punitive measures" against them for making a separate peace. The Allies, he noted, distinguished between people and government. He stoutly defended the British complaint against the Soviet armistice negotiations without previous Allied consultations as a breach of the September 4, 1914, treaty. Just because that treaty was made with an autocratic government did not mean it had no binding force on a successor government. Otherwise, international relations would have no stability. Britain repudiated the new doctrine but had no desire to hold an unwilling ally to its previous commitments. Buchanan appealed to the so-called higher principles of a democratic peace, which he felt Russian democracy aspired to and which he felt could not be obtained from the Germans. Such principles had to be agreed to before any armistice. The German government, he assured the Russian press, had spoken not a word about such principles. Rather, the Kaiser's government contemplated an imperialist peace in its favor. The British would not send representatives until they were assured that a stable government had been recognized by the whole Russian people. They wanted to examine their mutual war aims and the possible conditions of a just and lasting peace. The British would continue to hold down enemy troops on its respective fronts, what Buchanan called "rendering Russia the most effective assistance." However, he asked, could the same be said of Russia, which daily attacked Britain in the press for its imperialist aims and responsibility for the slaughter? Without British intervention in World War I, Russia would have been defeated by Germany, hence no Russian revolutions and no Russian democracy. "The German army would have seen to that, and without our cooperation in the war Russia would have never won her freedom." That, Buchanan emphasized, ought to qualify Britain as a friend. Buchanan was openly critical of Lenin for his attacks on British rule in India, and he pointed out the dangers for British subjects then resident in Russia because of the hostile Russian press. Finally, he noted his own and his embassy's neutrality and noninterference in Russian politics, but he warned the War Cabinet about the Soviet's meddling in the affairs of the Allied countries. The ambassador's central point was that the British government could not discuss peace terms with a revolutionary regime.[38]

In a discussion with twenty-five journalists following his press release, Buchanan made it clear that the Allies must reach an agreement on principles before discussing any peace with Germany. To do that, Russia ought to have a legal government, though Britain would be flexible in defining it.[39] House's policy toward the Bolshevik government, carried out in Balfour's telegram to Buchanan and enunciated to the press by Buchanan, had triumphed. The Allies would await formation in Russia of a legal government, democratically elected, with which peace principles would be elaborated. If at that point the German government agreed to them, negotiations could begin. Until such a government was constituted, Allied relations with the Bolsheviks would be minimal; that is, the Allies would, to borrow Francis's terminology, do nothing for fear of indicating to the rest of the world de facto recognition. Aside from Buchanan's statement, the War Cabinet secretly weighed the advantages and disadvantages of the alternatives to de facto recognition against the possibility of either covert action or an energetic intervention to depose Bolshevism.

Meanwhile, Judson visited Knox a few days after his Trotsky interview and spoke with General Ernest Poole and his assistant, Banting; they were in accord with what Judson called his policy of "conciliating the Soviet Government to a certain extent with the object of saving what is possible from the wreck."[40]

Robins took a tougher attitude by working on Sisson to get Francis recalled. Robins wrote, "We are at last driving full speed ahead. Work in coding the message that will get the stuffed shirt."[41] While this dangerous plot against the ambassador was being hatched, Lansing took decisive measures against Judson. He asked Phillips to draft Francis a cable saying "take no steps with Lenin or Trotsky." The cable of December 6 read: "Referring press reports received here last few days concerning communications of Judson with Trotsky relative armistice, President desires American representatives withhold all direct communication with Bolshevik government. So advise Judson and Kerth. Department assumes these instructions being observed by Embassy." Lansing reminded Francis to take no action on his previous suggestions to request Allies to confer with a committee to be appointed by the forthcoming Constituent Assembly on the state of the nation, or that the Allies would call a conference to state war aims, and, finally, to make no responses to various statements by Trotsky.[42] The definitive statement on doing nothing had finally arrived.

By this time, Lansing had had enough of Judson. If his cables to Francis left any doubt, he visited Secretary of War Newton D. Baker and wrote, "Secy Baker on recalling Judson from Petrograd. Phillips on whether Francis authorized Judson to see Trotsky. Phillips with late telegram about Judson." Francis tried squirming out of his authorization of Judson, telegram #2050 of December 1, with his renunciation telegram, #2057 of December 2, by claiming only that he had approved of Judson sending a subordinate and was not aware of Judson's visit to Trotsky until afterwards. Lansing, exercised over Judson's visit to Trotsky, spent fifteen minutes discussing the issue with Wilson and afterwards remarked, "Col Judson's conduct in Petrograd." Judson's recall was at hand. On January 1, 1918, he received a cable relieving him and ordering him to report to the army's chief of staff in Washington.[43] Judson left Russia on January 22, 1918. Robins remained and championed his alternative policy.

Lansing wrote another long private memo further explaining policy. The only practical procedure was "to let things alone as far as it is possible to do so." This was because Russia was an unresolved riddle.[44] However much Wilson could or could not be faulted for his understanding of the Russian puzzle, it is fair to say that none of America's observers, as Lansing commented, even the well-trained ones, had been able to find a way out of the Russian enigma that would lead to satisfactory results. Could anyone in Washington at that time have done better? The Root Mission was too optimistic. All its premises had come to naught, though able men had served. Even Lansing would not hazard his own guess. This was because the Russian situation was so novel, with the Bolshevik anarchists rejecting nationality, advocating the overthrow of existing governments, and establishing on their ruins a proletarian despotism. "I cannot see," he continued, "how this element which is hostile to the very idea of nationality can claim that they are the Government of a nation or expect to be recognized as such." Recognition would, in Lansing's opinion, only encourage them and their followers in other lands. That would be a serious error—an error both France and Britain seemed tempted to make. Lansing included the French because a deal like Judson's might be cut between them and Lenin.

Policy, Lansing believed, should be "to leave these dangerous idealists alone and have no direct dealings. To recognize them would give them an exalted idea of their own power, make them more insolent and impossible, and win their contempt, not their friendship." The "Teutonic Powers" might achieve some temporary advantages in arranging peace and gaining supplies in order to remove their military forces elsewhere, but they would pay a heavy price. His solution was simple. If left to themselves the Bolsheviks would self-destruct: "I cannot see how unorganized and undirected physical power such as now dominates affairs in Petrograd can continue. It has in itself every element of destruction." It was true that "Up to the present, however, the logic of events has failed." He was persuaded that it was "unwise to give recognition to Lenine, Trotsky, and their crew of radicals." It was better to "sit tight and wait and see how the Germans came out." If they did not "burn their fingers," he would admit he was wrong. Even if Germany made peace, recognizing the Bolsheviks would not stop communism nor help continue the war. The Bolsheviks would make any kind of humiliating peace with the Germans. Thirty years later George F. Kennan turned Lansing's "logic of events" into a "vigilant containment."

Lansing conceded that Lenin and Trotsky were probably not German agents but misguided idealists who were "honest in purpose and utterly dishonest in methods." Since national and personal honor, truth, and individual rights meant nothing to them, no one could deal with them. They planned a social revolution by mob violence to destroy civilization. Russia would give way to separate states, some favorable and others hostile to

Bolshevism. This would result in the worst civil war in history in which the Russian terror would far surpass the French terror. Eventually a strong man would restore order with the help of the military. Certain leaders in the south such as the Don Cossack General A. M. Kaledin or General M. V. Alekseyev, former chief of staff of the Russian imperial army, might accomplish this, but Lansing was not overly confident. They appeared America's only hope at that moment. Lansing opposed giving them any open support, as the situation was too uncertain and chaotic. Lansing inferred that covert help was possible. He concluded, " 'Do nothing' should be our policy until the black period of terrorism comes to an end and the rising tide of blood has run its course."[45] Lansing rejected all the various suggestions and initiatives that had come to him via Petrograd up to that time. Lansing and Wilson closed the door to the Judson-Robins alternative.

5.

The emergence of a British policy alternative came almost simultaneously with Lansing's suggestion of a sub rosa policy of covert action to aid Generals Kaledin and Alekseyev. Buchanan was ordered to backtrack, and within weeks after his press conference was recalled. He left Russia on January 7, 1918. On December 7 the British War Cabinet examined Commander Oliver Locker-Lampson's scheme. He had led a British armored-car squadron for General L. G. Kornilov in September at the time of the general's failed putsch against Prime Minister Alexander Kerensky's government.[46] The commander suggested a more forceful alternative than proposals made at the Inter-Allied Conference. His policy called for the Japanese and Americans to send a force to Vladivostok to guard Allied military stores and secure control of the Trans-Siberian railway and, by a far-reaching extension, open communications with southern Russia. A small British force should be sent to Murmansk to protect munitions and provide refuge for Entente nationals. Here was one of the first clearly enunciated and overtly interventionist policies, foreseeing the lines of operation it must take. In addition, the new government at Tiflis, Georgia, would be encouraged, and an effort would be made to constitute an Armenian army.

The British government wondered whether occupation of Vladivostok would do more harm than good. It would strengthen Russian opposition and threaten the lives of British nationals in Russia. Japanese expansion was a concern. It would be a risky policy. The War Cabinet decided to solicit Washington and Tokyo about stern measures to secure the Trans-Siberian railway and supply food to Russia. Would either government think it favorable for the dispatch of a police force to Vladivostok? A definite British policy had to be adopted and only two alternatives appeared: recognize the Bolsheviks and make the best arrangements possible, or refuse recognition and take open and energetic steps against them. The British seemed in no mood to do nothing. Though British alternatives were frowned on as dangerous, the latter alternative of taking energetic steps to directly secure Vladivostok and the Trans-Siberian railway seemed preferable.[47]

With the emergence of an Allied policy—recognize a stable Russian democratic government, otherwise do nothing—it was time to bring unity between the ambassadors and their staffs in Petrograd. A Lansing cable to Francis indicated changes. The secretary of state warned of cables at variance with Washington's policy. The State Department preferred messages to come from Francis as an expression of his personal views. The day before Lansing had wired John Mott, reprimanding one of Mott's YMCA secretaries, Jerome Davis, who was in charge of YMCA activities in Russia. Mott was admonished not to allow unauthorized persons to get diplomatically involved.[48]

Notwithstanding Francis's dalliances in the Matilda de Cram affair, Lansing kept the ambassador on, though it was clear he had erred on Judson's visit to Trotsky. Indeed, Francis had taken great comfort in Lansing's cable of December 6. It had pointedly referred to the president's "desire," in reality, a strict order: American representatives were to stop all direct communications with the Soviet government, especially General Judson, Lieutenant Colonel Kerth, and the embassy—a policy the ambassador had been advocating for almost a month. Francis welcomed Lansing's cable and correctly claimed that it was his policy the secretary approved.[49]

Judson interpreted Lansing differently: "cable from Washington to-day states the President desires American representatives to withhold all direct communication with the Bolshevick Government." Judson discounted it by saying that the cable was probably based on hostile American press reports, especially from Louis Edgar Browne of the *Chicago Daily News*, who was unfriendly to what was perceived as Judson's attempt to reach out to Trotsky. Judson's plan had been to assure Trotsky that if negotiations at Brest failed, Trotsky could count on America's help with troops and practical aid. In Judson's opinion this would make the Russians less willing to give in to the Germans. It was only the press, so Judson thought, that stood in the way.[50] He still did not realize that his alternative had been pushed aside.

Judson further proposed that he be authorized to promise "instantaneous action" if the Brest negotiations collapsed. What would this entail? This new plan of Judson's was another alternative to the earlier one offered to

Lansing. If the Bolsheviks accepted it as it would be negotiated by Judson, then they could expect the following:

> All American troops the Trans-Siberian Railway can transport; a real American railway advisor with a great staff or a railway administrator with same; American operation of the Trans-Siberian System and in so far as may be practicable of the trunk lines thence to Odessa, Moscow, Petrograd and the front; utmost efforts largely to increase shipments of railway material to the port of Vladivostok; assistance on a large scale of every other character; the creation in Russia of American Plenipotentiary Commission of three, empowered within wide limits to direct, not request, action in or material from the United States for Russia.[51]

Judson cabled the War College asking if the Allies would support Trotsky should his negotiations with Germany fail. As late as December 31 Judson reported that Trotsky still asked what the United States would do in this case.[52] Judson received no response to his latest alternative.

It was hardly a propitious time for such a proposition by Judson. The president and secretary of state were busy exploring a contemplated British and French covert policy alternative that aimed at keeping Russia in the war and at the same time giving the Bolsheviks a better opportunity to self-destruct or yield to Russia's democratic forces. The British, with French help, secured Wilson's backing of this alternative. The War Cabinet again met in early December to give further consideration to its Russian policy. It had before it a Balfour memorandum. In discussing that memorandum, the War Cabinet first maintained that Britain need not concern itself primarily with the local aspirations of the Bolsheviks or other competing political parties. Rather, its purpose was "to keep Russia in the war until our joint war aims were realised," but, failing that, "to ensure that Russia was as helpful to us and as harmful for the enemy as possible."[53] If the Bolsheviks were successful in making peace, then Britain should do everything to keep Russia in London's favor. That meant not antagonizing the Bolsheviks needlessly so that they would be thrown into Germany's arms. By now, Chicherin and Petrov had been released from Brixton prison, but what about British support of General A. M. Kaledin, a counterrevolutionary Don Cossack leader in southern Russia? It was pointed out that support to Kaledin was aimed against the Germans, supposedly, and not against the Bolsheviks. Certainly, this was a very fine distinction for Kaledin and those around him, as was well known to the British, were actively seeking to destroy the Bolshevik government. Kaledin's efforts, so the British contended, were to help Romania.

These conclusions were reached because Balfour's memorandum argued against treating the Bolsheviks as enemies: "I am," said Balfour, "clearly of opinion that it is to our advantage to avoid, as long as possible, an open breach with this crazy system. If this be drifting, then I am a drifter by deliberate policy." The safety of the British colony in Russia had required the release of Chicherin and Petrov. The Bolsheviks, Balfour pointed out, were not going to fight Germany, nor probably anyone else. Why drive them into Germany's hands? Without active Russian cooperation, Russia could not be easily organized or overrun, especially when German troops could not readily be spared. It would not be for many months that German needs could be supplied. Avoiding antagonizing the Bolsheviks must extend over that period.[54]

In a memorandum to Wilson, Lansing finally, like Balfour, drew up a policy diverging from the do-nothing attitude. It disregarded advice from some Americans in Russia. Now the Bolsheviks had determined to take Russia out of the war. The longer they were in power, the more anarchy. Russia would be eliminated as a fighting force, the war prolonged by two or three years. If Bolshevik domination could be broken, then Russia's armies might be reorganized and readied for action by the following spring or summer. Only a military dictatorship backed by troops could ensure stability and military participation. Lansing summarized his latest alternative: "the only apparent nucleus for an organized movement sufficiently strong to supplant the Bolsheviki and establish a government would seem to be the group of general officers with General Kaledin, the hetman of the Don Cossacks."[55] Based on these conclusions, Lansing considered whether to encourage Kaledin and, if so, how to do so.

Kaledin and his associates, Lansing thought, knew less about American policy than vice-versa because their information came from Bolshevik and German sources. They believed America recognized the Bolshevik government and concluded that further resistance was useless. Lansing knew that "to have this group broken up would be to throw the country into the hands of the Bolsheviki and the Germans would freely continue their propaganda which is leading to chaos and the actual disintegration of the Russian Empire." It was crucial to get a message to Kaledin by courier through Tiflis explaining the true situation. This message would communicate America's "readiness to give recognition to a government which exhibits strength enough to restore order and a purpose to carry out in good faith Russia's international engagements." Lansing advised Wilson to approve communicating with Kaledin quickly; otherwise by inaction the United States would be playing into Bolshevik hands. Lansing hoped "the situation may be saved by a few words of encouragement, and the saving of Russia means the saving to this country of hundreds of thousands of men and billions of dollars."

He had to admit, "I do not see how we could be any worse off if we took this course because we have absolutely nothing to hope from continued Bolshevik domination."[56]

When Wilson's cabinet met, Secretary of the Navy Daniels recorded that Wilson hesitated "to do nothing about Russia but puzzled to know how to take hold." Secretary of the Interior Lane interrupted: "Perhaps Constituent Assembly may point the way. [Wilson:] No, neither party will have majority. Lansing: The Bolsheviks permit soldiers to vote wherever they are and charge them so they will have a majority for their party—civil war possible. Everything now too chaotic to make move." Wilson seemed puzzled and Lansing spoke of chaos. Yet the following day the president accepted Lansing's memorandum: "This has my entire approval."[57] It contemplated covert action in support of the British and French initiative against the Soviet government that he refused to recognize.

This memorandum, which Lansing drafted and Secretary of the Treasury McAdoo approved, acknowledged that Kaledin held the best chance for success in reestablishing the Eastern Front and creating a stable government in Russia. Lansing cabled Ambassador Walter Hines Page in London with a note for Oscar T. Crosby, assistant secretary of the treasury and the department's delegate to the Inter-Allied Council on War Purchases and Finance. It authorized him to take up the matter of potential financial aid to the French and British governments in their quest to help Kaledin. Since Kaledin was not an acknowledged de facto government, U.S. law prevented direct loans to him. Lansing's cable simply enabled Crosby to find out "whether or not they [British and French] are willing to adopt the course above outlined and if so, to what extent financial aid will be required." Lansing asked for this inquiry to be timely, but stressed the "importance of avoiding it being known that the United States is considering showing sympathy for the Kaledin movement, much less of providing financial assistance." Lansing entertained covert action.[58]

As to this American money passed to the French and British, the U.S. Treasury exchanged more than a little. Initially, Crosby cabled Page, "have reason to believe that British effort will accomplish all that can now be considered valuable in this direction. Since this effort was made quite independently of even French, both Ambassador and I feel it unnecessary for us to offer just now to share liability though British have been given to understand we will consider sharing in any wise effort." Page added, "I should go further than Crosby and decline to risk money in any enterprise so doubtful and about which so little is known either by British Government or ourselves. I should surely wait till these people give some hopeful evidence of their strength and spirit."[59]

The matter temporarily ended for America. It had a painful consequence for Britain and France. Both powers had to exercise care to not so anger the Bolsheviks that their nationals in Russia would be endangered. They needed to fill the vacuum that would be left by the imminent departure of Russian armies from the Eastern Front. The Romanian armies had been reconstituted by the French military mission under General H. M. Berthelot after their 1916 defeat. They would need to secure Ukrainian food supplies and have allies in their rear. For continued Allied support and assurances, King Ferdinand of Romania, who had fled to Jassy in December 1916 after the fall of Bucharest, would try to link with the Cossacks in southern Russia and the British in Mesopotamia. House favored Jassy as the center for southern Russia but did not wish to support overtly any particular Russian group. David Lloyd George, Britain's prime minister, agreed. Yet there was confusion over just how strong Kaledin's forces were. House was ambiguous on the question of encouraging Kaledin without any definite program, yet he admitted to Lansing that if he were not helped his forces might go to pieces. France, Italy, and England needed more information in order to send a British military mission from Romania to Tiflis and on to Kaledin's headquarters at Novocherkassk to confer with him. A mission was sent though Buchanan was against it and Knox reported Kaledin had no strength.[60]

In the middle of this activity, with Balfour still in Paris, Lloyd George and the War Cabinet decided to give Kaledin money. This risky action occurred even at a time when Trotsky had considered arresting Buchanan. The War Cabinet, desperate to preserve some semblance of an Eastern Front, approved two financial advances totaling £10 million sterling and put another undisclosed amount at the disposal of Sir Charles Marling, British ambassador at Teheran. This effort culminated in the convention of December 23, 1917. Lord Robert Cecil, undersecretary for foreign affairs, and Viscount Alfred Milner, then minister without portfolio, left for Paris with a memorandum for French Prime Minister Clemenceau and his foreign secretary, Pichon. The memorandum became the "Convention between France and England on the Subject of Activity in Southern Russia." This agreement assigned an English sphere of influence to the Cossack territories—the Caucasus, Armenia, Georgia, Kurdistan—and a French sphere of Bessarabia, the Ukraine, and the Crimea. Expenses were to be pooled and regulated by an inter-allied organ though it was admitted that French money had already been allocated for a 100-million-franc credit. By the end of 1917 Great Britain and France were involved in southern Russia, and their action became the basis of the Anglo-French convention of December 23. It was done against the most expert advice.[61]

U.S. Consul DeWitt Clinton Poole in Moscow was dispatched on the covert mission by Consul General Maddin Summers; Poole arrived in Rostov under the pretense of establishing a consulate and went to Novocherkassk to call on Generals Kaledin and Alekseyev, who represented a group called the "League for the Defense of our Native Land and Liberty." He contacted the French military mission for Romania, which had granted Alekseyev a 100-million-ruble credit for restoring Russia and continuing the war.[62]

Poole remained in Novocherkassk for a month. He distinguished three groups: Alekseyev and the Volunteer Army, composed mainly of officers from the old Imperial army, Kaledin and the Don Cossacks, and the Southeastern Federation—the last representing other Cossacks and the Caucasus. The league had Kaledin's support. As hetman [chief] of the Don, he had General Hucher's French credit. The arrival of Boris Savinkov, former terrorist and member of Kerensky's discredited regime, complicated things. Alekseyev maintained that though it was impossible to bring together what remained of the old Provisional Government, there was the nucleus of an "organization which would sooner or later proclaim itself to be the Provisional Government of Russia." Alekseyev understood that the job of this government would be to stabilize Russia so that free elections could be held for a constitutional assembly with southern Russia's military force at its disposal. Another group was forming around General Kornilov, and in January it joined the other three, with a ruling council that included Savinkov. The council was broadened with three Social Democrats, two Social Revolutionaries, and some liberals such as Paul Miliukov and Peter Struve, leading Kadets. The league planned a proclamation to the people accusing the Bolsheviks of failing to fulfill their promises of peace and bread and of suppressing the Constituent Assembly. The proclamation would ask the people to support a new Constituent Assembly as well as to continue the war.

Poole recommended American support of the league because the latter met what he considered to be two fundamental American requirements: holding as many enemy troops of the Central Powers as possible on the Russian front and assisting Russians in establishing orderly government. He voiced concern over the league's probabilities for success. Poole noted the social unrest in southern Russia, particularly between Bolshevik elements and disaffected Cossacks. There was growing Bolshevik military action in the area. Poole stated, "The Volunteer Army now organizing includes as yet no infantry to speak of, and what artillery exists is practically without ammunition. From a military point of view the position of the Don government is lamentably weak." To succeed it needed money promptly, as well as ammunition and equipment. A more permanent solution to its problems would be essential. Contact with the Allies through Siberia and over the Trans-Siberian railway would be the key. Without such aid, Poole emphasized, "the league can not develop its possibilities in any important measure."[63]

Poole returned to Moscow in late January. He was convinced of Alekseyev's sincerity but doubted the quality of his troops, who appeared to be already defeated.[64] Yet Poole told Francis that the league was a serious attempt at saving a part of Russia. Though Poole thought his evaluation of that situation correct if balanced with his report's cautious notes, he later reflected, "We didn't yet see clearly how thoroughly the Russian people were defeated, and that no government could hope to survive in Russia at that time on a basis of continued resistance to the Central Powers. The Russians were just plain licked, and that was the basic fact and controlling fact, but we always hoped, naturally."[65] Meanwhile, the debate for a viable public alternative to doing nothing continued in Washington.

Without seeing a definite public policy toward the Soviet government, former members of the Root Mission argued with one another and with the administration. Phillips mentioned that Root had been in for a chat. Root was out of patience with the president's policy of doing nothing, and advised getting in touch with anti-Bolshevik forces, lending them money, giving them comfort, and in this way preserving southern Russia for the Allies. Bertron wrote Wilson to ask for a brief meeting with several mission members. He was worried that the Germans might use Russian resources to prolong the war. Bertron pestered Joseph P. Tumulty, the president's private secretary. Tumulty reported that Bertron brought to him a memorandum from Ambassador Bakhmetev containing one more alternative. Bertron "seemed to feel piqued that nothing had been done."[66]

Bakhmetev's memorandum suggested yet another policy alternative for Wilson to consider. He began by calling attention to the chaotic situation in Russia and its dangerous nature. The conflicting aims and movements, even the threat of civil war, took a back seat to the Bolshevik triumph and Lenin's ability to suspend active military operations at the front and lead Russia out of the war. Bakhmetev cautioned, "One should not regard Russia solely as a military factor, as a presumably 'lost' link in the allied war machine." However distressing, "Russia, if withdrawn from the war, is left face to face with a Germany which has not yet consumed the process of democratization and the Masters of which are full of aspirations for economic, if not direct, conquest." Russia would provide Germany with the possibilities of dismemberment and domination. Eastern Europe would be deprived of a "Great Unified Democratic State." Germany's control of Russia's resources and commercial penetration of its sphere would strengthen its autocratic claim to world leadership and dramatically change the world's geopolitics. Bakhmetev speculated that a situation might arise in which the resources of Russia and Asia Minor would enable Germany to preserve its political stability in the war's aftermath, while at the same time western democracies would enter a period of instability and internal reverses. This imminent danger of German autocracy's success could be paralyzed if the process of further political and economic disintegration in Russia was stopped and followed by a constructive movement for political unity, democratic stability, and economic progress. How could Russia, Bakhmetev asked, not be lost as a partner in the society of democratic nations?[67] Bakhmetev saw the fateful consequences of failed American policies in Russia.

Bakhmetev wanted to avoid German domination of the East. Only an active and deliberate policy of assisting non-Bolshevik Russia could save Russia's democratic forces. American help had to go to the Russian people and not the Bolsheviks. This was an important distinction that Wilson would subsequently use. It was necessary to have an effective policy for the constructive elements of Russia so that they could achieve political stability and an orderly democratic government. This policy had to be exercised through propaganda, economic organization, and relief. By propaganda, Bakhmetev meant explaining to the Russian people the real aims and intentions of the democracies against those of German autocracy. It should also include moral relief and comfort such as that afforded by the YMCA. By economic organization, Bakhmetev meant the reestablishment of production and distribution, especially the railways and agriculture. As to relief, this meant supplying everyday commodities.

To whom should this entire endeavor be directed? This was, he emphasized, the most delicate part of the problem. It should be given to those carrying authority and restoring order. This was the consolidating work of democratic elements. But for the moment, they had "seceded for the time being into self-dependent communities, revolutionary, military dictatorships, effectuating strong rule for a clear defined aim of saving the liberties of the people." Each particular case would have to be judged on its merits. For that purpose, a special committee had to be formed and authorized to make decisions. It would be named by the government and would represent various political factions. "This committee, acting on behalf and on account of the United States Government, should be given the disposal of the necessary funds and authorized to carry out the whole of the material and executive work in regard to Russia."[68] Bakhmetev's solution amounted to American economic intervention on a grand scale, administered by an autonomous committee. Wilson so far had only authorized a backdoor, covert intervention through monies as credits to the Russian embassy through the National City Bank and Crosby's possible laundering of money to Britain and France—the latter predicated on Poole's report, not Bakhmetev's advice.

Bakhmetev indicated that the committee should inherit all the orders pending for the former Russian government and decide the best course for each of them, including all credits. Actually, these finally fell to the Russian embassy. Though Bakhmetev did not indicate the general composition of the special committee, it probably would have been made up of American nationals, including members of the Root Mission and Stevens Railway Commission. Perhaps that committee would have had several Russians as ex officio members, including, of course, Bakhmetev, though the Russian ambassador did not specify. However that may be, the concerns expressed by former Root Mission members and in Bakhmetev's memorandum went unanswered.[69]

By this time House had returned from Europe and cabled to arrange a meeting with Wilson. Wiseman had sent House a secret cable to congratulate his friend on the mission to Europe. He emphasized the need for American manpower to hold the line against the German spring offensive. He called attention to the importance of Wilson's speech of December 4, which had stressed a fight to the finish as an antidote to Lord Lansdowne's *London Daily Telegraph* letter advocating a negotiated peace. All Russians wanted peace, he related, and there was little hope of assistance to Romania because Russian troops were no longer there. Sir Cecil Spring Rice, British ambassador, had said much the same thing. The British ambassador revealed that the War Cabinet was anxious about the rapid transfer of German troops from the Eastern to the Western Front. House arrived and reported on all his European activities. He shared Wiseman's cable with Wilson; in regard to aiding those movements in the East still willing to fight, he mentioned to Wiseman that although Wilson "has no power to lend money direct to such un-organised movements he is willing to let France and England have funds to transmit to them if they consider it advisable."[70] Once more, Wilson indicated his willingness to use laundered monies.

However much Crosby and Page objected to the president's and the secretary of state's decision to follow the British and French lead in supporting Kaledin, there is no reason to believe that their opinion swayed Wilson or Lansing. House strenuously objected to such a covert policy, while Phillips was relieved that "Our policy in Russia seems at last to be clearly defined." But Phillips emphasized that it was a gamble and that "Col. House is violently opposed and has so advised the President." It seemed that where Britain led, Wilson followed, though nothing as of yet came of it. Crosby did not make an offer. This was because of impossible monetary exchange problems. Though it seems no sizable amounts of American money reached Kaledin by laundering through the French and British, covert action remained a possibility.[71]

House had influenced Wilson to some degree, though probably not to the extent he claimed. When referring to Lansing and the British and French ambassadors, House quoted Wilson as saying, "I suppose it is well to let them feel they are doing something now and then."[72] He took up the question of Lansing: "I find the President still antagonistic to Lansing. Lansing constantly does something to irritate him, and generally along the line of taking action without consultation." Almost in the same breath, he continued: "I have about come to the conclusion that it is George Creel who is prejudicing the President against Lansing." House speculated on Creel's grand propaganda policy based on a broad declaration of war aims that would unite the world against Germany and help the Russian situation. House's think tank, The Inquiry, could elaborate war aims.[73]

Many alternatives for dealing with Bolshevism confronted President Wilson in December 1917. Ambassador Francis supported the watching and waiting policy of Wilson and Lansing. Judson and Robins preferred offering an olive branch to the Bolsheviks in the hopes of keeping them in the war or belligerently neutral. Wilson rejected the olive branch alternative. The British and French supported aiding counterrevolution. Wilson put that alternative on hold. Poole's investigation of Kaledin, though promising, came too late. Then General Kaledin committed suicide in February 1918. Similarly, Secretary Lansing's speculations, though Wilson inclined toward them, remained speculation for the time being. What intrigued Wilson was House's suggestion. Mobilize, democratize, and rejoin Russia through an appeal to ideals. The president must wage a propaganda campaign to this end similar to Creel's strategy. That campaign must stress the fairness and reasonableness of Wilson's gospel for all belligerents: territorial integrity and self-determination. All that remained was for Wilson to speak directly to the Russian people, promising them their territorial integrity and self-determination while bypassing the Bolsheviks. In this effort he would get the support of House, Creel, and Sisson.

Five

January 1918
Point VI of XIV

Bolshevik clamor for a clear enunciation of Allied war aims forced a statement out of President Wilson. There was a chance that the Bolsheviks might remain in the war if they feared German peace terms and believed in a fair deal from the Allies. Recognition and massive aid were essential components of any deal. Wilson countenanced neither. Instead, he intended to offer all belligerents territorial integrity and self-determination. These principles, applied to Russia, constituted Wilson's famous "acid test" of Allied goodwill in point VI of his Fourteen Points Address of January 8, 1918. A last-minute reprieve of Raymond Robins for Lenin failed. The Soviets ratified the Treaty of Brest-Litovsk. The German army, finally freed in the East, mounted its great spring offensive of 1918 in the West. Secretary Lansing's anti-Bolshevik view now began to prevail in the Wilson administration. Wilson's Allies threatened military intervention in Russia to reconstitute the Eastern Front, thereby relieving German military pressure in the West. If President Wilson failed to intervene in Russia, perhaps Japan would. Victory over the Central Powers seemed to hang in the balance. All eyes focused on the president, beginning with the eyes of the Bolsheviks.

Commissar for Foreign Affairs Lev Trotsky taunted the peoples and governments of the Western Allies and especially the United States by touting the Bolshevik peace program: "every nationality independently of its freedom and the level of its development," he announced, "would receive an entire liberty of national development." It was incumbent upon President Wilson, whose role at this most critical historical moment was widely recognized by leading statesmen as the most important of factors, to answer the Bolshevik peace challenge.[1] The Allies had not joined the negotiations between the Central Powers and Russia at Brest-Litovsk for reasons, according to Trotsky, which they obstinately declined to announce. He suggested that Germany seemed ready to evacuate Belgium and France, so the Allies could not claim that the war continued for liberation of territory in the West. "It is necessary," Trotsky said, "to say clearly and precisely what is the peace program of France, Italy, Great Britain, the United States." If it was necessary to liberate Alsace-Lorraine, Galicia, and Poznan, then what about Ireland, Egypt, and India? The Russian Revolution granted self-determination to Finland, Ukraine, and Belorussia. It was necessary to construct the international basis for peace on self-determination for all peoples.

Trotsky ridiculed the Allies for not entering into a democratic peace because of their class character. Their attitude toward national self-determination was suspicious. He believed Germany and its allies had renounced their intention to incorporate territories seized during the war. (In February 1918, to his dismay, Germany would insist on its conquests. Trotsky then labeled this as imperialism.) And what was the program of the Allies? He warned that if the Allied governments continued to sabotage the cause of peace, then the Soviet government would sign a separate treaty with Germany.[2]

No sooner had Trotsky thrown down the gauntlet before the Allies than he discovered that the Germans proposed retention of their conquests in Eastern Europe. The Germans also refused to allow the Russians to check the prohibition of troop transfers or permit commercial navigation on the White Sea. These German proposals threw the Bolsheviks into a fury. Speeches at the executive committee of the Soviet indicated a readiness to resume the war.[3]

General Judson reiterated his alternatives to his colleagues: "We discussed two papers for the Ambassador's action: one designed to indicate how far Robins could go in promising Trotsky the Ambassador's recommendation of support, to enable Trotsky to face a break with less apprehension; and the other a proposed cable to the Department [of State] requesting approval of the course he is proposing to take." When Edgar Sisson had brought Judson the first armistice document, Judson had reported it as an Allied military disaster by exclaiming, "German troops of two fronts massed now on one front—the Western! . . . The Russians have been tricked, as I told Trotsky they would be."[4]

The prospects of a break at Brest-Litovsk seemed great. Ambassador Francis confessed to Lansing that he was willing to "swallow pride, sacrifice dignity, and with discretion do all that is necessary to prevent Russia's becoming an ally of Germany." The ambassador suggested establishing relations to influence peace terms, prevent Allied stored munitions from falling into German hands, and keep Russian resources unavailable to Germany.[5] For these initiatives Francis needed Robins, who had managed to gain the confidence of the Bolsheviks. Robins had already found it expedient to ignore State Department strictures on contacts with Trotsky, including a prohibition extended to the Red Cross mission. Expedience dictated Robins's actions as a go-between, though they caused embarrassment to Washington.

Robins had become the one and only indispensable intermediary. Without him, there was absolutely no American contact, official or unofficial, with the Bolshevik leadership. And the Bolsheviks, like it or not, controlled the destinies of Russia.

Yet Trotsky followed up his propaganda coup over Judson with another over Robins. He stated that the chief of the American Red Cross (now Robins, since Thompson had left for home) had told him that "in Russia there had never been any such strong government as ours" and that America would provide all the supplies Russia needed with the exception of munitions. Francis supposed Trotsky was referring to Robins, but Robins denied he had said this. Francis had asked Lansing, "Are Red Cross members wearing uniform included in your 1883, December 6, 2 p.m., which says, 'The President desires American representatives withhold all direct communications with Bolshevik government?'" Lansing cabled back, "Red Cross members in uniform certainly included in instructions Department's 1883, December 6. Red Cross is so advising Robins."[6] So at the same time that Judson and Robins were being prohibited from relations with the Bolshevik leadership, Francis found it both necessary and convenient to use Robins for embassy purposes of keeping in contact with the Bolsheviks.

1.

It is important to follow the meanderings of American diplomacy at this very critical moment when everything seemed to devolve upon a few unlikely persons in Petrograd who, it then appeared, might save the Eastern Front by talking the Bolsheviks into staying the Allied course with the promise of U.S. recognition and massive American aid. Short of that goal, Lenin might have been persuaded only to make a peace that was highly favorable to him because he could threaten large-scale American help and, therefore, be a hostile neutral on the German's eastern flank, always a threat to reenter the war. That secondary goal would go a long way in blunting the collapse of the Eastern Front. But it required Allied, mainly American, cooperation. It was a very desperate game that was played out in an almost Byzantine fashion.

Perhaps the Brest negotiations would now fail. Clearly the clause dealing with transfer of troops was futile. Judson was prevented from going to Trotsky for clarification. Yet Robins repeatedly saw the commissar for foreign affairs and reported that Trotsky boastfully assured him that strategic transfers would continue to be prohibited. But Robins saw through this troop transfer deception. Judson then remarked on the connection of Robins with Trotsky: "Robins promised to look further into these matters. He said his position with Trotsky might grow weaker if he continued able only to talk, without authority to promise or deliver anything." Robins later spoke with Judson. Trotsky had given assurances, he told Judson, concerning nontransfer of troops. Incredible as this seemed to Judson, the general remarked, "I am sure Robins is doing good work in presenting these matters so ably to Trotsky." And Robins wrote, "Last night the Armistice terms to be translated. The end is racing in. The blow falls. The text falls short. We now have a difficult plan of work." The following day he continued: "Genl. J. and my letter and the word of the other folks. The terms of the treaty of Armistice and all the plans so far made for each." Robins's role as an intermediary now increased.[7]

Francis needed support, and Robins was it. Lansing told him that recognition was not possible but said that Robins could visit Trotsky: "Department desires you to continue the course you have pursued in the past and which it has approved. Department relies on your good judgment to persevere in difficult situation."[8]

To sense the pressure exerted on Robins, one has only to read his diary: "All morning on Smolny [Trotsky] task. Get train started at 5:10 pm — first drink in Russia. All clear and Trotsky is the power." Francis had to recognize Robins's importance as America's negotiator. As Francis later recounted, "I sent to Col. Robins. I said to him, 'I have this order [Department of State's #1883].' He said, 'I have a similar order.' I said, 'I think it unwise for you to sever your relations abruptly and absolutely; that is, I mean to cease your visits up there. Furthermore I want to know what they are doing, and I will stand between you and the fire.'"[9]

More than a month after Judson's fiasco with Trotsky, even Francis himself, in his role as dean of the diplomatic corps, had to visit Lenin to secure the release of Romanian Ambassador Count Constantine Diamandi from the infamous tsarist jail of the Peter and Paul fortress, regardless of State Department orders. The Count was being held due to the Romanian detention and possible execution of Bolshevik agitators on the southwestern front. The principle, Francis directly explained to Lenin, was diplomatic immunity. When Lenin asked to discuss the matter further, Francis flatly refused and left Lenin's office in a huff. The ambassador's daring secured Diamandi's release without the recriminations accompanying Judson's conversations with Trotsky.[10]

President Wilson was aware of Robins's role, though he disliked him. In a New Year's greeting to Lansing he wrote, "I am writing to ask your opinion as to the most feasible and least objectionable way (if there is any) in which we could establish similar unofficial relations with the Bolsheviki." No doubt he referred to R. H. Bruce Lockhart, unofficial British agent to the Bolsheviks. Disliked or not, America had its unofficial agent in the person of Robins. [11]

About this matter, Robins dolefully concluded sometime later:

> How shall I write of the events of the past months? So much that is tremendous and almost incomprehensible. As you know when Thompson left I was given command and promoted to the rank of Lieut. Colonel. Since then I have been the centre of the American relationship with the Bolshevik Government and the only man in Petrograd who was at home in both the Embassies and the Smolny. Military missions and all official groups have been working through me as the intermediary. It is most extraordinary. I sometimes rub my eyes to see if I am awake or dreaming. For days I was the only American of power—I believe the only ally—who thought there was any salvage in the entire Bolshevik government. At last all have come to agree more or less with my point of view. It is however very late in the day. [12]

The president had William Boyce Thompson's memorandum concerning a deal with the Bolsheviks. Secretary of the Navy Daniels had remarked to Wilson that Thompson, a Wall Street tycoon, had invested a million dollars in propaganda to sustain Russia's war effort and reported Wilson's snide response that "spending money in R[ussia] for propaganda was like pouring water into a bottomless hole."[13] Conversation in the cabinet turned to southern Russia, for Crane said that there was no "cement" left in other portions of the country. Daniels quoted Wilson: "We are left with E [England] and F [France] giving all aid possible to those in 'Little Russia' where there is a fight against Germany and Anarchy. Summers, consul at Moscow, says the only hope is in the men fighting in So. Russia. Baker said War College proposed, not recognition of the Bolsheviki, but acceptance as the best way to keep Russia from coming under the dominion of Germany."[14]

What to do about the military stores at Vladivostok and exertion of control over the Trans-Siberian railway? Those 648,000 tons of stores included 136,000 tons of railway material, 60,000 tons of nitrate of soda, 15,000 of explosives, 58,000 barbed wire, 70,000 shells, 43,000 phosphate, 27,000 metals, 78,000 of tea, rice, cotton, rubber.[15] The British fear was that Bolshevik troops in Vladivostok would seize the stores, send them to Petrograd, and sell them to the Germans.

In order to land a force sufficient to safeguard the military stores, the British could supply two companies from Hong Kong, but most of it would have to be Japanese troops. An American contingent would be necessary to prevent the Bolsheviks from claiming that it was an attempt by the Japanese to occupy Russian territory. When Lord Cecil brought this matter to the attention of the Japanese ambassador, the latter reacted unfavorably. Cecil thought the amount and value of the stores made it necessary to run any risk. At the first War Cabinet meeting of 1918, it was believed that these stores would "very probably fall into the hands of the enemy and be used against us." In December a cable had been sent to Washington, but the United States refused to take action. General Sir William Robertson, Chief of the Imperial General Staff, voiced his support for sending a force, entirely Japanese if need be. The War Cabinet decided on sending the cruiser *Suffolk*, arranging for the troops in Hong Kong to go, informing Japan that a joint action was being proposed, and telling House to inform Wilson of the dangers and the necessity for cooperation.[16]

Lansing spoke to the Japanese ambassador in Washington about a "possible necessity of protecting Siberia from German domination." The American consul in Vladivostok, John K. Caldwell, had sent information that the "Red Guard has been formed and armed for looting and rioting." The local Japanese consul, he reported, was asking for naval support. Importantly, Caldwell noted that German prisoners of war "may even attempt to seize munitions of war here for shipment to Germany." Lansing gave the Caldwell cable to Daniels and asked that the *Brooklyn* under Admiral Knight go to Vladivostok, that it should arrive unannounced and should avoid landing marines unless to save American lives.[17]

The British Foreign Office urged on the Americans the necessity of holding Vladivostok. "If we can get them to Vladivostok we may then be able to continue a move along the Siberian Railway." Cecil complained that an Allied landing was essential, not just Japanese or Japanese-and-British, because the Russians would then conclude that Japan was finally realizing its goals and the British government its desired control of the Siberian railway.[18] These plans and counterplans for Vladivostok marked the first extensive discussions of a direct intervention in Russia. They came, along with everything else, on the eve of Wilson's Fourteen Points speech designed to answer Trotsky's challenge for Allied war aims by appealing over the Bolshevik's heads and directly to the Russian people.

In pursuit of a clear enunciation of Allied war aims, Colonel House arrived in Washington and went into conference with the president "concerning the proposed message to Congress on our war aims which I have urged ever since my return, and upon which I advised by cable from Paris that nothing be said by the President until after he had seen me."[19] House and Wilson were aware of Trotsky's challenge. Then followed the Fourteen

Points speech. It revealed House's influence for moderation as opposed to Lansing's hard line. House and Wilson had worked on it the evening of January 6, and the following day House called it "remarkable." What the colonel meant was that they were busy "remaking the map of the world." They had first elaborated the points in the placard style recommended by Sisson and Creel, putting general terms at the beginning and following with territorial adjustments, with the exception of the "peace association," which would be last, as the president wanted to mention certain things with it and "it would round out the message properly."[20]

President Wilson's Fourteen Points were enunciated in an address to a joint session of the Congress on January 8, 1918. They came to be regarded as the distilled expression of Allied war aims. They were certainly an answer to Trotsky's demand that the Allies tell the world that their war aims were something different than the greed expressed in the secret treaties he had published from the tsarist archive he had just ransacked. Wilson introduced the Fourteen Points with a renunciation of any material gain for America. The gain would be a world made safe for the peaceful and free development of nations. The placarded points, that is, open covenants openly arrived at — freedom of the seas, free trade, and so forth — all rested on four overarching Wilsonian principles: peace without victory, the triumph of democracy, the rights of self-determination with territorial integrity, and an international peacekeeping institution.

Within this general context, the president developed his ideas for Russia. Surveying the speech's position on Russia, House had urged the president to be at his best here, and then submitted to the president phrasing of his own that Bakhmetev had approved. It suggested that there was no Allied resentment because the job now was to segregate Russia as far as possible from Germany. And a promise of more substantial help could do this, in House's opinion. "There was no argument about this because our minds ran parallel, and what he wrote about Russia is I think, in some respects, the most eloquent part of his message."[21]

House's account of the Russian part of the speech does not mention the memorandum prepared by The Inquiry, the colonel's think tank. That memorandum squeezed Russia into a Part VI and gave an analysis of the significance of the Russian moderates and an argument about Orthodox Russia as antagonistic to Protestant Germany. It advocated a diplomatic offensive that would state war aims as a means to intensifying propaganda.[22]

The actual address opened with an analysis of problems raised by the parleys at Brest-Litovsk, especially that of answering Trotsky's challenge for the Allies to make explicit their war aims. This consumed half the address, not counting Point VI dealing specifically with Russia. Wilson told

Congress that Russian representatives at Brest (he avoided the term Bolshevik) "presented not only a perfectly definite statement of the principles upon which they would be willing to conclude peace, but also an equally definite program of the concrete application of those principles."[23] He castigated the Central Powers for proposing no concessions either to Russian sovereignty or its minorities. In this he meant that Germany and its allies planned to hold everything they had occupied. "The Russian representatives were sincere and earnest. They cannot entertain such proposals of conquest and domination." In using Russia as a foil to Germany, Wilson could not find enough nice things to say about these "Russian representatives," otherwise he would choke on the "B"—Bolshevik—word. "The Russian representatives have insisted, very justly, very wisely, and in the true spirit of modern democracy, that the conferences they have been holding with the Teutonic and Turkish statesmen should be held within open, not closed doors, and all the world has been audience, as was desired."[24] There was a need for definitions, and the Russian voice "more thrilling and more compelling" called out, though Russia was prostrate and helpless. It would not be subservient, or yield in its principles. In fact, Wilson said, "Their conception of what is right, of what is humane and honorable for them to accept, has been stated with a frankness, a largeness of view, a generosity of spirit, and a universal human sympathy which must challenge the admiration of every friend of mankind; and they have refused to compound their ideals or desert others that they themselves may be safe." The president indulged in wishful thinking about the Bolsheviks. He hoped to help the people of Russia attain liberty and peace. When they called on others to be candid about war aims, it was his desire to respond with "utter simplicity and frankness."

In Point VI the president argued for evacuation of Russian territory and settlement of questions affecting Russia that would give "unhampered and unembarrassed opportunity for the independent determination of her own political development and national policy and assure her of a sincere welcome into the society of free nations under institutions of her own choosing; and, more than a welcome, assistance of every kind that she may need and may herself desire."[25] This treatment, he insisted, would be the "acid test" of goodwill, unselfishness, and understanding. Russian policy, his test, was restoration and settlement of borders, internal and external self-determination, accessibility to the world, and assistance to meet Russia's needs.

The speech concerned what happened to a country, here Russia, when Germany had it by the throat, and what the course of rectifications would be if justice were to prevail at a future peace table when the Allies had the upper hand. The president listed wrongs by the Central Powers led by

German militarism and autocracy. Russia could, he was implying, expect to have its throat slit if it did not stay the course of the war. What happened to Russia would happen to other countries seeking to negotiate with Germany and its allies from a position of weakness.

The speech's reception was interesting. Lenin told Sisson, "it is a great step ahead toward the peace of the world." Sisson commented that Lenin was "as joyous as a boy over the President's humanly understanding words to Russia, and his recognition of the honesty of Bolshevik purpose." Yet Lenin found fault: "This is all very well as far as it goes, but why not formal recognition, and when?"[26] Wilson caught Lenin's attention, but it was too much to hope that by such statements Russia might reenter the war and rectify Allied policy failures during the time of the Provisional Government.

This reaction was not so much hostile as querulous, as Lenin was grasping at any straw to avert an imposed and humiliating peace. He was satisfied, or he would not have sent Wilson's speech to Trotsky at Brest. He allowed Sisson to print it in handbills, posters, and pamphlets. "The appearance in the *Izvestiia* alone," wrote Sisson, "guarantees that every Russian soldier will get the message, for the *Izvestia* is read aloud to soldiers who do not read." Sisson triumphantly cabled Creel: "President's speech placarded on walls of Petrograd this morning. One hundred thousand copies will have this display within three days. Three hundred thousand handbills will be distributed here within five days. Proportionate display Moscow by end of week. . . . *Izvestiia*, official Government newspaper, with nearly a million circulation through Russia, printed speech in full Saturday morning with comment, welcoming it as sincere and helpful." Creel told this to Wilson, adding: "He reports utmost harmony and is not concerning himself with anything but the presentation of America's aims and objects." Later Sisson noted that "none of my distrust of Lenin was lessened. . . . On Robins the effect was different. Some fire in him was lighted." Both purportedly saw Lenin for the first time. If so, the whole episode received scant attention from Robins: "Smolny and Lenin and the word goes to Brest. Again we see the great idea." Robins, like Sisson, believed Wilson and the power of his winged words to transform Russia into a fighting machine despite the Bolsheviks. Of course, that is what Wilson and House intended. Lansing cabled Francis concerning the Fourteen Points: "Have it conveyed unofficially to Trotsky." Francis replied: "Robins reports had an interview with Lenin who has wired President's message textually to Trotsky at Brest. Lenin said that he approved of message and thought it potential agency in promoting peace." Francis was jubilant: "Think effect great, far reaching." Judson wrote that Wilson got a "most responsive and appreciative comment in the Soviet press, with the exception of *Pravda*."[27]

From this moment a rift opened between Robins and Sisson. Robins believed that a deal could still be struck with Lenin, and Sisson felt that propaganda could separate the Russian people from the Bolsheviks.[28]

In the United States the speech was inspiring. Senator Robert L. Owen of Oklahoma called it a "magnificent statement" of war aims. Thompson told Polk that the "President's message accomplished nine-tenths of what he had in mind, and was very anxious there should be a change in the Ambassador." Charles Crane said he was "entirely content" with the message. William Wilder of New York thought it a "master stroke" and that it would "strike through and past the Bolsheviki phase of the Russian Revolution." Wilder came closer to what both Wilson and House had in mind. General John J. Pershing, head of the American Expeditionary Force in France, reported that "In Russia Maximalist press published full text of President's speech calling his conditions a great victory in the struggle for democratic peace." Charles W. Eliot, retired president of Harvard, wrote, "the most striking thing in your address to Congress on January 8 was what you said in the two paragraphs about Russia. So far as I can judge from what I have heard and read during the last two months, your wisdom on this subject is a very rare wisdom." For Eliot, acid testing may have been akin to the golden rule. Wilson answered Eliot: "You may be sure that I wrote the passages about Russia in my recent address to Congress from the heart. I wish most earnestly that it were possible to find some way to help, but as soon as we have thought out a working plan there is a new dissolution of the few crystals that had formed there." William Allen White, well-known journalist, was quoted as saying, "the best thing in your peace terms is your consideration of Russia and the Russian views and rights in the matter."[29]

Samuel Gompers of the A. F. of L. suggested that Wilson send a greeting to the Constituent Assembly. He was unaware that it would meet only for a day, January 18, 1918, before being forcibly dispersed. Wilson responded, "I like your suggestion about a message to the Russian Constituent Assembly, but apparently the reckless Bolsheviki have already broken it up because they did not control it. It is distressing to see things so repeatedly go to pieces."[30]

Grant Smith, American chargé in Copenhagen, proposed that one of the Allies, perhaps the United States, should recognize the Bolsheviks in order to understand and influence them. This would be to the advantage of the others, who would get the necessary information while remaining aloof. Wilson wrote Lansing, "Here is the ever-recurring question. How shall we deal with the Bolsheviki? The particular suggestion seems to me to have something in it worth considering, and I am writing to ask what your own view is."[31] Lansing did not reply, indicating that he remained unconvinced, unsympathetic, and anti-Bolshevik.

Wilson explained to Sir William Wiseman that his statement of war aims "was largely due, he believed, to the outrageous conduct of the Bolsheviks in publishing the secret treaties, and the consequent fear of the people that they were being exploited for some imperial or capitalist purpose." Comments that had been made before and during the war by the powers were closely guarded secrets. This feeling of frustration carried over in Wilson's comment to Senator Robert L. Owen of Oklahoma. Wilson wrote Lansing to consider Owen's ideas, as he was "very earnest about the enclosed suggestions and I have promised him that I would discuss them with you."[32] What Owen had in mind was along Smith's lines, some sort of quasi or de facto recognition. This would allow for influence to be exerted over the Bolsheviks from the inside in order to counter German intrigue. The United States could send supplies and swell the number of consular officers for a greater grass-roots contact with various Russian centers. Inside influence was what Robins and Judson were pushing for and what Wilson would, with pressure from Lansing and the State Department, consistently reject.

Senator Owen recommended reviving the Stevens Railway Commission, especially improving the Siberian railroad, courier services, and communications in general.[33] Basil Miles wrote a memorandum on Owen's suggestions for Lansing. He thought de facto recognition was impossible because of the extreme views of the Soviet government as well as its repudiation of all foreign obligations. Miles did think Owen was correct in suggesting that America needed a way to deal unofficially with all parties in Russia. He considered sending more supplies for Red Cross distribution and the expansion of consular and courier service. He was not sanguine about the situation in the south or the prospect of an early reconstruction.[34] In other words, Miles, the State Department's resident Russian expert, was not optimistic about either of Wilson's Russian initiatives taken since November 7, 1917—possible laundered money to General Kaledin and Ambassador Bakhmetev or the "acid testing" of goodwill to Russia enunciated in Point VI—but he left the door open for Robins short of any form of recognition.

The New York financier Thomas W. Lamont begged the president to give Thompson an audience. Thompson only got as far as Frank Polk, who wrote, "Discussed Russia and urged that something be done to bring this country nearer to Russia." Thompson wrote Wilson, "I am in Washington for a few days and am still so vitally interested in the whole Russian situation that it would please me very much if you felt that you could give me a little time to talk with you direct in regard to it." Wilson had a bad cold, but hoped to see him subsequently when "things become a little more clear from the governmental point of view in the Russian situation."[35] For a man who had spent a million dollars of his own backing Russian liberal causes that Wilson himself dallied about belatedly supporting through Creel and Sisson, Thompson got short shrift. It is true that Wilson had been pulled an inch in Thompson's direction by the balm of House's advice, but the president was still not prepared for any versions of recognition.

Not much came from point VI of the speech in terms of America's Russian policy, probably because of Wilson's growing discontent regarding Lenin and those who believed they could deal with him. The president wrote Baker, "We are having hard luck with our military attaches at Petrograd, are we not. I should think that being sent to Petrograd would drive most men to drink, but anyone who is so driven is the very man who cannot be trusted to do the real job there, am I not right?" In the same vein he replied to Lamont, "Some day I hope I shall be able to have a deliberate talk with him [Thompson], but just at present the changes taking place in Russia are so kaleidoscopic that I feel that information and advice are futile until there is something definite to plan with as well as for." He meant by this, of course, an alternative to Bolshevism. To be viable, that alternative had also to block Japanese ambitions while preserving a shred of principled legitimacy for a future peace conference. There is no evidence that Lenin ever took seriously the Fourteen Points as an expression of American good faith, or that acid testing changed anything in his or Trotsky's view of Wilson's motives.[36]

Wilson made two more statements at this time. House suggested the first. It was made February 11, 1918, to Congress. In it, the president denounced the unfortunate bilateral nature of the negotiations and the fate awaiting Baltic nationalities. In the second, he dispatched a message to the Congress of Soviets, then considering ratification of the Brest treaty. The president indicated that America was unable to render "direct and effective aid" at that very moment. Nevertheless, he assured the Soviet Congress that America would eventually aid Russia in securing its "complete sovereignty and independence." The Fourth All-Russian Soviet Congress, meeting in Moscow on March 14, received Wilson's message with great applause and responded with a message of its own. It expressed its appreciation to the American people for Wilson's message, but it then used the occasion to state its conviction that soon the laboring masses would overthrow the capitalist yoke. Despite the applause, Wilson received a resounding slap in the face from the delegates for his supposedly lukewarm support of Russian sovereignty and territorial integrity. In fact, Francis later wrote that when Gregorii Zinoviev, Lenin's trusted lieutenant, returned to Petrograd and made a speech, he said that "We slapped the President of the United States in the face."[37] Not only had Wilson's propaganda efforts of the Fourteen Points, his address to the U.S. Congress, and his message to the Soviet Congress so far failed with Russia, but he had been sharply rebuked. However, Wilson could be content that he had laid the basis for a future peace conference.

2.

About this time the German army opened its feared spring offensive in the West, on March 21, almost a week after the Soviet government ratified the Treaty of Brest-Litovsk. Two options seemingly remained for Wilson's Russian policy. The first was to deal with Lenin in the hopes of a very belated Judson-Robinsesque holding action to restrict Germany's activity in Russia; the second was some form of intervention ranging from various covert activities to a full-scale landing of Allied forces to rally non-Bolshevik Russia while protecting Allied interests. Far Eastern intervention required Japanese support. The first option played out in a dazzling way.

Back when Germany had renewed its military advance against Russia on February 18 due to the rejection of Trotsky's "no peace, no war" initiative that ended the first Brest armistice, the American embassy was in immediate danger. Various Allied ambassadors, five in all, decided on February 21 to depart from Petrograd. Francis wanted to keep the flag flying and remain in Russia by retreating to Vologda at the junction of the Trans-Siberian and Moscow-Archangel railways. It was Robins who arranged with Lenin for the exit of Francis with his staff and files on two railway cars. Francis and his group departed for Vologda on February 27 and arrived on the twenty-eighth. Robins accompanied him. However, Robins returned when he heard the news from Smolny that negotiations supposedly had been broken off. That message had been signed by Lenin and addressed to Francis, dated March 2. When word reached Vologda that the peace actually had been signed, Robins was eager to be in Petrograd.[38]

Raymond Robins, in an effort to prevent the Bolsheviks from making peace with Germany, arrived in Petrograd on March 5 and went straight to Trotsky. "Do you want," Robins asked, "to prevent the Brest peace from being ratified?" Trotsky replied, "Lenin realizes that the threat of the German advance is so great that if he can get economic cooperation and military support from the Allies he will refuse the Brest Peace, retire, if necessary, from both Petrograd and Moscow to Ekaterinberg, reestablish the front in the Urals, and fight with allied support against the Germans." Robins asked for that in writing and arranged to see Lenin. Alexander Gumberg acted as his translator and stenographer. The resulting document was based on extreme contingencies: *if* the peace were broken, *if* the offensive were renewed, would help be forthcoming, and, *if* Japan occupied Vladivostok and took the Trans-Siberian railway, to what extent could the United States assure British aid through Murmansk and Archangel? Through Colonel James A. Ruggles, American military attaché, Robins tried to send the document to Francis, but Ruggles unaccountably delayed its sending for about two weeks. At the same time, R. H. Bruce Lockhart had seen Trotsky that same morning, March 5. Trotsky also told him of his fear of Japanese intervention. Lockhart counseled against the British encouraging the Japanese to intervene and pleaded for authority to "inform Lenin that the question of Japanese intervention has been shelved." If various kinds of support were offered, it was just possible that the Bolsheviks would abort Brest and stay in the war. Francis did send two cables on March 9 opposing a Japanese intervention.[39]

Meanwhile, Robins pleaded with Lenin for more time to get a reply from Washington, a reply that would offer to trade aid and recognition for Russia's continuing the war. Lenin's postponement of the Soviet Congress for two days led Robins to assume that it was for his benefit. On March 8, 1918, Robins went to Vologda to get Francis's support. Francis then delayed sending Lenin's statement—the March 5 document of extreme contingencies—to Washington and merely emphasized the Bolshevik fear of a Japanese advance into Siberia. Due to a coding problem, according to Robins and Gumberg, the statement originally given to Ruggles for transmission came back to Petrograd on the sixth and then was given by hand to Francis on the eighth in Vologda. Ruggles sat on his version of it, and Francis never sent the whole of it to the State Department. Thus only Wilson's formal message to the Soviet arrived in response, but there was never any acknowledgement of the extreme contingencies document.[40]

Robins left two accounts of this failed initiative. One was from his pocket diary and the other was his testimony before a congressional committee in March of 1919. In his entry he exclaimed, "What an hour this is." He went on to explain: "See Lenin and put the issue of the non-intervention of J[apan] and American attitude. He is not convinced. Meeting of Congress of the Soviets. Power everywhere. 8'45 the meeting opens (called for 6). Sverdlov in the chair—Steinberg of Justice against peace then Kamkov against peace then Zinovieff for and then Lenin for in a complete mastery of the crowd." Robins continued by giving the flavor of that historic meeting: "We find the chandeliers. Galleries and stage. Presidium and the Czars of old. Lenin and the crowds peasants soldiers workingmen and sailors. The two boy butcher lads and their idea of freedom." And along the side of the same page, Robins scribbled: "Lenin easy, but a clear, good voice perfect pose."[41] Naturally, Trotsky was absent as his policy of "no peace, no war" at Brest had failed with the renewed German military march on Petrograd back in February. The next day, Robins noted the "heat of the last days" and informed Francis by direct wire. "The voting goes on," he wrote, "desultory work." A few lines later, in his wretched scrawl, he mentioned, "Treaty being translated. Great stuff for propaganda." And a few more lines down, he finished, "The day of the ratification of the peace. What an hour it is in the world." Upon reflection the following day, Sunday, March 17, he noted, "Reaction is rife." And at the bottom of the page, he wrote about a curious contrast: "What an hour this is. Strange and beautiful purposes and powers of life. Exemption from the costs of an earlier purpose and power."[42]

These impressions make an interesting contrast to Robins's recollection a year later. He reported that Lenin had motioned him over and asked him if he had heard anything from the American government. Robins had replied that he had heard nothing. According to his testimony, Lenin said, "I am now going to the platform and the peace will be ratified." Robins then told the committee about Lenin's speech on the "shameful peace" and "protection of the revolution." Robins concluded that ratification was approved by an overwhelming vote. These words suggested that "had Robins been able to tell Lenin, at that moment, that his government had responded favorably to Trotsky's questions, the treaty might never have been ratified." Strange that Robins made no reference to Lenin's gesture in his diary.[43] After all, according to Robins's later testimony, the Eastern Front might have been saved.

The issue was thus settled. Lansing sent Francis the following message: "Your 7, March 12, 5 p.m. Department considers President's message to Russian people and address to Congress adequate answer." The secretary was referring to a cable by Francis confirming that Consul General Summers had Wilson's most recent message to the Fourth Congress and would send it, though it was delivered by Robins, as well as a condensation of the Trotsky-Lenin questions taken down by Gumberg on March 5: what kind of support, what way rendered, especially from the United States, and what practical steps the Allies, and particularly America, would take to prevent a Japanese invasion and assure uninterrupted transport along the Trans-Siberian railway. In the document Lenin was also interested in knowing what support the British would render through Murmansk and Archangel. Naturally, the document concluded, the policies of the Soviet government would remain socialist. Francis noted that he had received this document at midnight on the eighth and sent it at 2 P.M. on the ninth, as paraphrased by himself. It was received in Washington on March 15 at 5:33 P.M., which was by then too late as Brest was just in the process of being ratified. Lenin was getting ready to mount the platform and give his speech recommending ratification. As to Ruggles's bungling or inaction, Francis telegraphed Robins on March 11: "Ruggles returned after satisfactory interview with Trotsky and chief of staff but no definite program adopted. Ruggles talked to him on same lines as you in accordance with my instructions consequently interview had good effect." Ruggles, for whatever reasons, delayed transmission of the original message, which did not arrive until the twenty-second, or perhaps the twentieth. It seems that Robins only found out about this delay in the sending of the apparent Bolshevik offer to resume the war, sometime on March 19 at the earliest.[44]

In all this frenetic activity, what drew Lenin's eye, and Robins's as well, was what America was prepared to do about the rumored Japanese occupation. The question of making peace at Brest-Litovsk surely had already been resolved, no matter how much Trotsky pouted about the Brest peace because his "no peace, no war" formula had failed, while absenting himself from the Fourth Congress. It may even have been that Trotsky played his own double game with Lenin and used Robins for political advantage on the all-important Brest gambit. If Robins had succeeded with Washington, then Trotsky's "no peace, no war" formula might also have succeeded. The Brest Treaty might not have been signed.

3.

The second option, the matter of intervention, in this particular case Japanese intervention to protect Allied stores at Vladivostok or to secure the Trans-Siberian railway, became an intense concern in the aftermath of the Fourteen Points. When Polk asked the Chinese ambassador if he thought that the Japanese wanted to land in Siberia, the ambassador told Polk that they would be glad to have the opportunity. Polk spoke to Boris Bakhmetev, still recognized as Russia's ambassador to the United States. He believed the Japanese were eager to land at Vladivostok and would use any excuse. Bakhmetev feared that they would never leave. The ambassador was disturbed about the Japanese. The cagey diplomat told State Department counselor Breckinridge Long that the Japanese were already making preparations for occupying Vladivostok and Khabarovsk. He insisted that decisions made and actions taken be Allied and not Japanese alone. That would checkmate Japan's activities.[45]

Some American officials were eager to bring participation to the Far East. For instance, even DeWitt Clinton Poole's recommendation that the administration help forces in southern Russia included a Siberian connection of support from Vladivostok to Omsk or Samara. Informal agents to be dispatched to Omsk, Irkutsk, and other Siberian centers would be in contact with the movement for the formation of a Siberian government. A friend of House, Richard Washburn Child, suggested that since Japan could not possibly be stopped in the Far East, it was better that an ally, rather than the Germans, dominate Siberia.[46]

There was persistent British pressure for participation in a landing at Vladivostok to protect Allied stores and to secure the eastern sections of the Trans-Siberian railway. The British recognized the necessity of trying to limit the Japanese, but were prepared, if necessary, to allow the Japanese to act alone, for the Allies and Britain would be willing to risk the consequences. Foreign Secretary Arthur James Balfour wrote Lord Alfred Milner, British minister for war, that if Allied action were required, the Japanese would be the proper ones to carry it out. Lansing and Wilson realized that Japan had strong territorial ambitions in the area and that made the State Department pessimistic on this subject. Without Washington's consent, Britain or France could not invite Japan. Yet Balfour remarked that an overwhelming necessity would modify this attitude.[47] Locker-Lampson's suggestion of early January could now bear fruit.

A War Cabinet meeting held at the end of January considered possible Japanese intervention in Siberia. Japan might occupy eastern Siberia, the War Cabinet admitted, but it might then refuse to undertake Britain's main object of communications with southern Russia through control of the entire Siberian railway from Vladivostok to the Cossack country. Ambassador Page told Balfour that the American government hoped that the Japanese would not take possession of Vladivostok, much less the whole Trans-Siberian railway. Nevertheless, the War Cabinet felt "recent events in Petrograd and the bad behavior of the Bolsheviks might go far to cause the American Government to change its view."[48] The British realized that the introduction of the Japanese would, along with all the other dangers, probably involve a war with the Bolsheviks, and that risk would have to be faced. It might be acceptable because the Bolsheviks were a growing world menace. The British could count on French backing. The Japanese government would only act on its own initiative regarding the occupation of Vladivostok, not beyond, unless it clearly understood what was expected. The War Cabinet decided to go for a plan of opening communications between the southeast and Vladivostok by the Trans-Siberian railway. The Japanese role in this enterprise was to take control of the railway from Vladivostok on the Pacific Ocean to Cheliabinsk in the Ural Mountains. Washington and Paris would be urged to support such a plan. The British rationale remained to prevent Germany from controlling Russia by using local forces, which had sprung up in the south and southeast, especially the

Cossacks north of the Caucasus and the Armenians south of them. The areas to be controlled were the richest in grain-growing and contained almost all the coal and iron. It was hoped that the Armenians could block the Turanian movement. The difficulty lay in how to reach these local movements. Since the Baltic and Black Seas and Persia were no longer effective routes, there remained only the Siberian railway. "Our General Staff are strongly of opinion that this line ought to be used, and that it could be used if the Japanese will give us their assistance."[49]

Balfour assumed that participation was possible and argued that it would be more acceptable to the Russians, that is, the non-Bolshevik forces in the south, if the Allies did it rather than the Germans. German occupation would neutralize the Allied blockade and be a peril. The cable sent to British embassies in Paris, Rome, and Washington concluded, "We think that the scheme outlined above is the only way of averting these consequences and provides the only machinery by which such militant forces as South-East Russia still possesses may be effectively aided in their struggle against German influences on the West and Turkish attacks on the South." Wiseman, as usual, paraphrased it and gave it to House for forwarding to Wilson.[50] Thus it was that the president got the first direct British pressure for American participation in intervention.

Wilson was meanwhile reacting to the nagging problem of Vladivostok. Sensitivity to Japanese involvement was great. Daniels and Polk discussed the presence of two Japanese ships at Vladivostok and the question of Russian resentment. Admiral Austin M. Knight, Commander in Chief of the U.S. Asiatic Fleet, and Ambassador Roland S. Morris in Tokyo cabled on the advisability of sending Knight's flagship, the USS *Brooklyn,* and suggesting the removal of one Japanese ship. This action was recommended by Secretary of the Navy Daniels and sent for Wilson's permission. Wilson wrote Polk, "This cable to Morris has my approval." Polk's note to Wilson showed the gravity of the matter presented by the two Japanese ships at Vladivostok, as did Morris's cable. Disorder elsewhere might be repeated in Vladivostok. The Japanese had no objection to the presence of the *Brooklyn* at Vladivostok, but as Morris indicated, "If . . . conditions should hereafter require occupation of Vladivostok and the lines of the Chinese Eastern and Amur railways, Japan asks that this task be left to her alone and has definitely requested the British Government to agree to this as evidence of confidence of the Allies in her good faith, and is greatly pleased at reported refusal of our Government to a suggested plan [of] joint occupation if conditions should require more drastic action." Morris recommended keeping the *Brooklyn* in readiness to counter threatening conditions if they should occur in Vladivostok. Daniels gave the flavor of the tense discussions with

Wilson and Polk: "Is Japan trying to get a foothold in Russia? Shall we send a ship to V [Vladivostok] or trust Japan alone? Delicate question. No solution reached."[51]

Lansing responded to a French plan for sending a force to Harbin and Irkutsk. "It is believed that it would be likely to offend those Russians who are now in sympathy with the aims and desires which the United States and its cobelligerents have at heart in making war and might result in uniting all factions in Siberia against them." Polk reminded Morris of this and sent a copy of that cable to Wilson. The idea was that Japan and England would each maintain a ship at Vladivostok, the Japanese withdrawing all but one to "keep Russia from feeling allies were disposed to make invasion." Morris's cable indicating large-scale actions, which the Japanese seemed to be contemplating, received strong rebuke from Wilson. If such an action indicated coming events, it made an uncomfortable impression on him: "It seems to me clear," Wilson wrote, "that we should show very clearly in our reply that we should look upon military action in that quarter with distinct disapproval."[52]

Polk's cable to Morris temporarily ending the matter reminded him of America's rejection of the French plan and the idea that any occupation of Russian territory would be construed as hostile and likely to unite all factions against it. Morris was directed to tell the Japanese foreign minister that the "presence of more than one Japanese war vessel at Vladivostok at present is likely to be misconstrued and create a feeling of mistrust as to the purposes of the Allied Governments."[53] When Polk sent Wilson the views of the Japanese minister which suggested that Japan should do everything in terms of an intervention, the president wrote back, "I dare say that for the present we may let this matter stand as it does; but I hope that we shall soon have new material for judgment in the shape of further information from our Ambassador at Tokyo. I do not think that it will be safe or wise to leave the Japanese government in any doubt as to the impression such an attitude on their part makes on us."[54] Gunboat diplomacy at Vladivostok was restrained by Wilson for the time being.

At the beginning of February Wiseman had reported to Sir Eric Drummond, Lloyd George's personal secretary, that Wilson feared an intervention in Siberia because it might be used as propaganda by the Germans to consolidate Russia against the Allies. House had told Wiseman that the president doubted that any military advantage that might be gained was worth the political risk. Wiseman suggested that Wilson cable General Tasker Bliss, America's representative on the Supreme War Council in Paris, for his opinion. Wiseman warned Drummond that unless Bliss was strongly for intervention by the Japanese the whole plan would fail. He quoted House: "I have asked the President to reconsider the matter most carefully." Lansing cabled Bliss for his opinion on the military advantages of the scheme: "British Government are strongly urging that Japan should be asked by the Allies to occupy Transiberian Railway in their behalf. From the political point of view I think this would be dangerous and would be used by the Germans to consolidate Russian opinion against the allies."[55]

Pressure continued. Balfour cabled Wiseman to thank Colonel House for underlining the necessity for caution and emphasizing the progress of the Semënov expedition. Gregorii Semënov, a twenty-seven-year-old Trans-Baikal Cossack, was leading a force of 750 men in the northern part of the Chinese-Eastern railway zone. The Japanese would not be invited to occupy the Trans-Siberian railway until it was known how this Cossack fared. House wrote Wilson that he had never changed his opinion that it would be a great political mistake to send Japanese troops into Siberia. He saw no military advantage that would offset the harm. That harm, discounting Bolshevik ill will, was the race issue. Wiseman interviewed Wilson, who explained his concerns. Wilson noted that Ambassador Kikujiro Ishii thought the Japanese would not agree to the method or scale of the intervention. The risks would not outweigh any military advantages since anti-Allied and even pro-German sentiment might be created. The president promised Wiseman he would keep an open mind on the subject as he was "anxious to cooperate in any scheme for improving the conditions in Russia."[56]

Wiseman repeated to Balfour that the president could be persuaded to agree if Bliss conceded that intervention was practicable, and if the Japanese were approached confidentially. The president was anxious not to appear to be obstructing any plans. Wiseman asked Polk how he felt about the scheme. Polk replied that it was a mistake to ask the Japanese to land at Vladivostok. Balfour confided to Wiseman that the Japanese already had agents in Siberia reporting on the situation. The Japanese would take all necessary measures to secure Allied stores, including independent action. For Balfour that meant that his "mandatory" proposal, that is, Japan acting as the sole intervenor in behalf of the other Allies, deserved careful examination. France approved. Since this policy could create a reaction in Russia and objections from America, the French asked that it be accompanied with a clear declaration and guarantees to meet these difficulties.[57]

Lansing turned to colleagues in the State Department for opinions on Japanese military operations in Siberia. As a result, Breckinridge Long and E. T. Williams prepared a memorandum for the president. Wilson already emphasized that there was "nothing wise or practicable in this scheme" and that the United States "ought very respectfully to decline to take part in its execution."[58] In their memorandum, Long and Williams argued that things in Russia might change for the better without foreign intervention, and that, if intervention were undertaken, it ought to be by international cooperation and not any one power acting as the mandatory of the others. It was also noted that Japan had asked for a free hand in occupying the Chinese Eastern and Amur railways, that both Britain and France had acceded to this request, and that Britain asked the United States to permit Japan to occupy the whole of the Trans-Siberian railway. Oppositely, Ambassador Vasilii Maklakov, Bakhmetev's counterpart in Paris, believed as did Wilson that threatening Russian territories by Allied armed forces, especially by Japan, would have a disastrous effect on Russia and the Allied cause.[59]

Balfour had presented a long memorandum to the War Cabinet surveying Russia's situation. He started out with the blunt assumption that the Eastern Front had already collapsed prior to the Brest treaty due to the peace arranged with Germany by the breakaway Ukrainian Rada government and the public announcement by the Bolsheviks that they proposed to fight no longer. No further military cooperation could be expected. Even in areas where the British had made efforts to maintain their interests—Ukraine, Romania, the Cossack districts, the Caucasus, Siberia, and Archangel—the results were not much to boast about. Balfour could only point to Siberia and, especially, Vladivostok, where local resistance to the forces of disorder had some success. This was important; Siberia could become a great source of food for the Central Powers, and Vladivostok held immense stores of Allied munitions that the Bolsheviks could sell to Germany. Semënov had so far been successful in eastern Siberia with the British supplying him arms and money, but the best to be hoped for was the status quo. All these efforts only amounted to a rear guard action, which delayed the enemy's advance but did not check it. To arrest and reverse this action, a new effort would have to be made. Otherwise, only one thing remained: a Japanese troop incursion on a grand scale, acting as an Allied mandate, that would penetrate as far as the Urals in order to deny the Siberian railway to the enemy while simultaneously opening it up as a route to supply Cossacks of the southeast and Caucasus. Such a policy had already been accepted by the British and French, considered but not yet approved by the Americans and Italians, but not "officially" communicated to the Japanese. "The immediate question of policy," said Balfour, "is whether we should press President Wilson, against his natural inclination, to give his assent to the scheme. Without that assent the policy is impracticable; though unfortunately the converse proposition is by no means certain."[60] The key was how far Wilson's natural inclination for acid testing, his fairness policy for Russia, could be pushed this way or that.

Balfour thought it certain that the "President will yield only under the strongest pressure from the Allies, and I feel very reluctant to take any share in exercising this pressure unless we are certain that the Japanese will carry out their allotted role." Balfour had to admit that it was doubtful that Japan would carry out the role assigned to it and prevent German control of the eastern Siberian railway. Though the Japanese would readily occupy eastern Siberia, "I am extremely doubtful whether they would consent to go as far as the Ural Mountains, or to be shepherded on their way by representatives of their four great Allies." The scheme required a large force and the diversion of much Japanese tonnage to unprofitable work. This would be expensive and involve a serious military risk, little glory, perhaps open war with the Bolsheviks, and might even throw Russia into Germany's arms. Balfour was aware of Maklakov's aversion to the scheme. Here were all the arguments for and against. It was time to make a decision about whether or not to go forward. That would mean putting maximum pressure on Wilson, if the War Cabinet decided for it. Already the president, under some duress, had requested that Admiral Knight return to Vladivostok with the *Brooklyn* to observe conditions there.[61]

Pressure on Wilson was underway. Lord Reading, as of January the new British ambassador at Washington, reported on a long interview with Wilson. The U.S. government, the president said, was against Japan as a mandatory of the Allies. There should be international cooperation, for instance, if an emergency required sailors and marines. Wilson was sure that the Japanese would not undertake the task of guarding the railway alone. Moderates in Russia would prefer the protection of a German rather than a Japanese intervention. If the Japanese did intervene, Nippon should do it on its own, thus leaving the Allies to make representations later.[62]

General Bliss reported on the permanent military advisers' recommendation to the Supreme War Council in adoption of Joint Note 16:

> The Military Representatives are of the opinion, first, that the occupation of the Siberian Railway from Vladivostok to Harbin, together with both terminals, presents military advantages that outweigh any possible political disadvantages. Second, recommended that this occupation be by a Japanese force, after obtaining suitable guarantees from Japan, together with a Joint Allied Commission. Third, the question of the further occupation of the Railway shall be determined by the Allied Governments concerned according as circumstances develop.[63]

He spoke about the advantages and disadvantages of intervention. The main advantage was that it secured military supplies at Vladivostok and Harbin and prevented the Germans from using them. Nor could German submarine bases use the Asiatic coast. However, Bliss thought that the project of Japanese intervention involved grave dangers, while the resulting military advantages would only be transient. Since all the advantages came from occupying Vladivostok, the danger would be less if no attempts were made to proceed farther west, or at most to Harbin. Russian opinion, at that point, could be ascertained.[64] Bliss turned to a secret document, the confidential paper that American Ambassador William G. Sharp in Paris had cabled to Lansing, which he had received from the chief of the British military section. He called that document's assessment of the situation that would result from the occupation of the Trans-Siberian from Vladivostok to Cheliabinsk very optimistic. The plan would tend to organize Russian resistance and would require a larger force than the estimated six and a half divisions. As to the pin-pricks that the Japanese objected to if they had to contend with "show the flag" detachments, Bliss argued that the Japanese would regard the request for guarantees as something more than pin-pricks. The question of when and how to get a big Japanese force, distributed over a large part of Siberia, out was especially important. The frank convention of the sort debated—the mandatory—would not bring the Japanese any farther out than they already were. Any great military advantage resulting from moving west of Vladivostok to consolidate anti-Bolshevik sentiment, Bliss contended, was a question of high politics.[65] The general would not concern himself with counterrevolution.

Bliss called the direct military advantages of intervention "relatively small, or quite problematical."[66] The British recognized the action as secondary, that is, securing military supplies, railway materials, and prevention of German submarines. Bliss said, "it seemed to me doubtful whether any supplies would be left there that would compensate for the ultimate risk resulting from Japanese intervention." The British were advocating occupation of the entire length of the Siberian railroad by a Japanese intervention throughout Siberia. Bliss noted that the British agreed that it was a desperate measure with only a gambler's chance.

Parenthetically, no one even knew exactly what the aim of Japan was in World War I except that the Japanese would do whatever seemed best for their own interest, even if that meant cutting a deal with Germany.

All the permanent military advisers believed that the situation was desperate and recommended the adoption of Joint Note 16. Bliss confined the note to the question of Vladivostok and Harbin. He sensed "in regard to this whole Russian matter, that the feeling over here has become somewhat 'panicky.' " The Allies realized that German forces in the East were their last important body of troops. Yet Bliss thought that until the Allies knew the German intentions, no one should make panicky speculations and schemes.

Even a superiority of several hundred thousand men might not be enough to force the lines in the West back, and the Germans might suffer upwards of a half million losses. Germany might try a move into Macedonia and Italy or patiently consolidate in the East. The result of all these speculations was "a matter of anxious thought here, resulting in a feeling of almost desperation." That was Bliss's explanation of all these schemes. He wondered whether, if Japan did go into Siberia without selfish and ulterior purposes, its action would stop the German withdrawal of troops on the Eastern Front. The General concluded, "what is the value of that 'if'?" Bliss pointed out that the British believed that "there must be intervention; therefore, likely that strong pressure will be brought to bear on the United States."[67]

Balfour tried to place his scheme for a Siberian intervention into a moderate position between that of the French, who saw Japan as the only means of countering German influence, and the Americans, who, "apart from jealousy and suspicion of Japanese enterprises, considered the Japs as the worst possible agents of the Allies in Russia."[68]

All the while Lockhart continued semi-official relations with Bolshevik authorities on a basis similar to Robins's. "My instructions," he wrote, "were of the vaguest. I was to have the responsibility of establishing relations. I was to have no authority." The internal affairs of Russia, Balfour claimed, were of no concern to Britain except as they affected the war. If large portions of Russia preferred Bolshevism, that was Russia's business, not Britain's. Neither complete recognition nor a rupture of relations was desirable. So long as relations remained semi-official and informal, Lockhart should continue to act as Britain's representative. Balfour referred to the Bolsheviks as the de facto government. He saw no point in delving into past transgressions, broken treaties, repudiated debts, or abandoned military stores. Likewise, such a relationship would be entered into with other de facto governments that existed in Russia. Whatever the differences between Britain and the Bolsheviks, both could agree not to overlook militarism in central Europe. The Bolsheviks would refuse supplies to Germany on that basis. That would also allow Britain to send necessary supplies to Russia without fear that they would fall into German hands. Lockhart insisted that the Allies' cooperation with Lenin should be based on calculation, not love.[69] The British were free to support any troops in Russia likely to offer resistance to the Central Powers, even if this were only a shadowy chance, as in the Ukraine with the Cossacks, the Caucasus, or Romania. The Ukrainian Rada, the noncommunist government of the Ukrainian separatists, had thrown its lot with Germany, and the Cossacks seemed worthless. However, Britain could not pledge to the Bolsheviks abstention from action in Russia if it might help to win the war. Some sort of commercial arrangement might also be made with the Bolsheviks, but not one in which the hundreds of thousands of tons already sent benefited only Germany.[70]

The British had realized that since the Bolsheviks had signed the peace treaty with Germany, maintaining an embassy staff to influence Russian policy was useless. Balfour met with the Japanese ambassador to ascertain his position regarding Siberia. He was informed that Foreign Minister Viscount Ichiro Motono indicated his government was "anxious to proceed at once to seize the junction of the Amur Railway."[71] The Japanese felt that such an effort would safeguard Vladivostok. This action meant occupation as far west as Chita, where the Amur River and the Trans-Siberian railway crossed. From Chita the Trans-Siberian branch went north along the Amur River to Khabarovsk and then south along the Ussuri River to Vladivostok. The other branch, the Chinese Eastern Railway, proceeded through Manchuria, crossing the Sungari River at Harbin and then to Vladivostok. This made Chita the jumping-off place for either route to Vladivostok. When Balfour raised the question of Japan being the mandatory, Japan's ambassador to London replied that the "Japanese fully understood that they would go in as the mandatory of the Allies, simply as a move against Germany, and would disavow any intentions with regard to annexation." The Japanese were vehemently opposed to Allied detachments accompanying them, as this would adversely affect Japanese public opinion and injure Japanese *amour propre*. The Japanese, Balfour realized, would only accept Semënov's help. Most important, reported Balfour, "This being the case, we should have a difficult task in persuading President Wilson to agree to our policy." The War Cabinet agreed to send Reading a cable which stated that His Majesty's Government approved the Japanese intervention in Siberia all the way to Cheliabinsk on the east flank of the Urals and which asked him to get the president's approval.[72]

House and Wilson did not come to an easy conclusion. They worried that Japan's intervention would be analogous to the current German occupation of western Russia. The British War Cabinet decided not to approach the Japanese ambassador in London any further until Wilson's views had been obtained. French Ambassador Jusserand presented the State Department with an urgent request that the United States approve Japanese intervention; he noted the vulnerability of Allied supplies at Archangel. The British sent a similar message to Wilson. An announcement followed that enemy prisoners in Siberia had been organized to cut the railway. For Balfour, that demonstrated the extreme urgency of Japanese action. He asked whether John F. Stevens of the U.S. railway commission, with or without Semënov's help, could do something to protect the line. Balfour implied that the Japanese would eventually act and that this was the best time to put some restrictions on them.[73]

Wiseman urged the president to act, but Wilson expressed his fear that the Russian people would regard the Allied approval of Japanese intervention as being on a par with similar manifestos issued by the Central Powers. In this way the Allies could lose the moral force of their position. The president asked for more time to consider, but Wiseman pointed out that even Lansing understood that the French note somewhat altered the situation because it indicated Motono's willingness to make a public pledge.[74] House stuck by Wilson. The Allies needed caution and time to consider what was by now known as Balfour's scheme.

The Japanese problem revolved around what backing Wilson was willing to give. Reading saw Lansing about the proposed Japanese expedition and discovered that he had no objections to the Allies' request, but felt that America could not join in because the Senate would raise doubts.[75] House had The Inquiry's memorandum on this question sent to Polk. The Inquiry believed America's high moral position would be damaged because it would create another obstacle to a future peace settlement. That problem would be how to get Japan out of Siberia after the war. America's fear of Japan's joining Germany was a tacit admission that the United States thought Japan desired to annex Siberia. Nor could America object to the German occupation of western Russia if the United States were to allow Japan's occupation of eastern Russia.[76]

Everything came down to a proposal by House, a memorandum telephoned to the White House by his son-in-law and aide, Gordon Auchincloss. In it House spelled out a diplomatic tactic for Wilson: tell the Allied ambassadors where this venture might lead and send a note to the Japanese. At the same time, the Japanese should explain their reasons for military intervention. House also suggested sending a note to Balfour outlining the difficulties and dangers.[77] This activity proceeded when Wilson asked whether his memorandum to Japan had been readied by Lansing before House sent a note via Auchincloss.

The significance, according to House, was that "The President was much disturbed over my letter and has stopped, for the moment, the memorandum or note which was to go to Japan." Actually, Wilson had already drafted an aide-mémoire and handed it to Lansing. In it he responded to the tremendous pressure put on him by Balfour, Reading, and Wiseman to give Japan a free hand as a mandatory to protect Allied interests in Siberia, namely, the preservation of military stores in Vladivostok and the vast agricultural resources west of Lake Baikal. Indeed, Balfour had insisted that Japan would intervene with or without Allied consent to protect itself against the consequences of the Brest Treaty in Siberia. Lansing sent his own evaluation to Wilson along with the strongest cable from the French government. It asked for immediate acceptance of Motono's pledge of disinterestedness and willingness to act as far as the Urals. But it was Wilson's draft aide-mémoire that the secretary informally made known to the Allied embassies. In it Wilson assured the Allies that America had given all its energy in every direct action of the war that it was capable of giving: "it should leave itself diplomatically free wherever it can do so without injustice to its associates." Therefore, the president explained, "the United States has not thought it wise to join the governments of the Entente in asking the Japanese government to act in Siberia."

Wilson excluded American participation. He mistakenly opened the door to others: "It has no objection to that request being made, and it wishes to assure the Japanese government that it has entire confidence that in putting an armed force into Siberia it is doing so as an ally of Russia, with no purpose but to save Siberia from the invasion of the armies and intrigues of Germany and with entire willingness to leave the determination of all questions that may affect the permanent fortunes of Siberia to the Council of Peace." Wilson let the Japanese squeeze in, however much he would try to push them out later. The Allies came to realize that Wilson's mistake would, perforce, involve American intervention. They redoubled their pressure on him.[78]

It is interesting to compare that draft note to the one finally transmitted to the Japanese. Wilson made it clear that the United States intended to remain free wherever it could without doing an injustice to its allies. That was why the United States would not join in the request of the Allies in asking Japan to act in Siberia. America did not object to that request, for it had confidence that the action had one purpose: saving Siberia from German invasion and leaving its future to a peace council. As to the second note, House commented, "He told Polk he had written the new note and held up the other under my advice and after receiving my letter." It was unfortunate only because the State Department showed the first note's substance to the Japanese and Allied ambassadors. House added, "I believe the President was wise in changing it and substituting the note written yesterday." Wilson laid out his concern that Siberia was in danger of anarchy, German invasion, and domination. He allayed Japanese feelings by saying that the United States had "utmost confidence" in Japan and would "entrust the enterprise to it." What Wilson doubted was not Japan, but the value of intervention, even with explicit assurances. Germany would assert the same mission in western Russia. Such discrediting, along with Russian resentment, would play into the hands of revolutionary Russia's enemies.

Despite the president's protestations, Japan was not allayed. Britain and France pressed harder.[79]

Gone were the phrases about keeping a free diplomatic hand for the United States and approving of the request even though America chose not to join. In their place was a statement on the conditions prevailing in Siberia and a frank criticism of intervention, even with its guarantees, retained from the first note, plus two additions: "hot" Russian resentment toward intervention as contemplated and American "sympathy" for the Russian revolution, whatever unhappy and unfortunate turns it took. The second note ended on America's "warmest friendship and confidence" in Japan. Wilson had moved his argument away from criticizing Japan and onto a higher plane: attacking the value of intervention.[80] Wilson might intervene, but only if it met his "acid test" of fair play for Russia and Russian sovereignty and self-determination, as he had explained in Point VI of his Fourteen Points address.

House reported that Jusserand reluctantly agreed with the second note; Reading was talked out of his position. On both counts House deluded himself. Morris cabled to Lansing the Japanese reaction: Foreign Minister Motono expressed deep appreciation for its frankness and friendly spirit. Morris also noted that the British ambassador to Tokyo, Sir W. Conyngham Greene, informally suggested the advisability of Japan's intervention as far as the Urals. Britain, France, and Italy might later make a formal request for Japanese intervention. Motono regretted public opinion was not sufficiently favorable toward Greene's suggestion. Balfour told House that Britain would independently ask Japan to reconsider. Greene reported that the attitude of the United States made it impossible for Japan to obtain financial and material assistance from America. Until the Allies could count on Wilson's support, Japanese action must be deferred.[81]

The War Cabinet complained about Wilson's attitude. Hope should not be abandoned; the Americans would change their minds, according to Wiseman. Bliss reported that Lloyd George proposed that the prime ministers take up the question because of its important political character. They decided to send Wilson a message asking the president to reconsider the issue. It emphasized that Russia was too weak to help itself and needed the assistance of friends to prevent German domination. Japan had helped Russia throughout the war, would continue as a friend, and could act as a mandatory of the other Allied powers. Yet without American support, such a policy could not be executed.[82] Japanese intervention as an Allied mandatory had failed Wilson's "acid test" for the time being. President Wilson's point VI had failed by the middle of March, even though he stubbornly refused either collaboration with the Bolsheviks or Allied intervention against them.

Six

Northern Russia and Siberia

In the early months of 1918, American officials began to fear that munitions stockpiles in Murmansk and Archangel would fall into German hands. To protect these munitions was no easy task, however, given the political turmoil within Russia and the Allies' lack of formal relations with the Bolshevik government. The waiting period for Bolshevism's collapse so that Russia would continue its war effort had ended with the ratification of the Treaty of Brest-Litovsk by the Congress of Soviets just after Lenin's late-evening speech on March 15–16, 1918. Therefore, President Wilson's propaganda initiative to get Russia back into the war by point VI of his Fourteen Points Address had also failed. The great German offensive against France had begun on March 21, 1918. Allied pressure to resurrect some sort of Eastern Front or prevent Germany's full exploitation of Russian resources intensified. Wilson held the key to Allied hopes in Russia because intervention would require American resources. Hence, the Allies relentlessly applied that pressure on him for direct military intervention in northern Russia and Siberia.

1.

The situation in northern Russia had been calm compared to that in the rest of the country. Murmansk and Archangel were free of German control. Near Archangel on the White Sea the Allies had stockpiled 162,495 tons of supplies. British Rear Admiral Thomas W. Kemp had remained there until mid-December 1917, when the War Cabinet withdrew its naval personnel to Murmansk on the Kola Peninsula. Kemp left behind explosives, stores of metals, shells, tractors, motor cars, clothing, and other valuables. These could fall into German hands.[1]

Murmansk was a tiny place with a population of five thousand. Its protection was in the hands of Kemp's squadron. There also were Russian ships under Admiral K. F. Kyetlinski. Two American vessels carrying Red

128

Cross supplies had arrived. Raymond Robins detailed Red Cross Major Allen Wardwell to look after them. The major found that the local Russo-British shipping company had taken care of the supplies so that they would be duty-free. Admiral Kyetlinski arranged a guard. Wardwell went to a meeting of the Murmansk Soviet and made a speech about the supplies, and he sent seven railway cars of canned milk to Petrograd. Ambassador Francis ordered a passport control officer, Hugh S. Martin, to Murmansk. He was the first American official on regular duty there.[2]

Kyetlinski was murdered at the beginning of February 1918. Kemp, the British consul, and Kyetlinski's aide formed a group to control the port. Kemp reported a serious situation in Murmansk. The attitude of the Bolshevik garrison was mutinous and the Finns were a threat. The Finns acted at the instigation of the Germans, who proposed their advance along the Petrograd-Murmansk Railway. Refugees from Petrograd, as well as Russian soldiers and sailors who had been prisoners in Germany and Austria-Hungary, further complicated the situation. In Admiral Kemp's opinion "the occupation of Murmansk will probably be necessary." He requested a British force of at least six thousand men. The admiralty did dispatch a cruiser and two other ships. The French also sent a cruiser.[3]

Robins's assistant, Wardwell, told of a local Soviet agreement whereby Murmansk was to be under British, French, and Russian officers. "It apparently follows the answer to instructions from Trotsky to accept foreign aid. Learned of the proposed landing of British marines tomorrow." The next day he told Kemp that Ambassador Francis thought that "the only reliance was in the Soviet power, and suggested that the landing of Marines here might have an effect on that policy." As he left the HMS *Glory* he saw marines lined up, ready to go on the tender. "The marines actually came ashore about two o'clock and went up to the barracks near the naval base." Wardwell noted that another warship arrived on March 7, 1918. Two hundred French soldiers came from Petrograd.[4]

What prompted this garrisoning of troops on Soviet soil? The Murmansk Soviet, fearing an advance by Germans and Finns, wired the authorities in Petrograd, calling attention to the danger: "Representatives of friendly powers, the French, American and English missions stationed at Murmansk, continue to show themselves well disposed towards us and are ready to furnish aid ranging from food supplies to active military force, inclusively."[5]

Trotsky had the impression that the German offensive was about to begin and that Petrograd would fall. He telegraphed the city that "It is your duty to do everything for the protection of the Murmansk railway line. Everyone who leaves his post without fighting is a traitor. The Germans are advancing in small groups. Resistance is possible and obligatory. Nothing should be

Map 2: North Russia

left to the enemy. Everything valuable should be evacuated, if not possible — destroyed. *You are obliged to accept any help from the Allied Missions.*"[6]

Lansing was soon sending Wilson information from Colonel Ruggles in Vologda, to which the embassy had moved, concerning British action in Murmansk. Francis had recommended that an American vessel go to Murmansk. Ruggles cabled the War Department concerning reports that British and French troops were cooperating with the local soviet because of a threat by Finnish White Guards. The local soviet had asked for American representation. Francis confirmed that a French cruiser had arrived and that marines had landed from Kemp's cruiser.[7]

Counselor Frank Polk now asked Secretary of State Lansing for directions: "The attached memorandum has to do with sending a warship to Murmansk. Several of the high military officers are strongly in favor of this step. I will be very much obliged if you will let me have your views."[8] Lansing forwarded to Wilson a memorandum from Basil Miles saying that Francis recommended an American warship at Murmansk. The British and French were cooperating with the Murmansk soviet and the effect would be good. Miles confirmed that a French cruiser had joined the British there and landed two hundred troops. Finnish White Guards and German officers supposedly threatened the Murmansk railway. Miles's memo concluded, "It is to be noted that the British Embassy requested this Government to send a warship to Murmansk about two weeks ago. The Department is informed that the original landing of the British at Murmansk was made with the full consent and approval of Trotsky."[9]

President Wilson sent a memorandum to Secretary Lansing early in April, in which he asked that a navy ship proceed to Murmansk, if available. "I am willing to have its commander cooperate there," the president wrote, "but I think it would be wise to ask the Secretary of the Navy to caution him not to be drawn in further than the present action there without first seeking and obtaining instructions by cable from home." Secretary Daniels responded that ships in European waters were active, but that if the presence of the flag would have influence on events at Murmansk a ship would proceed. Wilson answered, "I had hoped that there might be some vessel on this side that could be sent over that would be sufficient force to command respect." The ship proved to be Admiral Dewey's flagship at Manila Bay, the USS *Olympia,* which arrived in Murmansk on May 24.[10] In this small way Wilson took his first move toward intervention.

Ruggles explained to the army's military staff that Trotsky had sent a letter requesting a unit of railway engineers for Moscow, another for European Russia, and one for Siberia. It looked as if the Bolsheviks might ask for Allied intervention. What was happening appeared to be part of a larger pattern.

An Anglo-Japanese landing of April 5 at Vladivostok was to make a great impression on the Bolsheviks. Trotsky set conditions upon any cooperation with the Allies: noninterference in internal politics, collaboration with the Bolsheviks, Allied rather than exclusively Japanese intervention; he also offered the possibility of concessions. Yet the Allies still believed there was collusion between Germans and Russians.[11]

The Supreme War Council met in Paris and adopted a report on "Allied Intervention at Archangel and Murmansk." It admitted that neither military nor naval resources could be spared, and advised all possible steps to "destroy stores at Archangel to prevent their falling into enemy hands, that naval steps being taken with respect to Murmansk be continued in order to retain the place for the Allies as long as possible." They added, "No action by American Government required." Though the War Council required no American help at that moment in northern Russia, Francis had suggested that possibility. In late April he came back to the subject while discussing with Lansing another possible move to Archangel.[12]

Francis did not realize that Major General Frederick C. Poole, "British Military Representative in Russia," had been aboard the *Olympia,* prepared to take command of Allied forces. He was to organize a Czech corps of twenty thousand expected there shortly. He found at Murmansk a force consisting of four hundred French soldiers, six hundred British Royal Marines, two thousand Russian railway troops, and twelve hundred Serbians.[13]

At this time Trotsky considered an Allied intervention by invitation to secure help in building the Red Army in order to prevent the Germans from destroying the Soviet government. The Allies desired a Bolshevik invitation rather than acting against Bolshevik wishes. According to a Bolshevik report guarantees would have to be made that "other allied forces were present" and there would be no objection to Japanese troops. Lockhart thought the Bolsheviks had changed their attitude toward the Allies. They believed war with Germany and counterrevolution inevitable.[14] Nonetheless, the day after three Japanese civilians were shot by Russian soldiers in Vladivostok on April 4, Japan landed five hundred marines to protect the lives and property of its nationals, and the British put fifty ashore. Then Trotsky had second thoughts about agreeing to intervention and gave orders to resist invasion. The president, Ambassador Reading assured Foreign Secretary Balfour, would not take part "unless there is at least something in nature of request from Russian government for this assistance."[15] It was this "something in the nature of a request" that had given Wilson confidence in his decision to send a vessel to Murmansk: the Murmansk Soviet had requested help after Trotsky had approved such a step.

Balfour played on this prospect of a request. After all, he reasoned, some observers noted that more than half the Russian people regarded Allied intervention as their only hope of rescue from either German domination or anarchy. Balfour continued, "Trotsky himself has given indications that he is inclining to this view but he seems reluctant to take so decisive a step as to request intervention." Balfour estimated that Germany was in the midst of transferring another forty divisions westward from Russia and that the creation of a pro-Allied force might prevent this. Disorder in Russia was increasing to such an extent that sooner or later the population might prefer German intervention to a continuance of those conditions. There was, as Balfour put it, a "considerable amount of supplies of all sorts" that might become available to Germany. Because there were great food resources in western Siberia and additional large stores in Petrograd, Moscow, Archangel, and Vladivostok, these resources could pass into German hands and prolong the war. Balfour thought it might be possible to persuade Trotsky to allow intervention, because "A bold and determined policy is required in the face of all these dangers. The presence of Allied Forces at ports such as Archangel, Vladivostok and Murmansk would be of some use in preventing the seizure by Germany of the stores in these towns." If a Russian army could be created, it could be supplied from the stores at Archangel and Vladivostok. "Of late a very significant change has come over attitude at any rate of its M.F.A. [Minister for Foreign Affairs] Trotsky towards Allies." As evidence of this, Balfour noted, "he has approved of Allied co-operation at Murmansk and has suggested that British naval officers should assist in restoring discipline in Black Sea Fleet." If this assessment was correct, then the only course in the Far East was to use Japanese strength with the Allies participating effectively. In northern Russia, "We should be prepared to make a naval demonstration at Murmansk and Archangel which would hold ports as bases and serve as rallying points for anti-German forces."[16]

Balfour's optimism concerning Trotsky's possible invitation to the Allies to intervene rested on the information that Trotsky had authorized Lockhart to send to London, namely, that Trotsky recognized the inevitability of a renewed war with Germany and suggested Allied help. He asked for a plan. This committed him to nothing but was a "skillful move, probably designed only to increase the desperately-needed breathing space and room for manoeuvre."[17]

The British ambassador in Washington, Reading, met with Wilson late in April. In regard to Trotsky's initiative, the president suggested that Reading watch for a trap. Wilson stated that he was expecting documents alleging that Lenin and Trotsky were German spies. Wilson was referring to the so-called Sisson documents, which purported to prove that the Bolsheviks were German agents. Wilson felt that care was called for in making any deals with the Bolsheviks, and he suggested that Lockhart be asked for further information. Wilson had heard that Trotsky's position in the Soviet government had weakened.[18]

Jusserand reported to Lansing that the French ambassador to Russia, Joseph Noulens, then in Vologda, had told him that the Germans were broadening their action in Finland, with White Guards attempting to blow the Kem bridge and proceed north to Kandalaksha to establish a submarine base. Inter-Allied landings at Murmansk and Archangel should complement any intervention in the Far East.[19]

Wiseman cabled House to take no action, though that would allow Germany to withdraw troops from the Russian front. Intervention at the Bolsheviks' invitation was the best course, but it was unlikely because Germany would regard it as a hostile act and turn Lenin out. Then Bolshevik influence in Russia would collapse. Wiseman even thought that Kerensky should form a government in Manchuria and do what Trotsky would not do—invite Allied intervention. Intervention without anyone's invitation, against Bolshevik wishes, was a last resort.[20]

Bliss reported that Joint Note 25 had been passed on April 27, 1918. Military representatives focused on getting the Czech Legion—Czechoslovak soldiers who had fought in the tsar's army against the Central Powers and now were trapped in Russia—to France. With Trotsky's agreement, Czechoslovak troops were en route to Vladivostok for transport to France. Those not already beyond Omsk were to concentrate at Murmansk and Archangel, where they could defend the two ports as well as guard the Murman railway.[21]

By the beginning of May, the president still was unconvinced of the need for intervention, even if Trotsky gave approval. Wilson had no confidence in Bolshevik leadership. Lansing had apparently heard that the Bolshevik government intended to ask for the withdrawal of British troops from Murmansk. "This new development," Reading cabled Balfour, "does not encourage the President to believe in Trotzky's good intentions towards the Allies. If this news had not arrived this morning I am convinced the President's answer to you would have been the same. He remains unconvinced that the balance of advantage and disadvantage is in favour of action at present."[22]

Thomas G. Masaryk, the refugee Czech leader, moved the president toward intervention. Richard Crane, the son of Charles and a State Department official, wrote the president in early May pronouncing Masaryk as the "greatest living authority on Central Europe." The Allies, Masaryk believed, should recognize the Bolsheviks if only to influence them, a line General Judson and Raymond Robins had taken. The Allies must not support monarchists. Nor for that matter did Masaryk feel the Kadets or Social Revolutionaries would have much success against Lenin. He did not wish to see support of counterrevolutionary generals. The Bolsheviks would maintain power longer than their adversaries supposed, though he thought their power would end because of their dilettantism. A coalition of socialist parties including the Bolsheviks might provide a lasting government. Eastern Europe needed a strong Russia to avoid being at the mercy of Germany. An independent Ukraine would be a source of conflict. The German threat had to be countered in every way, including the use of Japanese troops. "I succeeded in organizing in Russia out of our Bohemian and Slovak prisoners a corps of 50,000 men. I agreed with the French Government to send it now to France." Masaryk was on the verge of organizing a second corps. A Russian army would take six to nine months to be organized. French Ambassador Noulens reached an agreement with Trotsky to surrender a corps of Slovak and Teschen arms to the Soviets in exchange for the right of passage along the Trans-Siberian railway to Vladivostok under command of General Mikhail K. Dietrichs, formerly quartermaster of the tsar's army. Crane asked Wilson to meet Masaryk, "the wisest and most influential Slav of our day." Wilson delayed but indicated that he had read Masaryk's memorandum.[23]

The Supreme War Council considered using the Czech Legion: "The general view of the Military Representatives," Bliss noted, "is that it is still possible to make arrangements with the Russian Government by which these troops (who will not fight Russia but who will fight with the other allies against Germany) shall be transported to Archangel and Mourmansk, thence to be carried by water to the Western Front." He added, "Personally, I think that now the question has been put up (by the British Government) the above is about the only answer that we can make, although I doubt whether much material result will come from it."[24]

Reading presented Wilson with another cable which he had received, saying that the German ambassador in Moscow, Count Mirbach, had told the Bolsheviks that they must demand withdrawal of the forces at Murmansk because of the aggressive moves of Admiral Kemp. In Lockhart's view, "A position is now being reached at which it is impossible longer to avoid a definite decision. In my opinion there seems to be only one possible course of action, that is, to make urgent military preparations for landings at the earliest possible date at Archangel, Murmansk and in the Far East."

He thought that any collective Allied proposal to the Bolsheviks would be accepted. "It is, in any event, necessary to push forward intervention with the greatest possible rapidity."[25]

Lansing informed Wilson:

> I pointed out to Lord Reading that the problem had really become two problems in that intervention in western Russia in no way involved the racial difficulty which had to be considered in regard to Siberia. I further told him that intervention at Murmansk and Archangel would receive far more favorable consideration on our part than intervention in Siberia, for the reason that we could understand the military advantage of the former but had been unable, thus far, to find any advantage in sending troops into Siberia.[26]

He thought Trotsky favored such an intervention, especially since Balfour was convinced of this based on Lockhart's telegram.[27]

Reading understood the administration's attitude in separating the problems in northern Russia and Siberia. Regarding northern Russia, Reading noted Trotsky's supposed change of attitude and "some indication of Trotzky turning to the Allies for cooperation and assistance at Murmansk."[28] Reading thought that Lansing "certainly led me to believe that the President would be ready to cooperate with the Allies in the intervention in the North which should take place without the assistance of Japan." When Reading asked what the United States might be prepared to do in northern Russia, Lansing answered that "there were great difficulties as to shipping more especially to provide food and such supplies as could not be found at Archangel or Murmansk." Reading understood the president's feelings on Siberia: "He closed the door although he did not bolt it."[29]

Lansing told the president, "I have had another seance with Lord Reading on the question of intervention in Russia." Lansing reiterated that intervention was divided in two halves. Each half deserved separate treatment. Siberia depended on a military benefit as yet not evident — reconstituting the Eastern Front. Murmansk differed, "since it was a question of ability to land a sufficient military force" to secure stores of munitions. Reading insisted on getting the United States to unite with the Allies in trying to obtain a request from Trotsky that a Siberian intervention would be conditional on Japan declaring that occupied territory would be restored unconditionally after the war. Lansing saw no objection in securing a request from Trotsky for intervention at Murmansk.[30]

Lockhart reported that Lenin realized that Russian and Allied interests were similar in the face of the German danger. Yet Lenin was afraid of Allied intervention because "he believes that their real purpose is the destruction of the system of Soviet Government." Lenin sought guarantees that the Soviet system would be recognized. Lev M. Karakhan, assistant to George Chicherin, newly appointed commissar for foreign affairs when Trotsky became commissar for war, reminded Lockhart that the Germans threatened to occupy Petrograd if British troops remained in Murmansk. General Peyton C. March, U.S. Army Chief of Staff, and his personnel were against intervention because it would not be strong enough to amount to anything without taking shipping and manpower from the West. To all this Wilson replied that northern Russia and Siberia were questions that "must not and cannot be confused and discussed together."[31]

Reading gave Lansing more telegrams; they presented nothing new. Balfour's optimism about Trotsky's apparent favoring of the contemplated northern Russian intervention was reviewed and Lockhart strongly recommended a simultaneous intervention in the Far East and northern Russia. Miles favored Lockhart's recommendation and Francis pressed for preparations.[32]

As this information came to the president, Reading managed another interview. Wilson was apparently adamant in opposing intervention. The president did not wish to appear stubborn, but he thought that the force available would be insufficient to divert German troops from the West and would be resented by Russians:

> President thinks Trotsky and his Government may be amenable at one moment and may be prepared to give an invitation or an assent or a promise not to object but President regards him as absolutely untrustworthy and is convinced that any action Trotsky or his Government may take would be simply and solely for his or their own ends. The President's expression was that the only certainty in dealing with such a man was that he would deceive you.[33]

Francis had recommended intervention in northern Russia. General Bliss now added his voice. Expecting a joint note, beginning with discussion by the military representatives of Britain, France, and Italy who would probably decide on occupation of Murmansk and Archangel, Bliss indicated "a land force of not more than four or six battalions of British, French and possibly Americans. In view of pressing danger to these ports I propose to agree with my colleagues unless instructed to the contrary." General March confirmed Wilson's position: "The President is heartily in sympathy with any practical military effort which can be made at and from Murmansk or Archangel but such efforts should proceed, if at all upon the sure sympathy of the Russian people and should not have as their ultimate object any restoration of the ancient regime or any other interference with the political liberty of the Russian people."[34]

Balfour acknowledged the fact that "intervention at Archangel and Murmansk is regarded by the United States as a different question from that of intervention in the Far East." Balfour asked Reading to "urgently impress upon the United States Government and upon the President" that American assistance was required to retain Murmansk, "if we desire to retain any possibility at all of entering Russia." The British were sending small marine and military forces, though clearly an insufficient number even though the situation there was so dangerous. A brigade plus a few guns, even if not completely trained, would suffice, as operations would only be of an irregular nature. Secretary of War Baker informed Bliss that Wilson finally concurred in the recommendations of Joint Note 25 and suggested Czechoslovak contingents be used. The only catch to using American forces in northern Russia was the president's insistence that Field Marshal Ferdinand Foch, Supreme Allied Commander, approve the "diversion of troops and the necessary shipping for that purpose from those now going to France." Ambassador Noulens pressed for two American battalions.[35]

Early in June the Supreme War Council issued Joint Note 31, which stated that recommendations for northern Russia, agreed to in principle by Wilson, would be confirmed by Foch. The note maintained that the situation in the northern ports had altered since March when Joint Note 17B suggested an inter-allied expedition to protect military stocks and expressed confidence in Admiral Kemp. Finland had come under German domination and the Finns had claimed Karelia and the Kola Peninsula. An advance on Petrograd was being prepared. Occupation of Murmansk and its conversion to a submarine base would make the sea route to Archangel impractical, while its occupation by the Allies would protect Allied flanks. It was agreed that the Allies should hold Murmansk and if possible Archangel and that the National Czecho-Slovak Council should keep a small force in the area.[36]

Lord Milner, British Secretary of State for War, asked for three American machine-gun battalions, three companies of engineers, and two field gun batteries. He appointed General Frederick C. Poole commander and suggested that marines might be preferable to infantry because the operation was amphibious. Poole was appointed "because he is not only an able soldier but is very familiar with Russian conditions as he has spent the last two years in the country, gets on well with Russians and is on the spot." Milner had consulted Foch during a visit to Paris and had obtained the Marshal's assent. Foch recognized the importance of keeping Murmansk and Archangel in Allied hands and thought that if the Americans were willing to help, such a force would be advantageously employed. Milner's request differed from the Supreme War Council's in that instead of four to six infantry battalions, Milner requested three infantry *with* machine-gun units and preferred marines, but asked for three companies of engineers, presumably to maintain the roads. He asked for two batteries of artillery. Officers, specialists, medical and administrative backups were presumed in each request, that is, Milner's and the Supreme War Council's.[37]

Foch agreed with the Supreme War Council and thought that the dispatch of one or two U.S. battalions in June or July would not retard the arrival of American forces in France. He focused on the occupation of Murmansk, though Archangel was also contemplated. Foch assumed that twenty thousand Czechoslovaks would arrive in the northern ports and could be stiffened by not more than six Allied battalions. Foch took some small exceptions to Milner's revisions, as did Bliss.[38]

Wilson was on the verge of committing troops. Bliss reported that Sir Eric Geddes, First Lord of the Admiralty, had just returned from a conference in Murmansk with General Poole. Poole, with three British warships, twelve hundred British troops, two hundred French artillerymen and fifteen hundred Serbians, wanted six additional battalions, two batteries of artillery, and three companies of engineers. Since the British could not contribute, they asked Washington for these units and believed that request in accord with Poole's plans for occupying the northern ports in substantial accord with Joint Note 31. "With this force," Bliss noted, "as a nucleus he believes he can rally one hundred *thousand* Russian troops between Archangel and Vologda inclusive." The Supreme War Council asked the Allies, especially the United States, to dispatch forces. Bliss was requested to seek his government's concurrence and stress the necessity of immediate action. Bliss added, "I had conference with Lord Milner and General Pershing. General Pershing authorized me to say that he approves sending the infantry and engineers from troops now in France. . . . I recommend concurrence as to our participation in general plans and suggest prompt decision."[39]

Reading reported to Balfour that the president was worried that expeditions to northern Russia and Siberia would tax America's commitment in Europe. When he pointed out that Murmansk was a small matter, Wilson replied that it was small but could increase.[40]

Wilson wrote Lincoln Colcord, correspondent for the *Philadelphia Public Ledger,* that "Your thoughtful suggestions about Russia are always welcome and you may be sure I am trying to think out the right action. I hope and believe, too, that I am close upon the heels of it." If Wilson was "close upon the heels" of deciding what to do, it was not because of the efforts of the Supreme War Council, which he held in low esteem: "Speaking of War Councils advice on Russia," recorded Daniels in his diary on July 9, "he [Wilson] said they proposed such impractical things to be done immediately that he often wondered whether he was crazy or whether they were."[41]

The prime ministers judged Milner's request to be in substantial agreement with Joint Note 31. Because the total force remained the same, Bliss went along on the assumption that "no military movement from these places to the South can be made if Russians are not sympathetic." He warned of friction unless the United States adopted a policy: "It seems to me that there are evidences that our Allies want the United States to commit itself to expeditions to various places where after the war they alone will have any special interests." America should keep its army as intact as possible, and the sole object should be to defeat Germany, not to tie itself to those Allies with many other objects.[42]

Baker asked Wilson to approve "our fair part." Baker inquired whether General John J. Pershing, commander of the American Expeditionary Force (AEF), should send three infantry battalions and three companies of engineers, artillery being out of the question. If the British could supply the guns, the United States could send personnel. The president directed Pershing to select the troops and allow them to embark once Foch had approved. On July 22, March sent a terse memo to Bliss that Wilson permitted three battalions of infantry and three companies of engineers provided Foch and Pershing could spare them, but that the artillery had not been approved.[43]

At the end of July, Pershing detached the forces permitted by the president, the 339th Infantry Regiment of three battalions along with the First Battalion 310th Engineers, the 337th Field Hospital, and the 337th Ambulance Company, under command of Colonel George Stewart. The troops were known as the American Expeditionary Force, North Russia (AEFNR). Francis cabled Lansing early in September that forty-eight hundred troops had landed.[44]

2.

The decision to put troops in Vladivostok stretched over the spring into midsummer. It was one of the president's most misunderstood policies. Wilson received opinions from a variety of sources. In the end the decision was his, and he worked it over and gave Polk a chance for suggestions. Thereafter he would not enlarge the missions in northern Russia or Siberia.

Lansing had made clear that the problem of intervention could be divided. There was badgering by the British and French. A suggestion by the American ambassador to China, Paul S. Reinsch, caught the president's attention. Reinsch suggested that the situation seemed favorable for what he called "effective joint action of Allies and American initiative." He had in mind a "commission authorized to command moderate financial support" that would reconstruct at least Siberia. "Should America remain inactive longer friendly feeling is likely to fail." The idea gained ascendancy when pushed by William Bullitt, Colonel House, and Gordon Auchincloss. Bullitt recommended it to House as early as May 20. The complications arising over finding a satisfactory administrator and giving protection, as well as difficulties arising in Siberia, prevented its enactment. Reports of the arming and use of German and Austrian prisoners by the Bolsheviks, and the threat of Allied use of Japanese, with or without consent, added to the tension. Even after the Czechoslovak seizure of Vladivostok on May 28, Jusserand cabled that Reading had seen Wilson about the "Japan-Siberia question" and "renewed his entreaties and based his arguments on the disturbing news now reaching us, but, from what he told me, all this was to no avail." Wilson was less disposed than ever to agree with his Allies. He spoke of "letting events take their course." He seemed to think that Siberia would form a government, with Allied technical and economic help.[45]

Wilson thought that some of the Czechoslovaks should be retained because of familiarity with Russia. Jusserand began to notice a shift in the president's attitude. He talked of a shipment of American troops or stated that Wilson was no longer maintaining "the same absolute opposition as before." By mid-June both Lansing and House were still pushing a relief mission with Herbert Hoover, former head of the commission for Belgian relief, at its head. House complained that "Someone has been here almost every day since I arrived to talk about this vexatious problem, and try to get me to transmit their views to you." The colonel related that Hoover was willing to serve. Wiseman outlined an economic plan. As late as June 16, Reading wired Balfour that it was difficult to persuade Wilson because no adequate military plan had ever been presented to him and he believed the Russians would resent the entry of the Japanese into Siberia.[46]

Wilson made an intriguing comment when he sent Lansing the suggestion by Reinsch: "There seems to me to emerge from this suggestion," he wrote, "the shadow of a plan that might be worked, with Japanese and other assistance. These people are the cousins of the Russians."[47] Reinsch stated the opinion of Allied representatives in Peking that "it would be a serious mistake to remove the Czech-Slovak troops from Siberia. With only slight countenance and support they could control all of Siberia against the Germans. They are sympathetic to the Russian population, eager to be accessories to the allied cause, the most serious means to extension of German influence in Russia, their removal would greatly benefit Germany and further discourage Russia. If they were not in Siberia it would be worth while to bring them there from a distance."[48]

In that case, neither a large American nor Japanese force would be required since the "cousins" of the Russians were already there. An Eastern Front would not need to be reconstituted as it would be enough to deny Germany supplies from Siberia. Such an action might lead to a Siberian government compatible with the western democracies and, thus, one that could be aided.

On June 19 Wilson had a meeting with Masaryk and afterward wrote Lansing, "By the way, I saw Professor Masaryk today and he seemed to think well of the plan." Wilson was referring to the "shadow of a plan" mentioned to Lansing.[49] During this forty-five-minute conversation the president had expressed "sincere interest" in the Czech and Slovak peoples and was glad to have an opportunity to talk with Masaryk about a "serious problem," Russia and how to "help" her. He explained that the Allies wanted to use the Japanese for intervention, the effect it would have on Russians, and whether they could use the Czechoslovak Legion. Masaryk was unenthusiastic about intervention, especially by the Japanese, but he approved the "shadow of a plan."

The Reinsch proposal had been transmitted to Lansing on June 13. Included in Wilson's remarks regarding the plan were cooperative societies, an idea sent by the American consul in Moscow, DeWitt Clinton Poole, who had taken Maddin Summers's place on May 4, 1918, when the consul general died. Lansing had asked Poole to find out the attitude of Russian cooperative societies concerning Russian conditions. This was the other part of the "shadow of a plan" that had caught Wilson's attention. It had long been discussed in Washington as an economic mission to be led by Hoover. In the Reinsch formulation, the ambassador to China referred to representatives of the Moscow Central Supply Committee who were in Peking, describing their organization as "elective in its communal district and central bodies devoted to task of filling crying needs Russian population, saving lives, resisting extension of German influence, preventing supplies to regions under German control." Then came Reinsch's important remark: "They seem an organization which allies could support with good results." Like the Moscow Central Supply Committee, the Russian cooperative societies appeared to be the organization Wilson had been hunting for as the goal of his democratic aspirations for Russia. As he told Lansing, "This despatch has interested me very much. These associations," no doubt referring to those mentioned by Poole and the one spoken of by Reinsch, "may be of very great service as instruments for what we are now planning to do in Siberia."[50]

Poole wrote of the All Russia Union of Cooperative Societies that included many other associations, some in Siberia, led by Alexander Birkenheim, a Russian businessman who refrained from politics, yet spoke for the rank-and-file of Siberian cooperatives. The cooperative's sympathies were with the Allies, and "In Siberia, where the cooperative societies represent the people here in the fullest measure, there is a special feeling of friendliness fixed and upholding in America. On the other hand, there is distrust of Japan." Cooperatives had no way of stopping the Germans and the Allies were the only means of resistance. As a practical man, Birkenheim asked what the compensation for Japan would be, and the manner and date of intervention required. Speed was essential.[51] The "shadow of a plan" was now a plan. Wilson had the military and economic ingredients for his aide-mémoire, which he would write on July 17, 1918.

Until then the president demanded another note from Foch agreeing to intervention. French Prime Minister Clemenceau warned that intervention had to occur before the end of October and the onset of winter, and emphasized the prevention of the "slaughter of the Czechs." Wilson told Jusserand that a quotation from Foch was insufficient and that he required "a direct expression from General Foch about this perplexing matter." The president was eager for Foch to commit himself to the idea that it was justifiable to send American troops to Russia even if it involved a "subtraction of that number of men from those whom we could send to France."[52] Foch committed:

> In my opinion the sending by you of American troops to Russia is justified, for no appreciable diminution of the number of troops to be sent to France will result therefrom. I conceive the expedition to Siberia as having to be mainly formed with Japanese elements. The Allies' contingents would be reduced to modest numbers: some 12,000 men or thereabouts. America could supply at once two regiments and the Allies the rest. Under those conditions the American troops sent to France would only be reduced in an insignificant way.
> More than ever, in the interest of military success in Europe, I consider the expedition to Siberia as a very important factor for victory, provided action be immediate, on account of the season being already advanced. I take the liberty of insisting on this last point.[53]

Jusserand cabled Pichon that the president was satisfied.[54]

Wiseman wrote, "The most absorbing topic in Washington is intervention in SIBERIA, and it is full of enthusiasts who are seeking interviews with the President." Baker assessed men and material in the Philippines. Robins, recently returned from Russia, made suggestions that Wilson thought "much more sensible than I thought the author of them capable of. I differ from them only in practical details." Robins was against intervention without an invitation, and only for economic cooperation.[55]

On June 29 the Czechs seized Soviet buildings in Vladivostok, placing Bolsheviks under arrest. This action forced the fresh landing of Allied troops to guard consulates and supplies, even though the Czechs controlled the city.[56] The Supreme War Council believed that the "recent action of Czecho-Slovak troops has transformed the Siberian situation." The British thought that Siberia was no longer pro-Bolshevik and could be occupied all the way to the Urals. Russia would rally around the Czechoslovaks and create a new army "to reform an Eastern Front or at least to sustain a vigorous spirit of independence in the occupied territories behind the German line as well as compel Germany to maintain large bodies of troops in the East."[57]

Reading found Wilson still considering an economic commission, adamant about recreation of an Eastern Front, and considering only seven thousand Americans as the maximum contribution. Wilson recognized the obligation of the Allies to help the Czechoslovaks. The Siberian question had for Wilson a remarkable parallel to, in Wiseman's view, Wilson's earlier Mexican policy and "more than a passing political question, but a matter of principle." Wiseman thought that British traditional policy was up against a "new conception of foreign policy which no amount of argument will reconcile with." He recognized that Wilson's military advisers were against the whole scheme but that the Czechoslovaks had changed everything.[58]

Wilson now held a White House conference consisting of Lansing, Baker, General March, and Admiral Benson. They debated the Supreme War Council's views, deciding that an Eastern Front was impossible even if beyond the Urals; that an advance west of Irkutsk did not seem possible; that the Czechoslovak situation required the Allies to aid them in forming a junction with troops in western Siberia; and that "on sentimental grounds and because of the effect upon the friendly Slavs everywhere would be subject to criticism if it did not make this effort and would doubtless be held responsible if they were defeated by lack of such effort." Because the United States could not furnish any considerable force soon, these measures should be adopted if Japan agreed to furnish rifles, machine guns, and ammunition to the Czechoslovaks at Vladivostok: the United States to share the expense and supplement supplies as soon as possible; to assemble in Vladivostok a force of seven thousand Americans and a like number of Japanese to guard communication with the Czechoslovaks, the Japanese sending their troops immediately; to land American and Allied forces to hold Vladivostok in cooperation with the Czechoslovaks. A public announcement would be made that intervention was to aid Czechoslovaks against German and Austrian prisoners and that there would be no interference with Russia's internal affairs and a guarantee not to impair Russian sovereignty.[59]

Daniels informed Admiral Knight that the United States desired Vladivostok to be "available as a base for the safety of CZECHS, and as a means of egress." Knight was to use his forces and request similar action by Allied naval forces. He was to avoid actions that might offend Russians. Wilson wanted to help the Czechoslovaks, avoid a large Japanese intervention, and send a small American-Japanese force, so that the Czechoslovaks could join with their brethren a thousand miles in the interior. He also noted that Baker feared the Japanese, that Wilson did not think the Germans could get Russian help for at least eighteen months, and that the president still wanted to send an aid mission. The British agreed to get the Czechs whatever rifles and ammunition they had on hand.[60]

Wilson wrote House that he had been "sweating blood" over what to do in Russia and that every time he handled the question it went to pieces "like quicksilver under my touch." Reading was disappointed with such a small force and lack of unity of action, and he wondered why Wilson got Japanese approval before consulting Britain and France. Lansing commented, "Throughout this conference I felt that the French Ambassador and in a measure the Italian approved of our program, but that the British Ambassador was not entirely favorable because he felt Great Britain had been ignored."[61]

Reading explained away his doubts about Wilson to Balfour on the president's assurance that once the Japanese agreed everyone would be consulted. Lloyd George remained skeptical of the Wilsonian program. He was happy over intervention, but felt fourteen thousand men insufficient. Furthermore, such a small force would not guarantee that the "Czecho-Slovaks will not have their throats cut by German and Austrian prisoners." The force should be large enough to secure Siberia to the Urals, otherwise "It is repeating fatal error of Khartoum expedition to relieve Gordon and unless it is modified it might end in exactly the same tragic results."[62]

While awaiting the Japanese agreement, Wilson wrote an aide-mémoire, which he drafted for review by Polk, who added a paragraph concerning freedom of the Allies to define their policies. Wilson asked Polk to communicate the amended document to the Allied governments. The memorandum "embodies our most conscientious consideration of questions which we felt obliged to test by every practical consideration." He believed that the memorandum was of so confidential a nature that "I have, as you will see, written it myself on my own typewriter."[63]

The aide-mémoire was a remarkable proposition. It began with an emphasis on the main American agenda, winning the war in the West, which, it stated, might force it to decline other obligations. America had been asked to make additions to an already immense wartime program. It could not slacken since the crisis in the West remained. It was in France that the instrumentalities were created to sustain an American force, at great cost. The only diversion was the Italian front because it was part of a single line.

Russian intervention would add to the confusion, injure Russia, and be of no advantage to the main design. It would make use of Russia without serving her, and foreign armies would drain her substance. Military action in Russia could only be rationalized to help the Czechoslovaks, steady any Russian efforts at self-government or self-defense they might be willing to accept, guard military stores, and render such aid as would be acceptable to Russians. The necessity was to help the Czechoslovaks. This action was what the Russian people desired. The United States was willing to contribute a small force in Siberia as well as Murmansk. "But it owes it to frank counsel to say that it can go no further than these modest and experimental plans. It is not in a position, and has no expectation of being in a position, to take part in organized intervention in adequate force from either Vladivostok or Murmansk and Archangel."[64] If other purposes developed, Wilson maintained, the United States would feel obliged to withdraw the troops.

Wilson used Polk's addition to note that these conclusions were not to criticize other governments. All that was intended was a frank statement of policy. By securing the rear of the Czechoslovaks, America wished to assure the people of Russia "in the most public and solemn manner." Wilson concluded by offering at the earliest opportunity to send an economic commission that would follow but not interfere with the goal of safely removing the Czechoslovaks.[65]

Polk looked for a Japanese statement. No response was forthcoming until seventeen days later. He reported that France agreed and the British and Italians were forthcoming, but he wrote, "I have heard nothing from the Japanese Ambassador, although he told me late yesterday afternoon that he expected to receive a message from his Government today."[66] He desired a statement to the press by Wilson but suggested changes concerning an Eastern Front: say nothing and keep the Germans guessing, while stressing Allied efforts in the West.

Issued on August 3 when the Japanese reply was finally in hand, that statement included a final paragraph noting the hope of the United States that its Allies would actively aid the contemplated military and economic plans. Wilson omitted "explicit" from the draft. The word had occurred in the penultimate paragraph dealing with guarantees of noninterference or intervention in the political life of Russia and that there should be no impairment of Russia's territorial integrity: "The Japanese Government, it is understood, will issue a similar *explicit* assurance."[67]

While Wilson awaited a definite Japanese reply, the British went along with the aide-mémoire. Reading explained to Lloyd George that the best course was to accept Wilson's "proposals simplicities" and to "let situation develop." Balfour told Reading that although he was satisfied with the American decision, he and the War Cabinet viewed the size of the American-Japanese force as inadequate.[68]

On July 24 Ambassador Viscount Kikujiro Ishii finally brought Polk his government's answer. Political reasons had prevented Japan from binding itself to a force of seven thousand because the Japanese people would feel imposed on by a lack of confidence by America. The Japanese government, Ishii explained, realized that there was no lack of confidence, though it, too, felt the suggested force too small and planned to send in a division of twelve thousand. As Polk remarked, "I suppose the number of troops they intend to send now is not as important as their reserving the right to send more later." The Japanese document differed with Wilson's in terms of what constituted "suitable forces" and, if called on by further exigencies, whether or not to send another detachment. Japan reaffirmed the policy of "respecting the territorial integrity of Russia and of abstaining from all interference in her internal politics."[69]

Clemenceau's special envoy to Washington, Henri Bergson, well-known philosopher, observed that the Japanese had delayed in giving a clear yes or no, and that Ishii had made one vague statement after another. The Japanese wanted enormous supplies, especially steel. Wilson told Bergson that America could say yes only to the money. House also reported on Wilson's uneasiness over the Japanese delay: "The President is fretted with the Japanese attitude." House cited the Japanese failure to limit the size of their forces, their lack of altruism, and all their excuses. House continued: "The President sent rather a peremptory note to our Ambassador at Tokyo, telling him that unless they would agree to intervene upon our terms, there would be no intervention at all with our consent." The Japanese counterproposal had agreed only that Japan "send troops to Vladivostok but reserve the right to send other troops elsewhere appears to represent the minimum offer of the present Ministry."[70]

In an interview with the Japanese ambassador on July 25, 1918, Polk made plain that the United States would accept a Japanese division of ten to twelve thousand and the fact of the Japanese having command, but "We felt that by sending troops in not only without any limitation as to number, but even indicating that more troops would be sent if the occasion demanded, the natural impression would be created in the Russian mind that this was an expedition which had more in view than merely assisting the Czechs." The United States would probably be unable to participate in a larger expedition. When Admiral Knight requested reinforcements, the president told Daniels, "I wish I could give Knight the information he desires about the troops to be sent to Vladivostok, but unhappily the Japanese Government is trying to alter the whole plan in a way to which we cannot consent, and for the time being at any rate the whole matter is in suspense."[71]

The Japanese came sufficiently close to President Wilson's position that he agreed and gave out a press release confirming the agreement. Ishii offered Polk Japan's assurances that no more troops than necessary would be sent to help the Czechs. Though his government continued to think a larger force was necessary, "for immediate action, and in view of the attitude of this Government, his Government authorized him to say that they accepted our proposals, reserving the question as to the sending of additional troops to Vladivostok or elsewhere until circumstances should arise which might make it necessary." Polk had asked Ishii two or three times whether the Japanese would be limited to ten or twelve thousand, and Ishii thought, "there was no question."[72]

It was not until August that the War Department cabled the Philippines for the Twenty-seventh and Thirty-first Infantry Regiments, a field hospital, and an ambulance company, asking that they embark for Vladivostok. Major General William S. Graves was to bring an additional five thousand men from the Eighth Division at Camp Fremont, California. This would raise the total force to seven thousand. The peak size of U.S. forces ultimately serving in northern Russia was 5,710, those in Siberia 8,388. The Twenty-seventh Infantry arrived in Vladivostok on August 16 and two days later the Thirty-first arrived. On September 1 Graves and the remainder of the force sailed into Golden Horn Bay.[73]

The combination of diplomatic pressure and appeals from the Supreme War Council became too much for Wilson to ignore. The president also felt pressure from within the American government. March noted the "tremendous drive" to get America committed. The president had "been pulled and hauled." Baker said the government had "been literally beset" by the Russian question. The president himself wrote that he had "been sweating blood over the question of what it is right and feasible (possible) to do in Russia." Lloyd George was to tell the War Cabinet later, commenting on the failure of Allied policy in Russia, that he "did not think we should blame the Americans, as they had always been very much against undertaking operations against the Bolsheviks, and what they had done up to date was only on account of the pressure which had been brought to bear on President Wilson."[74]

3.

In summary, pressure for American support of intervention in northern Russia and Siberia, especially from the British, was continual. It is useful, therefore, to review the nature of that pressure, as it was the one decision of Wilson's that caused the most controversy in his entire Russian policy. Had there been no Allied pressure, there probably would have been no American intervention. London's interest in intervention derived from a fear of German victory, concern about investments, alarm as to German or Bolshevik advances into British possessions (especially India), and, of course, the threat of Bolshevism.[75]

The British did not waste time with Ambassador Walter Hines Page in London, concentrating instead on the president and the people who had immediate access to him. Reading visited Wilson and other Americans, such as Lansing and House. Wiseman obtained interviews with the president. He strove to persuade each government that the other's position on Russia was "somewhat similar to its own," even though the positions actually differed measurably.[76]

The campaign's object was always the same—to bring about American intervention. The British believed American participation necessary if intervention were to have success, as the Americans would have to provide manpower, supplies, and the finances. There were feelers as early as December 1917 concerning American and Japanese willingness to protect the Trans-Siberian railway and to supply food to Russia. Lansing hoped no action would be necessary, especially by the Japanese. Already Wilson and Lansing had established the first theme of American policy toward Russia after the revolution: "Do nothing."[77]

At the same time the Supreme War Council was urging the president to intervene. This constituted the other half of the Allied effort. The War Council had an extended discussion in late November, when the maintenance of the Eastern Front was of the utmost concern. House visited the council, where he expressed little interest in Allied projects to aid such anti-Bolshevik Russians as General A. M. Kaledin in southern Russia. Military representatives soon drew up a memorandum on "The Situation in Russia," which urged support for groups that proposed to keep fighting, but the plan came to nothing. By January 1918, however, the council had of necessity become preoccupied with restoration of the Eastern Front. From January until July the U.S. military representative to the council led an uncomfortable life. He found himself a holdout against action in Russia.[78]

In late January the British cabled Wilson the details of a plan to control the Trans-Siberian railway. Wilson put them off. He told Wiseman he detected no military advantage and believed the Japanese unwilling to participate. He did agree to seek General Bliss's opinion about the plan. Wiseman came away from the interview convinced that the president could be persuaded if Bliss would testify to the plan's military value: "President is particularly anxious not to appear as obstructing any of your [Balfour's] schemes."[79]

Asked by Wilson about intervention, Bliss called a meeting of the military representatives to the Supreme War Council, resulting in Joint Note 16, "Japanese Intervention in Siberia," which supported Japanese occupation of part of the Trans-Siberian railway. A joint Allied mission would administer the occupation. Bliss doubted that military advantage would result but found that his colleagues favored "an immediate occupation of the entire length of the Siberian Railway." He thought that he had limited the plan to the area near Vladivostok and believed that he had to concur for the sake of "morale." German gains in Russia and their impending strike in the West had resulted in a feeling of desperation—the probable explanation for such propositions." There had to be "yielding at times on the part of each Representative or else nothing would be accomplished." Washington's reaction was immediate. Wilson refused to approve because such inter-allied projects threatened his war aims and peace plans. Bliss understood Wilson's decision but responded that it was "likely that strong pressure will be brought to bear on the United States" on this topic. At this same time, it was apparent to Balfour that the president would consent to participation in any Siberian plan "only under the strongest pressure from the Allies."[80]

Wilson's advisers fortified his opposition. Lansing, House, Baker, Bliss, and March all opposed involvement. When the British pressed for a Japanese intervention, the president decided not to help, although he said that the United States would not obstruct the plan. The president changed his mind, and informed the Allies that he hoped no action would be necessary. The president believed even indirect approval would damage his ability to postpone settlement of political issues until the war ended. Reading soon cabled London that pressure on House might bring some change.[81] The British plan then came to center on converting those personages around Wilson to intervention, believing that they would convince the president.

Given this Allied campaign, it is possible to understand better the president's reaction to the Russian situation. Wilson's initial response in late 1917 was confused. He was concerned that "all sorts of work in Russia now is rendered extremely difficult because no one channel connects with any other." His inclination was to let events run. When House urged that criticism of the new government stop and the United States pursue its own policy, separate from the Allies, the president agreed. Wilson expressed some leniency toward the Bolsheviks by praising in his Fourteen Points speech their negotiators at Brest-Litovsk for sincerity and earnestness in demanding that the conference be held "within open, not closed, doors."[82]

The reaction in the State Department to the events in Russia circum-scribed certain options for the president. While opposed for some time to American military intervention, State Department officers were anti-Bolshevik. Lansing was alarmed about the implications of this. By early December, Lansing had decided it would be "unwise to give recognition to Lenine, Trotsky and their crew of radicals." He thought events would "far surpass in brutality and destruction of life and property the Terror of the French Revolution." Lansing gained the president's support for financial aid to Britain and France in their efforts to extend support to Kaledin in southern Russia, though that came to little. Wilson did put limits on Lansing and the department. He refused to send Major Stanley Washburn on a forty-day speaking tour to expound his anti-Bolshevik views. In late December, the president rejected an intensive propaganda battle inside Russia against the Bolsheviks. The president wrote Creel, "You are taking just the right position. It must be our position for the time being, at any rate, and must wait to see our way before pushing forward any faster."[83]

One of the issues dividing Wilson and Lansing concerned contacts with the Bolsheviks. Wilson wondered about a statement to the Bolshevik lead-ers, through unofficial channels, about the American attitude. Lansing countered that Creel's representatives could distribute the message. The president thought a recommendation that one of the Allies establish rela-tions "with the Bolshevik de facto government, the others holding aloof," well worth considering. The State Department insisted on nonrecognition. Wilson shortly forwarded to the State Department a suggestion by Senator Robert L. Owen that the United States recognize the Bolshevik government as de facto. He told Owen that "what you recommend has constituted no small part of my thought in recent weeks." State Department reaction came swiftly. Miles noted that "it seems to me quite impossible to recognize as de facto authorities a Government which includes among its extreme views a repudiation of all foreign obligations."[84]

Differences between the president and his secretary of state continued. Wilson wrote Lansing, "As I understand it, our official representative in Petrograd is keeping in touch with the Bolshevik leaders informally. Am I not right?" Miles was quick to straighten the president out: "The Depart-ment has steadily refused to allow the Embassy or Consulate at Petrograd to enter into any relationships with the Bolshevik authorities, either formally or informally."[85] There had been contacts, but the State Department had done all it could to stop them. Wilson was increasingly unhappy with the activities of Robins, especially during the period in which the Bolsheviks and the Germans negotiated to end the war on the Eastern Front. It was "very annoying to have this man Robins, in whom I have no confidence whatever, acting as political adviser in Russia and sending his advice to private individuals." But Wilson realized that as there were no official or unofficial negotiations between the American diplomats and the Bolsheviks, Robins served a certain purpose and might remain "until things clear up a bit in that unhappy country." The president discussed with House in mid-February the possibility of recognizing the Bolsheviks and even sought British opinion, but opposition came from both Britain and the State Department.[86]

Perhaps the most revealing example of State Department attempts to move the president from possible contact with the Bolsheviks occurred when Wilson drafted a statement in early March 1918 to greet the convening of the Congress of the Soviets. The State Department qualified this indication of goodwill. Wilson said that Americans were sympathetic to the Russian people, especially as Germany had tried to "turn back the whole process of revolution and substitute the wishes of Germany for the purposes of the people of Russia." At the State Department's suggestion, "whole process of revolution" became "struggle for freedom." And while Wilson's draft had said, "I beg to assure the Congress" that the American people supported Russian sovereignty and independence, the State Department revised the message to read "I beg to assure the people of Russia through the Congress." Both changes represented the differences between Wilson and the State Department. Polk was the one who made the changes in the message. He was afraid that it could be considered "an official communication" and be treated "contemptuously" by the Soviets.[87]

Wilson was not pro-Bolshevik, by any means, and he was not, as already shown, even deeply interested in events in Russia. This, of course, helps to explain his lost opportunities of 1917. He usually allowed the State Department to handle operations concerning Russia, perhaps showing that Wilson had assigned a lower priority to that country. He gradually displayed flexibility in regard to the Bolsheviks, partially, no doubt, because they also were not at that time of the highest priority with him. That changed. In this case the State Department's attitudes may have limited his options. Any Wilsonian negotiation with the Bolsheviks would have to take place against the backdrop of active opposition from Lansing and the State Department. Both Wilson's and Lansing's appreciation of Russia matured in the caldron of World War I.

The State Department's anti-Bolshevism was most important because House and Baker, who had frequent access to Wilson and could have worked against intervention, were neutralized. Wilson did not seek House's advice on Russia as on other topics. He was reacting to House's friendship with Reading and Wiseman—associations which probably led the president to conclude that House's advice would support British objectives. House did not know what to advise. He told the president what courses were open. House came to support the British position and told Wilson so. Baker was consistently opposed to sending troops to Russia. But his position was weakened by sensitivity to Allied pressure exerted through the Supreme War Council and concern that the Allies were losing faith in the United States—a concern he passed on to the president.

Given these circumstances, Lansing and the State Department emerged as a force shaping Wilson's decisions on Russia simply because, on the one hand, Lansing could control the daily diplomacy that the president could not hope to micro-manage and, on the other hand, Wilson always considered Russia of lesser importance than the Western Front. When pressure emanating from within the government coincided with the pressures coming from the Allied diplomats and the Supreme War Council, Wilson was to find himself isolated.

Almost immediately following the Treaty of Brest-Litovsk, the great German offensive broke out in March 1918. It revived the question of intervention within the Supreme War Council. Without Bliss, military representatives decided to support action in northern Russia at Murmansk and Archangel and began to query the American government. A small contingent of British troops landed, with the agreement of the Murmansk Soviet, to help protect the city from German attack. Trotsky seemingly gave approval.[88]

In early April, the military representatives adopted Joint Note 20, "The Situation in the Eastern Theatre," calling for intervention by the Japanese with assistance from the Czechoslovak Legion. Bliss refused to sign, although he promised to forward the note to Washington. He told his colleagues that such matters were "for diplomatic negotiation by his Government." The reaction was predictable. Baker informed Wilson that Bliss felt "embarrassed, being one of the military advisers, to sit into the conference on this subject when he knew that you regarded it as more political than military, and that he was equally embarrassed in refusing to participate in the discussions, since refusal by one nation's representative to discuss one question might be a precedent for similar action by others, ultimately disintegrating the Council."[89]

British diplomatic pressure persisted. The British began to press for involvement.[90] Following the Treaty of Brest-Litovsk, London asked again for the president's approval of Japanese intervention. Wilson refused, but House was weakening. He told Wiseman that he was "inclined to agree that, apart from intrinsic value of the scheme, it may be advisable, even necessary, to put it into effect for the sake of allied morale." By the end of April, Reading was convinced that the "best way to gain President's assent is by first convincing House." Reading met with Wilson on April 25. The president again expressed doubt about the plans for Siberia, but the ambassador sensed some movement: "His attitude is different, from that hitherto adopted and is more favorably disposed."[91]

Wilson's policy from January until May, however, was to let events work themselves out and to oppose every plan to intervene. Events were moving too fast—they were "kaleidoscopic," so he told Thomas W. Lamont. Writing to Charles W. Eliot, he unburdened himself: "I wish most earnestly that it were possible to find some way to help, but as soon as we have thought out a working plan there is a new dissolution of the few crystals that had formed there." During the months between January and April 1918, he had become increasingly unhappy with the Bolsheviks, especially when they broke up the Russian Constituent Assembly in January and signed a final treaty with the Germans in March. But his policy still was to do nothing. Waiting for some pattern to emerge, he showed a reluctance to speak to people about Russia. He refused to see Thompson because he felt that "information and advice are futile, until there is something definite to plan with as well as for."[92]

He was especially irritated when the Allies tried to involve themselves in the internal politics of Russia. In February he had seen nothing "wise or practicable" in the British plans for Siberia. And when a *New York Evening Post* writer suggested intervention, he said that the correspondent "entirely misinterpreted the spirit and principles of the Government if he thinks it possible for it to propose to interfere" in any other country. When he backed away from approval of Japanese involvement in Siberia in early March, Polk actually argued the question with him, but without success. Long suggested a plan for intervention in Siberia, but Wilson did "not think that it would be practicable." When the British pushed for an American presence in Siberia in late March, the president could not find "sufficient cause for altering our position."[93]

In April and May, Wilson realized he would have to give in on Russia. He considered possible intervention in northern Russia. That campaign had more—though not much more—military value; it bypassed the Japanese; it had the possibility of being approved by the Bolsheviks; it had more support from the American military; and, so he thought, it could be severely limited, thus blocking any possible Allied plans for intervention in the civil war there. Wilson may have hoped that he could forestall Allied pressure by concessions in northern Russia. He wrote Daniels that he favored sending a warship "if it can be done without sacrificing more important objects," especially on the Western Front. The United States should send a vessel of "sufficient force to command respect and afford real cooperation." Even here, it will be recalled, he cautioned the commander "not to be drawn in further than the present action there without first seeking and obtaining instructions by cable from home." The mission of the vessel was to assist in recovering the Allied stores and to protect Allied interests in northern Russia.[94]

A strong Allied push for American participation in Russian intervention began with adoption by the Supreme War Council of Joint Note 25, "Transportation of Czech Troops from Russia." The note called for Allied support of the Czech troops, which were to concentrate at Vladivostok, Murmansk, and Archangel. These plans caused Bliss a good deal of anguish. He warned Baker that Japanese troops would throw the Russians into the arms of the Germans.[95] The president insisted on the principles of Russian territorial integrity and political independence. Intervention via Vladivostok, the president told March, was impracticable "because of the vast distance involved, the size of the forces necessary to be effective, and financing such an expedition would mean a burden which the United States at this time ought not assume." The president approved "any practical military efforts which can be made at and from Murmansk or Archangel." Even in northern Russia such efforts had to have the "sure sympathy of the Russian people and should not have as their ultimate objects any restoration of the ancient regime or any other interference with the political liberty of the Russian people."

The meeting of the Supreme War Council on June 1–3 concerned both northern Russia and Siberia. Seizing on Wilson's concession on northern Russia, the council adopted Joint Note 31, "Allied Intervention at Russian Allied Ports," dated June 3. Allied troops were to take Murmansk and Archangel. Allied pressure had finally drawn Wilson's reluctant concurrence to the operation. Even here the president insisted that Foch go on record in support of the operation. Dutifully, Foch replied that the value of the planned occupation was "indisputable."[96] The Allies moved quickly on Wilson's concession. Soon Allied troops were in northern Russia. As already noted, Wilson gave in to Allied pressure and eventually dispatched several thousand American troops to northern Russia.

If the beleaguered president thought that his concession on northern Russia would be enough, he was mistaken. The Allies wanted intervention in Siberia and decided to discover whether the Japanese were prepared to carry it out. British plans for Siberia were reinforced by a turn in American opinion, which now seemed to favor intervention. Documents brought from Russia by Sisson purported to show that Bolshevik leaders were in the pay of Germany, though these documents were later proven to be forgeries. The

Czechoslovak Legion gained sympathy. British pressure remained. Wilson told Wiseman that no military man had convinced him an Eastern Front could be restored. He remarked that "he would go as far as intervening against the wishes of the Russian people—knowing that it was eventually for their good—providing he thought the scheme had any practical chance of success." But the only result would be to rally Russians against the Allies. Wilson's solution in early June was to "watch the situation carefully and sympathetically, and be ready to move whenever the right time arrived."[97]

Lansing and House decided to support some action in Siberia. On June 21 House told the president that a decision on the Russian problem was "a question of days rather than months." Once House became convinced that some action in Siberia, preferably economic action, was necessary, he even advised the British and French representatives in America which arguments they should bring up in their discussions with the president and which they should omit. At House's suggestion, Wilson conferred with Reading, who came away believing that the president recognized the impossibility of sending any kind of relief to Siberia without military backing. Reading's view, so he informed Balfour, was "that if only a small force perhaps not more than fifteen to twenty thousand men of which the larger number should be Americans were once introduced into Siberia there would be little difficulty hereafter in getting the president's agreement to a more advanced policy of military intervention." While the president still had not agreed, Reading became convinced that he was moving in that direction. The canny envoy even advised Balfour to keep Kerensky in Britain because his planned visit to the United States might have a "bad effect."[98] Meanwhile, the British also did what they could to publicize the difficulty the Czechoslovak Legion had encountered in its movement eastward along the Trans-Siberian railway.

The French also were busy. Jusserand had seen Lansing several times during the first half of 1918, leaving communications favoring intervention that were forwarded to the president. General H. M. Berthelot, head of the French military mission to Romania, and Marcel Delanney, recently appointed ambassador to Tokyo, met with the president and discussed Siberia. Wilson told Delanney that he "would try to be" convinced of the need for intervention for the sake of Allied unity and told General Berthelot that he awaited "the advice of General Foch; I have been the first to desire unity in the High Command. It is not for me to give a bad example and refuse to recognize his authority."[99] While Wilson seems to have been unaware of these differences in French governmental circles, he became aware of the French support for intervention.

The Allies prepared well for the July meeting of the Supreme War Council. Foch anticipated Wilson's desire for his approval, cabling the president,

"More than ever, in the interest of military success in Europe, I consider the expedition to Siberia as a very important factor for victory, provided action be immediate." The Japanese agreed to intervene as far as Irkutsk, provided the U.S. government approved. The Allies now presented their most forceful case. The British, French, and Italian prime ministers appealed directly to Wilson.[100]

All the while Wilson had hoped that Russia would solve its own problems. Now he realized that the Allies would not stop the pressure until there was action in Siberia. He began to consider a "kind of relief expedition for Russia." After it became clear that relief without military aid would fail and the Allies had made plain that relief was not enough, he seized on the Czechoslovak issue, even gaining Masaryk's concurrence. When the American minister to China, Reinsch, cabled Wilson about Czechoslovak troops, Wilson finally saw "the shadow of a plan that might be worked." Wilson viewed the Czechoslovaks as an instrument to end Allied pressure.[101]

The president set severe limits on intervention and attempted to restrict political involvement. He did not accept Lansing's suggestion of a "political High Commissioner." He agreed to provide a limited force to guard supplies in northern Russia and to assemble seven thousand troops at Vladivostok, along with that many Japanese, to guard stores and help the Czechs embark for France. His aide-mémoire claimed that victory would be won or lost on the Western Front.[102] Furthermore, no sooner had Allied intervention begun in September 1918 than World War I ended in November. A major part of the Allied rationale for its troops being in Russia collapsed.

Seven

1919
Paris in the Spring

At the Paris Peace Conference during the long months from January until the signing of the treaty with Germany late in June 1919, the president sought to do something, he was uncertain what, to resolve what he and everyone else denominated "the Russian problem," that is, what to do about the Bolsheviks. A critic, Herbert Hoover, watched him move from one solution to another, and he might have described him as uncharitably as he did Russia: "a specter which wandered into the Peace Conference almost daily."[1] To be sure, this was unfair, for the president was accomplishing some things and attempting others. But the "Russian problem" persisted. Wilson in the end tried three initiatives: Prinkipo, the Bullitt mission, and the Nansen relief plan. None of them got much beyond the planning stages.

When the Supreme War Council met on the eve of the opening of the great conference at Paris, on January 12, a heated discussion ensued over Marshal Foch's plan for moving Polish troops from France to the new Poland, to face forces of the Red Army. This could have been the beginning of a large Allied invasion of Russia. The president saw the challenge, and as the minutes recorded his wrath, in words that doubtless were not altogether his, he "pointed out that perhaps it might be unwise to express an opinion on the subject by itself because it would form a part of a much vaster problem; there was great doubt in his mind as to whether 'Bolshevism' could be checked by arms."[2]

It was the beginning of meetings that took place even before the conference's opening, and the antagonists were careful. French Premier Clemenceau said the case should be postponed until Bolshevism could be dealt with. Foreign Secretary Balfour asked whether this contingency was not provided for in clause sixteen of the armistice, which conferred wide powers on the council. Foreign Minister Pichon thought it important to repatriate Russian prisoners of war. If they were allowed to cross the frontier, Prime Minister Lloyd George said, they would be "asked by Bolsheviks either to join their party or to have their throats cut." It was not merely a question of feeding them, but whether they could be moved to the Ukraine or any other safe part of Russia. Foch asked that a committee study the question and report. Again Wilson spoke up, "that Russia itself was in a condition that the Allies did not like and could not control; Russia being in the condition in which she was, he did not believe it possible to introduce such a decision into the terms of the armistice." The meeting acceded to Foch's suggestion to form a committee.[3]

As for recognition of Russia, Pichon noted that several groups purported to represent Russia. Should the counterinsurgent Omsk government under the White Admiral Alexander V. Kolchak send delegates? The Bolshevik government was recognized by two-thirds of the Russian people, he said, and was a de facto government. Wilson agreed that White Russian leaders, generally all those who opposed Lenin and were then in Paris, should not be admitted to the conference.[4]

The president favored a British scheme to summon the factions to Paris to meet each other. Others thought the idea that Lenin and his opponents could discuss anything was ludicrous. A breakthrough came on January 18. In December the Bolsheviks' envoy, Maxim Litvinov, had asked to see representatives of the Allies in Copenhagen to negotiate a settlement of the civil war. It was decided to send the American attaché in London, William H. Buckler. He met with Litvinov on January 14–16. The Soviets were willing to pay the foreign debt, protect foreign enterprises, and grant concessions. "The conciliatory attitude of the Soviet Government is unquestionable."[5] The debt would take time. So would protection and concessions. Propaganda in foreign countries would cease. Amnesty would extend to all Russians. There would be self-determination for Finland, Poland, and the Ukraine.

A correspondent for the *Manchester Guardian* and a sympathizer close to the Bolshevik leadership, Arthur Ransome, believed that the Bolsheviks would consent to the Urals as a boundary. Ransome thought that no non-Bolshevik government could exist in Siberia without intervention. The Allied commander in Eastern Europe, General Franchet d'Esperey, told Bliss that the time for intervention in European Russia had passed.[6]

In the Council of Ten, which evolved from the Allied Supreme Council and consisted of two ranking delegates from each of the five great powers, Wilson offered to ask the factions to send representatives to some other place than Paris, perhaps Salonica. Lloyd George had pointed out the advantage of Salonica or Lemnos: Russian representatives could pass through the Black Sea without entering other countries. When the Italian Foreign Minister, Baron Sidney Sonnino, mentioned that Russian representatives were in Paris and could be heard, the president replied that they ought to be heard, but that it would be "desirable to get all these representatives in one place, and still better, all in one room, in order to obtain a close comparison of views." Sonnino countered that the parties in Paris did not wish to hear the Soviets and besides, "The Allies were now fighting against the Bolsheviks who were their enemies, and therefore they were not obliged to hear them with the others."[7]

Clemenceau did not favor conversations with the Bolsheviks because he felt that they were criminals; he threatened to resign if they were invited to Paris. Bolshevism was spreading to the Baltic and Poland, Budapest and Vienna; Italy was in danger. "If Bolshevism, after spreading in Germany, were to traverse Austria and Hungary and so reach Italy, Europe would be faced with a very great danger." He favored erecting barriers. But "in the presence of his colleagues he felt compelled to make some concessions as it was essential that there should not be even the appearance of disagreement amongst them."[8]

Lansing indicated that the president would draft an appeal to the factions to "lay their cases before an international commission." The following day he stated, "Agreed on an address drawn by Pres't. to Russian factions which was discussed this a.m. Delegates are to meet at Isle of Princes on Sea of Marmora." He was not sanguine. Wilson's physician, Cary T. Grayson, wrote privately that the president had prepared an outline of what he called the "Prince's Island Invitation." He noted, "It was an invitation to all of the factions in Russia to declare a truce, and to send delegates to meet in February to determine whether they could reconcile their views and thus secure representation at the Peace Conference." He added that the president insisted on "no interference with internal affairs of Russia, but that the Allies would do everything possible they could to help the Russian people from the outside."[9]

The Council of Ten adopted the president's proclamation of January 22 — to invite representatives to confer with the associated powers — by February 15. By February 12 the last replies were received, almost all negative, two days before the brief departures for home of Wilson and Lloyd George from Paris.[10]

The Bolsheviks again focused on loans, credits, and concessions, giving no attention to a cessation of hostilities, aside from the fact that they agreed to attend a conference. Commissar for Foreign Affairs Chicherin sent a radio-telegram complaining that he had only received a press account of an invitation. It was not until February 4 that a response from the Soviet government was received. The Bolshevik acceptance — "evasive," "somewhat insulting," and "after the fashion of early Soviet diplomatic communications" — failed to promise a stop to the advance of Soviet troops into Poland and the Baltic area. No wonder that Wilson was quoted as saying that the Soviet reply was "studiously insulting."[11]

With the exception of the Soviets and Estonians, the other factions rejected the offer. The Provisional Government of Archangel found the invitation impossible. The Omsk government seemed willing to comply if ordered, but otherwise opposed the offer. Ukraine made attendance dependent on withdrawal of the Red Army. The Omsk government then decided that under no conditions would it attend because it "rejected any possibility of an agreement with the Bolsheviks as well as any negotiations with them." The governments of Siberia, Archangel, and southern Russia made clear that never would they exchange ideas with Bolsheviks.[12]

Given these responses, these refusals from all but the Bolsheviks and Estonians, Wilson found that belligerents could not be ordered to a room and left to fight it out—an activity he often suggested. No one in Paris had the power to make them attend a conference.[13]

William Bullitt of The Inquiry, now a member of Wilson's peace commission in Paris, had written House that it was important to withdraw American troops from northern Russia to show that the Prinkipo proposal was in good faith. British Brigadier General Marlborough Churchill thought that six icebreakers could accomplish the move by sea, from Archangel to Murmansk, of twelve thousand American, British, French, and Russians. Bullitt claimed that unless action was taken, "we shall have another Gallipoli." Consul DeWitt Clinton Poole, now stationed in Archangel, reported that the new British commander at Archangel, Major General Edmund Ironside, said the military situation was critical. Bullitt scribbled a note for House: "The President can not act too quickly in this matter. He must get those troops out."[14]

Always against intervention, General Bliss asked of British General Sir Henry Wilson what proportion of reinforcements should be American to secure a safe withdrawal? What sort of U.S. troops? What were troops to do once they got there? He recounted his conversation to General Pershing and the two agreed "it would be a wise thing if the President were to demand that these reinforcements be used to assist in a withdrawal and concentration of our troops which are now badly scattered, provided this could be done with safety." Bliss had criticized Major General Frederick C. Poole's "wild expedition" that scattered troops in detached positions. He wrote the president: "I doubt the political or military wisdom of sending any more troops to North Russia except for the purpose of enabling the force that we now have there to concentrate at Murmansk and Archangel at the earliest moment that it can do so with safety." Bliss received a written request: two companies of railway troops, one for operating and one for maintenance, 720 men. Yet even for this small request, "My proposition to the President will probably be that as soon as these troops can be withdrawn to the ports, they should be so withdrawn and gotten out of Russia as soon as possible. They are not doing the slightest good there that I can see." Although ice at the entrance to the White Sea was two to three feet thick, merchant vessels could get through with the help of icebreakers. Bliss recommended the railway troops.[15]

Bullitt made a stronger recommendation: "In view of the possibility of a military disaster, it is respectfully suggested that the Allies should offer an immediate armistice on all fronts to the Bolsheviks."[16]

When Lansing tried to explain all this to Polk, the impossibility of the Russian situation became clear. The British, he thought, wanted to deal with the Bolsheviks. The French would have no dealings. Congress and the American press clamored to withdraw U.S. troops.[17]

Lloyd George's private secretary, Philip H. Kerr, wrote the prime minister of an astonishing conversation between Balfour and Clemenceau on the question of Prinkipo. Clemenceau had asked Balfour if he would do anything within reason for him, to which Balfour responded affirmatively. Then the premier said: "Will you postpone the Prinkipo question until after the President leaves?" The issue seemed dead. Yet it had to be brought up on Friday before Wilson left for his voyage home to sign legislation before Congress adjourned. Wilson would, then, return to Paris. Lloyd George said privately that Clemenceau would be happy to have Wilson out of town: "The old tiger wants the grizzly bear back in the Rocky Mountains."[18]

The British War Cabinet met on February 12, 1919, and Secretary for War Winston Churchill reported that the moment of decision had arrived: troops must now either be withdrawn, or, if plans for intervention were adopted, larger forces must be sent.[19] Lloyd George suggested the need for more military judgment. If withdrawal was decided, what effect would that have on the national states created in Eastern Europe? Since Wilson would oppose further intervention, the financial responsibility would be borne by Britain.

The showdown in Paris on intervention occurred February 14, just before the president left for America. Churchill came to Paris, supposedly to carry out decisions of the War Cabinet for Lloyd George, which meant getting Wilson to agree to a Russian course. He restated the concern over the proposed Prinkipo conference. The War Cabinet, he explained, believed little would come of it if only the Bolsheviks attended.[20]

Wilson had a clear opinion on two points: Allied troops were doing "no sort of good in Russia," that is, they did not know what or for whom they were fighting; they were not assisting any common effort to establish order. As far as Prinkipo was concerned, he claimed that the conference had been established to find out about the Russian situation and assist in the establishment of peace there as an "element of the world's peace." Information, he suggested, might well be gathered by an informal meeting between American representatives and the Bolsheviks, especially since their response to the invitation was, in the president's words, "uncalled for" and "insulting." Instead of answering to the points of the invitation concerning cessation of hostilities and withdrawal of troops, the Bolsheviks offered things not asked for, such as debt repayment and territorial compensation. The president concluded that if other Russian governments were unwilling to attend, the Allies should "imitate Mahomet, and go to them."[21]

Winston Churchill, Lord Milner's successor at the War Office, responded that though withdrawal was a logical policy, it would lead to the destruction of all non-Bolshevik troops in Russia: "Such a policy would be equivalent to pulling out the linch-pin from the whole machine. There would be no further resistance to the Bolsheviks in Russia, and an interminable vista of violence and misery was all that remained." The president said that Allied forces could not stop the Bolsheviks, nor were the Allies prepared to send more troops. Churchill countered that "volunteers, technical experts, arms, munitions, tanks, aeroplanes, etc." might be furnished. Wilson emphasized that not only in some areas would reactionaries be helped, but also in others no one could determine what was being supported, and "volunteers could probably not be obtained." There would be retribution, there would have to be a reckoning, because Allied troops would have to withdraw. He admitted he did not act alone and that if it were the Council's wish, he would "cast his lot with the rest."[22]

Churchill thought that if Prinkipo failed, Wilson was ready to do his share "with the other allies in any military measures, which they considered necessary and practicable to support the Russian armies now in the field." He added: "I consider this a very satisfactory note for him to end on and I conceive that we are entitled to count on American participation in any joint measures which we may have to take." He suggested an Allied Council for Russian Affairs and another note to the Bolsheviks giving them ten days to stop fighting.[23]

In Wilson's absence, Churchill tried to persuade the Supreme War Council that intervention was necessary. He sent an overly optimistic message to Lloyd George explaining Wilson's response to his suggestion that, if Prinkipo failed, the Allied and Associated Powers ought to have a well-thought-out military goal and ought to accomplish it if they decided to take action. Wilson, he believed, "would nevertheless if Prinkipo came to nothing do his share with the other allies in any military measures which they considered necessary."[24]

Churchill proposed a wireless to the Bolsheviks asking them to stop hostilities within ten days. If Prinkipo fell through, the Allies should have a military plan. But when the Prinkipo time limit passed, it seemed more prudent to set up a military commission, as he now called it, to prepare "a plan of war against the Bolsheviks."[25]

Churchill was advocating intervention. He wanted to bring troops into Russia and put down the "foul baboonery" of communism. The troops would have to be British and French, not American. And how serious was this sort of discussion with the American president absent? It was the sort of endless talk of alternatives that seemed to preoccupy Lloyd George and to amaze, perhaps disgust, or drive into silence and immobility the government of Clemenceau.

War bothered Lloyd George: "Am very alarmed at your second telegram about planning war against the Bolsheviks. The Cabinet have never authorized such a proposal. They have never contemplated anything beyond supplying armies in anti-Bolshevik areas in Russia with necessary equipment to enable them to hold their own, and that only in the event of every effort of peaceable solution failing." Churchill asked Balfour to accept March 15 as the end of the Prinkipo offer and to cable Lloyd George that Prinkipo could not be kept alive.[26]

Balfour was prepared to back Churchill but reluctant to take the lead. For English and American opinion, Prinkipo had merit. It seemed that the War Cabinet allowed Churchill to pursue the issue because, as Balfour saw it, "you are bathed in the atmosphere which prevails in Downing Street and have received directions immediately from there."[27]

Philip Kerr, secretary to the prime minister, sent news to Lloyd George that the conference would let the Prinkipo proposal lapse because no one had accepted its condition, the cessation of hostilities. That left Churchill's proposal; as Kerr put it, "you are bang up against Mr. Churchill's proposition of a war on the Bolsheviks with Allied volunteers, tanks, gas, Czechs, Polish and Finnish conscripts and the pro-Ally Russian armies."[28]

There was no enthusiasm on the American side. Bliss opposed anything that smacked of intervention. To Churchill's proposal that a military committee prepare a plan against Russia, Bliss wrote, "I think that it would be unwise if anything should be done with the consent of the United States which could be construed by anyone as indicating an intent on the part of the United States to take part in an intervention in Russia." If America could see all other problems resolved and focus on Russia, it might be willing to do its share. The Allies were free to do whatever they wished, but they must not assume America's participation.[29] Bliss was given to logical posturing.

House noted that Churchill was "persistent in pushing his plan for a military committee to examine into the question as to how Russia could best be invaded in the event it was necessary to do so." House explained his own and Balfour's subsequent victory: "I opposed this plan with the same vehemence. It was about to be adopted. . . . However, when I took my stand against Churchill, I suggested to Balfour a substitute resolution for the Churchill proposal." Lansing's notes make clear that "each delegation would consult its military representatives at Versailles on the points mentioned in Mr. Churchill's resolution, that the military representatives would talk the matter over in confidence with each other, and that they would then report to their respective delegation as soon as possible." House continued, "It was literally Balfour and myself against Churchill, the French and the Italians. We carried our point."[30]

House cabled the president that "Churchill not only wished to question as to what military action by the associated governments was practicable with respect to Russia to be referred to a military commission, but also a public statement to be made of this reference."[31] That Lloyd George had no connection with Churchill was proven by the prime minister's taking the measure of having Kerr show House all the instructions sent to Churchill. On February 17 the discussion was so anxious that it was deleted from the minutes of the Council of Ten. House was prepared to have Bliss state his view that "the United States could not employ any of her resources against Russia for we are not at war with Russia." Reference was made to the tie vote in the Senate on the resolution demanding withdrawal of U.S. troops from Russia. Vice-President Thomas R. Marshall had broken the tie.[32]

Two ideas now appeared, one about Prinkipo resulting from the collaboration of Wiseman and Auchincloss, the other a result of conversation between House and Lansing. The first concluded that nothing should be said about breaking off negotiations. The Allies would note that they wished neither to intervene nor to make loans nor to receive concessions. If the Bolsheviks failed to attend the conference, forces would be sent to neighboring states. It would be clear that the Allies were ready to meet all Russian delegates. The other idea resulted from House's conversation with Lansing on February 16 in which they discussed sending Bullitt to Russia. It was to be a fact-finding mission. Lincoln Steffens, the muckraking American journalist, later claimed credit for the idea. According to Bullitt, Lord Alfred Northcliffe, the British newspaper magnate, had dreamed it up.[33]

The president had stated in his last meeting at the Villa Majestic that if the

Russian governments would not come to Prinkipo, the Allies should imitate "Mahomet" and go to them. House was working on details of a commission to Moscow.[34]

House asked Bullitt to undertake a mission. Bullitt selected a Russian expert, Captain W. W. Pettit, and a naval secretary, R. L. Lynch. Steffens went along as "a friend of the Bolsheviks." The mission left on February 22. Just before its departure, Kerr handed Bullitt a note with a list of conditions. Kerr thought, and may have assumed Lloyd George did, that Allied governments might resume relations with Moscow, including withdrawal. "Kerr stressed that his paper had 'no official significance,' and it remains a matter of dispute as to whether he had cleared or discussed it with Lloyd George. As it turned out, the proposed agreement . . . conformed closely to the one set forth in the Kerr memorandum." Lansing did not know that Bullitt was a negotiator, rather than a fact-finder. House may have known. Certainly Wilson did not. Nothing was said to the French or other Allies. Neither Henry White, lone Republican on the peace commission and former ambassador to France, nor Bliss knew of the mission until after it departed.[35]

Discussion of the situation continued. At a War Cabinet meeting of February 24 the British prime minister again referred to Britain's Russian policy. Part of the problem was that five governments had to agree. The prime minister was prepared to press for a policy at the War Cabinet meeting.[36]

Balfour wrote a summary of that meeting: the great powers were not prepared to send increased forces to Russia; Bolshevism, if it survived internal difficulties, would be in a position to make a formidable attack on any part of non-Bolshevik Russia. Allied forces were too scattered to support one another; the conclusion was that Allied forces should be withdrawn as soon as weather permitted and other Russian governments could be warned. Though the conclusion was natural, Balfour felt it was wrong because its effect would be to discourage Russian friends and encourage the Bolsheviks. Friends would feel betrayed and might make Allied retreat difficult; that kind of policy would render a Bolshevik victory certain. It was "hard to believe that the fabric of Soviet Government stands on any very solid foundation."[37] It might even tumble in ruins. If the Bolsheviks were relieved of Allied pressure, they could devote their energies to the West; Foch's plan would have justification in using the small nations between the Central Powers and Russia assisted by western material if Bolshevism turned aggressive. "It hardly fits in, however, with the complete surrender to Bolshevism which the abandonment of Archangel, Siberia and the Don would seem to involve"; the consequences of evacuation meant "atrocious brutalities" by the Red Army toward those remaining, resulting in the most "embittered and enduring" consequences. Balfour recognized that the Allies' Russian friends made reckless charges. It would be a misfortune if the moderates felt that they not only had been abandoned but also suffered at the hands of the Allies.[38] No conclusions were reached.

House received word from Bullitt that his party had left Paris and was now in Stockholm, where it was to receive help from Ambassador Ira Morris to make contact with a Bolshevik agent, the Swedish communist Kil Baum. That Bullitt was unclear about his mission's purpose seemed evident: he asked House whether to send "a statement of the terms of the Soviet Government" and whether he should return or stay on. He kept referring to the hardest part of the task as being in Paris, where *"you have got to put it across."* For Wilson, and perhaps Lloyd George, the idea of a mission was to gather data. House may have had something in mind more like Kerr's note. There was ambiguity in the remarks of House. Chicherin met the mission in Petrograd and ascertained its seriousness, wired Lenin, and brought the mission to Moscow. Bullitt negotiated with Chicherin and Litvinov and finally, on March 14, received Lenin's conditions. They set April 10 as the deadline for an agreement. Lenin accepted Kerr's memorandum: de facto governments on Russian soil would remain; Allied troops would be withdrawn; there would be a cessation of military aid to de facto governments; repudiated debt would be recognized by the Soviets; and so forth. After a week in Moscow, Bullitt left, arriving in Helsingfors; from there he dispatched the conditions that he and the Bolshevik leaders had worked out. Here was an important offer not to be received indifferently, though Bullitt's procedure was probably unwise because it represented a fait accompli, leaving little room for further negotiation.[39]

Lansing wrote Pichon on March 15, announcing a small Russian mission consisting of Bullitt, Pettit, and Lynch. Unofficially it was to obtain "recent information concerning the true situation in Petrograd and Moscow." The French had not been informed, perhaps because it was thought that they had sabotaged Prinkipo. The mission was to be given "no notoriety or newspaper publicity to this affair lest its significance be exaggerated."[40]

In a "Text of Projected Peace Proposal By the Allied and Associated Governments," which Bullitt sent to Wilson, Lansing, and House, these were the conditions: cessation of hostilities for two weeks pending a conference; a conference of all de facto governments, which were to remain in power and not be upset by force; the economic blockade to be raised and trade relations reestablished, including the right of the Soviets to unhindered rail transit and use of port facilities; Soviet citizens and official representatives to have free right of entry to Allied and Associated countries as well as de facto countries on the territory of the former Russian empire and likewise for all those within Soviet territory; a general amnesty declared by all; withdrawal of all Allied military assistance and a reduction of armies by all states on the territory of the former Russian empire; and all such governments to recognize responsibility for obligations of the former Russian empire. Bullitt cited other items: the armistice was to begin one week after the proposal was announced, with a neutral country to host the conference; Germany was to leave alone and be left alone; Poland and all neutral countries were to be extended the same rights as the Allies; Soviet Russia should accept these proposals no later than April 10.[41]

This proposal Bullitt sent from Helsingfors. He explained that he had been in daily conversation with Chicherin and Litvinov, and that the executive council of the Soviet government approved the proposal. He had made clear that his visit was unofficial, but that he would bring this "absolutely secret" document to the attention of the Allies. He had found Lenin, Chicherin, and Litvinov "full of a sense of Russia's need for peace, and therefore, disposed to be most conciliatory"; he continued, "I feel certain that details of their statement may be modified without it being unacceptable to them."[42] In regard to supplies for the Russian people, the Allies would send inspectors to oversee distribution. This did not include diplomatic representatives. Norway was considered a preferable place for a conference. "Lenine, Tchitcherin, Litvinov and all other leaders of the Soviet Government with whom I talked expressed in the most straightforward, unequivocal manner the determination of the Soviet Government to pay its foreign debts, and I am convinced that there will be no dispute on this point."[43]

Bullitt had solved the Bolshevik riddle if the Allies were prepared to act on this document forcefully and not in the way in which they had allowed the Whites, with French support, to wiggle out of Prinkipo. It seemed that House's fault in the Bullitt matter was not to have made that initiative fully known to Wilson before or after he left France; or, if it had been a "trial balloon," it was Wilson's fault to have buckled under publicity. It appears that Wilson gave House latitude and was unaware of Kerr's unofficial list of conditions. House should have made him aware. After a flap in the press and in the British Parliament over the Bullitt mission had long passed, Wilson reacted to an article in the *Nation* by telling his secretary, Joseph Tumulty, that he knew of no such Allied terms penned by Kerr.[44]

Bullitt sent another memorandum for the "President and the Commissioners Plenipotentiary" dealing with conditions in Russia, presumably the only purpose of the Bullitt mission that Wilson claimed he was aware of. Bullitt blamed the distress in Russia on the Allied blockade. Industry was at a standstill, except for munitions. Bullitt believed that the destructive phase of the revolution was over, that the terror had ceased, that order had been established.[45] He claimed support for the government by the people. The Soviet form "seems to have become to the Russian people the symbol of their revolution." The position of the Communist Party was strong and had received support from opposition parties due to the blockade, intervention, and Allied support to anti-Soviet governments. As for the Communist Party, Trotsky and the generals felt that the Red Army should go forward, whereas Lenin was willing to compromise: "Lenin feels compelled to retreat from his theoretical position all along the line. He is ready to meet the western Governments half-way." It was Lenin who seized the opportunity. Bullitt emphasized that "no government except a socialist one could be set up." The Leninists were as moderate as other socialists. No peace could be made in Europe or in the world "until peace is made with the revolution." The blockade had to be lifted and supplies delivered if for no other reason than to diminish the hold of the communists. Intervention forced opposition parties to support Lenin. If Kolchak and Denikin were to win, an even bloodier purge would be carried out. The Red Army fought with "crusading enthusiasm." Lenin had become a legend, "a very striking man — straightforward and direct, but also genial and with a large humor and serenity."[46]

Rumors of Bullitt's mission began. Many were prepared to oppose the Bullitt-Lenin proposal and disagree with Bullitt's analysis. Within about a week, Auchincloss, of all people, leaked it to H. Wickham Steed, editor of Lord Northcliffe's *Daily Mail.* This may possibly have been engineered by House to test public opinion.[47] Sergei Sazonov, former Russian imperial foreign minister, had asked Henry White, former American ambassador to France and a peace delegate, if it were true that the American peace commission had sent someone to negotiate with the Bolsheviks. White denied the rumor, but later said, "I find, on inquiry, however, that Mr. Lansing permitted two Americans, who were anxious to go to Russia, to do so in a purely unofficial capacity and for information purposes only, provided they could make their own arrangements for getting into that country; but in no way as representing our Peace Commission."[48]

A division of opinion occurred among Wilson's lieutenants. Lansing confided that House seemed to favor, but that he and White opposed, Bullitt's proposal. There were other indications things might be going awry. The intent was to leave Pettit in Petrograd as liaison. The peace commissioners, who, with Lansing's approval, had sent the fact-finding mission, accepted Bullitt's recommendation to leave Pettit in Petrograd and then reversed themselves. Word came that Count Mihaly Karolyi's government of Hungary had been overthrown and that the Hungarian communist, Bela Kun, had come to power. This news, more than anything else, threw cold water on Bullitt's mission. Bullitt was on his way via Stockholm and London. Lansing gave Wilson reports of the alarming situation in Budapest. Kun was a "notorious communist," a proletarian army was being raised, and solidarity to Bolshevik Russia had been declared.[49]

The mission was becoming irrelevant. Playing with alternatives and sensitive to the changing political winds, House began flirting with an alternative plan involving food relief for Russia. The wily colonel was surely aware that the Bullitt plan could not succeed without Wilson's and Lloyd George's support, which, perhaps, the Auchincloss maneuver to Steed had aimed at testing. The president was already agitated by House's tendency for compromise, especially in giving the French what they wanted. Another plan was being put forward by Vance McCormick for food relief in the belief that it would undermine Bolshevism. The president suggested that House speak to Hoover, who had written a long letter on March 18 answering a request from Wilson for his opinion on the Russian problem. Calling attention to the legitimate social grievances that he felt were behind support for Bolshevism in Russia and elsewhere, Hoover addressed the unlikelihood that a military crusade, as suggested by Marshal Foch, would solve the problem. "This plan," Hoover remarked, "does not involve any recognition or relationship by the Allies of the Bolshevik murderers."[50] Hoover and Auchincloss approached the Arctic explorer, Fridtjof Nansen. Nansen was being substituted for Bullitt in the twinkling of the colonel's eye.

Wilson's altercations with Clemenceau over the German issue diverted him from "the Russian problem." The president suffered an attack of influenza in early April, perhaps a small stroke. He had refused to see Bullitt, at first because of a headache, eventually out of fear of publicity. Already Lloyd George complained to Bullitt about publicity, particularly that article in the *Daily Mail* by Steed which had been opposed to any kind of recognition. When talking to Bullitt at a breakfast in late March, Lloyd George used this article as evidence of the danger of proceeding. Had the colonel smoked the prime minister out? Lenin thought the Allies believed that since the Bolsheviks were grasping at straws, communism must be near collapse. The Allies often heard rumors in Paris that Kolchak's army would be in Moscow within a few weeks.[51] Kolchak's army never got near Moscow.

House noted that Bullitt had arrived in Paris. Bullitt told House everything that had transpired in Moscow. House admitted, "I can see a way out of that vexatious problem, that is, if we can get action by the Prime Minister and the President." He wrote, "I cautioned Bullitt against telling all he told me. . . . It is fear that will bring about a Russian settlement, not pity." He casually added, "While Bullitt was talking I was maturing plans which I shall begin to put in execution tomorrow."[52] He was preparing the Nansen scheme if Bullitt failed. The next morning he met with Vittorio Orlando, the Italian prime minister, and tried Bullitt's plan on him. Amazingly, "it succeeded admirably." House told Orlando that "Russia had become orderly and wanted to resume relations with the outside world." He suggested a treaty be drawn up on the Allies' terms and sent to Moscow. Nothing was said of a conference. To House's astonishment, Orlando agreed. But when House telephoned Wilson about this, the president was "against taking up this question at present." House blamed it on Wilson's "one track mind."[53]

Drummond suggested that if "the Bolshevik proposals brought by Mr. Bullitt are adopted many difficulties now encountered by the Conference will be solved." There would be modifications, but because of the Bolsheviks' position in Central Europe, it was Drummond's hope that a way might be found to accept the proposals. His reasons were simple and direct: Germany could no longer threaten a Bolshevik alliance if she disliked the Allied terms; the Baltic states could establish governments free of interference; future incidents such as the Hungarian would be eliminated; and, most important, Europe and Asia would be stabilized. Drummond did not refer to debts or concessions, two items Lenin was willing to compromise on. House might have been leaning in Bullitt's direction. Auchincloss reported the colonel's view that "we must in some way get in touch with the Soviet Government and present to them an armistice drawn up to suit ourselves."[54]

Lansing continued to dislike Bullitt's proposal. But then Bullitt was a radical, sympathetic to socialism. He "told of conditions which he painted rather rosily and praised the Bolshevik Lenine. Slid over terrible conditions and laid most everything on disorganized transportation."[55]

House was sufficiently encouraged that he took the Russian question up with the president, but he ran into problems: "I am trying something out that is workable," he lamented. "It is very difficult because no one wanted to deal with such as Lenine and Trotsky." This was evident in the president's suggestion that House "talk to Hoover and Robinson of the shipping board and see whether we could get ships and food to Russia in the event we wished to do so." Both, reported House, thought something in terms of food relief could be done within sixty days.[56]

In the United States the Bullitt mission had no support. As early as March 24 the *New York Tribune* carried an article, "Wilson sees Russia by Steffens' Eyes." It called Bullitt a "preacher of radicalism and a new social order" whose trip had been the result of State Department secrecy, and said that Steffens was acting as the "eyes and ears" of the president in Europe. The article claimed that the Allies were notified of the trip, "the subject of an explanation at the Hotel Crillon as the result of adverse criticism regarding its nature."[57] The record did not indicate who gave the explanation, but some felt "It was undoubtedly Colonel House." The *New York Sun* stated that Wilson was considering the Bullitt-Steffens plan favoring negotiations with Lenin and that the Big Four would follow along with Wilson's decision. The *New York Evening Post* of March 28 and the *New York Times* of March 29 both noted that the Bolsheviks requested recognition and, in a separate article by Charles Albert Selden of the *Times,* related a plan for dealing with the Bolsheviks. Richard V. Oulahan emphasized that Bullitt had given the Soviets a "clean bill of health" and that Lenin would have to be called to Paris before peace could be established.[58]

Tumulty's cable to Wilson on April 2, 1919, pointed out what was obvious: "The proposed recognition of Lenine has caused consternation here."[59] Tumulty's annoyance was due to George Rothwell Brown's article in the *Washington Post.* Brown thought that Lloyd George had decided on de facto recognition of the Soviets, that Clemenceau and Orlando opposed this, and that Wilson was in a halfway position. If recognition were conceded, Brown cautioned, Soviet embassies and legations everywhere would be centers of subversion. The article provoked "two scathing editorials" in the *Post* entitled "Proposed Recognition of Lenine" and "No Dealings with the Enemy." The first explored the dangers of de facto recognition while the second accused "treacherous Americans" of forwarding Lenin's cause and stated that such persons were defectives, "veritable birds of prey."[60]

Wilson received two long reports on the Hungarian crisis. One, from Lansing, emphasized the Bolshevik danger in Hungary and its effect in Germany; the other, from Bliss, cautioned the president on any kind of intervention in Hungary that could imply intervention in Russia.[61] The effect can be seen in House's diary. When he spoke with Lloyd George, the prime minister "scarcely touched upon the Russian question" except to delay any action until a "more matured plan" could be considered. The latter plan was none other than the Hoover-Nansen food-for-Russia scheme, which House talked over with Hoover that same day, in which neutrals would take the lead, on the condition that the Bolsheviks would accept a cease-fire on all fronts.[62]

An indication of just how quickly the Bullitt proposal was disappearing came when Lord Cecil related how Hoover stopped by with a memorandum he had handed the president, which Cecil summarized: it was useless to attack Bolshevism by force; it would be desirable for a neutral commission of, say, Swedes and Norwegians, perhaps Nansen and Karl H. Branting, to be consulted along the lines of the former Belgian Relief Commission for sending food into Russia if the fighting stopped; the president should publicly explain the "disastrous nature of Bolshevism, and the chaos and starvation which it had produced."[63]

Russians in Paris had already prodded Nansen to do something. He and McCormick discussed the issue. Cecil related that what Hoover had in mind was a Russian relief commission along the lines of his previously successful Belgian one. The president now had another alternative, especially if he did not wish to accept Bullitt's proposal on the one extreme or Foch's solution on the other: "an idea he has of forming a new Grand Armee to invade Russia," Cecil had related to Lloyd George, "and because neither Clemenceau nor Wilson nor Orlando nor myself could agree to it he sulked."[64]

Though Wilson steadfastly refused to see Bullitt, the latter's negotiation continued to concern him.[65] On March 31, thanks to Lansing's note and enclosure, the "Memorandum from the Russia Section," a unit consisting of Robert H. Lord, Chairman, Bullitt, and Captain Pettit reached the president's office. It started from the proposition that a continuing failure to deal with the Russian problem endangered the peace process. It made arguments in favor of a declaration to Soviet Russia; the German government might turn Germany over to the Spartacist-Bolshevik bloc just as the Karolyi government had done in Hungary; since no military barrier separated Germany or Hungary from Bolshevik troops, it was necessary to make an armistice, isolating Russia from Europe; a presidential declaration in favor of an armistice would go far in securing one. The independence of Estonia, Latvia, and Lithuania ought to be recognized in principle.[66]

Wilson never saw the memorandum, as House buried it. Wilson was in no mood to act on Bullitt's proposals. He needed Lloyd George's support. The prime minister did not have the public's or Parliament's support. Later Lloyd George told the Parliament that no approaches had been made: "We have had no approaches of any sort or kind." Articles by Steed may have cooled Lloyd George. Lloyd George's remarks were disingenuous. Bullitt did have breakfast with him and discussed the proposal.[67] Lloyd George's trial balloon had failed.

No one spoke of the Bullitt mission in the Council of Ten. House abandoned the proposal in favor of the food-relief scheme. He drafted a letter for the president's signature favoring the Nansen idea. Nansen called the president's attention to his idea of a "purely humanitarian Commission." The president asked for a program "without thought of political, military or financial advantage." Auchincloss and Hoover, at the colonel's urging, arranged for Nansen to send the president the letter. On April 6 Bullitt asked Wilson for fifteen minutes, a request denied. Bullitt prepared a telegram for Chicherin begging for a ten-day extension, but he never sent it. He suggested sending a cable hinting at food relief, to go out on the tenth.

In anger Bullitt resigned from the peace commission and told reporters that he would go to the Riviera, lie on the sand, and watch the world go to hell.[68]

President Wilson had considered three initiatives to solve "the Russian problem": Prinkipo, Bullitt, and Nansen. Each one failed. Only a White victory or truce in the Russian civil war could secure a possible return to Russian democracy. The price for either a victory or a truce was massive Allied aid in the form of arms and men. Europe was drained. America had to supply the aid. President Wilson was determined to see if Admiral Kolchak could secure Siberia on his own before America committed any substantial aid.

Eight

The First Cold Warriors

It was a short move from Wilson's Parisian disappointments in solving "the Russian problem" to his refusal to recognize Bolshevik Russia and to wait until it reformed or collapsed. The Wilson administration withdrew from intervention. There were no promises, no attempts at inside pressure along the lines suggested by General Judson, Raymond Robins, or William Bullitt. A diplomatic position consisting of outside pressure on Bolshevism to cease terrorism at home and propaganda abroad arose.

President Wilson had to be sure that Admiral Kolchak, the supreme ruler of Siberia, had no hope of defeating the Bolsheviks or establishing a stable government in Siberia that was secure from Moscow.[1] The president sent a high-level team to Omsk, capital of Kolchak's Siberian republic, to assess the likelihood of the admiral's success against the Bolsheviks before Wilson granted him substantial American aid. After the admiral failed, the Wilson administration chose an American policy of nonrecognition and quarantine of Soviet Russia. For the Wilsonians, the Bolsheviks either had to become honorable democrats or Soviet power had to collapse before the United States would recognize Russia. Thus, from August 1920 until November 1933, America's first cold warriors conducted a cold war with Soviet Russia.

1.

A Senate resolution in late June requested that the president inform it of "reasons for sending United States soldiers to Siberia, what duties are there to be performed by these soldiers, how long they are to remain, and generally to advise the Senate of the policy of the United States Government in respect to Siberia and the maintenance of United States soldiers therein." No sooner had Wilson arrived home from Paris than Baker reminded him that the resolution awaited an answer.[2]

At the same time, the adjutant general asked Major General William S. Graves to concentrate his forces in Siberia in order to minimize losses. Ambassador Roland S. Morris was preparing to proceed to Omsk, Kolchak's Siberian capital, with Graves "to carry out special mission directed by the President, leaving Tokio about July 7." Graves responded that a railroad strike prevented the trip: "I consider the present time inopportune for the trip to Omsk."[3]

In Wilson's League speech to the Senate, at the press conference afterwards, and in news reports, almost nothing was said of Russia. It was only alluded to in relation to Polish oppression. At the press conference, a reporter asked if Germany would be free to trade with Russia when the blockade was lifted; the president answered yes. Newspapers remained silent. Only the newly formed nations of Eastern Europe were discussed as well as the Shantung and Irish questions.[4]

"The Russian problem" remained, and the president was under some duress to answer the Senate's resolution concerning the presence of American troops in Russia. Resolution No. 13 had been introduced by Senator Hiram W. Johnson of California on December 12, 1918, and reported back as amended on May 20, 1919, then passed on June 27.[5] Between then and the president's reply on July 22, a considerable amount of Russian business occurred.

The first Russian item that Polk presented was a request to send five thousand tons of flour to Archangel from the Grain Corporation, to be paid for from the revolving fund for rationing northern Russia, to which $5 million had been originally allotted. Not only did Polk think that there was a moral obligation to continue assistance but also that "from a political point of view it is obviously unwise to let North Russia revert to Bolshevism through starvation, especially in view of Mr. Hoover's undertaking to supply Petrograd upon the overthrow of the Bolsheviki." Wilson approved. Polk asked Morris for his views on a comprehensive plan for "economic reconstruction in Siberia and ultimately for European Russia." Frank Polk requested Morris to consult with John F. Stevens, head of the Allied technical commission, and C. H. Smith, representative on the Inter-Allied Committee. Polk presumed that the president would submit such a plan to Congress.[6]

At last, Morris and Graves set out for Omsk to speak with Kolchak. Polk sent Wilson a revised policy regarding relations with the Omsk government, which the president had previously worked on with Vance McCormick: selling Kolchak on a credit basis army surplus, but with no recognition, formal or informal. It would furnish Kolchak with 200,000 uniforms, 500,000 rounds of cartridges, 2,000 machine guns, 400 heavy guns, 135 airplanes, and tanks. Polk hoped that American assistance would broaden to include food and medical supplies, along with technical assistance.[7]

Map 3: Siberia and Manchuria Insert

The State Department counseled a more active policy, while the War Department pressed the president to evacuate Russia. General Bliss and Secretary of War Baker were adamant on the subject, while Secretary of State Lansing and Frank Polk leaned in the opposite direction. Even when it was clear that troops were to be withdrawn from Archangel in July, Polk advised that one American warship be left to "make the withdrawal of our land forces from North Russia appear less pointed and abrupt." Wilson agreed.[8]

As the Czechs prepared to depart, the Council of Five asked Washington to secure the Trans-Siberian railway from Krasnoyarsk to Irkutsk. Bliss disagreed. Polk told the president that someone would have to guard that portion of the road, even as far west as Novosibirsk, and proposed that the Japanese do it. He pleaded for more medical supplies to Kolchak.[9]

Wilson's answer to the Senate gave a justification for troops. By then, Americans had departed from northern Russia and only two cruisers remained. The resolution had asked the president for the reason that he had sent soldiers to Siberia, the duties they were to perform, time there, how they were to be maintained, and what the policy was.[10] Wilson's reply told nothing of maintenance or time.

The reason for intervention, according to the president, was to defend the Czechoslovaks against German prisoners of war. Wilson made a case for helping them against that threat and for reestablishing law and order in Siberia. Ten thousand American soldiers were in Siberia by July 1919. The first contingents had arrived in September 1918, but the war was over in November 1918. The German threat against Czechs and Russians was thus over. Trade and aid would help. These required Siberian railroads. The Stevens Commission was revived in March 1918 and by February 1919 it operated under the Inter-Allied Committee. The crux of intervention had shifted from securing Czech withdrawal to defense of American railway engineers by doughboys. Intervention was nonpolitical, though it was recognized that Kolchak was the beneficiary. "All elements of the population in Siberia," the president said, "look to the United States for assistance." Nothing was mentioned of Bolsheviks. The Senate remained suspicious.[11]

The president's response was not borne out either by events or by reports from Siberia. The League of Nations debate spread to considerations of Russia as it was pointed out that it took the president more than three weeks to respond to Senator Johnson. Senator Henry Cabot Lodge of Massachusetts, chair of the foreign relations committee, complained that never since the Cleveland administration had the Senate's requests for information been treated in such "cavalier fashion."[12]

Wilson had stated the plan: Graves and ten thousand infantry, two companies of volunteer railway troops stationed around Vladivostok to help keep the Trans-Siberian railway open, humanitarian aid to Russians. The Senate fretted over the situation of the Czechs, whom Wilson had originally said were his reason for intervention. Did the Czechs need further aid? Were Americans really being used to defeat Bolshevism? Alternatively, were these American contingents there to offset Japanese influence? Was it because of some combination of these and other unspecified reasons that Wilson did not elaborate? Senators were puzzled by the Siberian situation and concerned that American soldiers were not rapidly withdrawn. The expected evacuation date of a few weeks was stretched. Not until October 1920 did the last contingent leave Russia.[13]

The day the president's message was read, he discussed the Czechs with Lansing. When he suggested that it might be better to send them through Bolshevik Russia, Lansing told him they would be murdered. This brought up the question of the safety of the Trans-Siberian railway. Lansing gave Wilson two cables. The first complained of Cossack interference and upheld the principle that only railway officials should operate the railway and that they would act solely under the Inter-Allied Committee with no interference from any Russian governmental agency. The second was a sharply worded telegram from Stevens: "It will be unfortunate if Japanese are utilized to take the place of Czechs guarding railway. Japanese preponderance and domination should be lessened rather than increased."[14]

In Siberia, all cables relating to the Trans-Siberian railway referred to difficulties resulting from American assessment of relations with Kolchak and policy toward Japanese intervention. In July and August, Morris went to Omsk with Graves. During that trip, the ambassador cabled Washington on the mounting crisis at Omsk.

Morris reported on July 10 that he had arrived in Vladivostok and would proceed to Omsk with Graves. Ernest L. Harris, consul general at Irkutsk, was already there. The president had ordered Morris to gain information about Kolchak's efforts to democratize his government, especially his proclaiming "order, liberty, and justice, promising to step down with the defeat of the Bolsheviks, and calling for a Constituent Assembly at that time."[15]

Wilson not only wanted the impressions of Morris and Graves; they also must convey to the Omsk government that though the United States took a sympathetic interest, America could not recognize Kolchak. Polk added restoration of the railroads: "your views as to a comprehensive plan for economic reconstruction in Siberia and ultimately for European Russia." Morris was to consult Stevens and stay in touch with the situation because "it is hoped the President will ask Congress for adequate appropriation in order to translate into action the genuine desire to assist the Russian people."[16]

Morris and Graves arrived July 22. Morris assumed that America would help to save Kolchak. The news he sent was discouraging: "I find the situation here extremely critical." Kolchak's Siberian army was demoralized and thousands of railway cars filled with White refugees were pouring eastward from areas surrounding Ekaterinburg and Cheliabinsk. He had expected to see strong sentiment in favor of Kolchak and anti-Bolshevik feelings. Instead, Kolchak failed to command anyone's loyalty except that of a small group of reactionaries, especially army officers of the old type. If the Czechs withdrew, that would be a signal for a "formidable anti-Kolchak if not pro-Bolshevik uprising in every town on the railway from Irkutsk to Omsk." Kolchak's failure to win support was due to the population's distrust of his Cossack leaders, the inability of civil and military officials to adapt to popular sentiment, the lack of measures to meet financial and economic conditions, peasants' resentment of conscription, and suppression of all local self-government.[17]

Morris met Kolchak's minister of foreign affairs, Ivan Sukine, who admitted to the seriousness of the situation. Sukine played on efforts of the Japanese to hold eastern Siberia, to control Semënov, and to discredit American activities. He pointed to the difficulties that would occur when the Czechs pulled out. Morris discussed the problems involved in producing a plan for the "strengthening and broadening of the Admiral's Government."[18]

Washington wanted the truth. Lansing sent Baker a message confirming the fact that the United States still recognized Boris Bakhmetev as ambassador and that Russia was legally a cobelligerent and eligible to purchase surplus war matériel with credits from the War Department. Lansing pressed Morris for his assessment: "definite misapprehensions it has received from reports by Harris, Hardley, Embry, Dr. Teusler, Major Emerson and other returning Americans." Lansing was interested in support for Kolchak west of Irkutsk and Kolchak's suppression of local government. Just how well-disposed Lansing was toward Kolchak, despite negative reports, could be summed up in his comment to Morris: "The Department has had the opinion the Kolchak reverses were result of over-extension and that present weakness is due to Kolchak supporters having placed almost entire emphasis on military effort. It would seem that no Government in Russia can survive except by demonstrating its power to give better conditions of general welfare than the Bolsheviki are affording."[19]

Morris's expedition to Omsk was important, not only as evidenced in Lansing's remarks to Baker but also in his comments to Morris on the State Department's attitude to Kolchak. The department had excused Kolchak's failures. The president telephoned Lansing to discuss Morris's "adverse report on Koltchak." He was referring to Morris's reports of July 22. Lansing's comments reflected the president's desire for information as well as his own tendency to be optimistic about Kolchak's reverses. Wilson directed that the State Department make Morris's reports available to the Supreme War Council. Philip Kerr wrote the prime minister regarding Morris's evaluations: "It is not a very pretty picture and the whole situation is evidently going to present considerable difficulty in the future." However, in Kerr's opinion, it was an American and Japanese problem only. As to the Japanese threat, Lansing played it down: "I have little patience with these people who are forever on the verge of hysterics about the deep and wicked schemes of Japan. They imagine some of the most preposterous things and report them as facts."[20]

Graves also reported, and Baker made this material available to the president. He had discovered that guarding the railroads was difficult because Russian soldiers were bitter toward the neutral position of American soldiers. General Dmitri L. Horvath, general manager of the Chinese Eastern

Railway and acting head of the Inter-Allied Railway Committee, blocked efforts to enforce security. Kolchak controlled supplies and transport of persons. He cheated the peasantry of food. "I am convinced in my own mind," Graves said, "that there is no possibility of settling this trouble by such oppressive, unjust and inhumane actions as are being committed by the Koltchak [*sic*] representatives here in Eastern Siberia." As to Grigorii Semënov, the Cossack leader, Graves stated, "In my judgment, Semenoff will have to be eliminated before the railroad can operate satisfactorily." Semënov's troops lived "by graft, theft, and money received from the Japanese." The Japanese controlled him, and "Semenoff is doing exactly what they want him to do."[21]

When Omsk called in the Kerensky rubles because the Bolsheviks were flooding European Russia with them, an immense number came from Vladivostok. General Graves concluded that this was not unexpected because Vladivostok was a center of corruption. Army officers without visible means of support lavished money on living in a high style. "If this money comes from the Omsk government, there is an immense leak somewhere." There was a large amount of propaganda in Siberia against the United States, probably directed by former German agents. "There is no question in my mind that these German representatives, the Japanese military, and the Russian army officer class, with a few exceptions, have an understanding as to their course of action." The propaganda insulted American soldiers, claimed Americans attacked them, and used "false and incorrect reports" sent out from Japanese headquarters.[22]

Graves brought up the painful relationship between himself and General Knox, now head of the British military mission in Siberia. He recalled that the British took credit for calling the Kolchak government into being by quoting a statement of Winston Churchill in the House of Commons on June 6. Knox and the British mission had taken a prominent role. He had "no hesitancy in expressing openly his antagonism to President Wilson's views . . . General Knox evidently thinks that the Ambassador in Tokio and I are responsible for the policy of the United States in Siberia." Knox asked John K. Caldwell, U.S. consul in Vladivostok, to "send a cablegram requesting that both of us be removed, as we were not representing the views of the United States." Graves asked Colonel John A. C. Somerville, who represented the British mission, to stop this "pin-pricking." This complaint got back to Knox, and he answered, "I was reported as having gone to Caldwell and said 'what a pity for America that you have such a rotten fellow as Graves for your representative out here.' . . . I write to you on Major Slaughter's advice to tell you that I never said anything of the sort to Caldwell." Knox continued, "I told Caldwell that I wished our Governments would come to some sort of agreement as to policy and give us instructions recalling either you or me if necessary."[23]

It was clear that the American task of guarding a portion of the rail-roads was compromised by Omsk, particularly by its military personnel and by Semënov, the duplicitous role of the Japanese, negative propaganda, corruption, and incompatible aims of Britain and America. Not only was Lansing wrong in thinking the Japanese benign but also Kerr was naive in thinking Siberia someone else's problem. The president was aware of these difficulties, as is clear in his remark to Baker: "Thank you very much for sending me Graves' report of June 21. You may be sure I shall give it a most careful reading."[24]

Morris met with Kolchak, who admitted that no new points were brought out in their talk. The admiral asserted that his sole objective was overthrow-ing the Bolsheviks; his government was provisional. Though the Russian people must accomplish this overthrow, he was in need of Allied assistance, especially in guarding the railroads. This would guarantee supplies; cred-its would enable his government to purchase aid and equipment. Kolchak recognized demoralization but attributed it to the sufferings of war and rev-olution. He approved "any plan of Allied supervision which would assure an honest distribution of the supplies which might be furnished." Kolchak backed Morris's suggestion that a plan be established. Morris thought a plan had to include the effective role of the Inter-Allied Committee, the guarding of the railroads, including the Czech question, military supplies and credits, commercial relief, Red Cross work, resolution of the German and Austrian prisoners of war problem, and a bill of rights for Siberians. He assumed that the action of the Supreme War Council in Paris pitted the United States and its associates against Bolshevism, and that therefore there was reason to hope Kolchak would survive with Allied aid. Because of this hope, Morris believed the United States was prepared to help if practicable.[25]

Morris discussed the railways with the Minister of Ways and Communi-cations. Problems remained: refusal of the Japanese authorities to protect representatives of the Technical Board, which was under Stevens's direction but was nominally directed by the Inter-Allied Committee, from carrying out duties; interference of military authorities in the operation by the rail-roads; rejection of railway personnel of the Technical Board's directions. This meeting included Sukine as well as the general in charge of military transportation and all key foreign representatives. They agreed on mea-sures to prevent interference: they required the military to get the Omsk government's Russian Railway Administration's approval to use the rails; that the railway administration would take its instructions only from the

Inter-Allied Technical Committee and all Russian laws in conflict with it would be removed; all Russian and other troops in the railway guard would support the Railway Administration; and the Technical Board and Military Committee would move to Omsk. Even the Japanese agreed to bring their present instructions into harmony with the agreed-upon measures.[26]

The Czech army was to be evacuated from Vladivostok. Given this decision, as well as the fact that Kolchak's troops could not be spared from the front, Morris estimated that the Allies would have to provide a guard of three divisions of infantry, a division of cavalry, three batteries of artillery, and forty thousand soldiers to replace the Czechs. Only Japan and America were in a position to consider such a request, and no arrangement with Japan would work unless the United States provided at least half of these troops. Morris asked that the United States "assume our full share of the protection which any further effort to help Russia necessarily involves, et cetera."[27] He reasoned that if this action were not taken, the Japanese would accomplish in Siberia what they had in China. "We cannot," he said, "meet this conspiracy and enforce the 'Open Door,' necessary for the economic salvation of Russia, merely by frank discussions and formal protests in Tokyo. We must speak our determined purpose in the only language the Japanese military clique can understand." This great number of troops would impress the Cossacks and others that the United States meant to protect American agencies at work in Siberia. All American aid to Siberia depended on the Czechs, but the war was over and it was not fair to ask them to remain. Morris concluded, "If our Government decides to adopt a comprehensive plan of help for Russia, including the further supervision of the railways, control over the distribution of supplies, Red Cross work, educational and agricultural assistance, we must have an adequate military police to protect these agencies until better order prevails."[28]

Morris sent cables describing frank discussions with Maurice Janin, the French general at Omsk, who had been designated supreme commander of the Czech army, and General Knox, commander of British forces in Siberia. Both, according to Morris, stated with brutal frankness the difficulties they had encountered over the last months in delivering supplies to Kolchak. They characterized Kolchak's army staff and supply departments as "completely disorganized, inefficient, corrupt and unsettled; that personal ambition, jealousy and intrigue prevailed; and that repeated appeals to the Admiral to correct the abuses had been without result because in their judgment he was powerless to act." Supervision and control over distribution and even organization of the army might be necessary. Morris was willing to grant that supervision over distribution of supplies was necessary, but not army organization, as that would involve "far-reaching obligations and create difficulties which in my judgment would be fatal to the success of the Kolchak movement." In another cable, he dealt with financing the Chinese Eastern and Trans-Siberian railways. The former paid for itself out of its receipts, but the latter, operating from Manchuria to the Urals, showed large deficits. Morris noted that a committee had been formed to report on this.[29]

Morris now assessed financial conditions and "personnel, the spirit and purposes, the efficiency and the present strength of the Kolchak government."[30] His reports gave a striking insight into Siberia's problems and a view to their solution with American help. The assessment started with Kolchak, whom he found honest and courageous but limited in experience of affairs, narrow in his views, and a poor administrator. He seemed oblivious to political and economic dangers, and had little knowledge of the army or experience with it. If this were not bad enough, Kolchak's ministers and staff were even less impressive. In the council of ministers, the acting minister of foreign affairs, Sukine, was the ablest. Mikhailov, minister of finance, knew nothing of finance. The civilian council members were earnest, politically moderate, but inefficient. Of military members, "nothing favorable can be said."[31] They were intolerant, reactionary, and corrupt. Morris believed that "The spirit and purposes of the Kolchak government are, I believe, moderately liberal and progressive." The military was reactionary. The problem was not spirit or purpose, but "utter lack of experience and efficiency." There was no civil administration; though ministers were clever in creating plans, they were incapable of carrying out a single detail. Because the government was unrepresentative, it had lost all contact with the population.

This ineptitude offered the military its opportunity to seize power, but in its zeal to raise a large army for the front, it had not considered the rear. This had resulted in a collapse, except for the Allied effort, with Czech support, to maintain the transport system. "To the mistakes of military policy must be added an incredible amount of corruption among individual officials which Kolchak has not seriously attempted to correct or punish." Kolchak's only strengths were honesty of purpose and patriotic motives against the current intrigue and corruption all around him. He had the support of Britain and France. There was no other alternative to him. As Morris had to admit, it looked "doubtful whether the Government can survive the present crisis . . . I find myself hoping that Kolchak will hold out long enough to permit the Allied Governments to give him the support and assistance which he will need and thus enable him to build on broader and sounder foundations."[32]

Morris expanded on his guarded optimism. Though Kolchak's government could not now withstand Bolshevism, "drastic changes in its personnel and methods would render it equal to such a task." He emphasized that it had to modify or control reactionaries, guarantee personal security, end speculation, and create a popularly elected council of peasant representatives. If it could survive its present crisis, it might reform, but it would be a long and arduous task.[33]

The State Department took a direct approach with Bakhmetev, who now represented the Omsk government in Washington. When on August 1 he called at the State Department, Long told him it was time to "speak to him very frankly and freely . . . that Mr. Morris' reports were not most encouraging; that the railroad situation and the conditions of its management had to be changed somewhat; that the populace in Siberia did not seem to be enthusiastically in favor of Kolchak." Long felt it a mistake to give Semënov the rank of full general. This would enable Semënov to interfere even more with Allied operation of the railroads. Kolchak seemed to be "approaching a crisis; that the only alternative to Kolchak was Bolshevism; and that there was a limit to the aid and assistance which we could give." He complained that Graves criticized Kolchak's military manner of controlling the railroads and the shipment of supplies and transport of persons. He mentioned abuses to persons. He thought that "such conditions made it almost impossible for the American and Allied representatives to deal with the situation." Bakhmetev confessed knowledge of this situation. Long continued, "unless such practice changed it would be almost impossible for us to be of any real assistance, because the ordinary peasants in Siberia would think that we were assisting the military authorities, even though they did represent Kolchak."[34]

Even with all the criticism, there was no one else to turn to in the struggle with Bolshevism, which the administration considered the greater evil and not likely to go away soon. The administration wanted to help Kolchak, but its counsels were divided. Morris and Graves told of Kolchak's liabilities and the great risks in getting further involved. Lansing continued to put pressure on the president to make a "frank declaration" against Bolshevik doctrines. Lansing even called on the president to do more than just issue declarations, to "assume the leadership against it to which your position and record entitle you." Concerning his advice, Lansing noted, "Wrote letter to Pres't urging him to attack Bolshevist movement. Sent him [DeWitt] Poole's memorandum." Lansing told Wilson that it might be useful as the basis for a presidential statement and serve as a way to clarify the "uncertainty in the attitude of the United States" toward Russia.[35]

Lansing's pleading for a "frank declaration" and Poole's statements of August 7 and August 21, 1919, were not lost on the president: "Thank you sincerely for having let me see the enclosed."[36]

Poole talked about the uncertainty in the attitude of the United States: "A statement from the President would have great moral weight." In his first draft of August 7, rushed to Wilson by Lansing, Poole vividly described the virulent Bolshevik propaganda of violence and unreason aimed at subverting foreign governments and provoking worldwide revolution. The Bolsheviks could not be counted on to honor their treaty commitments, and they followed a foreign policy of opportunism. They carried out a destructive reign of terror mainly against the middle classes, discriminated in food distribution, misgoverned the country, and produced economic ruin. Poole was concerned over the fate of Poland and the other newly created states in Eastern Europe: "The success everywhere of the healthy democratic movements of the day is endangered by an insidious suggestion of violence and unreason emanating from Moscow." Poole advocated a policy of humanitarian relief with assurances of its reaching the needy and, at the same time, hastening the end of Bolshevism: "Support will continue to be given to such elements in Siberia and elsewhere as are working for the restoration of order throughout Russia and the setting up of government under adequate democratic guarantees. Material relief will be provided in every possible way for the population of regions liberated from Bolshevik domination. Private enterprise desiring to trade with these regions will have the cooperation of the Government."

Between Poole's draft and his completed statement, Morris summarized his conclusions: "extend, if the present critical situation is successfully met within the next month, formal recognition to Kolchak and his associates, as the Provisional Government of Russia. Without this recognition and the substantial assistance which it implies, the Kolchak government, even though it should survive the present military crisis, could not, in my judgment, continue to function much longer." Morris asked for the granting of credits amounting to $200 million and that tokens circulating in Siberia be exchanged for Russian bank notes. Such notes were being held in Vladivostok; the remainder was to be printed by the American BankNote Company to nine billion rubles. Morris wanted to keep communication from Vladivostok to Omsk open for supplies purchased by credits. It was essential to increase the Inter-Allied railway agreement, inspectors and supply, to at least forty thousand more troops, of which twenty-five thousand would be Americans to replace the Czechs; Morris wanted another $20 million credit for the Inter-Allied Railway Committee. He stressed honest and efficient use of the credits and supplies. It was important to organize an Allied military supply committee with three hundred inspectors to supervise materials and create a committee of commerce to supervise and distribute goods purchased under the credit. He asked for diplomatic representation.[37]

Morris supplemented his plan as a result of Kolchak's return from visiting his northern army. Kolchak had made changes in his army's command and had decided on a retreat from the Tobol to the Ishim River, 170 miles west of Omsk. The Admiral requested Allied confidence for three or four more weeks, continued shipment of supplies, particularly rifles, and the continuation of talks for a comprehensive plan of assistance. Morris asked that the United States do everything possible. He included a suggestion that Wilson send a "purely personal message" expressing confidence.[38]

With these suggestions pouring into the White House, there was one thing the president would not, given the atmosphere in Congress, do: send more troops. In response to a request from Clemenceau, Wilson informed the American mission in Paris that no additional troops would be sent. "In reply to Mr. Clemenceau's recent telegram to the President as to whether this Government is disposed to furnish the needed number of troops to replace Czecho-Slovaks when the latter are withdrawn from Siberia please say that, with the utmost regret, the President finds it impracticable to furnish additional American troops for this purpose." This message was conveyed to Morris on August 12.[39] It was the beginning of the end of America's support for Kolchak and of the Siberian intervention.

Morris suggested commodity credits, keeping the military force at current level, and maintenance of Red Cross work. He continued to emphasize the things needed most by Kolchak: troops, credits, and inspectors.[40] None of these was forthcoming.

2.

The Siberian muddle came to a crisis as the scene in Washington over ratification of the League of Nations treaty reached the boiling point, forcing Wilson into his western tour—a speaking tour to promote the treaty. In thirty-three speaking engagements, the president sometimes reflected on his disillusionment with Russia, though he did not argue that a powerful League with the United States in it would be a bulwark against Bolshevism, as others such as former president Taft and Republican Senator Porter J. McCumber of North Dakota did. In Kansas City he came close to calling his Senate opposition "bolshevistically inclined." He digressed on the tragedy of Russia, where men in control refused to seek a mandate. In Des Moines he asserted that the Russian people had been deceived when the Bolsheviks did not call an assembly to frame a constitution and were ruled by a "little group of men just as selfish, just as ruthless, just as pitiless, as the agents of the Czar himself." In Sioux Falls he declared that the "Lenine-

Trotsky government" was composed of only a few men, "yet they worked their will upon the millions." Such a government "based upon violence or the threats of violence must fail." The United States would be opposed to those who ruled by force. In Minneapolis he continued his theme: "They have permitted a little handful of men — I am told there are only thirty-four of them constituting the real Bolshevist government — to set up a minority government just as autocratic and just as cruelly unmerciful as the government of the Czar ever was." In St. Paul he called Russia "pitiable" and declared that its lesson was that nobody could be free when there was no public order or authority. The old, distinguished, and skillful autocracy had been replaced by an amateur handful who exercised, he said, "without the slightest compunction of mercy or pity the bloody terror that characterized the worst days of the Czar." In Bismarck, North Dakota, he declared that the United States "could do nothing for that unfortunate nation until it had purged itself of the leaders who were far worse than the Czar ever had been." In Billings, Montana, he renewed these themes and added that the Bolsheviks maintained the sword by feeding only those who would fight for them and letting the rest starve. He made a prophetic statement: "there will be many a bloody year, I am afraid, before she finds herself again." Speaking of Bolshevik propaganda, he characterized Lenin's followers: "To be a disciple of Lenin means to be a disciple of night, chaos, and disorder." In Coeur d'Alene, Idaho, he complained that the poison infecting Russia was spreading throughout Europe. In Seattle he called the Russians "lovable people" who, in their anxiety to rid themselves of the autocratic terror of the tsar, had come under the terror of a minority using "intrigue, terror, informing, spying, military power" who dared not call a Constituent Assembly.[41] These remarks reflected the mood of anticommunism sweeping the nation.

When the president's train arrived in Portland on September 15, shocking news reached him. William Bullitt had given testimony before Senator Henry Cabot Lodge's foreign relations committee. Bullitt had the "most intense and almost pathological hatred" of Wilson as well as being "this frustrated young man," according to Lansing. Perhaps his behavior could be excused as a "lack of proportion." Regardless, his testimony undid almost everything Wilson might have accomplished in his swing westward. It renewed the growing distrust between Wilson and Lansing. It certainly added to the despair of Wilson in his mission. Bullitt's most sensational revelation was Lansing's hostility to the League of Nations. In six weeks of hearings on the League treaty and testimony from sixty witnesses, Bullitt had served Lodge's purposes best by embarrassing the president. Bullitt maintained that Lansing, House, Bliss, and White were not enthusiastic about the treaty: "It is no secret that Mr. Lansing, Gen. Bliss, and Mr. Henry White objected very vigorously to the numerous provisions of the treaty." He added: "I do not think that Secretary Lansing is at all enthusiastic about the league of nations as it stands at present." A memo of a conversation Bullitt had had with Lansing supposedly stated that the secretary of state had said that if the Senate and the American people really understood the treaty, "it would unquestionably be defeated, but I wonder if they will ever understand what it lets them in for." Bullitt's report on Russia, however, was a side issue for the committee. Bullitt turned it over to Lodge, though Wilson had earlier requested that it remain undisclosed. Wilson concluded that "Lansing was undermining and upsetting morale. And now here was verification of everything that he had suspected. 'Think of it!' he exploded to Tumulty. 'This from a man whom I raised from the level of a subordinate to the great office of secretary of state of the United States.' "[42]

Lansing responded. He explained how distressed he was about Bullitt's testimony. He recounted events surrounding Bullitt's resignation from the peace commission. He said that certain features of the treaty were bad, but that that was unavoidable and ought not to prevent its signing. American membership in numerous European commissions of the League might doom the treaty, especially because Senators Philander Knox of Pennsylvania and Lodge would use these to prevent ratification. He called Bullitt's conduct "most despicable and outrageous." The president was so angry that he never responded to Lansing's memorandum. "I am convinced," wrote Tumulty, "that only the President's illness a few days later prevented an immediate demand on his part for the resignation of Mr. Lansing."[43]

Wilson arrived in San Francisco on September 16. In a luncheon address he mentioned that despite Russia's losses in the war exceeding any other nation's, "poor Russia . . . got nothing but terror and despair out of it all." He went to San Diego and Los Angeles. While still in San Diego on September 19, he received a telegram from Phillips recommending that Baker sell to Kolchak on credit shoes, underclothing, and overcoats, as the British were supplying the White General Anton Denikin and the French the Czechs. If America refused, Phillips thought, its position would not be understood and that would help the Japanese. Phillips ended on a positive note: "The latest reports we have from Siberia dated September 11 indicate Kolchak's forces have resumed the offensive and are driving the Bolsheviki back towards the Urals." Phillips had reported on Polk's cables urging immediate repatriation of the Czechoslovaks; to do so would require an additional $12 million in credits to the Czech government and the necessary tonnage for about fifty thousand men. This request was repeated in September by Senator Carter Glass of Virginia, and Wilson replied, "Entirely approve loan to Czecho-

Slovak Republic under conditions named in your telegram of today." He had the same telegram sent to Phillips.[44] The subject of Russia did not occur again as the presidential train turned east, to Salt Lake City, Cheyenne, and on to Denver and Pueblo.

While Wilson was on his western tour, Long dealt with "the Russian problem." He met frequently with Bakhmetev. The difficulties of cooperating with the Japanese had made it necessary for the department in early September to consider withdrawing from Siberia. In a sharply worded note for Morris to deliver to the Japanese foreign ministry, Lansing stated, "the only course practicable for the United States to pursue is an entire withdrawal from all further efforts to cooperate in Siberia to be followed if need be by a public statement of the reasons for such action since it might be misunderstood if no explanation is made." The Japanese question had so pestered the department that, even notwithstanding the very real Russian difficulties, it was found necessary to threaten a departure. That note to Tokyo brought Bakhmetev to Long's office promptly. Would America, he asked, really withdraw? Long said no but indicated that "if Japan would live up to her agreements that we would not necessarily withdraw; that we wanted to remain but could not be placed in the position of being responsible for a situation for which we were not actually accountable." Bakhmetev understood but asked if any assurances had been sent to Kolchak, to which Long told him that "a message of encouragement from the President . . . was to be orally communicated to Kolchak." Long went on: "I told him that we wanted to help Deniken [*sic*] and Yudinich [*sic*] and any other movements on the soil of the old Russian empire which might be strongly against Bolshevism."[45]

The British noted that America was pursuing its Siberian policy more vigorously and attributed this to the aggressive Japanese policy aimed at excluding American influence. The Japanese chargé in Washington left two notes at the State Department. The first claimed that Mongolia and Manchuria were out of the operation of the Allied consortium and the second objected to Lansing's note to Tokyo. Japan thought it should have been advised informally.[46]

The British thought that enough was enough. A War Cabinet meeting on September 18 decided on the amount of "assistance in personnel, materials, and stores that should be given to General Anton Denikin, leader of the Whites in southern Russia, as the final contribution of the British Government to his cause in the struggle against the Soviet Government." House wired the State Department not to expect the great powers to meet in Paris without the heads of government there to handle the Russian situation, but that the foreign offices of each power had to deal with it on their own. The

British were proceeding in this direction. At the War Cabinet meeting, it was decided not to exceed £3 million for winding up the commitment of supplies to Denikin from existing stocks without replacement. A time limit would be placed on volunteers in service with the British mission in southern Russia. Lloyd George warned Churchill on October 10 not to promise Kolchak a decided effort by the United States to help his armies. Such a statement would irritate the Americans and would be used by Kolchak.[47]

On November 4 it was reported at a British cabinet meeting that General Denikin had been notified that after March 31, 1920, he would have to consider himself "self-supporting" and purchase his own supplies. In referring to its general Russian policy, the cabinet concluded, "the British Government were not out to destroy a revolutionary government in Russia, and had supported Admiral Kolchak and General Denikin because they had called their forces into being during the latter part of the war." British policy had been, the cabinet noted, an effort to get the "Americans and Japanese to be responsible for supporting the anti-Bolshevist forces in this theatre." The British cabinet meeting on December 15, 1919, let pass as an appendix to its transcript the policies decided at the Conferences of the Allied and Associated Powers and the British and French Governments held at 10 Downing Street: not to enter into any further commitments, yet to allow the purchase of war matériel by the anti-Bolshevists; each power to be free to leave or maintain its missions and "to leave Bolshevist Russia, as it were, within a ring fence"; to help to maintain a strong Poland; to call no conference of the anti-Bolshevist states for the time being; and to assist the border states in maintaining their freedom.[48] It was clear, therefore, that Britain, France, and the Associated Powers were washing their hands of Russia. The notion of a "ring fence" almost hinted at a British-style version of a containment policy.

The State Department was in despair over Siberia, which had, in Long's terms, "more or less blown up." He complained that Graves had sent a note to Omsk in "flagrant violation" of his jurisdiction and that the department was recommending his recall—nothing came of that—and that Morris's reports were "mixed," evidently referring to his change of heart to Kolchak. He was ordered to turn the remaining rifles over to Kolchak. Graves sent another scathing report on Kolchak and the Japanese to General March.[49]

Not until September 26 did Kolchak decide to call a zemstvo [land] council. Phillips reported on it to Wilson. Polk asked whether recognition was decided on. These last-ditch signs had no resonance in the Department of State. On September 30 Lansing had a conference with Long and Baker on the question of Siberia. They agreed to bring the troops home at the earliest possible moment, get the Czechs out, and arrive at some understanding with the Japanese concerning the railroads. Payment was arranged for the Czechs and German war prisoners, and the necessary tonnage was allotted. Lansing noted, "I favor strongly withdrawal of our troops and repatriation of Czechs, German and Austrian prisoners."[50] The fates of Kolchak and Denikin were sealed by actions in London and Washington. Russia would be left behind a "ring fence."

As a result of his massive stroke on October 2, 1919, the decline of the president until his last cabinet meeting of March 1, 1921, was steep and swift. Lansing wrote to Polk, admitting how distressing the Russian situation was because of "the illness of the President and his inability to take part in public affairs." When Wilson finally returned from his sickbed in January, Lansing characterized him as irritable, insolent, and resentful. In a letter to Wilson, Lansing admitted that it was true that he had held cabinet meetings. Lansing ended by saying, "I am of course ready, Mr. President, to relieve you of any embarrassment by placing my resignation in your hands." Wilson took advantage of this offer on February 11. Lansing tendered his resignation the next day.[51]

Lansing's resignation caused public indignation. He reflected on the reasons for it, one of them being "that I was running foreign affairs as I pleased." The president needed a lame duck secretary and on February 25 announced the nomination of Bainbridge Colby, a New York lawyer with no diplomatic experience. Wilson explained and justified his nomination to Polk: "[he] believes in the things that we believe in and really believes in them." House wrote that former Secretary of Agriculture David E. Houston had stopped by and that he had remarked, "He considers Alexander, new Secretary of Commerce, totally unfit for that place. He has an even stronger feeling as to the unfitness of Colby."[52]

Colby did not break new ground on Russia. He summarized the direction in which Russian-American relations had been headed under Lansing, especially when the Whites' cause had evidently been lost. It had been clear to Wilson and Lansing when they were in Paris that America could not for the foreseeable future deal with the Soviets. They had an inkling of this during the "watch-and-wait" days of "doing nothing" and only "trivial intercourse" with the Bolsheviks in November and December 1917. The recall of General Judson, the reluctance to use Raymond Robins, and the Bolsheviks' rejection of Wilson's initiatives indicated that the United States would have no truck with the Soviet government.

Russian affairs had continued despite Wilson's illness. During October, with the president close to death, key questions on the crisis in Russia arose and drifted as Dr. Grayson, Wilson's personal physician, and the president's wife, Edith Bolling Galt, received these questions but did not, and could not, respond. The ever-present Japanese problem persisted despite the ranting and raving of the State Department to the Japanese embassy and Morris's complaints to the Japanese foreign office. Graves repeatedly complained of Russian soldiers interfering with his operations in Vladivostok and the Cossacks in eastern Siberia doing so with the support of the Japanese. These complaints reached Grayson by way of Baker, but nothing could happen. Baker thought that U.S. troops either should be increased or withdrawn, that either the United States would open the Siberian door or the Japanese would close it. Lansing noted, "Secy Baker to say Grayson had read memo on Siberia who said we must insist on reply from Japan." There was no answer to Baker's two alternatives, and Lansing and Baker were exactly where they were before submitting the question to Grayson. General March told Graves that the president was too ill and the State Department would take up the question with the British ambassador, Sir Edward Grey. And that was where the matter remained.[53]

There was pressure from all sides to recognize Kolchak, but Lansing remained opposed and preferred to await developments. When Bakhmetev came to Long pleading for more troops, the answer was no. Hope ran high that Denikin might succeed and there was some talk of feeding northern Russia, including Petrograd. Finally, the question of a statement by the president on Bolshevism using Poole's memo turned up again at a cabinet meeting, but nothing came of it at that time.[54]

November was much the same, as the president's situation showed little improvement. The journalist Arthur Bullard told Morris, "If the State Department has any plans they are held up by the President's illness." When the question again came up as to what to do with Russian prisoners of war in Germany, Polk took the matter in hand to set up an Inter-Allied Commission. Lansing had realized that Kolchak was done for and America would gain nothing and help nobody by keeping forces there. Though the Japanese would grumble, they would send more forces to protect Semënov.[55]

December marked an improvement in the definition of Russian policy. The president began a slow recovery. Bakhmetev desperately appealed to Long that the president's forthcoming message to Congress should include provisions for military supplies for the anti-Bolshevik forces. Long countered by noting that the United States could not furnish supplies against an enemy with which America was not at war, nor act alone when the other Allies had not lived up to their promises. The United States, Long claimed, could not be held responsible for the fate of Russia. The League of Nations would have to do something for Russia. Bakhmetev acknowledged that he expected Kolchak's elimination from the government in Siberia and opposed sending him to Denikin. The ambassador asked that the United

States hold Kolchak's gold in trust. The Russian ambassador confronted Long on December 9, and Long refused military support of any kind. Long suggested economic assistance to the non-Bolshevik parts of Russia, saying that it might undermine the Soviets.[56]

Long realized that the power of the United States to aid Russia was about to end and that it would require congressional action for renewal. Lansing suggested that the time was right for a full report to Congress on America's actions in Russia and a presidential statement on future policy. Lloyd George suggested to Polk that "the time had come to see if it is not advisable to come to an understanding with Bolshevik Government." Lansing commented that past experience proved the futility of arriving at a satisfactory understanding with the Bolsheviks since their ultimate purposes were inimical to every established government and their opportunism compromised any of their promises. According to Lansing, they could never be forcibly ousted, and they would only give way very gradually to new leaders and evolve into a government which at some point America might deal with. Only at that moment, exercising the greatest care and judgment, would it be possible to recognize the Russian government. If recognition came sooner, it would only encourage extreme and uncompromising elements. Lansing warned that Lloyd George would make a serious tactical error if he recognized the Bolsheviks and would incur a great moral responsibility for doing so. From Lansing's point of view, "Lenin and his ill-advised disciples will never permanently forego [*sic*] the dream of world revolution or enter loyally into amicable relations with non-Bolshevik Governments."[57] This was the basis of America's nonrecognition policy.

Long reported in late December that Lansing had agreed to evacuate American forces from Siberia. It was an admission that the White cause was doomed and that Russia would be left to solve its own problems. Long was jubilant: "I have finally succeeded to get Mr. Lansing to agree to evacuate our forces from Siberia . . . I think I win. I have urged it for two months and do it now over the objections of the chiefs of my Russian and Far Eastern Divisions." Lansing recorded, "Long on policy of withdrawing troops from Siberia. I favor it." Polk could also be added to the list of those who opposed withdrawal. Long had the satisfaction that Wilson approved his memo, though Poole, now at the Russian desk, opposed it, and Polk was downright mad and requested a delay, which was rejected. Again, there was more jubilation from Long: "Lansing now agrees with me. So does Baker. Now does the President—and it is decided." General March immediately cabled Graves of the decision and its confidentiality until actual orders were received.[58]

Graves reported that Kolchak was imprisoned in Irkutsk, where he had been turned over to Social Revolutionists, according to General Janin's advice. On February 6 he was given to the Bolsheviks, who shot him on February 7. General Knox, who had left for England in early January, thought "the support given by the British Government to Admiral Kolchak has been the most disgraceful page in English history." He further blamed the Russian intelligentsia for being incapable of rallying round the admiral. So much for the maladroit admiral; so much for the pompous British general. It remained for Graves to pick up the pieces, keep the munitions intended for Kolchak, finish loading up the Czechs, Americans, and assorted German and Austrian prisoners of war, and deal with a new revolutionary government in Vladivostok. By February 19 he could report that only five thousand Americans remained and seventy-two thousand Czechs were withdrawing toward Vladivostok.[59]

This departure left the Japanese in control of the Maritime Provinces. In June Daniels wrote to Wilson, "The situation in Vladivostok has sufficiently developed to permit no doubt that the Japanese have firmly established themselves in Siberia and intend to remain, not only in Eastern Siberia, but also in Shantung and Manchuria and to dominate the government of China." The secretary felt that the situation would eventually lead to a war between America and Japan from the economic consequences of this occupation unless the great powers could force Japan to withdraw.[60]

3.

The cost of America's involvement had been twofold. First, there had been the credits of $450 million extended to various Russian governments after the tsar's fall. From July 6, 1917, to November 1, 1917, the amount of $191.4 million was expended. The total disbursement from December 1, 1917, to January 1, 1920, was another $77.3 million. Yet at least a third of the total, Bakhmetev claimed, was derived from sources other than American credits. If this was true, then the amount of U.S. money expended was approximately $179.1 million. Second, there were the expenditures related to the American participation in the northern Russia and Siberian interventions. The amount actually dispersed in northern Russia was $1.1 million, and another $1.9 million for a total of about $3.1 million was purchased from the British Supply Service in Russia. Added to this was the Siberian expenditure of $8 million. The grand total came to about $190.2 million. Baker told Senator James A. Reed of Missouri that some supplies were returned and salvaged.[61]

Graves turned in his final report on May 26, 1920. It was a detailed summary of events in Siberia. Baker wrote Graves that he had just finished reading the comprehensive report: "The Expedition having been completely withdrawn from Siberia, and its final operations now being a matter of record, I give myself the pleasure of congratulating you upon tact, energy and success with which you, as the commanding general of the Expedition, uniformly acted."[62]

Many excuses and apologies were offered for withdrawal. Lansing suggested that developments in Siberia were unexpected, contrary to the Wilson administration's hopes. Every man who could be drilled, Lansing argued, had to be sent to the Western Front; yet the Japanese could not be left alone to secure the eastward march of the Czechoslovaks and prevent German and Austrian prisoners of war from seizing the railroads as that would antagonize Siberians and unite all factions against them. The Supreme Command allowed ten thousand Americans for that purpose. Since the United States was not at war with Russia, America could not support one faction against another short of congressional action to declare war. Congress also was against the intervention in the first place and interfered every step of the way. It was a vain hope to believe that Kolchak's army, supplied by the United States, could replace the Czechs. Russians simply would not rally around him. Lansing concluded, "I wish you [George Kennan] to know that it was not lack of sympathy which prevented the deployment of a large active force in Siberia but conditions which simply rendered such a course out of the question. We were bound hand and foot by the circumstances."[63]

Bliss, in his final report to the Supreme War Council of February 6, 1920, explained that there had been a misconception as to the extent of revolutionary sympathy in Russia. The Allies thought that it would only take a few divisions to get possession of military stores at Vladivostok and Archangel and gain control of the Trans-Siberian railway as far as Cheliabinsk and furnish a nucleus around which orderly elements would rally and carry their influence to European Russia. The Germans would be prevented from getting military stores and Siberian grain. The restoration of order would lead to the rehabilitation of the Russian army so that it would again join in the struggle on the Eastern Front. Likewise, in northern Russia the Allies needed a point of support and access to western Russia in order to embarrass German efforts to check the Siberian intervention and allow supplies from two directions to Russia. Four to six battalions could do the job, with America sending one or two. It had been thought that orderly elements might rally around such a force, and an ice-free port at Murmansk might be held for a possible larger intervention. Wilson allowed three battalions of infantry and three companies of engineers to participate. When offensive actions began and the United States was urged to augment these forces,

Bliss insisted that the purpose was only defensive, that is, the retention of the ports. The United States refused an organized intervention into the Russian interior from northern Russia.[64]

Morris blamed the Siberian failure on Kolchak's "characteristic bad judgment" and the chicanery of French General Janin and British General Knox. As Morris aptly put it, "There is still much dispute as to what Janin told the Czechs to do but one fact is clear in the telephone conversation they handed Kolchak and, if you remember, the remaining members of the staff and guard to the Social Revolutionists who immediately locked him up in the Irkutsk prison. So ended the political career of the supreme ruler." Siberia to Irkutsk was controlled by the Bolsheviks; Irkutsk to the Pacific was under the Japanese.[65]

J. Van MacMurray at the Japanese desk of the State Department blamed Long for the decision, basing his criticism on Long's notion that the Siberian intervention had lacked popular understanding and sympathy.[66]

The ultimate question now arose in an acute form: what policy would America adopt toward Bolshevik Russia? Whatever statement would emerge, perhaps one sometimes urged by Lansing and based on drafts of a report by Poole, such a policy would now have to develop out of the backdrop of a Red Scare in America. The British ambassador, Sir Auckland Geddes, reported to the prime minister that "There is nothing that I know of that this country is so frightened of as Bolshevism. They have got a very large unassimilated foreign population that responds readily to Bolshevik and Socialist propaganda." Geddes had written approvingly to the secretary of state, Bainbridge Colby, of John Spargo's anti-Bolshevik book, *Russia as an American Problem*, just then published. He agreed with Spargo that Lenin was a great tyrant who made "dupes" of the working class to increase his power. "I do not imagine for one moment," he wrote Colby, "that he does anything but laugh in his sleeve at his dupes among the working class in Russia as well as in other countries."[67]

When replying to an inquiry by Samuel Gompers about the possibility of trade with the Soviet Union, Colby responded that there had been conferences on lifting the restrictions, but that the Soviet government was insistent on recognition as a precedent. Then Colby went on to lay down the basis of a future relationship between the United States and Russia: "While this government has no desire to interfere with the internal affairs of the Russian people or to suggest the kind of government they should have, the existing regime in Russia does not represent the will or consent of any considerable proportion of the Russian people. It repudiates every principle of harmonious and trustful relations, whether of nations or of individuals, and is based upon the negation of honor and good faith and every usage and convention underlying the structure of international law."[68] From this it was just a step to a full-blown and formal statement indicating to the world the consequences of this attitude.

Unwilling to accept the Curzon line as the eastern frontier of Poland, Marshal Jozef Pilsudski had swept into Ukraine and occupied Kiev on May 7, 1920. By June 11 Pilsudski was forced to evacuate Kiev. The Red Army threw the Polish army back behind the Bug River. The Reds tried to seize Warsaw. It was in this atmosphere that the Italian ambassador, Baron Camillo Romano Avezzana, asked what the American policy toward Soviet Russia was. Using this as the opportunity for a statement, Colby drew on the previous Lansing materials, the Russian desk of the State Department, and information supplied to him by John Spargo. Most important, as Herbert Hoover related, "The President at this time had passed the worst crisis of his illness, and Secretary Colby some years later informed me that he had gone over the draft of this message paragraph by paragraph with the President and that some of the expressions in it were introduced by the President."[69] It was only right that Wilson himself be the author of America's first formally announced cold war doctrine and, as such, its first cold warrior, though Lansing also was aptly qualified for that honor.

The result of these joint efforts was the note of August 9, 1920—a crystallization of Wilsonian diplomacy with respect to Soviet Russia. It represented the president's thoughts, reached by an arduous route: from his first known utterances on Russia, through his selection of an ambassador, to his recognition of the Provisional Government, to his "do-nothing" policy with the Soviets and reluctance to intervene, to his Paris failures, and, finally, to the withdrawal of forces.

The note began with an awareness of the Red Army's invasion of Poland and the necessity to guarantee "by all means" Poland's territorial integrity and independence through a specific armistice rather than through a general European conference, which would only serve to recognize Bolshevik Russia and dismember its territory. Colby then turned to "certain cognate and inseparable phases of the Russian question viewed more broadly."[70] This view rested on a history of America's relationship with Russia since March 1917. Colby noted that Russia's brief experiment in democratic self-government, a government first recognized by the United States, had gained the sympathy and help of America. America became the ally of Russia and gave moral and material support in order for her to carry on the war vigorously and simultaneously to reconstruct her national life. America exhibited a sincere friendship and gratitude to the "great Russian nation." Colby pointed out the tangible results: "we sent to Russia an expert commission to aid in bringing about such a reorganization of the railroad transportation system of the country as would reinvigorate the whole of its economic life and so add to the well-being of the Russian people." America deeply regretted Russia's withdrawal from the war at a critical moment, Colby continued, and the "disastrous surrender at Brest-Litovsk," for which the Russian people were "in no wise responsible." Rather, America retained a faith in the high character and future of the Russian people to overcome "anarchy, suffering and destitution" in order to restore a free and united country that upheld peace and justice. Until then, America would seek to uphold Russia's sovereignty over the former empire's territory, with the exceptions of Finland, Poland, and Armenia, as an "honorable obligation to the great nation whose brave and heroic self-sacrifice contributed so much to the successful termination of the war."[71] These illustrations, according to Colby, showed the consistency of America's policy toward Russia.

The United States would take justifiable steps to solve European difficulties peacefully, but it would not recognize Russia: "It is unable to perceive, however, that a recognition of the Soviet regime would promote, much less accomplish this object, and it is therefore averse to any dealings with the Soviet regime beyond the most narrow boundaries to which a discussion of an armistice can be confined."[72] The reason, Colby asserted, had nothing to do with any specific political or social structure the Russian people embraced, though the Bolsheviks seized power "by force and cunning" and ruled with "savage oppression." Rather, it had a wholly different basis: "The existing regime in Russia is based upon the negation of every principle of honor and good faith, and every usage and convention, underlying the whole structure of international law; the negation, in short, of every principle upon which it is possible to base harmonious and trustful relations, whether of nations or of individuals." These negations included signing but not observing agreements, instigating world revolution by every means including through their diplomatic agencies, and using the Third International whose agents received the support and protection of the Soviet government. The Soviet government promoted intrigue and propaganda against the institutions and laws of the very countries with which it was at peace. Given these circumstances, Colby concluded, there was no confidence, trust, or respect; hence, no recognition.[73] Nothing was said about trade, the repudiation of debts, or the nationalization of property.

There were two addenda: in August 1919 Wilson rejected participating in a joint Allied blockade of Russia in the Baltic Sea and stated that he preferred that each nation decide this issue on its own; and in June 1920 Wilson declared the freedom of the United States to trade with Soviet Russia on condition that the government took no responsibility for it.[74]

Conclusions

1921
The First Cold War

The Colby Note had adopted the nonrecognition policy advocated by Lansing and the State Department, and the Wilson administration had encouraged other countries to do likewise. Because the note was issued on Wilson's watch, it carried his immense intellectual respectability, a respectability only he could give it, not any of his advisers or, for that matter, any of his foreign colleagues. It was, as Winston Churchill later remarked, "upon the workings of this man's mind and spirit to the exclusion of almost every other factor" that the "history of the world depended." Americans supported such a policy. The note said nothing about trade, repudiation of tsarist and Provisional Government debts, or nationalization of American property in Russia. Though it castigated the Bolshevik regime, the possibility of trade remained. This was important because President Warren G. Harding's appointments of Herbert Hoover as secretary of commerce and Charles Evans Hughes as secretary of state not only agreed with nonrecognition but extended the Colby Note to trade. America had "quarantined" Russia and asked others to do so as well. In March 1921, Hoover issued a statement that trade was limited by communism because credits could not be extended to a government that repudiated private property. At a cabinet meeting three weeks after Harding's inauguration, Maxim Litvinov's appeal for a reversal of nonrecognition and an improvement in commercial relations failed. Hoover and Hughes spoke against Litvinov. Next, Hoover and Hughes extended the Colby Note into the Colby-Hoover-Hughes Doctrine by tying commerce to the question of recognition.[1]

The Republicans were more militant toward communism than their Democratic predecessors. Wilson had kept his silence toward Harding, but in April 1923 he produced a draft, "The Road Away from Revolution," a revised version of which appeared in the *Atlantic Monthly*. He called the Russian Revolution the outstanding event of the age. He stated that it was produced by the capitalist system and by no aberration of its own. Under the tsars Russians had been denied the right to be free. The Bolsheviks attacked capitalism. The way from Russia's Bolshevik fate lay in maintenance of standards for justice. Western civilization must reach beyond impartial rules to sympathy and helpfulness, to the general welfare. The age strove for these qualities and reacted against what it deemed to be capitalism's selfishness. Democracy had made the world safe from German autocracy. Wilson wrote that "democracy has not yet made the world safe against irrational revolution."[2] The supreme task facing democracy was the salvation of civilization. America as the greatest democracy must lead in the task. Republicans remained opposed to Wilsonianism and frozen in isolation.

Wilson's explanation for the mistakes of the Russian Revolution was deleted from the published article. In the draft he maintained that the Bolsheviks acted with haste, ignorance, and the passion of an elite suddenly possessing power to do as it pleased and not obliged to respect opposition. The future challenge was to redeem civilization without repeating Bolshevik mistakes. By finally and completely rejecting Bolshevism on all accounts, he had become the champion of the West — of Wilsonianism against Leninism.[3] But the champion had few followers.

His warning to Western capitalism that it might fall to Russian Bolshevism passed unheeded. America went through the twenties as it had during Wilson's time, without any real understanding of Russia. There was no intent to seek any kind of mutual respect until the "quarantined" Bolshevik contagion fell from power or changed its ways sufficiently to conform to Washington's standard of behavior. The Bolsheviks for their part would continue to see the world through the glasses of Marxism-Leninism. Soviet Russia was isolated by the Versailles system's *cordon sanitaire* of buffer states on its western rim and turned in on itself. A small amount of trade with the United States did occur through such Soviet organizations as Arcos and Amtorg, but the results were unsatisfactory. American travelers went to Russia to see the society of the future and tell Americans.[4] The United States refused to have anything to do with Soviet Russia, despite the fact that its former associates, Great Britain and France, had recognized the Bolshevik government by 1924; there was no opportunity for an American-Soviet dialogue.

Both powers, America and Russia, participated in the world that Wilson had created but that Americans refused to ratify. Russia made a treaty with Germany at Rapallo in 1922 and joined the League of Nations in 1934. America initiated the Kellogg-Briand Pact of 1928 and was an observer at the League. These actions inspired little dialogue; the hostility generated by intervention in Russia and expressed in the Colby-Hoover-Hughes Doctrine could hardly build respect. In the twenties Wilson's policy toward

Russia was sustained and deepened, mainly because Republican presidents
Warren Harding, Calvin Coolidge, and Herbert Hoover were not taken as
seriously as Wilson had been on large questions of foreign policy. This was
due not only to Wilson's high standing as a scholar but also to the fact that
America had been the holder of the balance of power during World War
I and Wilson had been the individual holder of that balance by virtue of
the power over foreign policy that a president possesses in the American
constitutional system. Wilson believed in that power to a greater degree
than had most of his predecessors.

If it had become clear that the Bolsheviks were there to stay, America
remained unconvinced. Wilson, Lansing, and Colby helped lay the foundations for the later Cold War and policy of containment. There was no
military confrontation, armed standoff, or arms race. Yet certain basics were
there: suspicion, mutual misunderstandings, dislike, fear, ideological hostility, and diplomatic isolation. America would find it easy to return to them.
Each side was driven by ideology, by capitalism versus communism. Each
country sought to reconstruct the world. When the world resisted, pressure
could be used. This was the very theme that Wilson's name and his intellectual respectability, if you will, lent credibility to. Recent reassessments
of Wilson credit him with setting the basics of American diplomacy for the
entire twentieth century. Frank Ninkovich asserts that all major American
foreign policies since 1939 have been extensions of Wilsonian principles:
Atlantic charter, Declaration on Liberated Europe, Truman Doctrine, Marshall Plan, and so forth. Tony Smith declares that America's winning of the
Cold War fulfilled Wilson's notion of a global order. And in a stunning essay, William R. Keylor agrees that the "Truman Doctrine was a Wilsonian
pronouncement par excellence."[5]

By the time of the presidency of Franklin Roosevelt, it had become evident
that isolation served no purpose. Roosevelt's hopes for a new relationship
with Bolshevism now displaced Wilson's intellectual respectability. America
could now play an inside game with the exchange of ambassadors and
counselors. The Soviet Union appeared likely to remain in place. The 1933
recognition seemed a start. The Russians pledged to refrain from subversive
activity, to protect all Americans in Russia (the problem that had led to the
abrogation of the 1832 treaty), and to negotiate a settlement of tsarist debts.
Few of these expectations came true, and only the slowing of American
overseas trade on account of the depression led to rapprochement with the
Soviet Union. The Soviets may also have considered that America might
help balance Japanese power.

American influence did not prevent the domestic evils that befell the Soviet Union in the thirties—collectivization and the great purges. Nor could

America look for enlightenment to Ambassador Joseph Davies, who succeeded William C. Bullitt, America's first ambassador to the Soviet Union. Davies's successor, Laurence Steinhardt, shared the hard line with those who felt that the Soviets only responded to force.[6] World War II did bring the two powers closer during the ambassadorship of W. Averell Harriman, but after the war policies again drove them apart. They maintained an uneasy relationship through the Cold War, but at least recognition allowed any attempt at modifying behavior. Recognition had not been an option under Wilson and his immediate successors. It was unnecessary in the 1920s when no one, not even the Bolsheviks, was sure the socialist experiment would work.

Through the years, however, there was a certain continuity of policy in regard to Russia, beginning with Wilson's "quarantine" and moving to containment as suggested by U.S. diplomat George F. Kennan and others such as White House counselor Clark Clifford. The most interesting aspect of Kennan's analysis was its assumption that the inside game, the one that had been represented by Robins, Judson, Bullitt, and, finally, Roosevelt, was useless in terms of gaining confidence and friendship.[7] Kennan's analysis rejected Roosevelt's notion that such a procedure would win over the Soviet dictator Joseph Stalin. Kennan's recommendations aimed at avoiding being a chum or assuming a community of aims. Goodwill got the United States nowhere. The "Clifford Report," submitted to President Truman in 1946, summarized Soviet diplomacy as aggrandizement designed to lead to "eventual world domination [by any means] considered . . . to be in the best interests of the Soviet Union in accordance with Soviet policy of increasing their power at the expense of other nations." Clifford's report went on to say, "The key to an understanding of current Soviet foreign policy, in summary, is the realization that Soviet leaders adhere to the Marxian theory of ultimate destruction of capitalist states."[8] One of Wilson's own experiences seemed proof enough. His message to the Fourth All-Russian Congress of Soviets had brought a rhetorical slap in the face from Grigorii Zinoviev.

What Kennan in the 1940s labeled modesty and patience were at the center of Wilsonian strategy; they were what Lansing termed watch-and-wait and what Colby called nonrecognition. The Wilsonians realized that a minority ruled Russia and that it must be distinguished from the masses. There was no idealism in that realization. Kennan said that the elite did not represent the people. Wilson found out the uselessness of intervention, as he had in Mexico. Kennan came to the same conclusion. Containment was not military, except as a last recourse. He emphasized "political containment of a political threat." Diplomacy had to be a "long-term, patient but firm and vigilant containment." The Colby Note recognized the danger of subversive activities. Kennan repeatedly drew attention to Comintern [Third or Communist International] actions. Kennan believed that if the United States had force and made clear its readiness to use it, it would rarely have to do so.[9]

Kennan's famous "X" article, "The Sources of Soviet Conduct" of July 1947 in *Foreign Affairs*, exploited this point of view. He referred to Marxist ideology and Marxists as "nebulous, visionary and impractical," reminiscent of Wilson's remark about the Bolsheviks as "fatuous dreamers" or Lansing's allusion to "dangerous idealists." Lansing and Wilson criticized those whom Kennan pointed out as Marxist ideologues who thought they knew what was best and who were willing to be duplicitous in pursuit of it. Wilson noted this tactic in his *Atlantic Monthly* article, and Kennan referred to "aggressive intransigence." Wilson would have needed no reminders in what Kennan characterized as the policy of secretiveness. Kennan remarked that there would always be Americans who felt that the Soviets changed; but he warned that such characteristics derived from the nature of the beast. Kennan reached almost the same conclusion that Wilson had, though it was extended to fit an even more powerful foe. Wilson had concluded that isolating the Soviets and protecting their neighbors by "quarantine" was the right policy, even if that meant an activist policy by his allies in Poland to prevent a Red Army victory in 1920, when General Maxim Weygand aided Marshal Pilsudski. Kennan sought a more active program of "firm and vigilant containment." He called for containment by "adroit and vigilant application of counter-force at a series of constantly shifting geographical and political points, corresponding to the shifts and maneuvers of Soviet policy." If this were done, Soviet power "bears . . . the seeds of its own decay, and . . . the sprouting of these seeds is well advanced."[10]

Shortly after Kennan's article, Walter Lippmann, the well-known political pundit and journalist, published articles in the *New York Herald Tribune*, later collected as a book, *The Cold War: A Study in U.S. Foreign Policy*. In it he opposed Kennan's containment and, by implication, the Wilsonian doctrine of quarantine. He did so by suggesting a wholly different alternative to fencing in Soviet Russia, what the British had called a "ring fence," whether it be by *cordon sanitaire*, "quarantine," or containment. He also popularized the term "cold war."

For Lippmann, containment — what he felt to be the heart of the Truman Doctrine, announced to the Congress by President Truman on March 12, 1947 — meant squandering power around the periphery of the Soviet Union in a kind of trench warfare, instead of focusing on the Atlantic community, including its Mediterranean offshoot. The objective of policy would be to negotiate treaties with Germany and Austria that would include evacuation of non-European armies, even if that meant paying a ransom to Russia in the form of reparations, concessions, and trade agreements. The Red Army had defeated Germany; its removal could liberate Germany. Removal would restore the balance of power, which Lippmann considered the goal of Soviet diplomacy, an extension of tsarist diplomacy. Withdrawal of the Red Army would be the "acid test," as he borrowed Wilson's words, of American diplomacy. "Our aim," he wrote, "will not be to organize an ideological crusade. It will not be to make Jeffersonian democrats out of the peasants of eastern Europe, . . . but to settle the war and restore the independence of the nations of Europe by removing the alien armies—all of them, our own included."[11]

Lansing and Wilson were cautious toward the Bolsheviks. They understood that Bolshevik goals varied from tsarist ones, that Marxist ideology made a difference. Fanaticism made Lenin and his colleagues opportunistic and intransigent and gave them what Kennan called aggressive intransigence. Lippmann was wrong. Kennan's analysis began with Marxism-Leninism, and Kennan concluded that for Lenin the "victorious proletariat . . . would rise against the remaining capitalist world," that capitalism was a menace to the socialist homeland and had intervened there, and that, in Kennan's words, the Soviets cultivated the "semi-myth of implacable foreign hostility," or what came to be known as the doctrine of the two camps. Because of the "innate antagonism between capitalism and Socialism," the Kremlin developed secretiveness, duplicity, suspiciousness, and unfriendliness. Kennan pointed to the backwardness of Russia and the problems of doctrine when a dictator made errors. What proved decisive in Kennan's critique was his analysis of the decay of the Stalinist system.[12] Lippmann ridiculed Kennan's calculation, but this was the one calculation, in retrospect, that was on the mark.

And it was only on that particular calculation that Kennan was, in a unique but important sense, a disciple of Wilson. They both believed that the Bolshevik system would collapse, though Wilson thought sooner rather than later. America had the ability, so the Wilsonians thought, to influence and to bring down the Soviet system. It should be noted that Kennan, after putting forward the idea, subsequently moved away from the most militant expressions of containment, while his successors at the State Department—for instance, Dean Acheson—implemented them. "The diplomat who had done so much in 1946 to convince official Washington that the Soviets had to be contained—by the threat of force as well as political and economic pressure—felt by 1948 that he had created a monster."[13]

The president of the World War I era was not willing to do everything to rid the world of communism. Yet he was just enough of an anti-Bolshevik pragmatist to try laundering a little money to Lenin's enemies, supporting a dose of espionage, and trying a very limited intervention. He was involved in a certain amount of conspiracy that one historian labeled a "secret war."[14] The British and French pressed him into intervention. He distrusted Japan and desired to help the Czechs. He drew a line to keep involvement small. Wilson was frequently misinformed, his attentions elsewhere, influenced by the British, sometimes a bit devious, high-handed, perhaps even conspiratorial. In the end, he was so frustrated by Bolshevik shenanigans that he decided on "quarantine," in the hope that others would follow.

Lansing and colleagues at the State Department had assumed that position all along. They preferred not to have any business at all with Bolsheviks. They rejected Judson, Robins, and Bullitt. The Bolsheviks wanted too much for their uncertain cooperation. In Wilson's view, recognition, trade, a presence in Russia, and diplomatic deals would accomplish little except to bleed the West, strengthen Soviet Russia, and leave the United States open to endless manipulation by the Bolsheviks. Wilson, finally and painfully, came to the same conclusion that would be reached by Kennan three decades later; it took two interventions and the Paris experience for Wilson to reach that point. On this issue, Wilson was a "realist."[15] By the time Secretary of State Bainbridge Colby came along, it was obvious that no dealings of the kind offered, no military adventures as pressed by the British or suggested by Foch and Clemenceau, would work. Colby's Note fixed American policy until 1933. There was then a fourteen-year hiatus during which Roosevelt tried to play the "inside game" recommended by Judson, Robins, and Bullitt. He lost. Kennan began a reversal of Roosevelt's wartime policy.

All this means that in 1920 Wilson had come close to the conclusion that Kennan arrived at after World War II. Wilson's notion of a policy to "quarantine" Bolshevism was broadly construed in the Colby Note and collective security and his own road away from revolution. America had to be strong, flexible, and patient. If Russia were contained, the system would collapse under the weight of its own contradictions. Kennan's policy was nothing if not exerted from the outside. It consisted of waiting and the use of counterforce. There was no sweet-talk, no promises.

Wilson's policy of informed containment had intellectual respectability. Because of this, it lent the policies of President Truman and Secretary of State George C. Marshall credibility, years before President Ronald Reagan's concept of an evil empire. It is possible to draw a relatively straight line from Wilson and his collaborators down to Kennan and Reagan. The Wilsonians were the first cold warriors, and in the era of Wilson the first cold war began.[16]

An Essay on Notes and Sources

Historians became interested in the relations of Wilson's administration to Russia with the publication of William Appleman Williams's seminal study of American-Russian relations a half-century ago, in 1952. No doubt this interest was a direct result of the start of the Cold War. George F. Kennan contributed a thoughtful analysis of the origin of Soviet-American relations a few years later. There have been numerous monographs to supplement these contrasting yet remarkable works. They were contrasting because Williams believed that Wilson intervened as well as initiated the Cold War due to his anti-Bolshevism; Kennan thought Wilson was pressured into intervention by the Allies and the need to help the Czechoslovak Legion. Among the various monographs, Betty Miller Unterberger's studies of the military intervention in Russia and the rise of Czechoslovakia, as well as John M. Thompson's research on the Russian question at the Paris Peace Conference, stand out. Students of this period are indebted to Arthur S. Link's publishing of *The Papers of Woodrow Wilson*. The present study owes much to a large and growing body of scholarship and the opening of relevant archives.[1]

Interpretations are often divided between what were labeled as "realists" and "idealists" or "orthodox" and "revisionists." As applied to Russia, these divisions represented those who sided with efforts at accommodation, even cooperation, with Russia, tsarist or communist, and those who viewed America's relationship suspiciously or with hostility. On both sides of the divide, scholars were called pragmatists, apologists, fellow travelers, true believers, doubters, irreconcilables, softs, and hards—to name but a few ill-fitting terms. More than fifty years of research and the end of the Cold War have taught us to begin putting aside these negative labels so that we may see the actual nature of the relationship Wilson established, however contradictory it may appear.

It is important for us to gain a clear understanding of Wilson's relationship with Russia because it contributed to a later rationale for the Cold War. It may come as a surprise to some that his administration employed similar Cold War tactics: ideological warfare, espionage, armed intervention, blockade, economic isolation, laundering money, and quarantine. There was no arms race. It may further startle students of the debate that at the same time that Wilson's administration employed these tactics, he himself insisted on Russia's self-determination and territorial integrity. On what grounds can we reconcile interference in the internal affairs of Russia and at the same time maintain that Wilson was true to his ideals?

Wilsonian tactics versus Wilsonian ideals make for a contradictory story. His tactics were aimed at reconstituting the Eastern Front in the first instance, and collapsing Bolshevism in the second. During the Cold War such tactics were used to prevent communism's worldwide penetration. The preaching of freedom and democracy went hand-in-hand with the use of dirty tricks. There was no causal relationship between Wilson's Russian diplomacy, with its contradictions and inconsistencies, and Cold War diplomacy, but some of his legacy could and would be employed again. Then and later ideological conflict between American capitalism and Russian communism as manifested in the Red Scare of 1919–1920 and the McCarthyism of the 1950s remained.[2]

The glaring contradictions in Wilson's Russian policy can be explained in a variety of ways. Wilson was sometimes poorly informed, even misinformed, about Russia. The result was that he often assumed an ambiguous position as he looked with bafflement on the Russian enigma, tsarist or commissarist. It could be argued that his Russian policy had inherited President Theodore Roosevelt's Japanese favoritism and President William Howard Taft's abrogation of the Russo-American commercial treaty of 1832, neither one a good start for Wilson. Wilson worsened further relations by waiting for more than a year before appointing two successive ambassadors, Henry M. Pindell and George C. Marye. Pindell lasted a day, Marye little more than a year. His third appointment, David R. Francis, had some success with the Tsarist and Provisional Governments but failed with the Soviets. That last failure owed much to his administration's cold-war-style tactics, diluted with vaunting idealism.

Students of this subject have struggled to understand Wilson's Russian policy. He made few clear pronouncements, and he acted in contradictory ways. For example, he denounced intervention and then authorized it. The opinions of his advisers, especially Secretary of State Lansing, were important. On some occasions, Wilson explicitly agreed with Lansing, but often his agreement was implicit. This was because the president liked acting as his own secretary of state, but he could not micromanage everything. He understood the general trend of his Russian policy, however unaware he might have been of its details. The president left us no memoirs, no diaries, no table talk. But there is a profusion of details that, taken as a whole, give a pattern to Wilson's Russian policy, especially after the Bolshevik Revolution.

The president avoided de facto recognition of Lenin in hope of Russia's democratic reconstitution and its military reestablishment of the Eastern Front. Wilson first intervened militarily in northern Russia after the Treaty of Brest-Litovsk on March 3, 1918, for the official reason of the protection of Allied supplies. He likewise intervened in Siberia with the additional argument that this would aid the Czechoslovak Legion's exodus from Russia. These Legionnaires had been recruited into the tsar's army during World War I and wanted to continue the struggle against Germany. It was British, and to some extent French, pressure that really forced Wilson's hand in each instance, with the later addition of Japanese complications in the Far East. At the Paris Peace Conference, the president attempted unsuccessfully to reconcile the Reds and the Whites, contenders in the Russian Civil War: he tried to get the Reds and Whites to negotiate a peace settlement at Prinkipo; William C. Bullitt went to Moscow to explore a possible deal with Lenin; the Allies offered food relief to Lenin through the auspices of Fridtjof Nansen; the president then adopted a watch-and-wait policy toward the counterrevolutionary Admiral Alexander V. Kolchak's Omsk government. He hoped it would succeed. It failed. All this time he preached the principles of Russian territorial integrity and self-determination.

Wilson never tried to abridge Russia's territorial integrity or limit Russian national sovereignty. To these principles he remained true. They help to explain why he vigorously resisted intervention and why, when the British and French pressed it upon him, he placed the strictest limitations on American military involvement. Wilson reluctantly went along with his Allies' wish for a reconstitution of the Eastern Front. But if Bolshevism had collapsed on its own or with a slight push, Wilson would probably have rejoiced.

It is unpopular to admit Wilson's anti-Bolshevism, though it became very clear by the time of his westward swing in support of the League of Nations in the fall of 1919. He reached this position painfully. What emerges is a very complex picture, but a picture of which Wilson could neither have been wholly unaware nor beyond reproach.

Wilson concluded that diplomatic relations with the Soviets, calling as they did for the destruction of capitalism, were impossible. Secretary of State Bainbridge Colby, Lansing's replacement in early 1920, announced nonrecognition as Wilson's final Russian policy. Colby's successor, Charles Evans Hughes, extended this to commerce. Both Colby and Hughes believed that their diplomatic and commercial quarantine would be imitated by other nations. It was not. Britain and France recognized Soviet Russia in 1924. Eventually, President Franklin D. Roosevelt did likewise in 1933.

Roosevelt's recognition broadened into wartime collaboration against Nazi Germany. In 1946 America reverted to a Wilsonian-like quarantine, some calling it containment, while at the same time the United States played the savior of freedom and democracy. Containment blossomed into a full-scale arms race.

It is in this sense that George F. Kennan, an architect of containment, was a disciple of Wilson. It is wrong to call Kennan a Wilsonian in any other sense, though the whole business about Kennan's realism now seems passé.[3] Kennan, while still calling on American foreign policy makers to "put away childish things" such as "self-idealization" and the "search for absolutes in world affairs," also contended that Bolshevik hostility to the West invited a similar reaction "equivalent to the creation of a state of war" that may even have been "part of the rationale for the Allied intervention in 1918." He pointed out that this was not the "classic concept" of a state of war: "[Russia] has not, in other words, sought to obtain its objectives by the traditional processes of open and outright warfare."[4] This nonclassical war, a variant of the later "Cold War," existed from Wilson's time throughout the twenties. Wilson met initial Bolshevik hostility in much the same way that his successors did, that is, by taking measures to contain the Bolshevik menace. Wilson's misunderstandings of Russia, his desire not to deal with Bolshevism, his various tactics to undermine or eliminate Bolshevism, and his high-flying idealism were foundation stones for the post-1945 Cold War.

It may seem contradictory that sometimes Wilson searched for accommodation with Russia. He was somewhat successful with the tsar, did not have a long enough time with the Provisional Government, and failed with the Bolsheviks. Exasperated, he finally moved to Lansing's position as exemplified in the Colby Note. Nonrecognition was broadened by the "Hoover-Hughes" doctrine of restricting commerce with Soviet Russia. In retirement Wilson acknowledged, as Williams stated it, the "broad challenge of the Bolshevik Revolution" and recommended facing its implications by embarking on an effort to improve capitalism. It should be noted that David McFadden took the lead in further investigating the unofficial or semi-official relations generally ignored or rejected by Washington—those avenues first explored by Williams.[5]

Wilson frequently fumbled his Russian policy by oscillating between reconciliation and hostility. Both sides of the historical argument for or against Wilson, therefore, draw inspiration or disillusionment from him. Williams titled his fifth chapter "The Birth of Containment," which chronicled U.S. policy from November 7, 1917, to March 3, 1918. Williams quoted George F. Kennan's "X" article: "The decision 'to promote tendencies which must eventually find their outlet in either the breakup or the mellowing of Soviet power' was not reached in 1945 or 1947—it was an established policy as of January 31, 1918."[6] Williams had it right, but his dating was too soon. It was not until Paris that Wilson decided on giving Kolchak a chance after being stymied by the Prinkipo, Bullitt, and Nansen initiatives. Ambassador Roland S. Morris, ordered to make the trip from Tokyo to Omsk in 1919, reported on the unlikelihood of Kolchak's success. Lansing and Long took notice. Morris's report also cooled Wilson.

Others explained Wilson's ambivalence by suggesting, as Betty Miller Unterberger did, that "his policies toward the Bolsheviks throughout the war consistently sought to uphold, within the limits of coalition diplomacy, the principles of nonintervention, anti-imperialism, the Open Door, and self-determination, principles that were fully compatible with American war aims in 1917."[7] Wilson's aide-mémoire of July 17, 1918, upheld Russia's self-determination and territorial integrity. Both sides, Williams and Unterberger, were correct to a certain extent. Wilson sat on the fence, leaning this way and that. This is why his Russian policy is so complex and controversial. Otherwise it would be impossible for two contemporary scholars, David S. Foglesong and Victor M. Fic, to reach opposite views after their exhaustive studies. Georg Schild noted Wilson's oscillation between his ideals and his pragmatic politics.[8]

Wilson may have initiated a "secret" war, as Foglesong contended; he certainly carried on a cold war. He may have been mistaken in not destroying Bolshevism, as Fic would have it, though at different times he moved in different directions. He played the good ally by intervening, but in the most limited way, and only gave proxies restricted help. Simultaneously, he tried to remain loyal to his most cherished principles, national self-determination and territorial integrity. Wilsonian Cold War tactics welded to high idealism were his legacy. They were enough for Kennan and all the other Cold Warriors to build on.

1. Western Historiography

In order to trace Wilson's earliest views on Russia, one should see Harley Notter, *The Origins of the Foreign Policy of Woodrow Wilson* (Baltimore: Johns Hopkins Press, 1937). As to America's first Russian experts, check Robert F. Byrnes, *Awakening American Education to the World: The Role of Archibald Cary Coolidge, 1866–1928* (Notre Dame, Ind.: University of Notre Dame Press, 1982) and Frederick F. Travis, *George Kennan and the American-Russian Relationship, 1865–1924* (Athens: Ohio University Press, 1990). The American ambassadors wrote their memoirs: see George T. Marye, *Nearing the End in*

Imperial Russia (Philadelphia: Dorrance and Company, 1929) and David R. Francis, *Russia from the American Embassy, April, 1916–November, 1918* (New York: Charles Scribner's Sons, 1921). As to the Russian ambassadors, see Norman E. Saul, *Concord and Conflict: The United States and Russia, 1867–1914* (Lawrence: University Press of Kansas, 1996) and Linda Killen, "The Search for a Democratic Russia: Boris Bakhmetev and the United States," *Diplomatic History,* vol. 2, no. 3 (summer 1978), 327–56.

Earlier works deal with the whole course of American-Russian relations and contain brief sections on the pre-Bolshevik period. Three such books are Foster Rhea Dulles, *The Road to Teheran: The Story of Russia and America, 1781–1943* (Princeton, N.J.: Princeton University Press, 1944); Thomas A. Bailey, *America Faces Russia: Russian-American Relations from Early Times to Our Own Day* (Ithaca, N.Y.: Cornell University Press, 1950); and William Appleman Williams, *American-Russian Relations, 1781–1947* (New York: Rinehart and Co., 1952). The Dulles book devotes eighteen pages to the pre-Soviet era. Dulles recognized tsarist bigotry and the lack of any sentimental attachment by Americans for Russia. He also noted the jump in commerce, after the war started, from an average of $8 million per year to $500 million from 1914–1916. Bailey analyzes abrogation and points to the hysteria whipped up in Congress and how detrimental it was to trade. Furthermore, he notes the failure of abrogation's objectives because it left the Jews and trade worse off. Williams insisted that the Jewish issue and resulting trade problems alienated Russian-American relations while drawing Russia and Japan closer, preventing American penetration of Asian markets by further closing the open door.

Wilson's dealing with the Provisional Government has received more attention from scholars. Of course, the above books treat this subject as well. So does an important early work by Robert D. Warth, *The Allies and the Russian Revolution: From the Fall of the Monarchy to the Peace of Brest-Litovsk* (Durham, N.C.: Duke University Press, 1954). Dulles had been critical of Ambassador Francis, as were subsequent writers. Dulles attributed much of the administration's complacency toward the Provisional Government to the optimistic cables of Francis. Dulles also felt that it was Wilson's principal task to convince the Provisional Government that Russia's newly founded democracy could only survive if autocratic Germany was defeated. But when Miliukov pressed Wilson for his war aims, it was doubtful that the president's message would say anything that could save the Provisional Government or keep it going in the war. Bailey concurred that Wilson was misled by Francis, whom he termed "amateurish and purblind." Warth called him "Babbittry personified" and quoted Lockhart that "Old Francis doesn't know a Left Social Revolutionary from a potato." Warth was very critical of the Root Mission. Though the mission was hopeless, a more liberal person than Root would have been better, according to Warth. Nevertheless, Root did have the acumen to recommend a large-scale propaganda campaign and a $5 million budget with one hundred thousand dollars for starters.

Warth was also critical of Wilson's tardiness in implementing the Root report. Warth noted that Lansing was personally pessimistic but that the State Department's naive optimism was buoyed by the glowing report of Root. Yet little money was forthcoming, and Thompson tried to shore things up with his own contribution of one million dollars, but "only propaganda on a large scale could make an impression." In fact, Warth reported that Wilson was not impressed by Thompson's cables pleading for money: "three million a month!" he exclaimed to Davidson. "What's the matter with your friend? Has he gone crazy?" (p. 146). That comment summed up the administration's view of the importance of Russia at the end of August, according to Warth. Sisson sailed for Russia with only a fraction of Root's request as a credit. Judson, Warth indicated, thought Thompson had delayed the advent of Bolshevism by four to six weeks [149]. As to the notion that Kerensky could crush a Bolshevik uprising, Warth believed that "The embassy circles still lived in a dream world in which the possibility of an armed rising meant only the opportunity to scotch the Bolshevik monster and thus, by some mysterious alchemy, restore the fighting vigor of the army. That the Bolsheviks might win and establish their own government was not considered a serious possibility" (152–53). Warth arrived at this judgment in 1954. It still stands.

Another book written along the lines of Warth's, and detailing the Allied reaction to the Bolsheviks, is Arno J. Mayer's *Political Origins of the New Diplomacy, 1917–1918* (New Haven, Conn.: Yale University Press, 1959) (republished as *Wilson vs. Lenin: Political Origins of the New Diplomacy, 1917–1918* [New York: World Publishing Company, 1964]). Mainly, Mayer insisted that the Fourteen Points were the "basis for a frontal psychological warfare assault on the Reich" (376).

In 1949 William Appleman Williams was engaged in doctoral research at the University of Wisconsin, which resulted in a dissertation finished in 1950, "Raymond Robins and Russian-American Relations, 1917–1938." Two years later he published a seminal work, *American-Russian Relations, 1781–1947* (New York: Rinehart and Co., Inc., 1952). The central chapters came from his dissertation. The book's most striking feature is its critical analysis of Wilsonian policies, backed by a mountain of evidence. Williams initiated a historiographical debate that has lasted to the present: Wilson's policy, he thought, was motivated by his anti-Bolshevism and had as its aim the destruction of the Soviet government and its replacement by a democratic one.

There are many aspects to Williams's wide-ranging analysis. His overall understanding of Wilsonian foreign policy was in its use of economic and military force to guarantee the creation and security of a government modeled on the Wilsonian vision of America. In Russia, as in Mexico, Wilson failed because the nation, especially the Senate, was not prepared to make the sacrifices necessary for a prolonged and substantial intervention. As a result, Wilson fell back on diplomatic and economic means to achieve his twin goals: abolishing the Soviet government and sustaining the open door against Japanese domination in Manchuria and Siberia. In both instances, by direct intervention or through indirect means, he failed.

In late 1963 and early 1964, Williams revisited this topic in a two-part series, "American Intervention in Russia, 1914–1920," *Studies on the Left*, vol. 3, no. 4 (fall 1963): 24–48; and vol. 4, no. 1 (winter 1964): 39–57. This series gave him a chance to address the outpouring of books on Wilson's Russian policy and the Cold War. Williams sharpened his original view and augmented his sources. He reviewed the ideology of the Wilsonians who believed in individualism, property rights, and a liberal democratic government. Peace, they felt, would establish their universality. Since revolutions disrupted such a program, they were to be opposed and so was socialism. How could the Wilsonians not oppose Lenin while not compromising their ideals? Williams asked. Lansing emerged as the architect of opposition to Lenin. That is not to say that Lansing led and Wilson followed, but the ideology of the two were so in sync that Lansing could determine the daily operations with only momentary shifts resulting from Wilson's moral scruples. Williams again claims that within five weeks of the Bolshevik Revolution, "Intervention as a consciously anti-Bolshevik operation was decided upon by American leaders" (fall 1963, 35). Furthermore, Lansing used the German agents' argument as a device to forestall dealing with the Bolsheviks. He never believed it.

Much of Williams's argument rests on Lansing's long memorandum of December 4, 1917, that the intervention was decided upon very early and was undertaken to provide "direct and indirect aid to the anti-Bolshevik forces in Russia. It was thus anti-Bolshevik in origins and purpose" (winter 1964, 55). Thus Bolsheviks were viewed as "dangerous radical social revolutionaries" threatening America and the international order. Though the Washington policy-makers also wanted to defeat Germany and check Japan, they repeatedly refused to collaborate with Lenin to achieve those objectives" (ibid., 56). Efforts to preserve the Eastern Front or anti-Japanese measures "could have been formulated and implemented through cooperation or collaboration with the Bolsheviks" (fall 1963, 41–42). Hence, Williams's central thesis: "opposition to the Bolsheviks claimed first priority. Anti-Bolshevism was the central causative and determining element in American intervention in Russia, an intervention which was in principle decided upon between December 10 and 12, 1917" (winter 1964, 42).

For more recent accounts that stress anti-Bolshevism as the main reason that Wilson agreed to send American troops to Siberia, see Lloyd C. Gardner's two books, *Wilson and Revolutions: 1913–1921* (Philadelphia: Lippincott, 1976) and *Safe for Democracy: The Anglo-American Response to Revolution, 1912–1923* (New York: Oxford University Press, 1984) as well as David S. Foglesong's *America's Secret War against Bolshevism: U.S. Intervention in the Russian Civil War, 1917–1920* (Chapel Hill: University of North Carolina Press, 1995).

Since Williams, other interpretations on intervention have emerged. A convenient summary of these interpretations, as well as the one by Williams, is Betty Miller Unterberger, ed., *American Intervention in the Russian Civil War* (Lexington, Mass.: D.C. Heath and Company, 1969). Unterberger stresses the influence of Japanese expansion on Wilson's Russian policy toward Siberia. She believed that President Wilson wished to protect the open door in Siberia and northern Manchuria from Japanese imperialistic designs. As Allied intervention loomed in Siberia, she contended that the president thought he could restrain the Japanese better by participating in the intervention than by opposing it. These views were best expressed in her article, "President Wilson and the Decision to Send American Troops to Siberia," *Pacific Historical Review* 24, no. 1 (February 1955): 63–74, and in her books, *America's Siberian Expedition, 1918–1920: A Study of National Policy* (Durham, N.C.: Duke University Press, 1956) and *The United States, Revolutionary Russia, and the Rise of Czechoslovakia* (Chapel Hill: University of North Carolina Press, 1989). Earlier, John A. White concurred in this view in his book, *The Siberian Intervention* (Princeton, N.J.: Princeton University Press, 1950). Two other works took the same tack: Pauline Tompkins, *American-Russian Relations in the Far East* (New York: Macmillan, 1949), a book heavily influenced by the events of World War II. Tompkins saw U.S. intervention as determined largely by the necessity to stop the Japanese drive for empire and defend Russia's sovereignty in the Far East. For a detailed study from Japanese sources of that country's decision to intervene, see James William Morley, *The Japanese Thrust into Siberia, 1918* (New York: Columbia University Press, 1957). A recent study by Carol Willcox Melton, *Between War and Peace: Woodrow Wilson and the American Expeditionary Force in Siberia, 1918–1921* (Macon, Ga.: Mercer University Press, 2001) agrees with Wilson's aide-mémoire, that is, to rescue the Czechs, restore commerce, communications, and transport, and tender humanitarian relief (208–9). However, her book takes an interesting line: "Wilson used the military in a new and untraditional manner; he used it not to wage war, but to restore peace" (211).

Another view suggested that Wilson's motive in sending troops to Siberia was to rescue the Czech Legion. These were largely volunteers in the tsar's army who were seeking to rejoin the fighting by getting to the Western Front, by going first through Siberia and thence shipping back to Europe. The best known study along this line was by George F. Kennan, who wrote that after rejecting various European attempts to bring American participation into the Russian civil war, the Czechoslovak odyssey finally forced the president to change his mind. Kennan completed two volumes on this subject, *Russia Leaves the War* (Princeton, N.J.: Princeton University Press, 1956) and *The Decision to Intervene* (Princeton, N.J.: Princeton University Press, 1958), taking the story from the Bolshevik Revolution to October 1918. Though he never wrote the projected third volume, he did touch on that part of the subject, October 1918 to the Colby Note, in *Russia and the West under Lenin and Stalin* (Boston: Little, Brown and Company, 1960) in chapters 5 through 10.

Two other interpretations, by Christopher Lasch and N. Gordon Levin, Jr., treated the Siberian intervention as part of the Allied strategy of the First World War. The former contended that the decisive consideration was the war with Germany. Wilson and the other Americans who made the decision believed the Bolsheviks to be German agents. Christopher Lasch wrote that the expedition into Siberia was understandable only as another way of defeating Germany, in his article, "American Intervention in Siberia: A Reinterpretation," *Political Science Quarterly 77*, no. 2 (June 1962): 205–23, and in his book, *The American Liberals and the Russian Revolution* (New York: Columbia University Press, 1962). The latter also maintained that the Wilson administration intervened because of a desire to support Russian "liberal-nationalism" against the threats of both German imperialism and Russian Bolshevism. On this, see N. Gordon Levin, Jr., *Woodrow Wilson and World Politics: America's Response to War and Revolution* (New York: Oxford University Press, 1968, reprt. 1978), where Levin viewed the decision to intervene in Siberia as also the result of Wilson's hope to steer the Allies, especially the Japanese, "into an anti-Bolshevik world order of liberal-capitalist harmony" (119).

Other historians considering American intervention in northern Russia have used some of the same interpretations as to motives, with two additions: this intervention was the result of Allied pressure, or it was an effort to prevent the Germans from gaining control of Allied supplies stored in northern Russia. Treatments of the northern Russian intervention are found in Kennan's second volume, *The Decision to Intervene,* and Leonid I. Strakhovsky's two books, *The Origins of American Intervention in North Russia (1918)* (Princeton, N.J.: Princeton University Press, 1937) and also his *Intervention at Archangel: The Story of Allied Intervention and Russian Counter-Revolution in North Russia, 1918–1920* (Princeton, N.J.: Princeton University Press, 1944). The latter book is a good study on the unrest in Archangel and the discontent among Allied troops. An excellent dissertation updating this subject is by John W. Long, "Civil War and Intervention in North Russia, 1918–1920" (Ph.D. dissertation, Columbia University, 1972), and the same author's article, "American Intervention in Russia: The North Russian Expedition, 1918–19," *Diplomatic History* 6, no. 1 (winter 1982): 45–67. Kennan wrote that Wilson's decision to send troops to northern Russia was a compromise. Wilson agreed because of the necessity of being a good ally. Kennan is correct, but he treats the northern Russian operation as completely separate from the Siberian intervention—which it was not. Strakhovsky emphasizes the concern in Washington about Germany and the hope that the Eastern Front could be reestablished. Long contended that the northern intervention was more representative of Washington's real intentions, that is, to secure Allied stores and to keep a window open to the Russian interior. Long also made the point of the importance of keeping the two interventions, northern and Siberian, separate.

Wilson did little serious thinking about Bolshevism after his decision to intervene until the time of the Paris Peace Conference, partly because he believed it was impossible to reshape any society from above. His inclination was to let the Russians get on with shaping their own future, confident that democracy would emerge. As to the Paris Peace Conference, John M. Thompson's thoroughgoing account remains the best study, *Russia, Bolshevism, and the Versailles Peace* (Princeton, N.J.: Princeton University Press, 1966). And for a sympathetic account of the Bullitt mission, see Beatrice Farnsworth, *William C. Bullitt and the Soviet Union* (Bloomington: Indiana University Press, 1967). Another work along the line of Paris, but focused on the struggle for the treaties, is Lloyd E. Ambrosius, *Woodrow Wilson and the American Diplomatic Tradition: The Treaty Fight in Perspective* (Cambridge: Cambridge University Press, 1987). The aftermath of Paris and the treaty struggle can be seen in Melvyn P. Leffler, *The Specter of Communism: The United States and the Origins of the Cold War, 1917–1953* (New York: Hill and Wang, 1994), where the author also focuses on the subsequent ideological clash from the days of Wilson. John Lewis Gaddis's recent book, *We Now Know: Rethinking Cold War History* (Oxford: Clarendon Press, 1997) seeks, perhaps, the earliest roots of the Cold War in the Wilson period.

Some recent accounts of Wilson and Russia take varying positions, such as Foglesong and Fic. Another interpretation is by Georg Schild, *Between Ideology and Realpolitik: Woodrow Wilson and the Russian Revolution, 1917–1921* (Westport, Conn.: Greenwood Press, 1995), in which Schild notes Wilson's ambiguity about Bolshevism and the complex nature of Wilsonian policy. His policies drifted "to and fro" between ideology and reality. Schild also takes into consideration the pressure exerted by the British and French. On British diplomacy, consult Richard D. Ullman, *Intervention and the War* (Princeton, N.J.: Princeton University Press, 1961), *Britain and the Russian Civil War: November 1918–February 1920* (Princeton, N.J.: Princeton University Press, 1968), and *The Anglo-Soviet Accord* (Princeton, N.J.: Princeton University Press, 1972). For the French, check Michael J. Carley, "The Origins of French Intervention in the Russian Civil War, January to May 1918: A Reappraisal," *Journal of Modern History* 48 (September 1976): 413–49, as well as his book, *Revolution and Intervention: The French Intervention and the Russian Civil War, 1917–1919* (Kingston, Ontario: McGill-Queen's University Press, 1983). Another work is David W. McFadden's *Alternative Paths: Soviets and Americans, 1917–1920* (New York: Oxford University Press, 1993), which chronicles the extensive efforts of semi-official and unofficial Soviet-American cooperation, especially the work of Robins. Furthermore, he challenges the views of Williams and Foglesong that anti-Bolshevism dominated American policy from the beginning.

A book appearing a year before ours is Norman E. Saul, *War and Revolution: The United States and Russia, 1914–1921* (Lawrence: University of Kansas Press, 2001). His is a vast story with encyclopedic detail. Saul's point of view is: "In contrast to most of the previous studies, mine provides a larger picture, linking the war itself with revolution and civil war and offering more of a sense of what was going on 'in the trenches,' among businessmen, reporters, and the various consular, diplomatic, and military staffs" (xiv).

Saul avoids two important points. First, he overlooks the Wilson administration's making of policy from the top—from Wilson and Lansing—down. If one were to believe Saul, U.S. policy was made from the bottom—by the likes of Charles Crane and Samuel Harper—up. Second, he neglects the intense historiographical disputes surrounding this topic. The Cold War vastly intensified these disputes. Saul does venture the opinion that Crane and his circle, especially Harper, were important influences on the president's Russian policies throughout, but paradoxically the Allies, especially the British, get short shrift as does Lansing and the State Department.

These omissions leave Saul in the interpretive positions reached by Kennan almost fifty years ago, but without Kennan's formidable analytical framework. Saul is content to compile the narrative history of the little people—countless YMCA and Red Cross workers—and socioeconomic data. One typical consequence of Saul's approach is his enumeration of the possibilities concerning Wilson's decision to intervene, where he puts British and French influence first, followed by the rescue of the Czechoslovaks. Few reasons are adduced.

Saul's conclusions range from the obvious — the slow awakening of American business to Russia — to missing the mark by suggesting Wilson's reliance on diplomats in the field and the State Department to commit America to intervention. There is some analysis of British and French pressure via Wiseman, Reading, Jusserand, and the role of House.

This narrative does tell an interesting story from the "trenches." However, from that angle it is hard to see why and how policy was made from the Oval Office where, finally, it had to be made.

2. Russian Historiography

The Russians have also studied the topic extensively. Two excellent reviews of these research activities are George F. Kennan, "Soviet Historiography and America's Role in the Intervention," *American Historical Review* 65 (1960): 302–22, a critique by one Soviet historian, S. F. Naida, and John M. Thompson, "Allied and American Intervention in Russia, 1918–1921," in Cyril E. Black, ed., *Rewriting Russian History: Soviet Interpretations of Russia's Past* (New York: Vintage Press, 1962), 319–80, a review of the Russian literature to the mid-1950s.

Some Russian works are fundamental, but many are often flawed by severe anti-Americanism. Mikhail S. Kedrov, *Za Sovetskii Sever* (Leningrad, 1927), by the commissar for Archangel at that time, gives his intimate insights on relations with the Allies. (All Russian titles are translated in the Bibliography.) One should also see his documentary collection: *Bez Bolshevistkogo Rukovodstva (iz Istorii Interventsii na Murmane); Ocherki* (Leningrad, 1930). An early two-volume work on the intervention in the Far East is G. Reikhberg, *K Istorii Interventsii na Dal'nem Vostoke* (Moscow, 1934), though it already began praising Stalin. For a militant Stalinist view of the intervention, there is G. A. Deborin, *Sovetskaia Vneshnaia Politika v Pervye Gody Sushchestvovaniia Sovetskogo Gosudarstva, 1917–1920gg* (Moscow, 1951). An example of early post-Stalinist historiography is G. V. Kuz'min, *Grazhdanskaia Voina i Voennaia Interventsiia v SSSR: Voenno-Politicheskii Ocherk* (Moscow, 1958), which is heavily patriotic and emphasizes the role of collective leadership in achieving victory. One must consult Andrei Gromyko and Boris Ponomarev, eds., *Istoriia Vneshnei Politiki SSSR 1917–1945*, vol. 1 (Moscow, 1980); they accuse the United States of trying to partition Russia.

Another interesting work is by I. I. Mints, *God 1918* (Moscow, 1982); he claims that America had its sights set on dominating Siberia.

Five of the most important Russian publications concerning this topic, more balanced in approach and excellent in their use of archives, are P. Ganelin, *Sovetsko-Amerikanskie Otnosheniia v Kontse 1917-Nachale 1918g* (Leningrad, 1975), which is a careful examination of events leading up to the intervention; L. A. Gvishiani, *Sovetskaia Rossiia i SShA (1917–1920)* (Moscow, 1970), a work by Alexei Kosygin's daughter, who had access to important documents; Z. Gershov, *Vudro Vil'son* (Moscow, 1983); A. Gromyko, ed., *Dokumenty Vneshnei Politiki SSSR*, 5 vols. (Moscow, 1957–1961); and A. Utkin, *Diplomatiia Vudro Vil'son* (Moscow, 1989). These works return to the moderation of earlier Soviet scholarship of the twenties.

Soviet historiography of Wilson's Russian diplomacy went through four phases. The first and last exhibited a high degree of objectivity. M. N. Pokrovsky, for example, in his *Vneshniaia Politika Rossii v XX Veke* (Moscow, 1926) emphasizes the desperate Allied need to keep Russian forces active and states that, therefore, intervention was more anti-German than anti-Bolshevik. M. N. Veltman (pseud. M. I. Pavlovich) in his *Sovetskaia Rossiia i Kapitalisticheskaia Amerika* (Moscow, 1922) notes that America was the most benign of the interventionists, and that Wilson wavered from indirect financial support of Kolchak to efforts at controlling the Japanese.

Historiographical moderation began to change with Stalin's ascendancy. Works by I. I. Mints in this period illustrate a shift to glorify the Red Army and Stalin's leadership. In his 1931 *Angliiskaia Interventsiia i Severnaia Kontrrevoliutsia* (Moscow, 1931), Mints places blame on Britain as the instigator of intervention and the manipulator of Wilson. It differs from the previous phase in that Stalin emerges as the hero. By 1933, Mints highlights Anglo-American strife, but still mentions U.S. disapproval of Franco-British plans to finance counterrevolution. (I. I. Mints, ed., *Interventsiia na Severe v Dokumentakh* [Moscow, 1933]). A year later, in I. I. Mints, comp., *Iaponskaia Interventsiia v 1918–1922gg v Dokumentakh* (Moscow, 1934), he labels Allied and, especially, Japanese interventionists as completely evil and deifies Stalin for vanquishing the imperialists. Mints comes close to Stalin's own *Kratkii Kurs'* (Short Course) (Moscow, 1938), which maintains that intervention was mounted solely to destroy the Soviet government.

Stalinist dogma abated during World War II. It reached a fever pitch again from 1948–1953. Then the United States became the sole organizer, leader, and financier-supplier of intervention. Simultaneously, earlier Soviet historians were chastised. Again, John M. Thompson's "Allied and American Intervention in Russia, 1918–1921," cited an article by A. Girshfeld, "O

Roli SShA v Organizatsii Anti-Sovetskoi Interventsii v Sibiri i na Dalnem Vostoke," *Voprosy Istorii* 4, no. 8 (August 1948): 3–32, as the piece that launched the virulent anti-American campaign. America's role was covert; it was the "chief supplier of money and arms to the anti-Soviet forces and also furnished deceitful 'democratic' programs designed to neutralize the genuine popular appeal of the Bolshevik revolution's progressive ideology." (Thompson on p. 364 characterizes Gershfeld's work.)

George F. Kennan's "Soviet Historiography and America's role in the Intervention," *American Historical Review* 65, no. 2 (January 1960): 302–22, shows how Soviet scholarship in 1958 still skewed the truth and distorted the record. He gives a close examination of a single work to illustrate this, S. F. Naida's *O Nekotorykh Voprosakh Istorii Grazhdanskoi Voiny v SSSR* (Moscow, 1958). Kennan cited ten instances of distortion, the most blatant by Naida being the allegation that "American interventionists in the most bestial manner obliterated the entire population of entire regions, acting in the same manner as the bands of Semënov, Kalmykov, the Kolchakovites and the Japanese." (Kennan's translation; he quotes Naida's book, 200, or 318 in his article.) After closely investigating this charge, Kennan states, "I am unable to find the faintest confirmation of an incident such as that described by Naida" (Kennan, 320).

As Thompson points out, after 1952 there was a gradual "abating" of attacks on America's role in the intervention (380). Actually, the opinions are a mixed bag, but a return to Lenin's view of things seems to prevail. M. I. Stishov's 1953 work, one point of departure, provides a bold relief of Stalinist literature.[9] In this account, Stalin played the major role in the defeat of the interventionists, who were led by the United States. One author, caught in the ideological shift between Stalin's death and the rise of Nikita Khrushchev, G. K. Seleznev, tried to moderate his earlier views. Others were trapped in the same dilemma. For example, in 1954 Seleznev published an article in the leading Soviet historical journal, "Ekspansiia Amerikanskogo Imperializm v Rossiu v 1917 Gody," *Voprosy Istorii* 10, no. 3 (Moscow 1954), in which he calls Wilson the lackey of U.S. monopolists and includes the United States as part of a plot to distribute spheres of influence in Russia as early as the London conference of June 1917. By 1963, in his book, *Krakh Zagovora Agressiia SShA Protiv Sovetskogo Gosudarstva v 1917–1920* (Moscow, 1963), Seleznev admits that there was insufficient information about attempts by America to aid bourgeois circles in Russia striving to destroy Soviet power. Nevertheless, he criticized American historians for supporting a "passive role" for the United States in the intervention.

It was during this same period, 1954–1963, that Kennan had cited Naida's completely unobjective work. By 1966 Naida was able to survey Soviet historiography more objectively as a result of Khrushchev's attack on Stalin, and to realize the detrimental effects of the personality cult on the question of intervention.[10] Works by Spirin, Gubelman, Tarasov, and Kondrashev were still very shrill. Kuz'min begins to talk about the collective leadership of the party in achieving victory, but he continues to place the major blame on the United States.[11] In 1960, one work by Stefankov went so far as to insist not only that it had been the United States that had obligated Britain and France to make loans to Kolchak but also that the leading role in directing Kolchak's movement belonged to General Graves.[12] That same year Ustinov and Zharov insisted that Britain and France were inspired to intervene by the United States.[13] The reason for this was the heavy financial involvement of the United States in Russia, according to V. A. Boiarskii in his 1961 book, *Vtorzhenie Imperialistov SShA v Sovetskuiu Rossiiu i Ego Proval* (Moscow, 1961). As late as 1971, Stepanova attacked Kennan, claiming that he was a "subjective realist," one who thought that Wilson was never very interested in Russian affairs, but wanted only to help the Russian people. She firmly disagreed with these assessments, stating that Wilson's peace program, the Fourteen Points, was actually a plan to partition Russia and destroy Soviet power. One cannot, she claimed, differentiate between U.S. interventionist policies and those of Britain and France. As to Kennan's assertion that the purpose of the U.S. and Japanese invasion of the Far East was to assure the safety of Czechoslovakian forces, in Stepanova's opinion, this was a "ludicrous" claim. That same year Skaba went so far as to suggest that the Allies wanted to "colonize" Russia.[14]

It was not until 1972 that the flavor of Soviet works on intervention returned to the normalcy of the 1920s and began to reassert the Leninist interpretation. While not specifically denying America's role in organizing the anti-Soviet offensive of the Allies, V. P. Naumov reviewed Soviet historiography by emphasizing Lenin's writings and dropping Stalinst claims: Lenin again became the director of the military struggle.[15] Both in 1973 and in 1980, Azovtsev focused his attention on Lenin's proclamations and the Red Army's successes. Instead of the United States receiving the most blame, it was the Allies who wished that American monopolists would give active financial and military aid.[16] More important, Ganelin in 1975 fully returned to the main interpretation of Pokrovsky and other scholars of the 1920s. Ganelin insisted that poor relations between the United States and Soviet Russia were not inevitable, but rather that Wilson's Russian policies were formulated at a slow pace and were closely tied to his World War I goals. According to Ganelin, the Sixth Point of the Fourteen Points indicated Wilson's tendency to recognize the Soviet government. However, in the face of internal opposition, Wilson quickly took a definite anti-Soviet position.[17] Kuz'min, who had already written disparagingly of America's role in the intervention in 1958, returned again to this subject in 1977.[18] He retained his hard line that the United States had played a particularly active role, anxious to establish a base in Siberia and seeking to destroy Soviet power. In this sense, his dissenting work in the late 1970s was reminiscent of M. Levidov's study in the 1920s, *K Istorii Soiuznoi Interventsii v Rossii* (Leningrad, 1925), in which Levidov had attacked Pokrovsky.

In 1979 Livshits virtually accepted Pokrovsky's view, that is, that the Allies were most concerned about the war and not about destroying the Soviets. Lloyd George was blamed for Japan's role as the "mandatory" and the United States, Livshits admitted, opposed Lloyd George.[19] Whereas Lebedev, like Kuz'min, retained a hard line against the United States in 1980, only two years later he saw Wilson's policy as an effort to neutralize Lenin as an "ideological counterbalance" to the Leninist Decree on Peace. Even Mints, by then the senior scholar of intervention, returned to his first formulations, that is, to the notion that intervention proceeded because of Russia's withdrawal from World War I and was aimed at resurrecting an Eastern Front, not destroying the Soviets. For example, in 1983 the United States could be treated even-handedly. Svetachev then maintained that Britain and France were the main culprits, and that they plotted to use American and Japanese strength in the Far East, but that Wilson had remained uncertain and was only moved to action by the presence of the Japanese.[20]

A 1989 Soviet dissertation by O. V. Terebov, "Partii i Politicheskaia Bor'ba v Kongresse SShA po Voprosam Amerikanskoi Interventsii v Sovet-skoi Rossii, (1918–1920)" (Moscow, 1989) captures the mood of research in Russia late in Gorbachev's era and throughout the Yeltsin period. In it the author first reviews and compares both Soviet and American historiography on the question of American intervention and then analyzes the opposition to intervention in the United States. He distinguishes three major trends among American historians: first, intervention was a result of Allied pressure on Wilson and Wilson's aid to the Czechs (Kennan and Strakhovsky); second, the explanation was a result of the necessity to neutralize Japanese expansion in the Russian Far East (White and Unterberger); and third, the ideological hostility to the Soviet state encouraged attempts to eliminate it (Schuman, Williams, Gardner). On the Soviet side, Terebov sees three periods: first, the United States was the least dangerous of the Allies and there were numerous contradictions in its policy (Veltman); second, the United States was portrayed as the main inspirer, organizer, and participant, planning partition and colonial-economic enslavement (Kunina,

Boiarskii, Seleznëv); and third, there was a reexamination and adoption of the views of the 1920s in which America was seen as wanting to restore the Eastern Front and hostile to Soviet power, but after the armistice America went against intervention in the Congress (Ganelin, Svetachev). Russian research is more promising, especially as access to Russian archives is becoming freer.

3. Western Archives

There are extensive American manuscript sources on Woodrow Wilson's Russian policy. The main collection of Wilson Papers is located in the Manuscript Division of the Library of Congress. It is an enormous collection, divided into a number of different series. An alphabetical index, available at the Library of Congress, makes the collection a little easier to use. Wilson frequently commented about current problems to many different people. The result is that the only reliable means of locating material on a certain topic is to go through the collection box by box, letter by letter. One cannot rely on certain correspondents or certain topics; also, though the Link edition of Wilson's papers is excellent, it is still important to check the manuscript collections.

The Manuscript Division at the Library of Congress includes many other collections that have in them materials that bear on the Wilson period and his Russian policy. Among those consulted for this study, though not all of them are cited here, were the papers of Carl Ackerman, the Adee Family, Chandler Anderson, Newton D. Baker, Ray Stannard Baker, Tasker H. Bliss, William Borah, Mark Bristol, William Jennings Bryan, Albert Burleson, Bainbridge Colby, George Creel, Josephus Daniels, Joseph E. Davies, Norman H. Davis, Thomas W. Gregory, Hermann Hagedorn — William Boyce Thompson, Herbert Hoover, Charles Evans Hughes, J. Franklin Jameson, Jules Jusserand, George Kennan, Philander Chase Knox, Robert La Follette, Robert Lansing, Breckinridge Long, Peyton C. March, William G. McAdoo, David Hunter Miller, Roland S. Morris, William C. Redfield, Elihu Root, Charles E. Russell, Hugh L. Scott, John F. Stevens, Oscar S. Straus, William Howard Taft, Stanley Washburn, Henry White, William Allen White, and the American Peace Commission to Versailles. Other than the Wilson papers, the most useful collections at the Library of Congress were those of Newton D. Baker, Tasker H. Bliss, Robert Lansing, especially for his desk diaries and private memos, and Breckinridge Long, who recorded a lengthy diary on American involvement in Siberia in 1918. The Elihu Root Papers contain relatively little on Root's mission to Russia in 1917.

Equal in importance to the collections in the Library of Congress are the numerous record groups in the National Archives that include material relating to this subject. The groups consulted for this study were Record Group #38—Records of the Office of the Chief of Naval Operations; #39—Records of the Bureau of Accounts—Department of the Treasury Records for Foreign Countries; #40—General Records of the Department of Commerce; #43—Records of International Conferences, Committees, and Expositions—Stevens Commission (The Russian Railway Service Corps); #45—Naval Records Collection of the Office of Naval Records and Library; #59—the vast and very important General Records of the Department of State, especially the Russian materials; #63—Records of the Committee on Public Information; #84—Records of the Foreign Service Posts of the Department of State—Selected Foreign Service Posts; #94—Records of the Adjutant General's Office; #120—AEF North Russia, Records of the American Expeditionary Forces (World War I), 1917–1923—American Section, Supreme War Council; #151—Records of the Bureau of Foreign and Domestic Commerce; #165—Records of the War Department General and Special Staffs—War Department, Office of the Chief of Staff; #345—U.S. Army Overseas Operations and Commands, 1898–1942, A.E.F. (American Expeditionary Force) in Siberia; and #407—War Department, The Adjutant General's Office, Central Decimal Files. Two other record groups consulted for this study are #182—War Trade Board; and #261—Records of Former Russian Agencies—Russian Consulates in the U.S. and Canada and the Russian Supply Committee and its successor, the Division of Supplies of the Russian Embassy.

Portions of the holdings at the National Archives are increasingly available on microfilm, and those that were have been consulted in that manner. They include M-316, Records of the Department of State Relating to Internal Affairs of Russia and the Soviet Union, 1910–1929; M-333, Records of the Department of State Relating to Political Relations between the United States and Russia and the Soviet Union, 1910–1929; M-340, Records of the Department of State Relating to Political Relations between Russia and the Soviet Union and Other States, 1910–1929; and M-367, Records of the Department of State Relating to World War I and Its Termination, 1914–1929, all portions of Record Group #59; and M-820, General Records of the American Commission to Negotiate Peace, 1918–1931, from Record Group #256. Of all this material from the National Archives, these items of the State and War Departments are by far the most important.

There are many other manuscript collections that include material on Wilson's Russian policy, which proved useful for this study. Both the Firestone Library at Princeton University and the Sterling Memorial Library at Yale University have a number of personal papers on this subject. Consulted at Princeton were the papers of Woodrow Wilson as well as the accession numbered documents gathered by Arthur S. Link et al. for the publication of *The Papers of Woodrow Wilson*, 69 vols. (Princeton, N.J.: Princeton University Press, 1966–1993); Ray Stannard Baker; Bernard Baruch; Arthur Bullard; Raymond Fosdick; the Selected Papers of Robert Lansing and John V. A. MacMurray; and Hugh L. Scott. The Wilson materials at Princeton are particularly important for the prepresidential years, and the library has collected extensively in this area. The Baker and Bullard papers are interesting, with the latter having extensive material on Bullard's service in Russia with the Committee on Public Information Papers. The Selected Papers of Robert Lansing complement the Lansing Papers at the Library of Congress, for the collection at Princeton, deposited by the Dulles Family, has many items unavailable in Washington, including some long personal letters by Lansing and some key documents on Russian affairs. The materials at Yale University are headed, of course, by the very large Edward M. House Papers, but they also include the Papers of Gordon Auchincloss, William C. Bullitt, Vance McCormick, Frank Polk, and William Wiseman, and the Records of The Inquiry. The House Diaries were very important for this study, as were the Auchincloss and Polk Diaries, which give much information on the making of policy in the State Department bureaucracy. The Wiseman Papers show the extent and intent of British pressures on Wilson concerning Russia. The Bullitt materials left at Yale, since the main body of papers were withdrawn a number of years ago, consist only of the Bullitt-House correspondence, available in microfilm.

The Hoover Institution at Stanford University also has extensive materials that proved helpful in doing the research for this study. Among the collections consulted were the Papers of the Allied and Associated Powers, American Red Cross, American Relief Administration, Nancy Babb, William Barrett, Philip Carroll, George Creel, William L. Darling, Benjamin Davis, George H. Emerson, French Army Telegrams—Major Pequin, Charles W. Furlong, Michael Giers, General William S. Graves, Ernest Harris, Paul A. Hill, the Hoover-Wilson Correspondence, Stanley Hornbeck, the Dmitri Khorvat Memoirs, Admiral Kolchak Correspondence, G. de Lastours, Roger Lewis, V. A. Maklakov—Russian Embassy in Paris, George Marye—French Telegrams from Russia, Hugh A. Moran, Bernard Pares, John F. Stevens, Russell Story, Supreme War Council—American Section, Sergei Ughet, Edward Willis, and the YMCA Special Collections. The collections at the Hoover Institution are strongest in materials on the Russian government at this time, such as the Giers, Maklakov, and Ughet materials, for collections of Americans who served in Russia for the State Department, the Red Cross, the YMCA, and the Stevens Railway Commission; and for the Papers of the Red Cross Mission to Russia and the American Relief Administration. The Giers Papers have some personal correspondence not available elsewhere.

Other repositories with multiple collections that were of use for this study were the Wisconsin State Historical Society in Madison and the various libraries at Columbia University. The Papers of George Gibbs, Alexander Gumberg, Morris Hillquest, Cyrus McCormick, Jr., DeWitt C. Poole, Paul Reinsch, Edward A. Ross, and especially Raymond Robins made the Wisconsin State Historical Society a fruitful research stop. The McCormick papers contain material on his service with the Root Mission as well as much evidence of the close relationship he had with his Princeton classmate from 1879 — Woodrow Wilson. The Robins and Poole papers also proved important for this study. At Columbia, the Nicholas M. Butler Library has the Lincoln Steffens Papers and Oral History Transcripts of DeWitt C. Poole and Boris Bakhmetev and Columbia University's Archive of Russian and Eastern European History and Culture, the Papers of Charles Crane and Allen Wardwell, including his valuable diary. Of these materials, the Crane papers shed the most light on this topic because of his intimate relationship with Wilson. The Houghton Library at Harvard has the Papers of David Houston, Walter Hines Page, William Phillips, John Reed, and W. W. Rockhill, with the notebooks in the Phillips papers proving to be the most helpful of these materials because of his service in the Department of State.

Other American collections consulted for this study that proved of value were the Papers of Henry Davison and the materials on the Red Cross Commission to Russia at the Library at the American Red Cross Headquarters in Washington; the YMCA Russian Service Records and the Paul Anderson Oral History Transcript for his Russian Service, formerly at the Library at the YMCA Headquarters in New York City but now at the University of Minnesota; the David R. Francis Papers at the Missouri State Historical Society; the very valuable William Judson Papers as well as the Graham Taylor Papers at the Newberry Library in Chicago; the Samuel Harper Papers at the Regenstein Library of the University of Chicago; the Papers of Herbert Hoover at the Hoover Presidential Library in West Branch, Iowa; the George Kennan, Nicholas Khrabrov, and Thomas Thacher Papers at the New York Public Library; the Hiram Johnson and E. T. Williams papers at the Bancroft Library at the University of California, Berkeley; the Warren G. Harding Papers at the Ohio Historical Society in Columbus; the Papers of John R. Mott, which were on deposit at the Library of the Princeton Theological Seminary but have been returned to Yale Theological Seminary; and the Papers of Paul B. Anderson at the University of Illinois,

Arnold Eugene Jenny, and the Rev. William L. Turner, all in private hands. Three collections consulted through the mail were the Papers of Edward Hurley at the University of Notre Dame Library; the Papers of Curtis Guild at the Massachusetts Historical Society; and the Swarthmore Peace Collection at the Swarthmore College Library. The Francis, Harper, Hoover, and Mott papers were of special importance because of the various services involving Russia performed by those individuals. For Cold War comparisons, the Harry S. Truman Library in Independence, Missouri, is useful.

British manuscript materials also have much on this subject and proved very useful for this study. Most important are the Papers at the Foreign Office and the Minutes of the War Cabinet and Cabinet in the Public Record Office (PRO). Of the Foreign Office materials, the most useful were those in F.O. 371, on the United States, Siberia, and Japan; and the personal papers collection in F.O. 800 of Arthur Balfour, Robert Cecil, George Curzon, Eric Drummond, Edward Grey, Ahlford Mackinder, Alfred Milner, Lord Reading, and Cecil Spring Rice. Other British collections consulted for this study were the papers of Arthur Balfour and Robert Cecil, at the British Museum; the papers of Andrew Bonar Law and David Lloyd George, in the Beaverbrook Library; the George Curzon Papers in the India Office Library; the Papers of Herbert H. Asquith and Alfred Milner at Bodleian Library, Oxford; and the Austen Chamberlain Papers at the Library of the University of Birmingham. These sources, plus the Wiseman Papers at Yale University, give a complete picture of the British interest in intervention, their hopes at the time of the Paris Peace Conference, and the pressure they exerted on Wilson.

4. Russian Archives

The Archive of the Foreign Policy of the Russian Empire (AVPRI) is affiliated with the Ministry of Foreign Affairs of the Russian Federation.[21] Two major funds were important for studying the development of the American foreign policy toward Russia: the Embassy in Washington (N 170) and the Office of the Minister of Foreign Affairs (N 133). The fund "Embassy in Washington" chronologically covers the periods of U.S. government relations with the Imperial, Provisional, and early Bolshevik governments. The period up to 1917 is presented by the political correspondence between the Russian Ministry of Foreign Affairs and the State Department, between the embassy in Washington and Russian missions and consulates in Chicago, San Francisco, and Seattle. The fund contains important material on Russian political and diplomatic relations, on the abrogation of the commercial treaty of 1832 and, directly connected with it, on the Jewish question, as well as the series of appointments of American ambassadors to Russia. The documents describe the evolution of American policy toward Russia after the beginning of World War I until the Bolshevik Revolution. They discuss the questions related to American neutrality concerning war supplies, war loans to Russia, and the reaction of the Russian government on American terms of assistance. They give evaluations of the relations between the two countries by both Russian and American officials and diplomats, analyze the circumstances and the possible consequences of the overthrow of the Tsarist regime, the coming to power of the Provisional Government, and the Bolshevik Revolution, and describe the activities of the Russian Railroad Mission to the United States, the American Railroad Unit in Siberia, and the Russian Information Bureau.

The period of 1917–1922 focuses mainly on American intervention in Russia through the correspondence of the Russian Embassy in Washington, its consulates, the State Department, and different public organizations. This part of the fund, "Embassy in Washington," also contains material on political émigrés, prisoners of war, the Brest-Litovsk Treaty, and the Omsk government.

The fund "Office of the Minister of Foreign Affairs" covers the period 1912–1917 and includes dispatches and letters of the Russian ambassadors in Washington, reports, memoranda, and telegrams and notes sent by the Ministry of Foreign Affairs, foreign diplomats in Russia, and different government and high-ranking officials abroad. It also contains correspondence of the Ministry of Foreign Affairs with Russian governmental bodies and officials, documents relating to the activities of international commissions and conferences, and reports and circulars of the Ministry of Foreign Affairs, which involve the discussion of the different aspects of relations between Russia and the United States.

The Archive of the Foreign Policy of the Russian Federation (AVPRF) affiliated with the Ministry of Foreign Affairs contains the documents on the relations between the United States and early Soviet Russia (1917–1920). Our interest was focused on three funds: G. V. Chicherin's Secretariat (fund 04/4), Assessorship on the United States (fund 0129/129), and Mission of the Russian Soviet Federated Socialist Republic in the United States.

The fund "Chicherin's Secretariat" contains materials concerning economic and political relations between the United States and Soviet Russia and the W. C. Bullitt Mission to Russia in 1919. The fund "Assessorship on the United States" includes documents on the Russian Extraordinary Railway Mission to the United States (Y. Lomonosov's Mission); on the organization of the Russian Information Bureau in the United States (1918); on

American participation in the Civil War and military intervention in Russia; on the American Red Cross Mission to Russia, and has the correspondence of statesmen on Russian-American relations. The third fund includes the documents on the activities of L. Marten's Mission in the United States.

The State Archive of the Russian Federation (GARF) contains important materials focusing on the relationship of the Wilson administration with the Russian Provisional Government and later with the Russian governments in Murmansk and Omsk.

The fund "The Administration of the Prime Minister of the Provisional Government" (N 1778) includes correspondence with various American representatives on the possibilities of a separate peace with Germany, materials regarding the "mobilization" of American capital for the improvement of Russian-American financial relations, and a letter by Theodore Roosevelt to the Russian Prime Minister A. Kerensky. The personal fund of P. N. Miliukov (N 579) contains several important documents, including the interview of 1915 given by Baron Rosen, former ambassador of Russia to the United States, relating to relations between the two countries during World War I, and Miliukov's speech in the Temporary Council of the Provisional Government on the war and its impact on Russia and the United States.

The fund "Administration of the Temporary Government of the North" (N 17) provides accounts by American representatives in Murmansk on the political situation in Russia in 1918–1919, which were sent to Washington in order to help formulate American policy toward Russia. The personal fund of N. B. Tschaikovsky includes his correspondence with the representative of the Northern government in the United States, the copies of important notes and telegrams signed by the Russian Ambassador B. A. Bakhmetev, and a series of articles written by the head of the Russian government in the north on Russian-American relations and the involvement of the United States in the intervention in Russia.

The fund "Russian Government in Omsk" (N 200) contains correspondence and telegrams of Kolchak's government with the Russian ambassador and consulates in the United States in 1918–1919 regarding the status of Russian-American relations, the political situation in both countries, and the prospects for American economic assistance, military loans, and supplies to Omsk.

The fund "Commission on the Research and Control of the War and Influence on the Economy of Soviet Russia" provides information on the losses of Soviet Russia from the American presence on its territory during the period of intervention.

The Russian State Military Archive (RGVA, former Central State Archive of the Soviet Army) contains the documents of the Red Army (funds

N 1 and 33987) and the headquarters of the White military units (funds N 39499, 39507, 39515) concerning the presence of the Allied and American troops on the territory of Russia. Among the most important materials are the report of the military headquarters of the Omsk government on American secret military supplies to Russia; the decoded telegrams of the military attaché of the Omsk government regarding the American policy toward Russia; the correspondence on the organization of the guarding of the Baikal railway with the participation of America and American military supplies to the Omsk government; the report of the headquarters of the All-Russian government concerning the interests of Japan and the United States in the Russian Far East; and documents on the activities of American public organizations in Siberia and the Far East. These materials suggest the controversial character of the relationship between American troops and the Omsk government, and provide important information regarding the growing antipathy of the Omsk government, White Army, and the Russian population toward the American military presence in Russia, and the activities of the Red Cross and YMCA on its territory.

Research in the Russian Center for the Preservation and Study of the Documents of Contemporary History (the former Central Party Archive) (RTsKhIDNI) was focused on three major funds: Lenin's fund (N 2), Secretariat of the Chairman of the Council of the People's Commissars and the Council of Labor and Defense (N 5), and Trotsky's fund (N 325).

Lenin's fund is represented by correspondence of the founder of the Soviet Russian state, V. I. Lenin, with R. Robins, L. Steffens, R. Keely, and some other Americans who visited Russia in 1918–1919 and expressed controversial impressions about the political situation in the country and the prospects of American relations with the Bolsheviks. It also includes an evaluation by the Soviet authorities of the differences between the Democrats and Republicans in their relations with Russia, the reaction of the Bolshevik government to the denial of the various representatives invited to the Prinkipo Conference, the Allied press coverage of the Paris Peace Conference, and U.S. strategic interests in Russia. Fund 5 consists of the documents regarding the contradictions between the United States and Japan in the Russian Far East and the possibilities of American support of the Bolshevik representation at the Prinkipo Conference in exchange for certain concessions from the Soviet government.

Trotsky's fund is focused on the civil war and Allied intervention in Russia. Trotsky's correspondence with other high-ranking Soviet officials points to the clear concern of the Bolsheviks regarding the military strengthening of the Japanese in the Far East, which they felt would inevitably damage both Russian and American strategic interests in this region. Fund 17 contains the documents explaining the goals of U.S. intervention as recounted by American officers, information on the reaction of Bolsheviks on American intervention, and so-called details of fraternization between Red Army and American soldiers on the Northern Front.

It should be mentioned that the Archive of the President of the Russian Federation (Arkhiv Prezidenta Rossiiskoi Federatsii—APRF) remains virtually closed to researchers.

Notes

Introduction. 1913: Russo-American Relations

1. Arthur S. Link, et al., *The Papers of Woodrow Wilson* (hereafter referred to as *PWW*), vol. 27, 149; see also "President Wilson: His Inauguration, Cabinet, and Problems," 553–58; Joseph Tumulty, *Woodrow Wilson as I Know Him*, 139. Link emphasizes Wilson's feelings about the uniqueness of Americans politically, socially, and morally. See Link's essay, " 'Wilson the Diplomatist' in Retrospect," in Arthur S. Link, *The Higher Realism of Woodrow Wilson and Other Essays*, 78.

2. There are good surveys of U.S.-Russian relations: Anna Babey, *Americans in Russia, 1776–1917: A Study of the American Travellers in Russia from the American Revolution to the Russian Revolution*; Thomas A. Bailey, *America Faces Russia: Russian-American Relations from Early Times to Our Own Day*; Norman E. Saul's three-volume work, *Distant Friends: The United States and Russia, 1763–1867, Concord and Conflict: The United States and Russia, 1867–1914*, and *War and Revolution: The United States and Russia, 1914–1921*; William Appleman Williams, *American-Russian Relations, 1781–1947*. Also see the interesting article by Harvey Wish, "Getting Along with the Romanovs," 341–59. As for Wilson's prepresidential views, see Harley Notter, *The Origins of the Foreign Policy of Woodrow Wilson*, especially 30, 42, 46, 78, 114–15, 179–80, 191, 196, 201. For "ambrosia," check 7d ser., box 5, Wilson Papers (hereafter WP), Library of Congress (hereafter LC); for "The case versus Russia," December 6, 1911, see 7a ser., box 8, WP, LC; House, Diary, November 10 and December 18, 1912, February 28, 1913, Edward M. House Papers (hereafter House Papers), Yale University Library (hereafter CtY); Charles Ernest Scott to President Woodrow Wilson (hereafter WW), White House Summary, March 1, 1913, WP; and an account of Russia in the *New York Times*, March 6, 7, 1913. For Wilson's interest in Russia, see George F. Kennan, *Russia Leaves the War*, 28.

3. Anna Viroubova, *Memories of the Russian Court*, 98–101; Miriam Kochan, *The Last Days of Imperial Russia*, 99–101, 163–67; Vladimir Kokovtsev, quoted in W. Bruce Lincoln, *In War's Dark Shadow: The Russians before the Great War*, 392. For Wilson's congratulatory note to Nicholas II, see WW to Tsar Nicholas II, March 6, 1913, State Department (hereafter SD), Record Group (hereafter RG) 59, 861.415/3, National Archives (hereafter NA).

4. Jacob Schiff to Adolph Ochs, April 29, 1911, quoted in Naomi W. Cohen, "The Abrogation of the Russo-American Treaty of 1832," 8n22. Cohen's is the most useful article in print on the activities of the American Jewish Committee in the abrogation campaign. For a more detailed presentation on the impact of Russian émigrés on American policy, see Richard D. McKinzie and Eugene P. Trani, "The Influence of Russian Émigrés on American Policy toward Russia and the USSR, 1900–1933, with Observations on Analogous Developments in Great Britain," 215–51.

5. Alexis A. Goldenweizer, "Legal Status of Jews in Russia," 85, 96–98, 106, 108. Popular expert George Kennan insisted that the Jewish blood spilled by peasants was on the heads of the oligarchy, for it was they who made the peasants believe that "Jews spit on and trample under foot the sacred pictures of the Madonna and Child. . . . and murder young Russian children in order to get Christian blood to mix with the dough of Passover cakes." George Kennan, "Alliance with 'Russian Barbarism,'" 26.

6. Ann E. Healy, "Tsarist Anti-Semitism and Russian-American Relations," 408–25, esp. 415. In a few cases, Roman Catholics and atheists also were denied visas. A compendium of State Department documents related to U.S. protests is in *The American Jewish Yearbook: 5665,* 283–305. A great many more documents, including relevant congressional testimony and resolutions, were published at the height of the abrogation dispute in *The American Jewish Yearbook: 5672,* 19–128.

7. Cyrus Adler, *Jacob H. Schiff: His Life and Letters,* vol. 2, 151–52; Charles Reznikoff, ed., *Louis Marshall Champion of Liberty: Selected Papers and Addresses,* vol. 1, 104; Cohen, "Abrogation of the Russo-American Treaty of 1832," 5–8. The Russian government did believe that domestic Jews would revolt if foreign Jews were not subject to Russia's restrictions; the foreign ministry also insisted that ordinary Russians would ignore any exemptions that officials might grant foreign Jews outside the Pale.

8. Naomi Cohen, the student of the treaty's abrogation, wrote, "Legally, Article I might be construed literally in Russia's favor, but there is no question that Russian practices on granting visas violated American institutions safeguarding liberty of conscience." Cohen, "Abrogation of the Russo-American Treaty of 1832," 18; for the text of the treaty, see William M. Malloy, *Treaties, Conventions, International Acts, Protocols and Agreements between the United States of America and Other Powers,* vol. 2, 1515ff.

9. *New York Times,* December 7, 1911; for the text of Wilson's speech see also Woodrow Wilson, *College and State: Educational, Literary and Political Papers (1875–1913),* edited by Ray Stannard Baker and William E. Dodd, vol. 2, 318–22. "Russia Hoodwinking U.S. about Passports for Jews," by Herman Bernstein, the lead article in the magazine section of the Sunday *New York Times,* July 25, 1911, is one of many articles that were "planted" by the American Jewish Committee. Notter, in his *The Origins of the Foreign Policy of Woodrow Wilson,* points out that Wilson claimed that "Russia's actions were intolerable, and that the intercourse should be broken unless agreements were observed 'in letter and in spirit'" [180]. Notter goes on to note that these remarks of Wilson "served to illustrate the type of approach by which he might be expected to meet diplomatic problems. He had asked pointedly for conformity to the terms 'covenanted' in the treaty, or alternatively, action in accord with our national dignity" [180–81]. From the Russian perspective, Wilson was either an ultra-radical or an extreme liberal; see G. P. Bakhmetev to S. D. Sazonov, January 6/19, 1912 [double dates refer to Old Style (OS)/New Style (NS) because Russia remained on the Julian calendar until the Gregorian (Western) was adopted on January 31, 1918] f. 133, d. 63, Archive of the Foreign Policy of the Russian Empire (hereafter AVPRI), and Bakhmetev to Sazonov, June 21/July 4, 1912, f. 133, d. 169, no. 56, AVPRI; Bakhmetev to A. A. Neratov, June 29/July 12, 1912, f. 133, d. 63, no. 29, AVPRI; and Bakhmetev to Sazonov, April 25/May 8, 1912, f. 133, d. 63, no. 20, AVPRI, on unfriendliness of Roosevelt and skepticism about Democrats. For the use of Russian abbreviations such as *f.* for *fond* meaning record group, *op.* for *opis* standing for inventory or part of a collection, *d.* for *delo* as a box

or package of documents, and *l.* for *list* as a leaf or page in a manuscript collection, sometimes referred to here as *no.*, see Patricia K. Grimstead's *Archives and Manuscript Repositories in the USSR: Moscow and Leningrad*, 385–91. The new names of Russian archives in the post-Soviet period are given in our text. For a discussion of Russian archives, check An Essay on Notes and Sources, pt. 4., "Russian Archives" of this book. All Russian titles are translated in the Bibliography.

10. Jeanette E. Tuve, "Changing Directions in Russian-American Economic Relations, 1912–1917," 57–59. Of course most everyone who respected rules wanted the commercial treaty renegotiated immediately. Foreign Minister Sazonov would not discuss the subject so long as "the passport issue" remained a part of it. One of the most interesting arguments for hastening toward a new treaty was that the past balance of trade in favor of the United States (as much as $55 million annually) depended on cotton and other commodities that Russians would produce for themselves now that the agricultural/industrial revolution had reached take-off. "Within five years," concluded an analyst in the *Political Science Quarterly*, it was "not improbable" that Russia could cut its imports from the United States by more than 90 percent. In that case, the trade advantage would be so much in Russia's favor that "Russia might well deem it advisable, simply on economic grounds, to refuse to renew that treaty." John V. Hogan, "Russian-American Commercial Relations," 631–47. Another indication that trade was little affected even by 1917 is a note from W. R. Tucker, Russian consul in Philadelphia, to Boris E. Shatzky of the Russian Information Bureau in New York City in April 1917, in which he states, "It is fair to say that since the abrogation of the Treaty of 1832, little inconvenience has been experienced, owing to the friendly relations existing between the two countries." See W. R. Tucker to Boris E. Shatzky, April 25, 1917, f. 296/1, 132, l. 7, AVPRI.

11. Curtis Guild, "Russia and Her Emperor," 713.

12. George Kennan, "A Voice for the People of Russia," 470; Kennan, "Russian Despotism," 753, 755; Kennan, "Alliance with 'Russian Barbarism,'" 26. The Pale of Settlement consisted of fifteen provinces in the southwestern parts of Russia and ten provinces of Russian Poland. By requiring residents to "register" with local authorities and then controlling the requirements for changed registration, the Imperial government controlled the movement of people within the Russian Empire. About 95 percent of the Jewish population registered in the Pale. Christopher Lasch considers Kennan the quintessential opinion maker on Russia; see his *The American Liberals and the Russian Revolution*, 8.

13. George Kennan, "The Attitude of the Russian People," 328–32; Kennan, "Russian Despotism," 751–55; Kennan, "Alliance with 'Russian Barbarism,'" 26; Frederick F. Travis, *George Kennan and the American-Russian Relationship, 1865–1924*, 381–83.

14. Babey, *Americans in Russia, 1776–1917*, esp. 70–79; see also Leonid I. Strakhovsky, *American Opinion about Russia, 1917–1920*; Robert F. Byrnes, *Awakening American Education to the World: The Role of Archibald Cary Coolidge, 1866–1928*, 122; *Report of the Librarian of Congress and Report of the Superintendent of the Library Building and Grounds for the Fiscal Year Ending June 30, 1905*, 17; ibid. (for the fiscal year ending June 30, 1906, 16–47).

15. Russia's ten top exports to the United States, in order of value, were (1) hides and skins; (2) raw wool; (3) rubber waste; (4) flax, hemp, and tow; (5) animal and human hair; (6) liquorice root; (7) wood pulp; (8) fusel oil; (9) manganese; (10) rugs. Hogan, "Russian-American Commercial Relations," 640. The most valuable U.S. items exported to Russia were (1) raw cotton; (2) agricultural equipment;

(3) wheat flour; (4) copper; (5) twine and cord; (6) finished leather; (7) rosin; (8) typewriters; (9) sewing machines; (10) rugs. See *The Russian Market: Its Possibilities and Problems*, 18; James K. Libbey, *American-Russian Economic Relations, 1770's-1990's: A Survey of Issues and Literature*, 13.

16. *The Russian Market*, 8, 9, 11, 16, 17; Curtis Guild to Josiah Quincy, November 8, 1912, Guild Papers, Massachusetts Historical Society (hereafter MHS), Boston, Mass.

17. *The Russian Market*. Because American exporters focused on specific Russian markets, a few items were significant in the Russian economy. Historians note that Russians bought 36 percent of their cotton and 20 percent of their farm machinery from U.S. suppliers. Gail L. Owen, "Dollar Diplomacy in Default: The Economics of Russian-American Relations, 1910–1917," 253; Consul North Winship, Petrograd, "Annual Report on Commerce and Industries for 1915," appended to the Inspection Report, Petrograd, October 25–November 13, 1916, SD, RG59, Inspection of Consular Posts, 1911–1929, NA. The disparities between U.S. and Russian statistics are revealed in the following tables, extracted from figures compiled by the American-Russian Chamber of Commerce in *The Russian Market*, 8, 9, 11.

According to Russian statistics:

Years	Russia's Imports*		Russia's Exports*	
	Total Imports	Imports from U.S.	Total Exports	Exports to U.S.
1901–1910	393.27	28.3%	547.21	3.0%
1911–1913	616.83	42.3%	761.51	7.4%

*yearly average in millions of dollars; rubles converted @ .51 cents

According to U.S. statistics:

Years	U.S. Imports*		U.S. Exports*	
	Total Imports	Imports from Russia	Total Exports	Exports to Russia
1901–1910	1,158.5	11.9%	11,616.2	16.7%
1911–1913	1,714.5	21.1%	2,325.3	25.4%

* yearly average in millions of dollars.

For the multiple figures on imports and exports, see Libbey, *American-Russian Economic Relations*, where he calculates Germany's share of Russia's total imports as 47.4 percent. Tuve, "Changing Directions in Russian-American Economic Relations," 54. As Tuve notes, it is impossible to compute the exact amount Americans had invested in Russia. She sets the figure at $60 million, about 5 percent of all foreign investments in the Empire.

18. See Albert Guirand, "German Capital in Russia," 39–51 and the strong statement by North Winship, "Annual Report on Commerce and Industries for 1915," dated April 15, 1916 (typescript), 13, appended to "Inspection Report, Petrograd, Russia, SD, RG59, Inspection of U.S. Consulates, 1911–1929, NA.

19. These comments appended to Inspection Report, Odessa, Russia, July 9–26, 1911, SD, RG59, Inspection of U.S. Consulates, 1911–1929, NA.

20. See N. Peacock, *The Russian Almanac 1919*, 173. See also note 17 previously. C. J. Medzikhovsky was sent to Washington as a commercial attaché in 1913 to promote direct trade ($9 million to America in 1913 and U.S. to Russia $25 million, though unofficially $30 million for the former and $80 million for the latter) in Tuve, "Changing Directions in Russian-American Economic Relations," 58–59.

21. Rachael West, *The Department of State on the Eve of the First World War*, 4, 10, 13–14.

22. Curtis Guild to Josiah Quincy, November 8, 1912, Guild Papers, MHS.

23. American and Russian diplomatic principals in 1913 were: [C = consul; VC = vice consul; CG = consul general].
U.S. American Ambassador to Russia: Curtis Guild, resigned in November 1912
Batum: Leslie A. Davis, C
Moscow: John H. Snodgrass, CG [Alfred Willoughby Smith, acting CG]
Odessa: John H. Grout, C
Riga: Douglas Jenkins, C
St. Petersburg: Jacob E. Conner, C
Vladivostok: John Jewell, C
Warsaw: Thomas E. Heenan, C
Russian Ambassador to the United States: George P. Bakhmetev
Mobile: Murray Wheeler, VC
San Francisco: Pierre Rogdestvensky, CG
Pensacola: Chipley Fannin, VC
Honolulu: August Marquis, VC
Chicago: Victor Chickkine, C
Baltimore: vacant
Boston: Joseph A. Conry, C
Philadelphia: William R. Tucker, C
Galveston: Carl C. Biehl, VC

24. Batum, 1913, SD, RG59, Inspection Reports on Foreign Service Posts, 1906–1939, NA.

25. Odessa, 1914, SD, RG59, Inspection Reports, NA.

26. Riga, 1913, SD, RG59, Inspection Reports, NA.

27. St. Petersburg, 1913, SD, RG59, Inspection Reports, NA.

28. Warsaw, 1913, SD, RG59, Inspection Reports, NA.

29. Moscow, 1913, SD, RG59, Inspection Reports, NA.

30. Vladivostok, 1913, SD, RG59, Inspection Reports, NA. Clearly, Inspector George H. Murphy intended to accent positive characteristics just as clearly as Alfred L. M. Gottschalk intended to ferret out weakness.

31. Batum 1913, Odessa 1913, St. Petersburg 1913, Vladivostok 1913, SD, RG59, Inspection Reports, NA. It could be said, from the Russian viewpoint, that Russian diplomats felt the same way about the extent of Russian representation in America because the Russian consulates in the United States were not enough to represent the interests of thousands of Russians in dozens of states. For example, Russian workers in America often got into trouble and were in dire need of representation by Russian officials. See T. Chirkov, Russian consul in Pittsburgh, to Bakhmetev, April 14/27, 1916, f. 170, d. 410–411, no. 205, l. 66–67, AVPRI. Jerome Davis later wrote extensively on this subject; see his book, *The Russian Immigrant*, especially chap. 6.

One. 1914–1916: Three Ambassadors for St. Petersburg

1. Curtis Guild to Josiah Quincy, November 8, 1912, Guild Papers, MHS.
2. Ibid.
3. Guild to WW, December 23, 1912, ser. no. 2, WP, LC; Guild to Secretary of State, March 4, 1913, ser. no. 4, Case File 64, WP, LC.
4. *Boston Commercial Bulletin,* August 1, 1914, ser. no. 4, Record File 403, box 246, WP, LC; *Boston Herald,* August 2, 1914; *Boston Globe,* August 2, 1914, ser. no. 4, Case File no. 403, Box 246, WP, LC; Guild to J. P. Tumulty, August 3, 1914, ser. no. 4, Case File no. 403, box 246, WP, LC; Notter, *The Origins of the Foreign Policy of Woodrow Wilson,* 203.
5. House, Diary, April 4, 1913, House Papers, CtY; for the quote, see Arthur S. Link, *Wilson: The New Freedom,* 102n28; Albert Parry, "Charles R. Crane, Friend of Russia," 26–28.
6. Bryan to WW, June 4, 1913, WP, LC; WW to Bryan, June 8, 1913, box 43, Bryan Papers, LC.
7. Friends of Crane understood Wilson to have agreed that "Mr. Crane can have the place whenever he feels he can leave the country." Oswald F. Schuette to Herman Nohlsant, September 25, 1913, Charles Crane Papers (hereafter Crane Papers), Columbia University (hereafter CU). As to Pindell, the "original" Wilson man, see Link, *Wilson: The New Freedom,* 102. Other names for ambassador to Russia floated through Washington's top offices. Even before Wilson's inauguration, Charles H. Sherrill, lately ambassador to Argentina, became the candidate of Jews interested in a new treaty that would pressure the tsar to lift more antisemitic ordinances. Although Wilson's advisers said nothing negative about Sherrill, he was a Republican appointment, and Jewish leaders at that moment had no particular power with the administration. Wilson briefly considered appointing Augustus Thomas, a playwright; Bryan wanted the president to consider Alva Adams, former governor of Colorado. House, Diary, April 30 and September 27, 1913, House Papers, CtY; Bryan to WW, July 19, 1913, WP, LC.
Apparently, Wilson decided to go along with any solution Bryan might devise until Crane was available. By September 24, 1913, he was "perfectly willing that we should offer Mr. Pindell the temporary appointment at St. Petersburg." WW to Bryan, September 24, 1913, WP, LC; see "Moore's Memoirs," 456–58, Moore Papers, box 217, LC. Bakhmetev saw this sordid affair of appointing "deserving" Democrats as a sign of a party delirious with success and behaving as though it had conquered the country. See Bakhmetev to Sazonov, April 5/18, 1913, f. 133, d. 111, AVPRI.
8. Link, *Wilson: The New Freedom,* 103n80; "Moore's Memoirs," 458, Moore Papers, box 217, LC; Charles R. Crane to WW, May 18, 1914, WP, LC. There was also pressure from the Russian government, which wanted someone other than Pindell. See S. D. Sazonov to G. P. Bakhmetev, November 24/December 7, 1913, f. 133, op. 105, d. 110, AVPRI.
9. Quoted in West, *The Department of State on the Eve of the First World War,* 106.
10. George Thomas Marye, *Nearing the End in Imperial Russia,* 18–19; Curtis Guild, "Russia and Her Emperor," 713.
11. *New York Times,* July 3, 1914.
12. House, Diary, September 25, 1914, House Papers, CtY.
13. Bryan to American Embassy, St. Petersburg, encl. in Bryan to WW, 1914, c.

August 4, 1914, WP, LC; Bryan to WW, August 28, 1914, Bryan Papers, box 43, LC.

14. Marye, *Nearing the End*, 17–19.

15. Bryan to WW, August 17, 1914, WP, LC and Bryan Papers, box 43, LC; WW to Bryan, August 18, 1914, WP, Letterpress Books, book 15, LC and Bryan Papers, box 43, LC; Marye, *Nearing the End*, 20, 21–22, 29–34.

16. Charles Wilson to Secretary of State, October 16, 1914, Telegram Petrograd, SD, RG59, 861.51/78, NA; Robert Lansing to WW, October 19, 1914, SD, RG59, 861.51/78, NA; WW to Lansing, October 20, 1914, SD, RG59, 861.51/78½, NA; for quote, see Wilson's insertion in Lansing to American Ambassador, October 20, 1914, SD, RG59, 861.51/78, NA (draft encl. in WW to Lansing, of same date and reference number). As to Lansing's qualifications for secretary of state and Wilson's interest or knowledge of Russian affairs, check Kennan, *Russia Leaves the War*, 28, 30.

17. Lansing to Wilson, October 20, 1914, SD, RG59, 861.51/74½, NA; Bakhmetev to Lansing, October 20,1914, and encl. to WW and Lansing Memo, October 23, 1914, encl. in Lansing to WW, October 23, 1914, all in SD, RG59, 861.51/74½, NA.

18. Marye, *Nearing the End*, 34–38, 40–41; *New York Herald*, November 20, 1914, and quoted by Lansing to WW, November 23, 1914, WP, LC; as for the quote in the text, see Lansing to WW, November 23, 1914, WP, LC.

19. House, Diary, January 13, 1915, House Papers, CtY; House to WW, March 27, 1915, WP, LC.

20. Charles Wilson to Secretary of State, July 31, 1914, *Papers Relating to the Foreign Relations of the United States* [hereafter *FRUS*], *1914, Supplement, The World War*, 26; James W. Gerard to Secretary of State, August 1, 1914, *FRUS, 1914, Supplement, The World War*, 27; Wilson to Secretary of State, August 1, 1914, *FRUS, 1914, Supplement, The World War*, 28, 30; Wilson to Secretary of State, August 2, 1914, *FRUS, 1914, Supplement, The World War*, 34.

21. Bryan to WW, March 5, 1915, Woodrow Wilson–William Jennings Bryan, Bound Correspondence, vol. 3, NA. As early as January 1915, Bakhmetev warned Sazonov that the Austrian ambassador had complained to Lansing that Marye was not able to do enough to improve the situation and assuage the sufferings of German and Austrian POWs and asked Lansing to issue a note to the Russian government about the "inhumane" treatment of POWs in Siberia. See Bakhmetev to Sazonov, January 16/29, 1915, f. 133, d. 60, no. 24, AVPRI. Bryan to WW, March 12, 1915, and WW to Bryan, March 12, 1915, Woodrow Wilson–William Jennings Bryan [hereafter WW-WJB] Bound Correspondence, vol. 3, NA; James W. Gerard to Secretary of State, March 11, 1915, *FRUS, 1915, Supplement, The World War*, 1011–12. On the efforts of the Y and Red Cross, see Donald E. Davis and Eugene P. Trani, "The American YMCA and the Russian Revolution," 469–91 and Paul B. Anderson, *No East or West*.

22. See Lansing to Bryan, March 16, 1915, Link Collection, no. 113281, Princeton University Archives (hereafter NJP); WW to Tsar Nicholas II, March 18, 1915, SD, RG59, 763.72114/534, NA; for Marye's delivery of the letter, see WW to Ben G. Davis, March 18, 1915, and Ben G. Davis to Marye, March 18, 1915, SD, RG59, 763.72114/534, NA; as to Marye's remark to the Tsar, see Marye to the President, April 15, 1915, *FRUS, 1915, Supplement, The World War*, 1019; on the language of reciprocity, check Sazonov to the American Ambassador, April 18/May 1, 1915, *FRUS, 1915, Supplement, The World War*, 1020–21.

23. Secretary of State to Marye, June 15, 1915, *FRUS, 1915, Supplement, The World War,* 1021–23; Link, *Wilson: The Struggle for Neutrality,* 421–26 on Bryan's resignation.

24. Marye, *Nearing the End,* 325–27.

25. WW to Schiff, April 1, 1915, Jacob H. Schiff Papers, Hebrew Union College, American Jewish Archives, Cincinnati, Ohio, and WW to Simon Wolf, April 12, 1915, WP, LC.

26. Alderman to Bryan, May 12, 1915, SD, RG59, 711.6112/8, NA; Crane to Bryan, May 16, 1915, SD, RG59, 711.6112/9, NA; Crane to Secretary of State, May 15, 1915, Crane Papers, CU; Bryan to WW, May 17, 1915, WW-WJB, Bound Correspondence, vol. 4, NA; Bryan to WW, May 20, 1915, WP, LC; Lansing to Marye, June 19, 1915, David R. Francis Papers (hereafter Francis Papers), Missouri State Historical Society (hereafter MOSHI).

27. Marye to Secretary of State, July 24, 1915, SD, RG59, 861.111/171–405, NA.

28. Marye, *Nearing the End,* 143, 190–91.

29. House, Diary, July 24, 1915, House Papers, CtY; Lansing to WW, July 26, 1915, SD, RG59, 711.612/242, NA; Secretary of State to Ambassador, Petrograd, July 27, 1915, Francis Papers, MOSHI; WW to Lansing, July 28, 1915, SD, RG59, 711.612/242½, NA; Lansing to WW, August 12, 1915, WP, LC.

30. *New York Times,* February 17, 1916.

31. House to WW, February 3, 1916, WP, LC.

32. Marye, *Nearing the End,* 243, 273.

33. Marye to WW, January 25, 1916, WP, LC; for his wife's comment, see *New York Town Topics,* February 23, 1916, Francis Papers, MOSHI; WW to Marye, February 17, 1916, WP, LC. An interesting comment on the nature of Marye's resignation is Lansing's own cable to him: "President, after most careful deliberation, has finally and irrevocably determined that interests of the government require immediate appointment of a new ambassador as successor of Marye. There are fundamental objections that can not be removed and that made it impossible further service for Marye. President in consequence . . . desires to save him from dismissal, and would accept his resignation by cable on such proper grounds, as Marye may set up." Lansing to Marye, January 11/24, 1916, f. 133, d. 120, no. 93, AVPRI. Marye responded: "Reasons of health require my resignation." Marye to Lansing, January 23/February 5, 1916, f. 133, d. 120, no. 168, AVPRI. House, Diary, December 15, 1915, House Papers, CtY; House to WW, February 3, 1916, WP, LC; *New York Town Topics,* February 23, 1916, Francis Papers, MOSHI.

34. House, Diary, December 15, 1915, House Papers, CtY; Whitlock to WW, February 28, 1916, WP, LC; Lansing to WW, February 10, 1916, Robert Lansing Papers (hereafter Lansing Papers), box 3, LC; C. H. Boynton to Tumulty, February 16, 1916, WP, LC; Wood to WW, February 16, 1916, WP, LC; Crane to WW, February 17, 1916, WP, LC; Crane to WW, February 22, 1916, WP, LC.

35. WW to Crane, February 21, 1916, Letterpress Books 27, WP, LC; Phillips to Francis, March 23, 1916, Francis Papers, MOSHI. Bakhmetev judged Francis as honest, but a provincial "new rich" as well as overconfident, narrow-minded, and without an adequate education or any diplomatic skills. See Bakhmetev to the Foreign Ministry, March 26/April 6, 1916, f. 133, d. 101, no. 81, AVPRI. As to a similar changeover in Washington, George P. Bakhmetev resigned as ambassador to the United States on April 4/17, 1917; see Bakhmetev to Foreign Ministry, April 4/17, 1917, f. 133, d. 69, no. 171, AVPRI. The embassy was then temporarily run

by K. M. Onu until Boris A. Bakhmetev took over in June 1917. (These men are not related.)

36. See Francis's on-board messages: Francis to WW, April 8, 1916, WP, LC; Francis to Senator William J. Stone, April 12, 1916, Francis Papers, MOSHI. Francis admitted he knew little about Russia. Check David R. Francis, *Russia from the American Embassy: April, 1916–November, 1918*, 3. The Russian attitude to his appointment fluctuated. At first Bakhmetev characterized him as well-educated, knowledgeable, wealthy, of high energy, and sympathetic to Russia. See Bakhmetev to Sazonov, February 11/25, 1916, f. 133, d. 101, no. 40, AVPRI. However, by March Bakhmetev referred to him as too cocky and superficial. Francis even appeared to be pro-German until it was confirmed that his son was ordered to sever any of his father's German business dealings to prevent a conflict of interest. See Bakhmetev to Sazonov, March 25/April 7, 1916, f. 133, d. 55, no. 33, AVPRI, and Bakhmetev to Sazonov, May 3/16, 1916, f. 133, d. 101, no. 121, AVPRI. Francis has fared badly in American historiography; see for example Robert D. Warth, *The Allies and the Russian Revolution: From the Fall of the Monarchy to the Peace of Brest-Litovsk*, 30, where Warth states: "Francis was Babbitry personified and hardly the man to change the prevailing view."

37. Francis to Perry Francis, May 1, 1916, Francis Papers, MOSHI. Actually, Francis called the embassy "inconvenient, ill-adapted, almost absolutely unequipped." He recommended spending $205,000 for a new embassy, because "We are now the creditor-nation, besides being a world power." His advice was disregarded. See Francis to Lansing, May 7/20, 1916, f. 133, d. 120, AVPRI. Francis to William Phillips, May 2, 1916, Francis to Lansing, May 2, 1916, and Francis to Frank L. Polk, May 3, 1916, Francis Papers, MOSHI. It was obvious that as long as neither side was willing to budge, a new commercial treaty did not stand a chance. For example, see Bakhmetev's cable back in 1913 where he indicated that a Jewish delegation had visited Wilson and insisted that Russia liquidate its current passport system before the United States sign a trade agreement, Bakhmetev to Sazonov, March 22/April 4, 1913, f. 133, d. 105, no. 14, AVPRI, or later in 1914 when he told Straus that no change on passport restrictions would be made until the end of the war (Bakhmetev to Sazonov, November 29/December 12, 1914, f. 133, d. 48, no. 238, AVPRI). Francis to Perry Francis, May 1, 1916, Francis Papers, MOSHI.

38. Polk to Francis, with handwritten comment by Francis, May 18, 1916, Francis Papers, MOSHI; WW to Francis, June 9, 1916, Francis Papers, MOSHI.

39. Francis to Stone, June 20, 1916, and Francis to Secretary of State, January 16, 1916, Francis Papers, MOSHI.

40. Francis to WW, with encl., July 7, 1916, WP, LC; Francis to Darwin P. Kingsley, July 10, 1916, Francis Papers, MOSHI.

41. Bogoyavlensky to Director of Second Department, Ministry of Foreign Affairs, June 9/22, 1916, d. 1151, l. 40–43; Bogoyavlensky to Director of Second Department, Ministry of Foreign Affairs, August 23/September 5, 1916, d. 1703, l. 19–21; L. Alurievsky to George Bakhmetev, November 12, 1916, d. 715, l. 32; and for quote, A. I. Sack to K. Yu. Medzykhovsky, January 10, 1917, f. 170, op. 512/1, d. 525, l. 16–18, all in AVPRI.

42. Francis to Secretary of State, July 23, 1916, in Jamie H. Cockfield, ed., *Dollars and Diplomacy: Ambassador David Rowland Francis and the Fall of Tsarism, 1916–17*, 35.

43. Francis to Perry and Dave [Francis], August 7, 1916; for the banker's remark,

Francis to Lansing, August 14, 1916, Francis Papers, MOSHI; Francis to Lansing, July 25, 1916, encl. in Lansing to WW, August 22, 1916, SD, RG59, 763.72/2835½, NA; Francis to Polk, August 30, 1916, Francis Papers, MOSHI.

44. Francis to Darwin P. Kingsley, July 10, 1916, in Cockfield, *Dollars and Diplomacy,* 33; for the exact terms of this arrangement, see Francis to Lansing, June 13, 1916, in Cockfield, *Dollars and Diplomacy,* 26; on the cable deal, which ended up not happening, see Francis to Senator Robert Owen, October 2, 1916, Francis Papers, MOSHI.

45. Francis to Phillips, October 16, 1916, Francis Papers, MOSHI.

46. For the opening of the Duma, see Francis to Secretary of State, November 18, 1916, SD, RG59, 861.00/267, NA; for possible revolution, see Francis to Nina, November 20, 1916, Francis Papers, MOSHI; for Trepov quote, check Francis to Lansing, November 28, 1916, Francis Papers, MOSHI.

47. Francis to Dave [Francis], December 11, 1916, Francis Papers, MOSHI; Francis to Leila [Francis], December 14, 1916, Francis Papers, MOSHI; Francis to Perry [Francis], January 2, 1917, Francis Papers, MOSHI; Francis to Secretary of State, January 4, 1917, SD, RG59, 861.00/270, NA.

48. Francis to W. M. Ledbetter, February 23, 1917, Francis Papers, MOSHI; Francis, Appointment Book, February 24, 1917, Francis Papers, MOSHI; Francis to Lansing, February 24, 1917, in Cockfield, *Dollars and Diplomacy,* 86.

49. Francis to Secretary of State, February 25, 1917, SD, RG59, 861.00/272, NA; Francis to Jane (Francis), February 25, 1917, Francis Papers, MOSHI; Francis to Polk, February 25, 1917, in Cockfield, *Dollars and Diplomacy,* 87. Francis, Appointment Book, February 26, 1917, February 27, 1917, and February 28, 1917, Francis Papers, MOSHI; as to the comments about Golytsin, Shulgin, and the Duma Committee, see Cockfield, *Dollars and Diplomacy,* 88–89, and Tsuyoshi Hasegawa, *The February Revolution: Petrograd, 1917,* 519 ff., concerning Shulgin.

50. Francis to Secretary of State, March 15, 1917, Francis Papers, MOSHI; Hasegawa, *February Revolution,* 508, 520–22; Francis to Secretary of State, March 14, 1917, encl. in Lansing to WW, January 15, 1917, SD, RG59, 861.00/273, NA. In this telegram Francis mistakenly wrote, "Rodzianko, president of the Douma, issuing orders over his own signature." In this same telegram, Francis noted that "Revolutionists have absolute control in Petrograd." It is this telegram that Lansing sent to the president with the comment: "My own impression is that the Allies knew of this matter and I presume are favorable to the revolutionists since the Court party has been, throughout the war, secretly pro-German." Lansing to WW, March 15, 1917, WP, LC. Francis to Secretary of State, March 16, 1917, SD, RG59, 861.00/279, NA.

51. House to WW, March 17, 1917, WP, LC; War Cabinet Meeting no. 98, March 16, 1917, Public Record Office (hereafter PRO).

52. Maurice Paléologue, *An Ambassador's Memoirs,* vol. 3, 243; Francis, "Memo on Events of the First Revolution," March 13–18, 1917, Francis Papers, MOSHI; Francis to Perry, March 19, 1917, Francis Papers, MOSHI; Lansing to WW, March 19, 1917, WP, LC; Secretary of State to Francis, March 20, 1917, Tele 1271, SD, RG 59, 861.00/284, NA.

53. Lansing, Private Memo, March 20, 1917, Lansing Papers, box 67, LC.

54. As quoted in Arthur S. Link, *Wilson: Campaigns for Progressivism and Peace, 1916–1917,* 424.

55. Francis to President of the Council of Ministers, March 22, 1917, Francis Papers, MOSHI.

56. K. M. Onu to Director II Department, Ministry of Foreign Affairs, March 14/27, 1917, f. 170, o. 119, d. 525, l. 78, AVPRI; for quote, see "Address delivered by Dr. B. E. Shatsky, March 28th, 1917," f. 170, d. 525, l. 65–66, AVPRI. Extract from the journal, no. 98, "A Separate Consultation on Transportation, from the 29 of March 1917," f. 158, o. 449, d. 129a., l. 32, AVPRI.

57. Supplement to no. 71/0, April 5, 1917, "Project of a Convention about the Establishment of the London Supply Bureau," f. 170, o. 512/1, d. 468, l. 72–75, AVPRI. In May, Onu reported that the U.S. administration had opened a $100 million credit. See Onu to Foreign Ministry, f. 133, d. 63, no. 265, AVPRI. General Zaliubovsky to General Manikovsky, April 7, 1917, f. 170, o. 512/1, d. 468, AVPRI.

58. Francis to Perry and Dave, March 28, 1917, Francis Papers, MOSHI.

59. Samuel Gompers to Francis, April 2, 1917, WP, LC. As earlier mentioned (note 35 previously), George P. Bakhmetev tendered his resignation on April 4/17, 1917. G. J. Sosnowsky to WW, April 7, 1917, WP, LC; Baker to WW, April 14, 1917, WP, LC; Lansing to WW, April 5, 1917, encl., War File, vol. 25, SD, RG59, 763.72/3787, NA.

60. Oscar Straus to Secretary of State, April 4, 1917, SD, RG59, 861.00/314, NA.

61. Kennan, *Russia Leaves the War,* 12.

Two. 1917: The Root Mission and the Stevens Railway Commission

1. Elihu Root as quoted by George F. Kennan, *Russia and the West under Lenin and Stalin,* 26. For the second Root quote, see Warth, *The Allies and the Russian Revolution,* 98; as for the Lansing quote, see Lansing to Amembassy [American Embassy], May 18, 1917, *PWW,* vol. 42, 369. The amounts are cited in Kennan, *Russia Leaves the War,* 19 and note 10 on that page where Kennan notes that another $125 million of credit was approved on November 1, 1917, but the Provisional Government fell on November 7, 1917.

2. Secretary of State to Francis, May 22, 1917, *FRUS, 1918, Russia,* 1: 110–11.

3. Miliukov to Bakhmetev, March 5/18, 1917, encl. in Bakhmetev to Secretary of State, March 18, 1917, *FRUS, 1918, Russia,* 1: 5.

4. Lansing to WW, April 9, 1917, with encl. William Phillips to Lansing, April 7, 1917, SD, RG59, 763.72/3799½, NA.

5. Oscar Straus to Secretary of State, April 4, 1917, SD, RG59, 861.00/314, NA; on the role of Straus, check Lasch, *The American Liberals and the Russian Revolution,* 42. House, Diary, April 9, 1917, House Papers, CtY.

6. House to WW, April 10, 1917, House Papers, CtY; Cecil Spring Rice, Memo, April 13, 1917, Cecil Spring Rice Papers (hereafter Spring Rice Papers), Public Record Office, London (hereafter PRO).

7. Lansing to WW, April 11, 1917, encl. Francis to Secretary of State, April 10, 1917, SD, RG59, 763.72/3771, NA; Josephus Daniels to Wilson, April 10, 1917, encl. Gatling on German socialists, Daniels Papers, box 13, LC.

8. WW to Lansing, April 12, 1917, SD, RG59, 763.72/3800½, vol. 25, NA; Lansing to WW, April 12, 1917, WP, LC.

9. House to WW, April 13, 1917, WP, LC; Lansing, Desk Diary, April 13, 1917, Lansing Papers, box 65, LC; Frank K. Lane to George W. Lane, April 15, 1917, in Anne W. Lane and Louise H. Wall, eds., *The Letters of Franklin K. Lane,* 248.

10. Lansing, Desk Diary, April 16, 1917, on McAdoo's visit, Lansing Papers,

box 65, LC; McAdoo to WW, April 17, 1917, WP, box 84, case file 64 B, LC, suggesting Root; Lansing, Desk Diary, April 17, 1917, on the cabinet meeting, Lansing Papers, box 65, LC; Josephus Daniels, *The Wilson Era: Years of War and After, 1917–1923*, 57–59, on his criticism of Root's appointment. As to Root being a "real friend of the Russian Revolution," see WW to Lansing, April 24, 1917, SD, RG59, 763.72/4031½, NA; Lansing, Desk Diary, April 24, 1917, Lansing Papers, box 65, LC; discussion with the president in Robert Lansing, *War Memoirs of Robert Lansing, Secretary of State*, 334.

11. Secretary of State to Embassy, April 14, 1917, SD, RG59, 861.00/336A, NA.

12. Lansing, Desk Diary, April 16, 1917, Lansing Papers, box 65, LC; McAdoo to WW, April 17, 1917, WP, LC; WW to Lansing, April 19, 1917, SD, RG59, 763.72/4031½, vol. 26, NA.

13. *New York Times*, April 10, 1917, sec. 3, p. 2. Root is quoted in Philip C. Jessup, *Elihu Root*, vol. 2, 356.

14. Lansing, Desk Diary, April 24, 1917, Lansing Papers, box 65, LC; Thomas W. Brahany, Diary, April 24, 1917, Franklin Delano Roosevelt Library, Hyde Park, N.Y.

15. Stephen S. Wise to WW, April 24, 1917, WP, LC; Meyer London to WW, April 28, 1917, WP, LC; Hiram W. Johnson to Mrs. Raymond Robins, July 17, 1917, Raymond Robins Papers (hereafter Robins Papers), box 12, State Historical Society of Wisconsin (hereafter WSHS); Oscar Straus to George Kennan, May 2, 1917, George Kennan Papers (hereafter Kennan Papers), box 4, LC; Francis to Edward B. Lilley, May 14, 1917, Francis Papers, MOSHI.

16. Taft to Root, April 28, 1917, Elihu Root Papers (hereafter Root Papers), box 166, LC; *New York Times*, April 7, 1917; for the quote, see *New York Times*, April 28, 1917.

17. Secretary of State to American Embassy, Petrograd, encl. in WW to Lansing, May 1, 1917, SD, RG59, 763.72/4377A, vol. 28, NA; Francis to Secretary of State, April 28, 1917, encl. in Lansing to WW, April 30, 1917, SD, RG59, 763.72/4377A, vol. 28, NA. After Bakhmetev's arrival in the United States, he spoke with officials, members of Congress, and the president. He remarked that although he had a very warm welcome, he sensed a certain reserve, especially on the part of Lansing. See Bakhmetev to Foreign Affairs Ministry, June 14/27, 1917, f. 170, op. 512/1, d. 507, l. 78–79, AVPRI. (George P. Bakhmetev tendered his resignation on April 4/17, 1917.)

18. WW to McCormick, May 1, 1917, C. H. McCormick Correspondence, LC; Root to Lansing, May 3, 1917, encl. in Lansing to WW, May 4, 1917, SD, RG59, 763.72/4524½, NA; N. Baker to Franklin Lane, April 26, 1917, N. Baker Papers, box 2, LC.

19. WW to Baker, May 1, 1917, N. Baker Papers, box 4, LC; Lane to Lansing, encl. in Lansing to WW, May 1, 1917, WP, LC; House to WW, May 2, 1917, WP, LC; Burleson to WW, May 2, 1917, N. Baker Papers, box 4, LC; and WW to Baker, May 3, 1917, N. Baker Papers, box 4, LC; quote of Wilson on Walling, WW to Lansing, May 3, 1917, SD, RG59, 763.72/ 4390½, vol. 28, NA; for attached list of names, see Lansing's list, May 3, 1917, SD, RG59, 763.72/4390½, vol. 28, NA; on Walling, see W. B. Wilson to WW, encl. in WW to Lansing, May 3, 1917, SD, RG59, 763.72/4390½, NA.

20. For N. Baker's announcement of Hugh Scott, see *New York Times*, May 12, 1917; as for Scott's "cheerfulness," see Scott, "The Russian Revolution," 2, Hugh Scott Papers (hereafter Scott Papers), box 84, LC; on his pessimism, see Scott to

General Albert Wheeler, May 15, 1917, as well as Scott to Mrs. H. L. Schelling, May 15, 1917, Scott Papers, box 29, LC. As for Daniels's selection of Glennon, see Josephus Daniels, Diary, May 10, 1917, Josephus Daniels Papers (hereafter Daniels Papers), LC, and Daniels to WW, May 10, 1917, WP, box 84, case file 64 B, LC.

21. On Gompers, see Lansing to WW, April 12, 1917, SD, RG59, 763.72/3800½, NA, and Samuel Gompers, *Seventy Years of Life and Labor: An Autobiography*, 398; on Gompers's recommendation, see Gompers to Lansing, May 4, 1917, SD, RG59, 763.72/4391½, NA, and Lansing, Desk Diary, May 5, 1917, Lansing Papers, box 65, LC, and Duncan to WW, May 7, 1917, SD, RG59, 763.72/4670½, NA; on Francis's inquiries of Miliukov and others, check Lansing to Francis, April 14, 1917, SD, RG59, 763.72/4001A, NA, and Francis to Lansing, April 19, 1917, SD, RG59, 763.72/4002, NA, and Francis to Lansing, April 17, 1917, SD, RG59, 861.00/407, NA, and April 20, 1917, SD, RG59, 763.72/4003, NA; on Meyers, see WW to Lansing, April 17, 1917, SD, RG59, 763.72/4031½, NA; on the opinions of Bertron and Harper, read Bertron to House, April 30, 1917, House Papers, drawer 3, CtY, and Harper to Crane, April 20, 1917, Samuel Harper Papers, envelope 9, University of Chicago [hereafter Harper Papers, UC]. On Washburn's involvement, check Lansing, Desk Diary, April 30, 1917, and May 1, 1917, Lansing Papers, box 65, LC, as well as Lansing to WW, April 30, 1917, SD, RG59, 763.72/4386½, NA; on the use of Brandeis, see Lansing, Desk Diary, May 1 and 3, 1917, Lansing Papers, box 65, LC. On Wilson's denial that the Russian government rejected a Jew, see WW to Tumulty, n.d., WP, box 84, case file 64 B, LC. For Lvov's denial, check the *New York Times*, May 30, 1917.

22. William B. Wilson to WW, April 30, 1917, SD, RG59, 763.72/4386½, NA; WW to Lansing, May 3, 1917, SD, RG59, 763.72/4390½, NA; Lansing to WW, May 3, 1917, SD, RG59, 763.72/4390½, NA; Root to Lansing, May 3, 1917, SD, RG59, 763.72/4524½, encl. in Lansing to WW, May 4, 1917, SD, RG59, 763.72/4524½, vol. 29, NA; on Walling's reluctance to serve, see Polk to Lansing, encl. in Lansing to WW, May 7, 1917, WP, LC; on Russell's acceptance, see William B. Wilson to WW, May 9, 1917, WP, box 84, case file 64B, LC, and WW to Russell, May 10, 1917, Charles Edward Russell Papers, book 6, LC; Link mentions the condemning of the antiwar sentiment of socialists by prominent members in Arthur S. Link, *Woodrow Wilson and the Progressive Era, 1910–1917*, 274, n. 59. For Russell's essay, check William E. Walling, ed., *The Socialists and the War: A Documentary Statement of the Position of the Socialists of All Countries; with Special Reference to Their Peace Policy.*

23. On Washburn, see Washburn to Baker, May 10, 1917, Stanley Washburn Papers (hereafter Washburn Papers), box 1, LC, and Lansing to American Consul, Vladivostok, May 17, 1917, SD, RG59, 763.72/4781B, NA. As to some of the others, see Daniels to Curl, May 9, 1917, WP, box 84, case file 64B, and Lansing to Willys-Overland, May 14, 1917, SD, RG59, 763.72/4609, NA, as well as all the names of the total membership of 26 on pp. 1–2, Mission Log, Root Papers, box 192, LC. Check also Secretary of State to Amembassy, Petrograd, May 16, 1917, SD, RG59, 763.72/4711a, vol. 30, NA.

24. On the question of the note, see Paul Miliukov, *Political Memoirs, 1905–1917*, 445–55; on the suggested alterations, check Robert P. Browder and Alexander F. Kerensky, eds., *The Russian Provisional Government, 1917: Documents*, vol. 2, 1109. Francis to Lansing, May 31, 1917, SD, RG59, 763.72/5173, NA; Lansing to Francis, June 3, 1917, SD, RG59, 763.72/5173, NA; WW to Lansing, June 1, 1917, Ray Stannard Baker Papers (hereafter R. S. Baker Papers), ser. I, box 11, LC; also

see Lansing to WW, May 28, 1917, SD, RG59, 861.00/362½, NA, for "Document" from Provisional Government; Joseph P. Tumulty to WW, May 21, 1917, WP, ser. 2, box 161, LC. The full text of the president's message can be found in Secretary of State to Amembassy, Petrograd, May 22, 1917, SD, RG59, 763.72/5171a, vol. 33, NA. For Wilson's note of May 22, 1917, see *PWW,* vol. 42, 365–67; Browder and Kerensky, *Provisional Government,* vol. 2, 1110, and John Ray to Lansing, June 16, 1917, SD, RG59, 861.00/446, NA. For Lansing's comment on Francis, see Lansing, Desk Diary, Sunday, June 3, 1917, Lansing Papers, box 65, LC, and for notes to change and complete text, see *FRUS, 1918, Russia,* 1: 86–89, 90–94, 96. For Lansing's comment on Francis, see Lansing, Desk Diary, Sunday, June 3, 1917, Lansing Papers, box 65, LC.

25. Daniels, *The Wilson Era,* 59, and E. David Cronon, ed., *The Cabinet Diaries of Josephus Daniels, 1913–1921,* 152. As to the Scotch, see Jessup, *Elihu Root,* vol. 2, 360.

26. Paul V. Harper, ed., *The Russia I Believe In: The Memoirs of Samuel N. Harper, 1902–1941,* 99. On Russia's high expectations for the Root Mission and the preparations for it, especially Russian public opinion, see Onu to the Foreign Ministry, May 3/16, 1917, f. 133, d. 63, no. 268, AVPRI, whereupon its reception, Onu thought, largely hangs the extent of aid Russia would get.

27. For the president's message and Gompers's greetings, see Francis, *Russia from the American Embassy,* 96–98; for credits and railway men, check ibid., 110, 124; as to the actual credits, again, consult Kennan, *Russia Leaves the War,* 19, esp. note 10. For the secretary of the treasury's cable, check McAdoo to Francis, draft, encl. in McAdoo to WW, May 16, 1917, WP, LC.

28. Francis, *Russia from the American Embassy,* 98–100, 110, 113–14; Francis to Secretary of State, April 21, 1917, Tele 1211, SD, RG59, 861.00/327, NA. Francis to Lansing, May 4, 1917, *FRUS, 1918, Russia,* 1: 40. On the "irksome war," see N. Winship to Secretary of State, May 8, 1917, *FRUS, 1918, Russia,* 1: 50; on the prediction as well as partisanship, check Winship to Secretary of State, May 13, 1917, *FRUS, 1918, Russia,* 1: 64. Francis to Lansing, May 13 and 14, 1917, *FRUS, 1918, Russia,* 1: 52–53; Francis to Lansing, May 20, 1917, *FRUS, 1918, Russia,* 1: 74.

29. Elihu Root et al., *America's Message to the Russian People: Addresses by the Members of the Special Diplomatic Mission of the United States to Russia in the Year 1917,* 22, 27, 67.

30. Ibid., 17.

31. Ibid., 17 and 33 for first quote; 45 and 79 for last quote.

32. Ibid., 17, 30, 33, and quote on 103.

33. Jessup, *Elihu Root,* vol. 2, 353, and R. S. Baker, *War Leader,* vol. 7, 109; Francis to Lansing, June 13, 1917, *FRUS, 1918, Russia,* 1: 116; Root to Lansing, June 17, 1917 June 18, 1917, *FRUS, 1918, Russia,* 1: 118–19, 123. For text of Root's speech, check Root to Secretary of State, July 17, 1917, WP, LC. Just as Root met with Russian officials in Petrograd, Bakhmetev claimed to have swayed Lansing to abandon his do-nothing policy; yet he observed that little tangible progress had been made on the matter of American aid. See Bakhmetev to Foreign Affairs Ministry, June 17/30, 1917, f. 133, d. 61, no. 364, AVPRI.

34. For quotes, see Wiseman to Drummond, June 20, 1917, FO 800/205, Balfour Papers, PRO; also check W. B. Fowler, *British-American Relations, 1917–1918: The Role of Sir William Wiseman,* 111ff. In all probability, what Wiseman had in mind was counteracting German propaganda influence through returning refugees of an Allied persuasion rather than a German one.

35. FO [Foreign Office] to Consul-General Bayley, June 19, 1917, FO 800/205, Balfour Papers, PRO.

36. Wiseman to Drummond, June 20, 1917, FO 800/205, Balfour Papers, PRO.

37. Scott to Newton D. Baker, June 14, 1917, and Scott to Baker, June 18, 1917, N. Baker Papers, box 3, LC.

38. Root's suggestion in Root to Lansing, June 17, 1917, *FRUS, The Lansing Papers, 1914–1920*, 2: 120–22; for reply, Lansing to Francis on agency, June 27, 1917, *FRUS, Lansing Papers*, 2: 127, and outlays, 128–29; for the role of the YMCA, check Davis and Trani, "The American YMCA and the Russian Revolution"; for German efforts, see *FRUS, Lansing Papers*, 2: 128–29. At this time, Bakhmetev reported on Lansing's pessimism about Russia, that is, a "certain reserve." See Bakhmetev to Foreign Affairs Ministry, June 14/27, 1917, f. 170, op. 512/1, d. 507, l. 78–79, AVPRI. In a cable of July 27/August 9, 1917, he criticizes the ineptitude of the Wilson administration and, particularly, the cabinet composed of "mediocre men." See Bakhmetev to Foreign Ministry, July 27/August 9, 1917, f. 133, d. 61, no. 441, AVPRI. Root to Lansing, July 2, 1917, and Polk to Francis, July 7, 1917, *FRUS, Lansing Papers*, 2: 128–29; "Report of the Special Diplomatic Mission to Russia to the Secretary of State," August 1917, *FRUS, 1918, Russia*, 1: 133; Root pressed for a credit extension in July. See Bakhmetev to Foreign Affairs Ministry, June 30/July 13, 1917, f. 133, d. 61, no. 387, AVPRI. Root persistently cabled for an extension of a $5 million credit.

39. George Creel to WW, encl. June 20 [Aug.] 1917, *PWW*, vol. 43, 526–30 (quote on 529 and estimate).

40. W. V. Judson to Burleson, June 24, 1917, WP, LC. For technical problems, see, for example, the minutes no. 98 of the Special Council on Transportation, March 29, 1917, where an "urgent" order is placed for 2,000 locomotives and 40,000 rolling stock cars, f. 158, d. 449, op. 129a., l. 32, AVPRI; of course, although factories had been found to cover the order in the United States, credits had to be available, supply coordinated with the Allies, and a means found to deliver the goods. See V. Nabokov to Ministry of Transportation, April 7, 1917, f. 170, op. 512/1, d. 173, l. 110, AVPRI. On those aspects, check Onu to the Foreign Affairs Ministry, April 8/21, where he reports on his meeting with McAdoo on a $3 billion loan's progress and notes McAdoo's comments on avoiding waste and the sending of technical experts. See Onu to the Foreign Affairs Ministry, April 8/21, 1917, f. 133, d. 63, no. 180, AVPRI. Finally, on delivery problems, see Bakhmetev to the Foreign Affairs Ministry, June 17/30, 1917, f. 133, d. 61, no. 363, where he notes that naval shipments are in a "critical" condition and puts a halt on new orders except for railroad materials until the Russian government sets priorities. See also Bakhmetev's cable to the Russian chargé in London in which he writes that because of the insufficiency of the cargo fleet tonnage, Russia should not be able to purchase a significant amount of supplies in the United States. See Bakhmetev to chargé in London, July 3/16, 1917, f. 170, op. 512/1, d. 477, l. 55, AVPRI.

41. Baker to Scott, July 1, 1917, N. Baker Papers, box 3, LC. Tereshchenko cabled the Russian embassy in Washington indicating his readiness to coordinate the war effort with the United States. See M. I. Tereshchenko to Embassy, July 15/28, 1917, f. 170, op. 512/1, l. 35, no. 3181, AVPRI. The new Russian ambassador, who presented his credentials on July 2/15, 1917, reported at this time that he had spoken with members of the administration and congressmen and that they had "very little acquaintance with Russian affairs." See Boris A. Bakhmetev to Foreign Affairs Ministry, June 14/27, 1917, f. 133, d. 61, no. 355, AVPRI. He found Lansing

more reserved, but a few days later he and Lansing agreed that Russia would be treated equally with the other Allies. See B. Bakhmetev to Foreign Affairs Ministry, June 19, 1917, f, 133, d. 61, AVPRI. In August he felt Lansing willing to discuss the Russian crisis and continuing to support Russia morally and materially, despite recent events. See Bakhmetev to Foreign Affairs Ministry, August 3/16, 1917, f. 133, d. 61, AVPRI. By mid-August he noted the administration's approval of a $100 million credit and of 1,500 steam locomotives and 30,000 rolling stock cars. See Bakhmetev to Foreign Affairs Ministry, August 10/23, 1917, f. 133, d. 61, AVPRI. By early November he could report that the U.S. Treasury provided Russia with another $125 million credit through January 1, 1918, bringing the sum total of American credits to $450 million. Bakhmetev to Foreign Affairs Ministry, October 21/November 3, 1917, f. 133, d. 61, no. 651, AVPRI.

42. Washburn to Baker, July 8, 1917, N. Baker Papers, box 4, LC.

43. Francis, Appointment Book, July 16/August 3 and July 17/August 4, Francis Papers, MOSHI; on the extent of Bolshevik complicity in the July Days, check chaps. 1–4 of Alexander Rabinowitch, *The Bolsheviks Come to Power: The Revolution of 1917 in Petrograd.*

44. House to WW, July 23, 1917, WP, LC.

45. Washburn to Baker, July 25, 1917, N. Baker Papers, box 5, LC; Lane to Baker, attached to Washburn to Baker, July 25, 1917, N. Baker Papers, box 5, LC; "General Scott's Report to the Secretary of War," July 25, 1917, Tasker Bliss Papers (hereafter Bliss Papers), box 174, LC.

46. "Report of the Diplomatic Mission to Russia to the Secretary of State," August 1917, *FRUS, 1918, Russia,* 1: 138–39, 144, 145; "Supplementary Report of the Special Diplomatic Mission to Russia to the Secretary of State," August 27, 1917, *FRUS, 1918, Russia,* 1: 147–53, 167–69. On implementation, see Lansing to Francis, October 29, 1917, *FRUS, 1918, Russia,* 1: 214–15. For YMCA, check note 38 previously as well as Donald E. Davis and Eugene P. Trani, "An American in Russia: Russell M. Story and the Bolshevik Revolution, 1917–1919."

47. Lansing, Private Memo, August 9, 1917, Lansing Papers, box 67, LC. (For a discussion of the importance of the memo, see note 63 to follow.) Bakhmetev reported that the Root Mission was favorably disposed to Russia but that he thought he needed all the help Root could provide. See Bakhmetev to Foreign Affairs Ministry, July 29/August 11, 1917, f. 133, d. 61, no. 451, AVPRI. Given Lansing's pessimism, it is interesting that Russian officials, certainly Onu and Bakhmetev, thought highly of Root's role for securing U.S. aid. Yet Root extricated himself from Russian affairs by declining the presidency of the Russian-American Society. See Root to Bakhmetev, September 25, 1917, f. 170, op. 512/1, d. 482, l. 56, AVPRI.

48. "Statement of William English Walling," encl. in WW to Lansing, August 24, 1917, WP, LC; War Cabinet Meeting no. 215, August 15, 1917, PRO; House to WW, August 15, 1917, WP, LC; War Cabinet Meeting no. 229, September 7, 1917, PRO; House, Diary, September 16, 1917, House Papers, CtY; McCormick to Scott, September 11, 1917, Scott Papers, box 71, LC.

49. William Phillips, "Notebooks," August 30, 1917, William Phillips Papers (hereafter Phillips Papers), Harvard University (hereafter HU).

50. Strakhovsky, *American Opinion about Russia,* 6–9; Morgenthau to Lansing, April 12, 1917, Lansing Papers, vol. 26, LC; *New York Times,* April 28, 1917; Lansing to WW, April 11, 1917, SD, RG59, 763.72/3771, NA.

51. War Cabinet Meeting no. 126, April 25, 1917, PRO; Lansing to Lane, April

25, 1917, Lansing Papers, vol. 27, LC; Summers to Francis, April 25, 1917, Francis Papers, MOSHI; Moran to Francis, April 13, 1917, Francis Papers, MOSHI.

52. Root to Lansing, May 6, 1917, encl. in Lansing to WW, May 7, 1917, SD, RG59, 861.77/97½, NA; WW to Lansing, May 7, 1917, SD, RG59, 861.77/98½, NA; Lansing to Root, May 9, 1917, Root Papers, box 136, LC. Root has received much criticism, as previously noted. Yet from the start Russians considered his future goodwill crucial and he was able to deliver even before he left on his mission. For example, see K. Onu's account of his conversation with Root where Root mentioned he had been able to insist on the immediate placement of the Russian railroad contract and the opening of a credit line to finance it. See K. Onu to Foreign Affairs Ministry, May 3/16, 1917, f. 133, d. 63, no. 264, AVPRI and also Onu to Foreign Affairs Ministry, May 3/16, 1917, f. 133, d. 63, no. 265, where he reports on the credit line opened at $100 million for railroad locomotives and cars.

53. Cronon, ed., *Cabinet Diaries of Josephus Daniels*, 125–26; Lansing to Francis, April 2, 1917, Francis to Lansing, April 9, 1917, Francis to Lansing, April 21, 1917, Lansing to Francis, April 21, 1917, all in *FRUS, 1918, Russia*, 3: 184–88; Stevens to WW, May 1, 1917, WP, ser. 4, box 84, 64C, LC; Lansing to WW, May 1, 1917, WP, ser. 4, box 84, 64C, LC; WW to Lansing, May 5, 1917, WP, ser. 4, box 84, 64C, LC; Lansing to Francis, May 3, 1917, *FRUS, 1918 Russia*, 3: 189, and for departure, see Baker, *War Leader*, 59, 61.

54. Lansing to Francis, May 15, 1917, and Francis to Lansing, May 15, 1917, *FRUS, 1918, Russia*, 3: 191.

55. Stevens to Root, July 1, 1917, Root Papers, box 136, LC; Franklin K. Lane to WW, August 10, 1917, WP, LC.

56. Stevens's Message to Russians, "Message to the People of Russia from the United States Railway Advisory Commission," July 4, 1917, *FRUS, Lansing Papers*, 2: 340–41; Lansing to WW, August 13, 1917, WP, LC; Lansing to WW, August 13, 1917, *FRUS, Lansing Papers*, 2: 339; WW to Lansing, August 14, 1917, *FRUS, Lansing Papers*, 2: 342.

57. Francis to Lansing, August 1, 1917, *FRUS, 1918, Russia*, 1: 171–72; Francis to Lansing, August 25, 1917, and Stevens to Lansing, received September 17, 1917, both in *FRUS, 1918, Russia*, 3: 197–98. Bakhmetev talks about assembling locomotives in Vladivostok as a constructive and positive use of American help. See Bakhmetev to Foreign Affairs Ministry, August 26/September 8, 1917, f. 158, op. 449, d. 129a., l. 351, 352, AVPRI. Black, "Memorandum for the Secretary of War," September 21, 1917, RG 407 (AG Office) Central Decimal Files, box 1381, NA; Black to Adjutant General, October 13, 1917, RG 407 (AG Office) Central Decimal Files, box 1381, NA; Lansing to WW, October 26, 1917, SD, RG59, 861.77/193, NA.

58. Francis to Lansing, September 28, 1917, Francis to Lansing, September 29, 1917, Lansing to Francis, October 15, 1917, Francis to Lansing, October 20, 1917, Francis to Lansing, November 11, 1917, Francis to Lansing, November 7, 1917, and Polk to Caldwell [consul at Vladivostok], November 14, 1917, all in *FRUS, 1918, Russia*, 3: 199–208. Stevens to Lansing, received November 26, 1917, *FRUS, 1918, Russia*, 3: 210. Stevens was frustrated by both governments. Bakhmetev recommended assisting him in every possible way because the reorganization of the rails was urgent. Bakhmetev to Foreign Affairs Ministry, August 28/September 10, 1917, f. 158, op. 449, d. 129a., no. 518, l. 410, AVPRI. Lansing to Caldwell, November 27, 1917, Caldwell to Lansing, December 4, 1917, Stevens to Lansing,

December 14, 1917, Stevens to Lansing, December 17, 1917, and Lansing to Scid-more [Consul General, Yokohama], December 19, 1917, all in *FRUS, 1918, Russia*, 3: 211–13.

59. House to WW, July 19, 1917, WP, LC on France and Russia; on House's conversation with Bakhmetev, see House to WW, July 23, 1917, WP, LC; for Narodny, check Narodny to WW, July 22, 1917, stated as Memorandum, July 24, 1917, The White House Files, and referred to the State Department. Bakhmetev reported that only extraordinary measures such as large-scale loans could prevent the bankruptcy of Russia. See Bakhmetev to Foreign Affairs Ministry, August 28/September 10, 1917, f. 133, d. 61, no. 519, AVPRI.

60. British Embassy Memo, encl. in Memo, August 5, 1917, WP, LC; Polk to Lansing, August 7, 1917, WP, LC; British Embassy Memo, encl. in Polk to Lansing, August 7, 1917, WP, LC.

61. E. Drummond to G. Buchanan, August 6, 1917, FO 800.383, Drummond Papers, PRO. For a work that stresses the Japanese influence on Wilson's Russian policies, see Pauline Tompkins, *American-Russian Relations in the Far East.*

62. War Cabinet Meeting no. 205, August 7, 1917, PRO; George Buchanan, *My Mission to Russia and Other Diplomatic Memories*, vol. 2, 157–205.

63. Lansing, Private Memo, August 9, 1917, Lansing Papers, box 67, LC. For an analysis of this important document somewhat contrary to the one presented here, see Williams, *American-Russian Relations*, 91–92. Whereas we point to the memo's ambivalence, Williams stresses Lansing's comment concerning *if* Root were wrong. From that, Williams concludes, "In August, 1917, the United States determined to abandon Russia of the March Revolution until the 'normal process' of revolt ran its course and order was reestablished 'by arbitrary military power'" (91). Williams credits Lansing with this policy though various sources warned that it was extremely dangerous (91). However that may be, Williams is right about Wilson's Russian policy being conceived with indifference, a helpless feeling, and distrust of Kerensky. We find it hard to believe that this document alone was the basis of Wilson's Russian policy at that time. However, Lansing's attitude in August 1917 may be the earliest statement of a future "cold war" approach to Russia. It is noteworthy that Link never cites this document in the *PWW.* Does this imply that Wilson never saw it or even was influenced by Lansing's attitude at this time? For more on Williams, see An Essay on Notes and Sources section of this book.

64. Lansing, Private Memo, August 9, 1917, Lansing Papers, box 67, LC.

65. Ibid.

66. Ibid.

67. House to WW, August 10, 1917, WP, LC; for quote, Page to WW, August 14, 1917, WP, LC.

68. War Cabinet Meeting no. 215, August 15, 1917, PRO.

69. Washburn to Secretary of State, June 29, 1917, encl. in WW to Lansing, August 14, 1917, and Washburn to Secretary of State, encl. in WW to Lansing, August 14, 1917, SD, RG59, 763.72/6504½, NA.

70. Washburn to Northcliffe, August 24, 1917, Washburn Papers, box 1, LC.

71. House to WW, August 5, 1917, WP, LC.

72. House to WW, August 19, 1917, WP, LC.

73. Mott to Lansing, encl. in Lansing to WW, August 27, 1917, WP, LC; Lansing, Desk Diary, August 28, 1917, Lansing Papers, box 65, LC.

74. Lansing to WW, October 3, 1917, WP, LC; McAdoo to Lansing, October 27, 1917, encl. in WW to Lansing, October 30, 1917, SD, RG59, 763.72/7666, vol.

52, NA; Lansing to WW, October 3, 1917, WP, LC; Lansing, Desk Diary, October 3, 1917, Lansing Papers, box 65, LC.

75. Cable, October 10, 1917, to William Wiseman, encl. in House to WW, October 15, 1917, WP, LC.

76. House, Diary, October 21, 1917, House Papers, CtY; L. S. Rowe, Assistant Secretary of the Treasury, quoting Francis, to Wilson, October 30, 1917, WP, LC. It is interesting that only a few days later the Russian Procurement Committee in the United States stopped its activities. See "Proekt postanovlenie Russkogo Zagotovitel'nogo Komiteta v Amerike," October 30, 1917, f. 170, op. 512/1, d. 469, l. 0208–0207, AVPRI. Frank Polk, Diary, November 2, 1917, Frank Polk Papers (hereafter Polk Papers), CtY.

Three. Wilson and Lansing Face Lenin and Trotsky

1. For Judson's appointment, see Scott to Lansing, July 9, 1917, William V. Judson Papers, box 4, Newberry Library (hereafter Judson Papers, NL). For a biographical account of General Judson, see Jane Gilmer Weyant, "The Life and Career of General William V. Judson, 1865–1923," especially for the period before November 1917, chaps. 1–4, and p. 74 for reference to correspondence between Burleson and Wilson. For a handy collection of Judson's messages, see Neil V. Salzman, ed., *Russia in War and Revolution: General William V. Judson's Accounts from Petrograd, 1917–1918.* The White House files indicate that on May 3 Burleson suggested giving Judson a place on the Root Mission. Wilson wrote Baker that he was inclined to give him consideration if there was no impropriety to other military appointments. See Memorandum, May 3, 1917, The White House Files, LC, and WW to N. Baker, May 3, 1917, WP, LC.

2. Judson, "Report on the Russian Situation," March 16, 1918, p. 6, Judson Papers, box 8, NL. As to Order Number One, see Rabinowitch, *The Bolsheviks Come to Power,* xxvi.

3. WW to Williams, August 13, 1917, J. S. Williams Papers, box 3, LC.

4. Williams to WW, August 10, 1917, WP, LC.

5. Judson to War College Staff [Warcolstaf], August 7, 1917, Judson Papers, box 4, NL; Judson to Scott, August 9, 1917, as quoted by Weyant, "The Life and Career of General William V. Judson, 1865–1923," 113. The "Kerensky Offensive" was the last major military effort of Russia against the Central Powers and began on July 1, 1917 (NS). British Embassy Memo, encl. in Memo, 1917, August 5, 1917, WP, LC; Judson to Warcolstaf, September 3, 1917, Judson Papers, box 4, NL.

6. Judson to Warcolstaf, October 7, 1917, Robins Papers, box 13, folder 2, WSHS; Judson to Francis, August 29, 1917, and September 3, 1917, Judson Papers, box 5, NL; Judson's paraphrase of Francis, Judson to General Peyton C. March, U.S. Army Chief of Staff, May 21, 1919, Judson Papers, box 6, NL; Francis to Lansing, August 30, 1917, *FRUS, 1918, Russia,* 1: 179–80; Francis to Lansing, September 6, 1917, *FRUS, 1918, Russia,* 1: 181; Francis to Secretary of State [SS], November 6, 1917, *FRUS, 1918, Russia,* 1: 221.

7. Memorandum for the Ambassador, August 29, 1917, encl. I, in Judson, "Report on the Russian Situation," March 16, 1918, Judson Papers, box 8, NL; Memorandum for the Ambassador, August 30, 1917, Judson Papers, box 8, NL;

Memorandum for the Ambassador, August 31, 1917, Judson Papers, box 8, NL; Memorandum for the Ambassador, September 3, 1917, Judson Papers, box 8, NL.

8. Judson to Warcolstaf, October 7, 1917, Robins Papers, box 13, folder 2, WSHS.

9. On Thompson's independent efforts, see Kennan, *Russia Leaves the War*, 56–61. Cable to Wiseman, encl. in House to WW, 15 October 1917, WP, LC; on House's access, see House, Diary, October 13, 1917, *PWW*, vol. 44, 380, 385 (italics ours).

10. Judson to Warcolstaf, October 7, 1917, *FRUS, 1918, Russia*, 1: 204–5.

11. Judson to Warcolstaf, October 28, 1917, Judson Papers, box 4, NL.

12. Ibid., October 28 and November 4, 1917.

13. SS to Francis, November 2, 1917, *FRUS, 1918, Russia*, 1: 217–18; Francis to SS, November 1, 2, and 4, 1917, *FRUS, 1918, Russia*, 1: 216, 219; Polk, Diary, November 2, 1917, Polk Papers, CtY.

14. Russell to WW, November 7, 1917, Creel Papers, WP, book 1, LC; WW to Russell, November 10, 1917, *PWW*, vol. 44, 558; WW to Creel, November 10, 1917, WP, LC.

15. Francis, Diary, November 6, 1917, Francis Papers, MOSHI; Francis to SS, November 7, 1917, tele Petrograd, WP, LC. This telegram was only received on November 20. Lansing wrote on it, "For the President."

16. Lansing, Desk Diary, November 8, 1917, Lansing Papers, box 65, LC; Francis, Diary, November 8, 1917, Francis Papers, MOSHI; Kennan, *Russia Leaves the War*, 80–81.

17. Speaking of newspapers, other colorful Americans such as John Reed and Louise Bryant, Reed's wife, were reporting from Petrograd at this time. In fact, Citizen Reed was appointed Soviet consul for New York City in January 1919. By early February, when Reed departed for the United States, Trotsky canceled his appointment as too great an affront to the U.S. See Kennan, *Russia Leaves the War*, 67–69, 405–10. Daniels, Diary, November 9, 1917, *PWW*, vol. 44, 556.

18. Morris to SS, November 8, 1917, *FRUS, 1918, Russia*, 1: 225.

19. An Address in Buffalo to the American Federation of Labor, November 12, 1917, *PWW*, vol. 45, 14.

20. WW to Frank Clark, November 13, 1917, *PWW*, vol. 45, 39.

21. August Heckscher, *Woodrow Wilson*, 463; Arthur Walworth, *Woodrow Wilson*, vol. 2, 144.

22. Francis, Diary, November 9, 1917, Francis Papers, MOSHI; Polk, Diary, November 10, 1917, Polk Papers, CtY; McCormick, Diary, November 12, 1917, Vance McCormick Papers (hereafter McCormick Papers), CtY. Bakhmetev believed the administration maintained a temporizing position to the Bolsheviks in order to keep Russia in the war as long as possible. See Bakhmetev to the Russian Ambassador in Paris, October 27/November 10, 1917, f. 170, op. 512/1, d. 508, l. 4–6, AVPRI.

23. William Appleman Williams, "Raymond Robins and Russian-American Relations, 1917–1938," 77–79.

24. Francis, Diary, November 11, 1917, Francis Papers, MOSHI; Lansing, Desk Diary, November 11, 1917, Lansing Papers, box 15, LC; Francis, Diary, November 13 and 14, 1917, Francis Papers, MOSHI.

25. Morris to Lansing, November 11, 1917, and Garrett to Lansing, November 12, 1917, *FRUS, 1918, Russia*, 1: 229–30; Francis to Lansing, November 12, 1917, R5/331; Francis to Lansing, November 13, 1917, R5/f326; and Francis to Lansing,

November 14, 1917, R5/f322, all in Paul Kesaris, ed., *Confidential U.S. Diplomatic Post Records, Pt. 1 Russia, From the Czar to Commissars, 1914–1918* (hereafter *Confidential*).

26. Francis to Lansing, November 13, 1917, Tele Petrograd, R5/f322, *Confidential;* Francis, Diary, November 13, 1917, Francis Papers, MOSHI; Francis to Lansing, November 14, 1917, R5/f326, 327 Tele Petrograd, *Confidential;* Francis, Diary, November 14, 1917, Francis Papers, MOSHI; Polk, Diary, November 14, 1917, Polk Papers, CtY. American companies continued buying Russian stocks as if they did not take the Bolsheviks seriously. See M. Karpovich to S. Tron, November 13, 1917, f. 170, op. 512/1, d. 478, l. 79, AVPRI.

27. Williams, "Raymond Robins and Russian-American Relations, 1917–1938," 89; Judson, Diary, December 5, 1917, Judson Papers, box 8, NL.

28. Judson to the Secretary of War (Baker), June 18, 1919, Judson Papers, box 6, NL; also see *The Reminiscences of DeWitt Clinton Poole,* typescript, Oral History Project, Columbia University, 88 [hereafter Poole typescript, CU], where Poole recognizes that the ambassador was quite a lady's man. The whole of this affair is recounted in Kennan, *Russia Leaves the War,* 38–40, 58, 114, 117, 126–28, 387–88, and 416. Judson to Baker, June 18, 1919, Judson Papers, box 6, NL; Lansing to Francis, November 14, 1917, rec'd. November 21, 1917; Judson, Memorandum, July 6, 1918, Judson Papers, box 4, NL; Judson to Baker, June 18, 1919, Judson Papers, box 6, NL.

29. For Francis on "message" and Wright's complicity, see Kennan, *Russia Leaves the War,* 117–18.

30. Judson to Burleson, April 10, 1919, Judson Papers, Box 6, NL.

31. Judson to Warcolstaf, November 8, 9, 11, and 13, 1917, Judson Papers, Box 4, NL. The question of security raised the issue of so-called trivial intercourse with the Bolsheviks.

32. WW to Burleson, November 14, 1917, WP, LC; Baker to WW, November 23, 1917, with Judson encl. for Burleson, November 14, 1917, *PWW,* vol. 45, 104.

33. Robins, Diary, November 9–14 and 16, 1917, Robins Papers, box 42, WSHS; Allen Wardwell, "American Red Cross Mission to Russia, 1917–1918, excerpts from diary and letters," vol. 1, 74–76, December 4, 1917, Allen Wardwell Papers (hereafter Wardwell Papers), CU.

34. Williams, "Raymond Robins and Russian-American Relations, 1917–1938," 83–85; the quote attributed to Robins is a paraphrase by Williams on 85. See Robins's testimony concerning his first meeting with Trotsky, U.S. Congress, Senate, 65th Cong., 3d sess., *Bolshevik Propaganda, Hearings before a Subcommittee of the Committee on the Judiciary, 1919,* 783–84; Robins and Thatcher to Gumberg, January 26, 1918, Robins Papers, box 13, WSHS. For an evaluation of Gumberg, see James K. Libbey, *Alexander Gumberg and Soviet-American Relations, 1917–1933;* for a detailed biography of Robins, check Neil V. Salzman, *Reform and Revolution: The Life and Times of Raymond Robins.* Thompson's stormy activity can be gotten from Herman Hagedorn, *The Magnate: William Boyce Thompson and His Time, 1869–1930.*

35. Robins, Diary, November 16, 1917, Robins Papers, box 42, WSHS.

36. Judson, Diary, November 27, 1917, Judson Papers, box 8, NL, for all three quotes.

37. See Kennan, *Russia Leaves the War,* 107, and from Judson, "Report on the Russian Situation," March 16, 1918, Judson Papers, box 8, NL.

38. Libbey, *Gumberg and Soviet-American Relations,* 29; also see Williams, "Raymond Robins and Russian-American Relations, 1917–1938," 88. Katherine Breshkovskaya, who received Thompson's dollars, was the "little grandmother of the

revolution" and a Social-Revolutionary, favoring Kerensky and continuing the war. See Libbey, 9–10, for more on her activity. Thompson to Robins, November 27, 1917, Robins Papers, box 13, WSHS.

39. Robins, Diary, November 14 and 15, 1917, Robins Papers, box 42, WSHS. The Robins quote is from R. H. Bruce Lockhart, *British Agent*, 222.

40. Francis to Military Attaché, Petrograd, attached to Francis to Lansing, November 20, 1917, Francis Papers, MOSHI. Thus, the phrase "trivial intercourse" was Judson's as quoted by Francis. Lansing was well aware of the phrase "do nothing."

41. Judson, Diary, November 20, 1917, Judson Papers, box 8, NL. Orlando Figes disputes the "right wing" generals' conspiracy theory; see his book, *A People's Tragedy: The Russian Revolution, 1891–1924*, chap. 10, sec. 3. Francis to Lansing, November 22, 1917, *FRUS, 1918, Russia*, 1: 244; see also facsimile copy as reprinted in Kennan, *Russia Leaves the War*, 114, insert of copy, dated November 7 and received November 8, 1917. On this Long commented: "a most remarkable specimen . . . preserving my copy as a souvenir." Long, Diary, November 24, 1917, Long Papers, box 1, LC. Judson, Diary, November 20, 1917, Judson Papers, box 8, NL. Russian representatives abroad were swift in their opposition to Trotsky's peace initiative and their hostility to the Bolshevik government. For instance, see Bakhmetev to V. Maklakov, November 16/29, 1917, f. 170, op. 512/1. D. 508, l. 61–63, AVPRI, where he rails against the legitimacy of Trotsky's proposal, or Maklakov to Bakhmetev, October 27/November 9, 1917, f. 170, op. 512/1, d. 508, l. 2, AVPRI, where he expresses the conviction that the new regime was absolutely illegitimate and would not last. Bakhmetev cautioned against any hasty moves in his cable to Maklakov, October 27/November 10, 1917, f. 170, op. 512/1, d. 508, l. 4–6, AVPRI, and expected U.S. policy to become more pragmatic though it maintained the appearance of optimism. Bakhmetev told Lansing that the Bolshevik government was "antinational and not representative of the will of the Russian people." See Bakhmetev to Lansing, November 24, 1917, f. 170, op. 512/1, d. 508, l. 103, AVPRI. Onu called for a collective protest by the Russian diplomatic corps. See Onu to Bakhmetev, November 23/December 5, 1917, f. 170, op. 512/1, d. 508, l. 103, AVPRI. Robins, Diary, November 20–22, 1917, Robins Papers, box 42, WSHS.

42. Francis to Lansing, November 24, 1917, *FRUS, 1918, Russia*, 1: 247; Francis to Lansing, cable no. 2006 of November 22, 1917, *FRUS, 1918, Russia*, 1: 244; Francis to Lansing, November 22, 1917, *FRUS, 1918, Russia*, 1: 245; Francis to Lansing, November 28, 1917, *FRUS, 1918, Russia*, 1: 252; Judson to Warcolstaf, November 26, 1917, Judson Papers, box 4, NL.

43. Judson, "Report on the Russian Situation," March 16, 1918, Judson Papers, box 8, NL.

44. Ibid.; Judson, Diary, December 10, 1917, Judson Papers, box 8, NL; the intercepted press message is as quoted by Judson in his "Report on the Russian Situation," March 16, 1918, Judson Papers, box 8, NL. Kennan corrects the amounts of the credit as actually standing at $137.7 million; see Kennan, *Russia Leaves the War*, 103. Though Judson mentioned Francis's approval of this letter, he also noted that "neither I nor the American Ambassador has as yet received from the United States of America instructions or information similar to that contained in the press report." However, he continued, "We are in daily expectation of receiving information similar to that conveyed by the above mentioned press report." Judson, "Report on the Russian Situation," March 16, 1918, Judson Papers, box 8, NL. None ever arrived.

45. Kennan, *Russia Leaves the War*, 103. Short of a thorough review of Central Committee documents in the Russian "Presidential Archive," closed to all researchers, we should not further speculate. See Judson, "Report on the Russian Situation," March 16, 1918, Judson Papers, box 8, where the letter is fully reproduced on 20. Judson, Diary, November 24 and 25, 1917, Judson Papers, box 8, NL.

46. Judson, "Report on the Russian Situation," 21, March 16, 1918, Judson Papers, box 8, NL; Judson to Warcolstaf, November 25, 1917, Judson Papers, box 4, NL; Allied Military Missions (Romania, France, Italy, Japan, England, Serbia) to Dukhonin, November 23, 1917, and Lt. Col. Kerth to General Dukhonin, November 27, 1917, in C. K. Cumming and Walter W. Pettit, compilers and eds., *Russian-American Relations, March, 1917–March, 1920, Documents and Papers*, 53 and James Bunyan and H. H. Fisher, *The Bolshevik Revolution, 1917–1918: Documents and Materials*, 245; Bunyan and Fisher, *Bolshevik Revolution*, 247. Lavergne's quote is as paraphrased by Bunyan and Fisher, *Bolshevik Revolution*, 247–48*n18*.

47. *Izvestiia*, November 27, 1917, as quoted in Bunyan and Fisher, *Bolshevik Revolution*, 250.

48. Statement by Trotsky regarding the Note of Lieutenant-Colonel Kerth, December 1, 1917, *Izvestiia*, December 1, 1917, as quoted in Cumming and Pettit, eds., *Russian-American Relations: March, 1914–March, 1920*, 54.

49. Krylenko's Report to the Sovnarkom, *Novaia Zhizn*, no. 189, December 13, 1917, 3, as quoted in Bunyan and Fisher, *Bolshevik Revolution*, 267–68; Judson, "Report on the Russian Situation," March 16, 1918, Judson Papers, box 8, NL; Judson, Diary, November 26, 1917, Judson Papers, box 8, NL; Buchanan, *My Mission to Russia and Other Diplomatic Memories*, vol. 2, 224.

50. Francis to Lansing, November 28, 1917, *FRUS, 1918, Russia*, 1: 253.

51. Summers to Lansing, November 27, 1917, *FRUS, 1918, Russia*, 1: 270–71; also consult Kennan, *Russia Leaves the War*, 155–56.

Four. December 1917: The Struggle for a Policy

1. Francis to Lansing, quoting Trotsky, December 1, 1917, *FRUS, 1918, Russia*, 1: 275. See also the interesting comments on Trotsky's position by Isaac Deutscher, *The Prophet Armed: Trotsky, 1879–1921*, 352–53.

2. *FRUS, 1918, Russia*, 1: 276; Kennan, *Russia Leaves the War*, 116. Kennan felt Francis had been left in the dark. Dzerzhinsky to [whomever], November 18, 1917, Alexander Gumberg Papers (hereafter Gumberg Papers), box 10, WSHS.

3. Robins, Diary, November 30, 1917, Robins Papers, box 42, WSHS.

4. Judson, "Report on the Russian Situation," March 16, 1918, Judson Papers, box 8, NL. Kennan claims this incident showed how impotent the "pathetic" Francis was. See Kennan, *Russia Leaves the War*, 115–16.

5. Edgar Sisson, *One Hundred Red Days: A Chronicle of the Bolshevik Revolution*, 80; for the armistice arrangements, see John W. Wheeler-Bennett, *Brest-Litovsk: The Forgotten Peace, March 1918*, 83. Kennan claims the conference ended "inconclusively" (see *Russia Leaves the War*, 118). Francis to Lansing, December 1, 1917, *FRUS, 1918, Russia*, 1: 279.

6. Francis to Lansing, November 30, 1917, *FRUS, 1918, Russia*, 1: 274; Judson, Diary, November 30, 1917, Judson Papers, box 8, NL.

7. Judson, "Report on the Russian Situation," March 16, 1918, Judson Papers, box 8, NL.

8. Ibid.; Francis to Lansing, December 1, 1917, *FRUS, 1918, Russia*, 1: 279.

9. Bakhmetev to Polk, November 27, 1917, Polk Papers, CtY.

10. House to Lansing, November 28, 1917, *FRUS, 1918, Russia*, 1: 271; also check Lansing to House, December 1, 1917, noting that U.S. papers printed little along those lines, *FRUS, 1918, Russia*, 1: 276–77.

11. Cecil to Bertie, November 28, 1917, Balfour Papers, British Museum (hereafter BM).

12. Miles to Phillips, November 28, 1917, and Lansing's addenda, November 30, 1917, SD, RG59, 861.00/753, NA.

13. Francis to Lansing, November 20, 1917, *FRUS, 1918, Russia*, 1: 238; Francis to Lansing, November 25, 1917, *FRUS, 1918, Russia*, 1: 268; WW to Lansing, November 28, 1917, SD, RG59, 861.00/703, NA; Lansing to Francis, November 30, 1917, no. 1873, *FRUS, 1918, Russia*, 1: 274; Lansing to Francis, November 30, 1917, no. 1874, *FRUS, 1918, Russia*, 1: 275.

14. Lansing to House, November 28, 1917, SD, RG59, 861.00/719, NA; House, Diary, November 29, 1917, House Papers, CtY; Polk, Diary, November 30, 1917, Polk Papers, CtY; Lansing to WW, November 30, 1917, WP, LC.

15. Buchanan, *My Mission to Russia and Other Diplomatic Memories*, vol. 2, 225; House, Diary, November 30, 1917, House Papers, CtY; House to WW, November 30, 1917, *PWW*, vol. 45, 166; House to WW, November 30, 1917, *PWW*, vol. 45, 166n1 and House to WW, December 2, 1917, *PWW*, vol. 45, 184–85; *PWW*, vol. 45, 173–74n1; Lord Lansdowne's letter of November 29, 1917, is quoted at length.

16. Tumulty to WW, with encl., November 30, 1917, *PWW*, vol. 45, 164–65; Josephus Daniels, Diary, November 30, 1917, *PWW*, vol. 45, 176.

17. Judson, Diary, December 1, 1917, Judson Papers, box 8, NL.

18. Judson, "The Russian Situation," March 16, 1918, Judson Papers, box 8, NL. For the actual terms of the armistice, see Wheeler-Bennett, *Brest-Litovsk*, 379–84, especially Article 2.

19. See note 8 previously, and also Judson to War Department, December 1, 1917, *FRUS, 1918, Russia*, 1: 279; Judson, Diary, December 1, 1917, Judson Papers, box 8, NL.

20. Judson, "Report on the Russian Situation," March 16, 1918, Judson Papers, box 8, NL.

21. Ibid.

22. Judson to Warcolstaf, November 30, 1917, *FRUS, 1918, Russia*, 1: 272–73.

23. Cumming and Pettit, eds., *Russian-American Relations, March 1917–March 1920: Documents and Papers*, 55: "Statement by the People's Commissariat of Foreign Affairs, regarding the Visit of General Judson to Trotsky, 1 December 1917."

24. Judson, "Report on the Russian Situation," March 16, 1918, Judson Papers, box 8, NL.

25. For the quote, see Judson, Diary, December 2, 1917, and for his comment about the press, check Judson, "Report on the Russian Situation," March 16, 1918, both in Judson Papers, box 8, NL.

26. Telegram in which Francis admits consenting: "Judson saw Trotsky today with my approval." Francis to Lansing, December 1, 1917, *FRUS, 1918, Russia*, 1: 279.

27. Francis to Lansing, December 2, 1917, *FRUS, 1918, Russia*, 1: 282 (includes translation of the *Izvestiia* article with Judson's supposed statement, ibid., 282–83).

28. Edgar Sisson, *One Hundred Red Days*, 82, 83; Morris to Lansing, December 3, 1917, *FRUS, 1918, Russia*, 1: 283. The Russian chargé in Copenhagen, Meindorf, angrily informed Bakhmetev of the reports in the Scandinavian press of Judson's visit to Trotsky and asked Bakhmetev to raise the matter with Lansing. See Meindorf to Bakhmetev, November 26/December 6, 1917, f. 170, op. 512/1, d. 508, l. 98, AVPRI.

29. War Cabinet Meeting no. 289, December 3, 1917, PRO; House, Diary, December 3, 1917, House Papers, CtY; House to Lansing (for the President), December 3, 1917, *FRUS, 1918, Russia*, 1: 256–57 (includes text of Balfour's telegram). House's note is as quoted by Richard H. Ullman, *Intervention and the War*, 27n90.

30. Jusserand to Pichon, December 5, 1917, *PWW*, vol. 45, 220–21.

31. Phillips to Lansing, December 3, 1917, Lansing Papers, box 2, NJP.

32. On the first inquiry of the availability of an army in the south, for whatever purposes, see Lansing to Francis, November 30, 1917, *FRUS, 1918, Russia*, 1: 273; also see two replies of Francis on this subject, Francis to Lansing, December 3, 1917, *FRUS, 1918*, Russia, 1: 284–85; as to the Creel propaganda initiative, see Lansing, Desk Diary, December 3, 1917, Lansing Papers, box 65, LC, and Lansing to Amembassy, Petrograd, December 3, 1917 (Creel to Sisson), WP, LC; for the new mission to Russia, see Lincoln Colcord to WW, December 3, 1917, WP, LC, and Wilson's response refusing the idea, December 6, 1917, *PWW*, vol. 45, 222. It was at this stage that Bakhmetev felt the "do-nothing" U.S. policy profitable, for no contracts had been canceled and the Bolsheviks would not last long. Bakhmetev to N. M. Khrabrov, December 3, 1917, f. 170, op. 512/1, d. 469, l. 0220–0222, AVPRI. For the role of Bakhmetev and the Russian embassy, check David S. Foglesong, *America's Secret War against Bolshevism: U.S. Intervention in the Russian Civil War, 1917–1920*, chap. 3. Especially important is Foglesong's account of Bakhmetev's use of loans to the Provisional Government, credited in the National City Bank, between $60 to $70 million, for the purchase of supplies that could be sent to anti-Bolshevik forces (60–64). Also, see the suggestion of Linda Killen, *The Russian Bureau: A Case Study in Wilsonian Diplomacy*, 17–21, especially the creation of the War Trades Board of the United States Russian Bureau, Inc. Also read her article on Bakhmetev's role, "The Search for a Democratic Russia: Bakhmeteff and the United States." Kennan also deals with the issue, but he tends to dismiss its ultimate influence and effectiveness. See George F. Kennan, *The Decision to Intervene*, 326–28. A very provocative article is Larry G. Hodge, "American Diplomacy towards Transcaucasia during the Russian Revolution, March 1917–March 1918." The author claims that two hundred tons of silver were purchased by the Provisional Government with U.S. credits and shipped for use in Persia between August and October of 1917. By early December another 2.6 million ounces of silver were purchased by the Provisional Government and made available to Britain by Bakhmetev (29). Bar silver, according to Hodge, was handed over to the British by Russians in San Francisco to be used in southern Russia (34). The author notes this contradiction to Wilson's Point 6 of his Fourteen Points (35–36). Hodge's article leans heavily on previous work done by Oleh S. Pidhainy, Loventrice A. Scales, and Alexander S. Pidhainy, "Silver and Billions: American Finances and the Bolshevik Revolution."

33. Francis to Lansing, December 1, 1917, received December 4, 1917, at 2:15 P.M., *FRUS, 1918, Russia*, 1: 279; Wilson, "An Annual Message on the State of the Union," December 4, 1917, *PWW*, vol. 45, 199.

34. Wilson, "An Annual Message on the State of the Union," December 4, 1917, *PWW*, vol. 45, 199.

35. Lansing, "Statement on Recognition," December 4, 1917, Lansing Papers, box 2, NJP.

36. Ibid. For a summary of "Cold War" definitions and characterizations, see William Dudley, ed., *The Cold War: Opposing Viewpoints;* for a provocative analysis, see John Lewis Gaddis, *We Now Know: Rethinking Cold War History.*

37. Buchanan, *My Mission to Russia,* vol. 2, 229. On Petrov and Chicherin, see Ullman, *Intervention and the War,* 33–36.

38. Buchanan, *My Mission to Russia,* vol. 2, 235, 236–37; Ullman, *Intervention and the War,* 30.

39. Buchanan, *My Mission to Russia,* vol. 2, 238.

40. Judson, Diary, December 4, 1917, Judson Papers, box 8, NL. An indication of the "wreck" was Trotsky's order to all Russian embassies to support a rapid peace or quit. See Trotsky to Bakhmetev, December 5, 1917, f. 170, op. 512/1, d. 508, l. 90, AVPRI.

41. Robins, Diary, December 4, 1917, Robins Papers, box 42, WSHS; on the complications of finding a code that the embassy would not recognize, see Kennan, *Russia Leaves the War,* 126.

42. Lansing, Desk Diary, December 5, 1917, Lansing Papers, box 65, LC; Lansing to Francis, December 6, 1917, *FRUS, 1918, Russia,* 1: 289; as to "press reports," check *London Times,* December 6, 1917. In this connection, Ira Morris also noted that Judson's visit to Trotsky had been causing a "great deal of comment in Sweden." Morris to Lansing, December 6, 1917, received December 7, 1917, *FRUS, 1918, Russia,* 1: 289. Again concerning reaction in the Scandinavian press about Judson's visit to Trotsky, see note 28 previously.

43. Lansing, Desk Diary, December 6, 1917, Lansing Papers, box 65, LC; Francis to Lansing, December 1, 1917, and December 2, 1917, *FRUS, 1918, Russia,* 1: 279, 282; Lansing, Desk Diary, December 7, 1917, Lansing Papers, box 65, LC; Judson, Diary, January 1, 1918, Judson Papers, box 8, NL.

44. Lansing, Private Memo, December 7, 1917, Lansing Papers, box 67, LC.

45. Ibid. This kind of rationale for dealing with the Bolsheviks, of course, leads directly to Kennan's "X" article. Kennan simply replaced isolating them so that, given time, they would self-destruct, with the more activist policy of "containment." See George F. Kennan, "The Sources of Soviet Conduct."

46. Ullman, *Intervention and the War,* 12.

47. War Cabinet Meeting no. 294, December 7, 1917, PRO.

48. Lansing to Francis, December 8, 1917, *FRUS, 1918, Russia,* 1: 292; Lansing to Mott, December 7, 1917, *FRUS, 1918, Russia,* 1: 289.

49. Lansing to Francis, December 6, 1917, *FRUS, 1918, Russia,* 1: 289; Francis to Lansing, December 10, 1917, *FRUS, 1918, Russia,* 1: 295.

50. Judson, Diary, December 10, 1917, Judson Papers, box 8, NL.

51. Judson to Warcolstaf, December 6, 1917, in Judson, "Report," March 16, 1918, Judson Papers, box 8, NL.

52. Judson to Warcolstaf, December 11, 1917, and December 31, 1917, Judson Papers, box 8, NL.

53. War Cabinet Meeting no. 295, December 10, 1917, PRO.

54. Ibid., and see its appendix.

55. Lansing to WW, December 10, 1917, SD, RG59, 861.00807a, NA. After studying these same documents noted previously, we are inclined to agree with Foglesong's thoughtful analysis, though there probably never will be an absolute proof as to what he calls the "direction, motives, and methods of Wilsonian policy

toward Russia in the first months after the Bolshevik Revolution." See Foglesong, *America's Secret War,* 77. The tendency of Lansing and Wilson, whatever may have been the objections voiced or obstacles encountered then and later, was there. It is simply not enough for Kennan to dismiss this effort because "So far as can be ascertained, no actual use was made of this authorization and no official American funds were ever placed at the disposal of any of the early centers of anti-Bolshevik activity." See Kennan, *Russia Leaves the War,* 178. However, it should be pointed out that others sharply disagree with Foglesong's analysis. For a summary of their views, check Betty Miller Unterberger, "Wilson vs. the Bolsheviks." Especially note her strong criticism of Foglesong's attempt to see this as a first effort in "providing a model for Wilson's 'secret war' against Bolshevism" (129–30 and *n12–13*).

56. Lansing to WW, December 10, 1917, SD, RG59, 861.008072, NA.

57. Daniels, Diary, December 11, 1917, *PWW,* vol. 45, 271; WW to Lansing, December 12, 1917, *PWW,* vol. 45, 274.

58. Lansing to Page (for Crosby), December 12, 1917, *PWW,* vol. 45, 274–75; Kennan, in *Russia Leaves the War,* 175ff, gives a very thorough accounting of the specific facts at issue.

59. Kennan, *Russia Leaves the War,* 178. Foglesong has also completely analyzed this affair and concludes that after all the hand-holding by Crosby and Page, contrary to what previous historians assumed, by February 1918, even after the collapse of Kaledin, "Crosby had begun to fulfill the U.S. pledge to reimburse the British." See Foglesong, *America's Secret War,* 103. Furthermore, the British drew on bar silver that Bakhmetev purchased from U.S. advances, and Willoughby Smith, the U.S. representative, advanced two million rubles to the British from sources in Persia. Crosby to Page, December 13, 1917, *FRUS, 1918, Russia,* 2: 591–92; Page to Lansing, December 18, 1917, *FRUS, 1918, Russia,* 2: 592.

60. House to Lansing, December 2, 1917, *FRUS, 1918, Russia,* 2: 584; Ullman, *Intervention and the War,* 52.

61. Buchanan, *My Mission to Russia,* vol. 2, 227; Louis Fischer, *The Soviets in World Affairs,* vol. 2, 836, quotes the entire document; Ullman, *Intervention and the War,* 57.

62. Francis to Lansing, January 24/February 6, 1918, with encl., dated January 26, 1918, of Consul Poole, *FRUS, 1918, Russia,* 2: 609.

63. Ibid., 609, 610–11, 613, 614, 619.

64. "The Reminiscences of DeWitt Clinton Poole," Poole typescript, CU, 151.

65. Ibid., 152, and quote from 154.

66. For Root, see Phillips, Notebooks, December 13, 1917, Phillips Papers, HU; for Bertron, check Samuel Reading Bertron to WW, December 12, 1917, *PWW,* vol. 45, 282–83; Tumulty to WW, December 14, 1917, *PWW,* vol. 45, 288.

67. Tumulty to WW, December 14, 1917, encl., n.d., Bakhmetev's Memo, *PWW,* vol. 45, 288–95.

68. Ibid.

69. Ibid. See also note 32 previously.

70. House to WW, December 15, 1917, *PWW,* vol. 45, 309; Wiseman to House, December 15, 1917, *PWW,* vol. 45, 311–13. See note 16 previously. On the pathos of Lord Lansdowne's letter of November 29, 1917, see Kennan, *Russia Leaves the War,* 145. Spring Rice to House, encl., December 17, 1917, *PWW,* vol. 45, 316; House to Wiseman, December 18, 1917, *PWW,* vol. 45, 322.

71. Phillips, Notebooks, December 26, 1917, Phillips Papers, HU; Kennan, *Russia Leaves the War,* 178 ff. See note 59 previously.

72. House, Diary, December 18, 1917, *PWW,* vol. 45, 323.

73. Ibid., 327, 324; for information on The Inquiry, see Lawrence E. Gelfand, *The Inquiry: American Preparations for Peace, 1917–1919.*

Five. January 1918: Point VI of XIV

1. Francis to Lansing, December 31, 1917, containing text of Trotsky's address, *FRUS, 1918, Russia,* 1: 406; Winston S. Churchill, *The World Crisis,* vol. 3, 234.

2. Francis to Lansing, December 31, 1917, 406–8.

3. Judson, Diary, January 1, 1918, Judson Papers, box 8, NL.

4. Ibid.; Sisson, *One Hundred Red Days,* 136.

5. Francis to Lansing, December 24, 1917, *FRUS, 1918, Russia,* 1: 325.

6. Francis to Lansing, December 12, 1917, *FRUS, 1918, Russia,* 1: 301; Judson, Diary, December 12, 1917, Judson Papers, box 8, NL; Francis to Lansing, December 12, 1917, and Lansing to Francis, December 20, 1917, *FRUS, 1918, Russia,* 1: 301, 319.

7. Judson, Diary, December 17 and 18, 1917, Judson Papers, box 8, NL. Robins, Diary, December 17 and 18, 1917, Robins Papers, box 42, WSHS; one example of Robins's useful role was in the infamous Kalpashnikov Affair, where the hapless Red Cross worker was arrested by the Bolsheviks for supposedly trying to send vehicles to Kaledin under the guise of the Red Cross. Robins's good offices probably saved Kalpashnikov's neck. See Kennan, *Russia Leaves the War,* chap. 10.

8. Lansing to Francis, December 29, 1917, *FRUS, 1918, Russia,* 1: 330; for Phillips's role in this, see also Williams, "Raymond Robins and Russian-American Relations, 1917–1938," 108 and especially note 50; Kennan, *Russia Leaves the War,* 212.

9. Robins, Diary, December 24, 1917, Robins Papers, box 42, WSHS; testimony of Mr. David R. Francis, March 8, 1919, *Bolshevik Propaganda, Hearings before a Subcommittee of the Committee on the Judiciary, United States Senate, 65th Congress, Third Session and thereafter Pursuant to S.Res. 439 and 469,* 956.

10. Francis's account of the incident is found in Francis, *Russia from the American Embassy,* 216–22. Francis adds that Diamandi was expelled from Russia and, on Soviet orders, just missed assassination at Torneo. Furthermore, Zalkind claimed that Francis had agreed to protest Romanian actions on the southwestern front in exchange for the count's release, which Francis denied.

11. WW to Lansing, with Balfour's encl., January 1, 1918, *PWW,* vol. 45, 417, 418.

12. Robins to Dearest Blessed One, January 21, 1918, Robins Papers, box 13, WSHS.

13. Daniels, Diary, January 4, 1918, *PWW,* vol. 45, 474.

14. Ibid., 474–75.

15. Cecil to British Embassy, January 1, 1918, *PWW,* vol. 45, 420.

16. Ibid.; War Cabinet Meeting no. 309A, January 1, 1918, PRO; also see FO to C. Greene (Tokyo), January 2, 1918, Milner Papers, box 112, Bodleiain Library, Oxford (hereafter BLO).

17. Lansing, Desk Diary, January 3, 1918, Lansing Papers, box 65, LC. This question had been on Bakhmetev's and Maklakov's minds; for example, see Bakhmetev to Maklakov, December 4/17, 1917, f. 170, op. 512/1, d. 516, l. 4, AVPRI, where he mentions that Allied consuls in Vladivostok considered bringing in contingents to protect supplies and foreign nationals from the Bolsheviks. Maklakov

responded that American objections to intervention could change given the threatening Bolshevik situation. See Maklakov to Bakhmetev, December 6/19, 1917,
f. 170, op. 512/1, d. 516, l. 6, AVPRI. Finally, on December 21, 1917, Bakhmetev cabled Maklakov that the efforts of Russian diplomacy should be directed
toward preventing the Japanese occupation of Vladivostok because it would cause
irreparable damage to the Allied cause in Russia. See Bakhmetev to Maklakov,
December 8/21, 1917, f. 170, op. 512/1, l. 7, AVPRI. John K. Caldwell to Lansing,
January 1, 1918, encl. in Lansing to Daniels, January 3, 1918, WP, LC; Phillips
to Polk, January 3, 1918, encl. Opnav (naval operations) to C in C (commander
in chief) Asiatic, WP, LC.

18. Sir George R. Clerk, Foreign Office Minutes of S.E. Russia, January 4,
1918, Milner Papers, box 109, BLO; War Cabinet Meeting no. 316, January 7,
1918, PRO.

19. House, Diary, January 4, 1918, *PWW,* vol. 45, 458.

20. Ibid.

21. House, Diary, January 9, 1918, *PWW,* vol. 45, 550–53.

22. "The Inquiry Memorandum," December, 1917, *PWW,* vol. 45, 464, 467.

23. Woodrow Wilson, "An Address to a Joint Session of the Congress," January
8, 1918, *PWW,* vol. 45, 534.

24. Wilson, "Address," *PWW,* vol. 45, 534–35. (Arno Mayer suggests that since
Wilson saw ideas as weapons, he would neither allow Germany to make "psychological capital" from Brest-Litovsk, nor let Lenin gain a "monopoly on blueprints"
for the post–World War I period [371]. Germany, he later remarked, realized "Wilson's passages pertaining to Russia were calculated to court a failing ally" [374].
See Arno J. Mayer, *Wilson vs. Lenin: Political Origins of the New Diplomacy, 1917–1918.*)

25. Ibid., 537.

26. Ibid.; for both quotes, see Sisson, *One Hundred Red Days,* 209. It should be
noted that the controversy over the implications of the Fourteen Points speech
has been hotly debated, particularly by William Appleman Williams and Betty
Miller Unterberger. Unterberger claims that Wilson's decision to intervene was a
principled one based on Point VI of the speech, that is, the "acid test" to protect
Russian self-determination from overzealous allies and Japanese empire builders.
See her article, "Woodrow Wilson and the Bolsheviks: The 'Acid Test' of Soviet-
American Relations." Williams sees the episode of the Fourteen Points speech as a
momentary lapse due to pressure from House on an otherwise anti-Bolshevik stance
adopted by Wilson within five weeks of the Bolshevik Revolution, resulting from
Lansing's and the State Department's pressure. See his two-part article, "American
Intervention in Russia, 1917–1920."

27. Sisson, *One Hundred Red Days,* 209, 211, 213; Sisson to Creel, January 13, 1918,
encl. in Creel to WW, January 15, 1918, WP, LC; Creel to WW, Memorandum,
January 15, 1918, WP, LC; Kennan, *Russia Leaves the War,* 259n19; Robins, Diary,
January 10, 11, 1918, Robins Papers, box 42, WSHS; Lansing to Francis, January
9, 1918, *FRUS, 1918, Russia,* 1: 426; Francis to Lansing, January 12, 1918, *FRUS,
1918, Russia,* 1: 426; Judson, Diary, January 11–13, 1918, Judson Papers, box 8,
NL.

28. Sisson, *One Hundred Red Days,* 214–15.

29. Owen to WW, January 8, 1918, WP, LC; Polk, Diary, January 8, 1918, Polk
Papers, CtY; Crane to Tumulty, January 9, 1918, WP, LC; William R. Wilder to
WW, January 12, 1918, WP, LC; Pershing to Adjutant General, January 17, 1918,
encl. in Memo of N. Baker, January 17, 1918, no. 505, WP, LC; Charles W. Eliot

to WW, January 17, 1918, WP, LC; WW to Charles W. Eliot, January 21, 1918, WP, LC; White as quoted by Victor Murdock to WW, January 19, 1918, WP, LC.

30. Samuel Gompers to WW, January 19, 1918, WP, LC; WW to Gompers, January 21, 1918, WP, LC.

31. W. H. Page to Lansing, January 15, 1918, encl. in WW to Lansing, January 20, 1918, R. S. Baker Papers, ser. 1, box 8, LC.

32. Wiseman, Notes on Interview with the President, January 23, 1918, Balfour Papers, BM; WW to Owen, January 24, 1918, *PWW,* vol. 46, 88; WW to Lansing, January 24, 1918, *PWW,* vol. 46, 88.

33. Owen to WW, encl. in WW to Lansing, January 24, 1918, SD, RG59, 861.00/1048½, NA.

34. Basil Miles, Memorandum for the Secretary of State, January 29, 1918, attached to Owen to WW, January 22, 1918, SD, RG59, 861.00/1048½, NA.

35. Lamont to WW, January 29, 1918, WP, LC; Polk, Diary, January 30, 1918, Polk Papers, CtY; Thompson to WW, January 31, 1918, WP, LC; WW to J. P. Tumulty, February 1, 1918, attached to Thompson to WW, January 31, 1918, WP, LC.

36. WW to N. Baker, January 31, 1918, N. Baker Papers, box 8, LC; WW to Lamont, January 31, 1918, WP, LC; Kennan, *Russia Leaves the War,* 260–61; see also Williams, *American-Russian Relations,* 123, where the author views the Fourteen Points as a "momentary disagreement with Lansing on Russian policy." By the end of January 1918, Wilson had adopted the policy of intervention toward Russia, according to Williams, and also wanted by this means to prevent Japanese expansion into Asia.

37. For Wilson's address to a joint session of the Congress on February 11, 1918, see *PWW,* vol. 46, 318–24; for the Russians, see Wilson, "To the Fourth All-Russia Congress of Soviets," March 11, 1918, *PWW,* vol. 46, 598. Sitting of the Fourth Extraordinary Congress of the Soviets, March 14, 1918, Robins Papers, box 13, WSHS; Francis, *Russia from the American Embassy,* 230.

38. Kennan, *Russia Leaves the War,* 372–76, 434–35, 491. For an exhaustive accounting of the U.S. Embassy's sojourn in Vologda, see Saul, *War and Revolution: The United States and Russia, 1917–1921,* chap. 5.

39. Kennan, *Russia Leaves the War,* 496, as reproduced from *Bolshevik Propaganda, Hearings,* 800–801. "Agreement," no heading or title, no date, probably March 5, 1918, in Gumberg's handwriting, Gumberg Papers, box 1, WSHS; also see note 43 to follow. Lockhart to FO, March 5, 1918, Robins Papers, box 13, WSHS. That the Bolshevik leadership was sincerely concerned by the possibility of the Japanese intervening can be seen from Trotsky's note to Chicherin of January 31, 1918, in which he suggests that Chicherin prepare a note warning against intervention and that the American embassy should get a copy. See Trotsky to Chicherin, January 31, 1918, f. 325, op. 1, d. 403, l. 13–14, The Russian Center for the Preservation and Study of the Documents of Contemporary History (the former Central Party Archive) [hereafter RTsKhIDNI]. Document on transmission problem, Robins Papers, box 13, WSHS; Francis to Lansing, March 9, 1918, *FRUS, 1918, Russia,* 1: 394–95, and Francis to Lansing, March 9, 1918, "Paraphrase of Special Cipher," Robins Papers, box 13, WSHS.

40. Kennan, *Russia Leaves the War,* 499–517. This is a brilliant analysis of Robins's claim that Lenin delayed the Soviet Congress against the weight of accumulated evidence. We must agree with Kennan's conclusion that "nothing in the available record supports such a suggestion in any way" (516). For a more recent discussion

of this question, see Salzman, *Reform and Revolution*, where the author concludes that "the proposals, if acted upon by the Allies, might have played a role in delaying or altering the terms of the peace. To dismiss their possible or potential importance at a time of such flux and crisis is hasty and incorrect." After all, the German army was rapidly approaching Petrograd. Check pp. 245–49 and the quote on 247. Also see the author's interesting comments in his notes on 422, especially notes 11, 14, and 17.

41. Robins, Diary, March 15, 1918, Robins Papers, box 42, WSHS.

42. Ibid., March 16 and 17, 1918. Lansing ordered Robins to leave Russia on May 15, 1918. See Williams, *American-Russian Relations*, 144. Robins wrote Lenin on April 25, 1918, expressing his appreciation for the Soviet government's assistance to the American Red Cross Mission. Lenin responded with the following handwritten note: "I am sure the new democracy that is proletarian democracy is coming in all countries and will crush all obstacles . . ." Robins to Lenin, April 25, 1918, f. 2, op. 1, box 5832, l. 1, RTsKhIDNI. For Lenin's handwritten response to Robins, see April 30, 1918, which is scribbled by Lenin on the reverse.

43. *Bolshevik Propaganda, Hearings*, 807. It is, essentially, this version that Robins repeated in his autobiography: William Hard, *Raymond Robins' Own Story*, 151–52. For careful reconstruction of this story as quoted in the Overman testimony, see Wheeler-Bennett, *Brest-Litovsk*, 303, and also Kennan, *Russia Leaves the War*, 515–17. Robins's "suggestion" is so pregnant with meaning that the authors have tried at some length to gain access to the Archive of the President of the Russian Federation (Arkhiv Prezidenta Rossiiskoi Federatsii, APRF) in order to check the Minutes of the Central Committee for March 1918. This request was brought to the director of the Presidential Archive by Professor Yu. S. Kukushkin of the history faculty at Moscow State University. Mr. Korotkov wrote Professor Kukushkin on November 25, 1994: "On behalf of the Head of the Administration of the President of the Russian Federation in the President's Archive, your inquiry was considered concerning access to the Archive of the American, Professor D. Davis, . . . working on the problem of Soviet-American relations, 1917–1920. The Archive of the President, according to its very status, does not serve foreign investigators. By order of the President of the Russian Federation, the documents of the historical section of the Archive are being transferred for preservation to the institution of the State Archival Service of Russia, where they, after declassification, will be accessible to investigators." Numerous other channels to this archive were tried, with no results. Davis again tried in 1996 and got nowhere.

Williams gives a detailed account of this episode, maintaining that in fact Lenin did postpone the IV Soviet Congress as well as his last-minute speech recommending ratification. Williams concludes, however, that the Allies always considered this entire matter a ruse. Whether or not the full document reached Washington until after ratification, Williams concludes that the delay was not significant because *"Top American leaders already had explicit knowledge of the Bolshevik interest in obtaining assistance from the United States."* Williams, "American Intervention in Russia, 1917–1920" (pt. 2), 41, especially note 78.

44. Lansing to Francis, March 19, 1918, *FRUS, 1918, Russia*, 1: 402; Francis to Lansing, March 12, 1918, *FRUS, 1918, Russia*, 1: 397–98; Francis to Robins, March 11, 1918, Robins Papers, box 13, WSHS. See handwritten note, probably George F. Kennan's, in R684622, Moscow Consul General, 1918, box 5, Division of Russian Affairs, Department of State, NA.

45. Wilson, "Address," *PWW*, vol. 45, 537. For a more general discussion of

the Japanese question, see John Albert White, *The Siberian Intervention*, 90ff; see especially James William Morley, *The Japanese Thrust into Siberia, 1918*, 129–35. Polk, Diary, January 9 and 10, 1918, Polk Papers, CtY. Long, Memo of Visit by Japanese Ambassador, January 10, 1918, Long Papers, box 183, LC.

46. Poole to Lansing, January 15, 1918, Russian Decimal Files, 7, SD, RG59, 861.00/271 3/4, LC; Memo to E. M. House from Richard Washburn Child, c. January 1918, in Note to President from House, WP, LC.

47. Balfour to Milner, January 18, 1918, FO 800/214, Balfour Papers, PRO.

48. War Cabinet Meeting no. 330A, January 24, 1918, PRO.

49. Foreign Office Telegram to British Embassies in Paris, Rome, Washington (Mr. Barclay, no. 538), January 26, 1918, Balfour Papers, BM.

50. Ibid. For paraphrase, see House to Wilson, January 31, 1918, *PWW*, vol. 46, 181–83.

51. Polk, Diary, January 18 and 19, 1918, Polk Papers, CtY. WW to Polk, January 19, 1918, *PWW*, vol. 46, 34; Polk to WW, January 19, 1918, *PWW*, vol. 46, 34; Morris to Lansing, January 17, 1918, enclosed in WW to Lansing, January 20, 1918, SD, RG59, 861.00/967, NA; Daniels, Diary, January 18, 1918, *PWW*, vol. 46, 34.

52. Lansing to Jusserand, January 16, 1918, *FRUS, 1918, Russia*, 2: 29; Polk to WW, encl. 2, January 19 [20], 1918, *PWW*, vol. 46, 35; Daniels, Diary, January 19, 1918, *PWW*, vol. 46, 41; WW to Lansing, January 20, 1918, *PWW*, vol. 46, 46.

53. Polk to Morris, January 19 [20], 1918, *PWW*, vol. 46, 35.

54. WW to Polk, with encl., January 28, 1918, *PWW*, vol. 46, 117–18.

55. Wiseman to Drummond, February 1, 1918, Balfour Papers, BM; "Following for Mr. Balfour from Col. House," in Wiseman to Drummond, February 1, 1918, FO 800/223, Lord Reading Papers (hereafter Reading Papers), PRO; Lansing to Amembassy, Paris, no. 3136, n.d., Department of War (hereafter WD), RG120, American Expeditionary Force (hereafter AEF), American Section, Supreme War Council, box 23, NA.

56. Tele to Wiseman, February 2, 1918, following from Mr. Balfour to Colonel House, Balfour Papers, BM; House to WW, February 2, 1918, WP, LC; Wiseman to Drummond, February 4, 1918, Balfour Papers, BM.

57. Wiseman for Balfour, Tele no. 44, February 4, 1918, Balfour Papers, BM; Polk, Diary, February 4, 1918, Polk Papers, CtY; Balfour to Wiseman, March 8, 1918, following from Mr. Balfour for Colonel House, Balfour Papers, BM; Lord Bertie to Balfour, February 8, 1918, no. 178, Balfour Papers, BM.

58. WW to Lansing, February 4, 1918, attached to Lansing to Wilson, February 9, 1918, SD, RG59, 861.00/1097, NA.

59. Ibid.

60. A. J. Balfour, Memorandum, February 14, 1918, Balfour Papers, BM.

61. Ibid.; Lansing to Daniels, February 16, 1918, SD, RG59, 861.00/2336a, NA.

62. Lord Reading to the FO, February 15, 1918, *PWW*, vol. 46, 355. Reading succeeded Sir Cecil Spring-Rice.

63. Bliss, Versailles, to Agwar, Washington, no. 32, n.d., WD, RG120, AEF, American Section, Supreme War Council, box 23, NA.

64. Ibid.

65. Bliss to Peyton March, February 20, 1918, Bliss Papers, box 75, LC.

66. Bliss to Baker, February 25, 1918, WD, RG120, AEF, American Section, Supreme War Council, box 24, NA.

67. Ibid.; Bliss to Agwar, February 25, 1918, no. 36, WD, RG120, AEF, American Section, Supreme War Council, box 23, NA.

68. War Cabinet Meeting no. 350, February 20, 1918, PRO.

69. Lockhart, *British Agent*, 199; Balfour to Wiseman, February 22, 1918, no. 52, Balfour Papers, BM.

70. Balfour to Wiseman, February 22, 1918, no. 52, Balfour Papers, BM.

71. War Cabinet Meeting no. 353, February 25, 1918, PRO.

72. Ibid.

73. House, Diary, February 25, 1918, House Papers, CtY; War Cabinet Meeting no. 354, February 26, 1918, PRO; Miles, Memo, encl. in Lansing to WW, February 26, 1918, WP, LC; Balfour to Reading, February 26, 1918, encl. in Reading to WW, February 27, 1918, WP, LC. For the rumor of German and Austrian POWs and their impact on decisions, see Christopher Lasch, "American Intervention in Siberia: A Reinterpretation." Balfour to Wiseman, February 28, 1918, Balfour Papers, BM.

74. Wiseman to FO, February 27, 1918, William Wiseman Papers, CtY; Lansing to WW, February 27, 1918, RG 59, 861.00/1165½, NA. Lansing's greater tolerance of the Japanese may have had something to do with his anti-Bolshevism. Also check note 45 previously, especially Morley, *The Japanese Thrust*.

75. Lansing, Desk Diary, March 1, 1918, Lansing Papers, box 65, LC.

76. Bullitt, Memo for Mr. Polk, March 2, 1918, WP, LC.

77. Memo given by House to Auchincloss to telephone the president concerning House's views on the invasion of Siberia by the Japanese, March 3, 1918, House Papers, CtY.

78. See Balfour to Reading, February 26, 1918, in note 73 previously and House, Diary, March 4, 1918, House Papers, CtY; Wilson, A Draft of an Aide-Mémoire, March 1, 1918, *PWW*, vol. 46, 498–99. Check Williams, *American-Russian Relations*, 138–39, and also his article, "American Intervention in Russia, 1917–1920" (pt. 2), especially 42–45, where Williams expands the story from the original account in his book by emphasizing House's intervention in this matter. House argued that Wilson risked the Japanese either staying in Siberia and/or moving into China. Either America would have to abandon the Open Door or go to war with Japan. That argument, along with Wilson's fear of provoking Russians to support the Bolsheviks, made Wilson reverse his policy of February 28, 1918. As Williams points out, he did so within seventy-two hours.

79. For a copy of the first note, see Wiseman to Drummond, March 4, 1918, *PWW*, vol. 46, 531; for the actual one that was transmitted, check Polk to Morris, March 5, 1918, *PWW*, vol. 46, 545. Wiseman to Drummond, March 14, 1918, *PWW*, vol. 46, 531; House, Diary, March 5, 1918, *PWW*, vol. 46, 553; Polk to Morris, Message to Japan (in re Siberia), March 5, 1918, *PWW*, vol. 46, 545.

80. Polk to Morris, March 5, 1918, *PWW*, vol. 46, 545.

81. House to WW, March 6, 1918, *PWW*, vol. 46, 555; Morris to Lansing, March 12, 1918, *PWW*, vol. 46, 620; Balfour to Wiseman, no. 62, For Colonel House from Mr. Balfour, March 6, 1918, F/60/2/46, David Lloyd George Papers (hereafter Lloyd George Papers), Beaverbrook Library (hereafter BL); Greene to the FO, March 7, 1918, *PWW*, vol. 46, 571.

82. War Cabinet Meeting no. 363, March 11, 1918, PRO; Bliss to Agwar, no. 49, March 14, 1918, WD, RG120, AEF, American Section, Supreme War Council, box 23, NA; For the President, Extended Session of the Supreme War Council,

March 16, 1918, *PWW,* vol. 46, 59–61; Balfour to WW, March 18, 1918, *PWW,* vol. 46, 61–63.

Six. Northern Russia and Siberia

1. Kennan, *Decision to Intervene,* 17n3; Henry Newbolt, *History of the Great War Based on Official Documents by Direction of the Historical Section of the Committee of Imperial Defence, Naval Operations,* vol. 5, 301–4, 312, 314.

2. Ullman, *Intervention and the War,* 109–15; Kennan, *Decision to Intervene,* 26, 28–30. See also Bakhmetev to Admiral Kyetlinsky, January 10/23, 1918, f. 170, op. 512/4, d. 27, l. 69, AVPRI, on the necessity of the Red Cross's participation to ensure fairness in distribution of supplies and, again, on February 5, 1918, in Bakhmetev to Ughet, f. 170, op. 512/4, d. 27, l. 98–99, AVPRI. Wardwell, Diary, January 19, 1918, 2: 15, Wardwell Papers, CU; Leonid I. Strakhovsky, *The Origins of American Intervention in North Russia, 1918,* 27.

3. Wardwell, Diary, 2: 19, 35, 36, Wardwell Papers, CU; Kennan, *Decision to Intervene,* 34–35, 44, and especially note 20; The British Embassy to the Department of State, March 4, 1918, *FRUS, 1918, Russia,* 2: 469; The British Embassy to the Department of State, March 5, 1918, *FRUS, 1918, Russia,* 2: 469; Newbolt, *History of the Great War,* vol. 5, 312.

4. Wardwell, Diary, March 5, 6, 7, and 8, 1918, 2: 47–48, Wardwell Papers, CU.

5. Strakhovsky, *North Russia,* 28, quoting the French version of the document as found in Alexandra Dumesnil (trans. and ed.), "L'Intervention des Alliés à Mourmansk. Documents," *Revue d'Histoire de la Guerre Mondiale,* 14, no. 1 (January, 1936), 44. Kennan quotes the same document but translates it from its Russian source, Mikhael Sergeevich Kedrov, *Bez Bolshevistkogo Rukovodstva (iz Istorii Interventsii na Murmanye),* 27; Kennan, *Decision to Intervene,* 45.

6. Kennan, *Decision to Intervene,* 46; Strakhovsky took his translation of Trotsky's telegram from the *Izvestia Murmankago S.R.i.S.D.,* no. 57, March 2, 1918, and Kennan from Kedrov, *Bez Bolshevistkogo Rukovodstva,* 28 (italics added by Kedrov). Trotsky quote is from Strakhovsky, *North Russia,* 29, with heading of telegram taken from Kennan.

7. Lansing to WW, March 25, 1918, including report of Ruggles to Warcolstaff, March 12, 1918, Lansing Papers, box 2, NJP; Francis to Lansing, March 28, 1918, *FRUS, 1918, Russia,* 2: 471; Ruggles to Milstaf, March 30, 1918, no. 10, WD, RG 407, Cable Section, box 94, NA; Francis to Lansing, March 31, 1918, *FRUS, 1918, Russia,* 2: 471.

8. Polk to Lansing, April 2, 1918, Polk Papers, CtY.

9. Basil Miles, "American Warship for Murmansk," April 2, 1918, encl. in Lansing to WW, April 2, 1918, Polk Papers, CtY.

10. WW to Lansing, April 4, 1918, *PWW,* vol. 47, 246; Daniels to WW, April 5, 1918, *PWW,* vol. 47, 263; WW to Daniels, April 8, 1918, *PWW,* vol. 47, 290, and note 1.

11. Ruggles to Milstaff, April 7, 1918, no. 12, WD, RG407, Cable Section, box 94, NA; Ruggles to Milstaff, April 8, 1918, no. 14, WD, RG407, Cable Section, box 94, NA. Chicherin complained to Robins about "counterrevolutionary" activities in the Far East, especially Vladivostok and the role of the American consul, John K. Caldwell. See Chicherin to Robins, n.d., f. 129, op. 2, d. 2, l. 5, AVPRF. Kennan dates this at or about April 26, 1918. See Kennan, *Decision to Intervene,* 342.

12. Bliss to Agwar (Adjutant General, War Department), April 12, 1918, no. 85, WD, RG120, AEF, American Section, Supreme War Council, box 23, NA; Ruggles to Milstaff, April 14, 1918, WD, RG407, Cable Section, box 94, NA; Francis to Lansing, April 30, 1918, *FRUS, 1918, Russia*, 1: 511.

13. Newbolt, *History of the Great War*, vol. 5, 318–19; Ullman, *Intervention and the War*, 178.

14. Paraphrase of telegram from Mr. Lockhart, March 28, 1918, handed by Reading to Lansing, April 2, 1918, and read by Wilson on April 4, 1918, *PWW*, vol. 47, 245–46.

15. Reading to Balfour, April 7, 1918, *PWW*, vol. 48, 281.

16. Balfour to Reading, April 15, 1918, *PWW*, vol. 47, 355–56; Balfour to Reading, April 18, 1918, *PWW*, vol. 47, 367, 368.

17. For Lockhart's message to Balfour of April 13, 1918, see Ullman, *Intervention and the War*, 160. (The quote is Ullman's opinion.)

18. Reading to Balfour, April 25, 1918, *PWW*, vol. 47, 440–41. The question of the authenticity of these documents is exhaustively treated in George F. Kennan, "The Sisson Documents." A further analysis that reaches the same conclusion is Helena M. Stone, "Another Look at the Sisson Forgeries and their Background." Francis requested twenty-five thousand dollars to pay for these documents, alleging that Lenin and Trotsky were German agents. See WW to Lansing, February 16, 1918, *PWW*, vol. 46, 358 and Lansing to WW, February 18, 1918, *PWW*, vol. 46, 372, where Wilson worries about the expenditure and then approves it. The documents, as it finally turned out, were forgeries.

19. Jusserand to Lansing, April 23, 1918, *PWW*, vol. 47, 430–31.

20. House to WW, May 3, 1918, encl. I: Wiseman to House, May 1, 1918, *PWW*, vol. 47, 503–4.

21. Bliss to Lansing and Others, May 3, 1918, *PWW*, vol. 47, 512–14, especially note 7, on 514, where Joint Note 25 is quoted in full.

22. Reading to Balfour, May 6, 1918, *PWW*, vol. 47, 544.

23. Richard Crane to WW, with encl., May 7, 1918, *PWW*, vol. 47, 548, 551, and especially note 5; Charles R. Crane to WW, May 8, 1918, *PWW*, vol. 47, 561, and note 1.

24. Baker to WW, May 8, 1918, with encls.: Bliss to Baker, April 27, 1918, *PWW*, vol. 47, 565; see Eugene P. Trani, "Woodrow Wilson and the Decision to Intervene in Russia: A Reconsideration," where the argument is made that British pressure forced Wilson's decision. If there had been no British pressure, then there would have been no American intervention. Various points of view are listed here. On these, also see Betty Miller Unterberger, ed., *American Intervention in the Russian Civil War*.

25. Lansing to WW, May 11, 1918, encl. I: Paraphrase of Telegram from the British Representative at Moscow to Mr. Balfour, May 7, 1918, handed to Lansing by Reading, May 11, 1918, *PWW*, vol. 47, 606.

26. Lansing to WW, May 11, 1918, with encls., *PWW*, vol. 47, 605.

27. Ibid.; also Balfour to Reading, May 10, 1918, encl. 2, of Lansing to WW, May 11, 1918, *PWW*, vol. 47, 607.

28. Reading to Balfour, May 12, 1918, *PWW*, vol. 47, 621.

29. Ibid., 622.

30. Lansing to WW, May 16, 1918, *PWW*, vol. 48, 37–38.

31. Lockhart to Foreign Office, encl. 1, April 23, 1918, *PWW*, vol. 48, 39; Lock-

hart to Foreign Office, encl. 2, May 8, 1918, *PWW,* vol. 48, 40; WW to Lansing, May 20, 1918, *PWW,* vol. 48, 73.

32. Lansing to WW, May 21, 1918, *PWW,* vol. 48, 99; Balfour to Reading, encl. 1, May 15, 1918, and Lockhart to Foreign Office, encl. 2, May 15, 1918, *PWW,* vol. 48, 99–104; Lansing to WW, with Miles's encl., May 21, 1918, *PWW,* vol. 48, 104–6 and Miles to Lansing, May 21, 1918, with encl.: Francis to SS, May 11, 1918, *PWW,* vol. 48, 112–14.

33. Reading to Balfour, May 23, 1918, *PWW,* vol. 48, 112–14.

34. Baker to WW, with encls., May 28, 1918, encl. 1: Bliss to Baker, May 26, 1918, *PWW,* vol. 48, 181; March to Bliss, May 28, 1918, *PWW,* vol. 48, 182.

35. Paraphrase of a Telegram from Mr. Balfour to Lord Reading, May 28, 1918, encl. in Lansing to WW, May 31, 1918, *PWW,* vol. 48, 207; Baker to Bliss, May 31, 1918, *PWW,* vol. 48, 219; Lansing, Memorandum, June 3, 1918, *PWW,* vol. 48, 236; Jusserand to Lansing, May 28, 1918, encl., Lansing to WW, June 4, 1918, *PWW,* vol. 48, 239.

36. Joint Note 31, June 3, 1918, "Allied Intervention at the White Sea Ports," *PWW,* vol. 48, 287–88*n*3.

37. Balfour to Reading, "Following from Lord Milner," June 11, 1918, *PWW,* vol. 48, 286. At the same time that the Allies argued over specifics to send to northern Russia, Chicherin sent an official protest to Poole concerning the presence of American warships at Russian ports. See Chicherin to DeWitt Clinton Poole, June 14, 1918, f. 129, op. 2, d. 2, l. 13, AVPRF. These complaints put Poole in harm's way; there were rumors of his imminent arrest. Chicherin cabled Joffe that he denounced reports in the European press of Poole's threatened arrest. See Chicherin to Joffe as late as October 19, 1918, f. 129, op. 2, d. 8, l. 4, AVPRF.

38. Baker to WW, June 20, 1918, encl.: Bliss to Secretary of War, June 18, 1918, *PWW,* vol. 48, 367–70.

39. Baker to WW, July 6, 1918, encl.: Bliss to Secretary of State, Secretary of War and Chief of Staff, July 5, 1918, *PWW,* vol. 48, 536, 537.

40. Reading to Balfour, July 8, 1918, *PWW,* vol. 48, 565.

41. WW to Lincoln Ross Colcord, July 9, 1918, *PWW,* vol. 48, 568; Daniels, Diary, July 9, 1918, *PWW,* vol. 48, 578.

42. Bliss to Baker and March, July 12, 1918, *PWW,* vol. 48, 601–2.

43. Baker to WW, July 20, 1918, *PWW,* vol. 49, 43–44; Baker to WW, July 21, 1918, *PWW,* vol. 49, 52; March to Bliss, July 22, 1918, *PWW,* vol. 49, 57.

44. John J. Pershing, *My Experiences in the World War,* vol. 2, 175–76. For an excellent account of north Russia, see John W. Long, "American Intervention in Russia: The North Russia Expedition, 1918–1919." Francis to Lansing, September 4, 1918, *FRUS, 1918, Russia,* 2: 519. While U.S. troops were in transit, N. I. Tschaikovsky, president of the North Russia Government, cabled Bakhmetev that the Bolsheviks were overthrown with Allied help in the north. See Nicholas Tschaikovsky to Bakhmetev, August 31, 1918, f. 170, op. 512/4, d. 110, AVPI, and Bakhmetev to N. Tschaikovsky, September 9, 1918, f. 170, op. 512/4, d. 110, l. 13, AVPRI, that the embassy would do its utmost to assure its "efficient" assistance. Already by September 29, 1918, Tschaikovsky cabled Wilson directly for more American troops. See N. Tschaikovsky to WW, September 29, 1918, f. 17, d. 29, l. 105, State Archive of the Russian Federation (former State Archive of the October Revolution) (hereafter GARF). It should be mentioned that Francis left Russia permanently on October 23 as he required surgery in London. Officially, he remained ambassador until his death in 1928.

45. On the separation, see Lansing to WW, May 16, 1918, *PWW,* vol. 48, 37–38. For an instance of badgering, see George Kennan to Lansing, May 26, 1918, *PWW,* vol. 48, 185; see also note 24 previously. Lansing to WW, May 20, 1918, encl. Reinsch to Lansing, May 16, 1918, *PWW,* vol. 48, 72; House to WW, May 24, 1918, encl. Bullitt to House, May 20, 1918, *PWW,* vol. 48, 145; Jusserand to Pichon, May 29, 1918, *PWW,* vol. 48, 202.

46. Baker to Bliss, June 1, 1918, *PWW,* vol. 48, 218–19; Jusserand to Pichon, June 6, 1918, *PWW,* vol. 48, 254; Jusserand to Pichon, June 9, 1918, *PWW,* vol. 48, 274; Lansing to WW, June 13, 1918, *PWW,* vol. 48, 305; House to WW, June 13, 1918, *PWW,* vol. 48, 306; House to WW, June 13, 1918, *PWW,* vol. 48, 307; House, Diary, June 13, 1918, *PWW,* vol. 48, 310; Wiseman to Drummond, June 14, 1918, *PWW,* vol. 48, 315–16; Reading to FO, June 16, 1918, box 118, Balfour Papers, BL.

47. WW to Lansing, with encl., June 17, 1918, *PWW,* vol. 48, 335; see the interesting article by Carl J. Richard, "'The Shadow of a Plan': The Rationale behind Wilson's 1918 Siberian Intervention," in which he reviews the six major explanations of Wilson's decision and backs the notion that Wilson proceeded mainly to support the Czechs, thus agreeing with Kennan's analysis in *Decision to Intervene.*

48. WW to Lansing, June 17, 1918, with encl. dated June 13, 1918, *PWW,* vol. 48, 335–36.

49. WW to Lansing, June 19, 1918, *PWW,* vol. 48, 358. Masaryk combined several of his conversations with Wilson in his memoir, according to Link; *PWW,* vol. 48, 358n1. See also Thomas G. Masaryk, *The Making of a State: Memories and Observations, 1914–1918.*

50. WW to Lansing, June 13, 1918, and note 1, *PWW,* vol. 48, 358; Lansing to WW, June 19, 1918, *PWW,* vol. 48, 359; Reinsch to Lansing, June 13, 1918, encl. in WW to Lansing, June 17, 1918, *PWW,* vol. 48, 336; WW to Lansing, June 19, 1918, *PWW,* vol. 48, 358.

51. Poole to Lansing, June 12, 1918, encl. 2, Lansing to WW, June 19, 1918, *PWW,* vol. 48, 360.

52. Clemenceau to Jusserand, June 24, 1918, *PWW,* vol. 48, 416; Jusserand to WW, June 24, 1918, *PWW,* vol. 48, 415; WW to Jusserand, June 25, 1918, *PWW,* vol. 48, 421.

53. Foch to WW, June 27, 1918, *PWW,* vol. 48, 445–46.

54. Jusserand to Pichon, June 29, 1918, *PWW,* vol. 48, 446.

55. Wiseman to Drummond, June 30, 1918, *PWW,* vol. 48, 470. Admiral Knight kept Washington informed on conditions in Vladivostok, Knight to Baker, June 29, 1918, *PWW,* vol. 48, 480. Baker to Wilson, July 2, 1918, *PWW,* vol. 48, 483–84; WW to Lansing, July 3, 1918, *PWW,* vol. 48, 489; Robins to Lansing, July 1, 1918, encl. in WW to Lansing, July 3, 1918, *PWW,* vol. 48, 489–90.

56. Balfour to Reading, July 3, 1918, *PWW,* vol. 48, 494.

57. Balfour to Reading, encl. 4, July 2, 1918, in Reading to WW, July 3, 1918, *PWW,* vol. 48, 493–501, quotes on 496 and 499.

58. Reading to Balfour, July 3, 1918, *PWW,* vol. 48, 511–14; Wiseman to Arthur Cecil Murray, July 4, 1918, *PWW,* vol. 48, 523–25.

59. Lansing, Memorandum of a Conference at the White House in Reference to the Siberian Situation, July 6, 1918, *PWW,* vol. 48, 542–43.

60. Daniels to Austin Melvin Knight, July 6, 1918, *PWW,* vol. 48, 543; Daniels,

Diary, July 6, 1918, *PWW,* vol. 48, 544; Baker to WW, with encls., July 7, 1918, *PWW,* vol. 48, 544–45.

61. WW to House, July 8, 1918, *PWW,* vol. 48, 550; Lansing to WW, July 9, 1918, *PWW,* vol. 48, 574–75.

62. Reading to Balfour, July 10, 1918, *PWW,* vol. 48, 586–87; Lloyd George to Reading, July 10, 1918, *PWW,* vol. 48, 587–88.

63. WW to Polk, with encl., July 17, 1918, *PWW,* vol. 48, 639 as well as the draft, July 16, 1918, 624–27, and the final copy, 640–43; see Betty Miller Unterberger, "Woodrow Wilson and the Bolsheviks: The 'Acid Test' of Soviet-American Relations," in which the author maintains that Wilson upheld the principles of nonintervention, anti-imperialism, the Open Door, and self-determination within the limits of coalition diplomacy. Wilson feared that any intervention would be construed as anti-Bolshevism and violate Point VI of the Fourteen Points, even though in rescuing the Czechoslovaks, "His basic object was to prevent his associates from turning the rescue mission into an anti-Bolshevik crusade" (90). In an earlier article, "President Wilson and the Decision to Send American Troops to Siberia," Unterberger insisted that Wilson "wished to preserve the open door in Siberia and North Manchuria, without interfering in the factional disputes of the Russians" (70). She reiterated this view by emphasizing the preservation of the open door in the Far East and the preservation of Russian territorial integrity in her article, "The Russian Revolution and Wilson's Far-Eastern Policy."

64. WW to Polk, with encl., July 17, 1918, *PWW,* vol. 48, 642.

65. Ibid., 640–43, usually referred to as the aide-mémoire. It should be noted that Wilson's action did not go unnoticed by Lenin. See Lenin's speech of July 29, 1918, "Rech' na ob'edinennom zasedanii VTsIK Moskovskogo Soveta, Fabrichno-Zavodskikh Komitetov i Professional'nikh Soiuzov Moskvy," that a state of war existed between the Soviet Republic and the Allied powers. Check V. I. Lenin, *Polnoe Sobranie Sochinenii,* vol. 37, 1–18. See also John M. Thompson, "Lenin's Analysis of Intervention." Thompson points out that Lenin maintained that there was a close class interest between the counterrevolutionaries and the foreign capitalists, that there was rivalry between Japan and the United States, and that there was a fear that at the war's end there could be a European crusade against Bolshevism (152, 153, 155).

66. Polk to WW, July 18, 1918, *PWW,* vol. 49, 5, and especially note 1; Polk to WW, July 20, 1918, *PWW,* vol. 49, 39.

67. Polk to Wilson, July 20, 1918, encl., July 20, 1918, *PWW,* vol. 49, 40 (italics ours). A Press Release, August 3, 1918, *PWW,* vol. 49, 171.

68. Reading to Lloyd George, July 21, 1918, *PWW,* vol. 49, 52; Balfour to Reading July 22, 1918, *PWW,* vol. 49, 57, and Memorandum, War Cabinet, July 22, 1918, *PWW,* vol. 49, 58.

69. Polk to WW, July 24, 1918, *PWW,* vol. 49, 75; Polk to WW, encl., July 20, 1918, *PWW,* vol. 49, 76.

70. Bergson, Notebooks, July 25, 1918, *PWW,* vol. 49, 96; House, Diary, July 25, 1918, *PWW,* vol. 49, 96. That telegram, Polk to Morris, July 27, 1918, *FRUS, 1918, Russia,* 2: 306–7, is a summary of Polk's interview with Ishii, July 25, 1918. Polk to WW, July 25, 1918, encl. 1, July 23, 1918, *PWW,* vol. 49, 107. For the painful Japanese reaction and delayed response to Wilson, see a detailed account in Morley, *The Japanese Thrust,* chaps. 12–13.

71. Polk to WW, July 26, 1918, encl. 2, July 25, 1918, *PWW,* vol. 49, 108, 109; see also Polk to Morris, August 1, 1918, *FRUS, 1918, Russia,* 2: 322–23, where Polk

states, "This Government believes that if the Japanese Government can not reach an early and favorable decision in regard to the proposed plan of action to secure the safety of the Czecho-Slovaks, the support of even the very moderate military force which this Government proposes should now be used will prove abortive." WW to Daniels, August 1, 1918, *PWW,* vol. 49, 149; Daniels to WW, July 31, 1918, *PWW,* vol. 49, 142; Polk to WW, August 1, 1918, encl. 2, July 31, 1918, "Telegram from Knight," *PWW,* vol. 49, 151.

72. See "A Press Release," August 3, 1918, *PWW,* vol. 49, 170–72; Polk to WW, August 3, 1918, *PWW,* vol. 49, 175, 176. Bakhmetev's reaction to the aide-mémoire and its lack of immediate consequences west of the Urals can be gauged from his statement to Lansing of September 30, 1918: "It is with deep affliction, that I have learned of the sad conclusion to which the government of the United States has arrived with regard to the military situation beyond the Ural mountains and the decision which it has reached upon the prospects of the Czecho-Slovak action in that region." See Bakhmetev to Lansing, September 30, 1918, f. 170, op. 512/4, d. 41, l. 64, AVPRI.

73. Williams S. Graves, *America's Siberian Adventure,* 34, 52, 55–57; United States, Army War College, Historical Section, *Order of Battle of the United States Land Forces in the World War, American Expeditionary Forces,* vol. 1, *General Headquarters, Armies, Army Corps, Services of Supply and Separate Forces,* 380–89, where the size of the north Russian and Siberian forces is listed.

74. March to Pershing, July 5, 1918, Peyton C. March Papers, LC; March to Bliss, July 8, 1918, and Baker to Bliss, July 8, 1918, Bliss Papers, LC; WW to House, July 8, 1918, House Papers, CtY; War Cabinet Meeting no. 601, July 29, 1918, PRO.

75. See Ullman, *Intervention and the War,* for the factors that influenced the British.

76. Lansing, Private Memorandum, "Rufus, Earl of Reading," April 1918, Lansing Papers, box 66, LC; Fowler, *British-American Relations,* 165.

77. War Cabinet Meeting no. 294, December 7, 1917, PRO; Cecil Spring Rice to FO, December 24, 1917, Milner Papers, BLO.

78. "The Situation in Russia," Supreme War Council, Joint Note 5, December 24, 1917, WD, RG120, NA; David Trask, *The United States in the Supreme War Council: American War Aims and Inter-Allied Strategy, 1917–1918,* 102.

79. Wiseman, notes of interview with WW, January 23, 1918, and FO to British Embassy, Washington, January 26, 1918, and January 31, 1918; FO to Wiseman, January 30, 1918; Wiseman to Balfour, February 4, 1918; Wiseman to Eric Drummond, February 4, 1918, all in the Balfour Papers, BM.

80. Japanese Intervention in Siberia, Joint Note 16, February 19, 1918, Bliss to Baker, February 25, 1918, and Bliss to War Department, February 25, 1918, all in WD, RG120, NA; Bliss to March, February 20, 1918, Bliss Papers, LC; Balfour, Memorandum, February 14, 1918, Balfour Papers, BM.

81. House to Balfour, March 4, 1918, and Balfour to House, March 6, 1918, Lloyd George Papers, BL; Wiseman to Drummond, March 4, 1918, and March 5, 1918, and Reading to Balfour, March 10, 1918, Balfour Papers, BM.

82. WW to C. E. Russell, November 10, 1917, WP, LC; speech of WW to the American Federation of Labor Convention, November 12, 1917, published in Ray Stannard Baker and William E. Dodd, eds., *The Public Papers of Woodrow Wilson: War and Peace,* vol. 1, 116–24; Lincoln Colcord to WW, December 3, 1917, and WW to Colcord, December 6, 1917, WP, LC; "The Fourteen Points Speech," January 8, 1918, published in Baker and Dodd, *Public Papers of Woodrow Wilson,* vol. 1, 155–62.

83. Lansing, Private Memorandum, December 7, 1917, Lansing Papers, LC; WW to Lansing, December 12, 1917, SD, RG59, 861.00/804D, NA; George Creel to WW, December 21, 1917, and Creel to WW, December 27, 1917, WP, LC; WW to Creel, December 24, 1917, and WW to Creel, December 29, 1917, Creel Papers, LC.

84. Lansing to WW, January 10, 1918, WP, LC; WW to Lansing, January 20, 1918, R. S. Baker Papers, LC; WW to Senator Robert Owen, January 24, 1918, WP, LC; Basil Miles, Memorandum for the Secretary of State, January 29, 1918, SD, RG59, 861.00/1048½, NA.

85. WW to Lansing, February 4, 1918, and Basil Miles, Memorandum, February 5, 1918, both SD, RG59, 861.01/14½, NA.

86. WW to Lansing, February 4, 1918, Lansing Papers, NJP; WW to Henry Davison, February 22, 1918, WP, LC; Wiseman to Reading, February 12, 1918, FO 800, Reading Papers, PRO.

87. The original draft of Wilson's message to the Soviet Congress is in the Lansing Papers, NJP. For Polk's thoughts, see Polk, Diary, March 11, 1918, Polk Papers, CtY.

88. Report of Military and Naval Representatives, March 23, 1918, WD, RG120, NA. For detailed treatments of this question, see Kennan, *Decision to Intervene,* and Ullman, *Intervention and the War.*

89. "The Situation in the Eastern Theatre," Joint Note 20, April 8, 1918, and Bliss to War Department, April 12, 1918, WD, RG120, NA; N. Baker to WW, April 25, 1918, and May 2, 1918, N. Baker Papers, LC.

90. See Robert Cecil to Balfour, March 10, 1918, Balfour Papers, BM; War Cabinet Meeting no. 360, March 6, 1918, PRO.

91. FO to Balfour, March 16, 1918, Balfour Papers, FO 800, PRO; Wiseman to Drummond, March 27, 1918, Balfour Papers, BM; Reading to FO, April 22, 1918, FO 800, Balfour Papers, PRO; Reading to FO, April 25, 1918, FO 800, Reading Papers, PRO.

92. WW to Thomas Lamont, January 31, 1918, WW to C. W. Eliot, January 21, 1918, and WW to Samuel Gompers, January 21, 1918, all in WP, LC.

93. WW to Lansing, February 4, 1918, SD, RG59, 861.00/1097, NA; WW to Lansing, March 22, 1918, SD, RG59, 861.00/1433½, NA; WW to Tumulty, February 23, 1918, WP, LC; Polk to Lansing, March 5, 1918, R. S. Baker Papers, LC; WW to Breckinridge Long, March 14, 1918, Long Papers, LC.

94. Lansing to WW, April 11, 1918, SD, RG59, 861.00/1464½, NA; WW to Lansing, May 20, 1918, SD, RG59, 861.00/1895½, NA; WW to Daniels, April 8, 1918, Daniels Papers, LC; WW to Lansing, April 4, 1918, Polk Papers, CtY.

95. "Transportation of Czech Troops from Russia," Joint Note 25, April 27, 1918, Bliss to War Department, May 26, 1918, and March to Bliss, May 28, 1918, WD, RG120, NA.

96. "Allied Intervention at Russian Allied Ports," Joint Note 31, June 3, 1918, and Bliss to War Department, June 18, 1918, WD, RG120, NA.

97. Wiseman to Drummond, June 3, 1918, FO 800, Reading Papers, PRO. As to the forged documents, see Kennan, "The Sisson Documents."

98. House to WW, June 21, 1918, WP, LC; House, Diary, June 21, 1918, House Papers, CtY; for Lansing's conversion to action in Siberia, Lansing to WW, June 23, 1918, SD, RG59, 861.00/2164½, NA. See also the two documents from Reading to Balfour, both dated June 25, 1918, FO 800, Reading Papers, PRO.

99. Jusserand to WW, March 13, 1918, WP, LC; Jusserand to Lansing, March

12, 1918, encl. in Frank Polk to WW, March 14, 1918, SD, RG59, 861.00/1676, NA; Jusserand to Lansing, April 8, 1918, encl. in Lansing to WW, April 11, 1918, SD, RG59, 861.00/1464½, NA; Jusserand to Lansing, April 23, 1918, encl. in Lansing to WW, April 25, 1918, Lansing Papers, NJP; Jusserand to Lansing, March 28, 1918, encl. in Phillips to WW, June 4, 1918, WP, LC; Jusserand to Paris, June 19 and 20, 1918, copies in SD Records of the Office of Eastern European Affairs, NA. Michael J. Carley, "The Origins of French Intervention in the Russian Civil War, January to May 1918: A Reappraisal," shows the different attitudes that the French Ministry of War and the Quai d'Orsay had concerning collaboration with the Bolsheviks until April 1918, when the French government became committed to overthrowing the Bolsheviks; also check Carley's book, *Revolution and Intervention: The French Intervention and the Russian Civil War, 1917–1919.*

100. Foch to WW, June 27, 1918, N. Baker Papers, LC; Memorandum to WW from Allied leaders, July 2, 1918, encl. in March to WW, July 3, 1918, *PWW,* vol. 48, 503–6.

101. WW to Daniel M. Barringer, June 10, 1918, and WW to William C. Redfield, June 13, 1918, WP, LC; WW to Lansing, June 17, 1918, SD, RG59, 861.00/2145 1/2, NA; Lansing to WW, June 23, 1918, SD, RG59, 861.00/2164½, NA.

102. Lansing, Private Memorandum, July 4, 1918, Lansing Papers, LC; Lansing, "Memorandum of a Conference at the White House in Reference to the Siberian Situation," July 6, 1918, SD, RG 59, 861.00/2240½, NA; WW, Aide-Mémoire, July 17, 1918, SD, RG59, 861.00/3130a, NA.

Seven. 1919: Paris in the Spring

1. For quote see Herbert Hoover, *The Ordeal of Woodrow Wilson,* 115–16.

2. Notes of a Meeting of the Supreme War Council at Quai d'Orsay at 2:30 on January 12, 1919, WP, LC; for an overview of Allied efforts, see Kennan, *Russia and the West Under Lenin and Stalin,* 121–22. He listed five efforts. For the definitive study of the Russian problem at Paris, check John M. Thompson, *Russia, Bolshevism, and the Versailles Peace.* Chicherin sent a radio-telegram to the State Department on January 12, 1919, repudiating reasons for U.S. troops to be in Russia and declared his continuing readiness to negotiate all outstanding issues. See Chicherin to State Department, January 12, 1919, f. 0129/129, op. 3, p. 2.a., d. 1, l. 6–7, AVPRF. As Wilson was wondering about the efficacy of arms, so was Chicherin: "We are therefore at a loss to understand how the further maintainance [*sic*] of American troops in Russia can be justified."

3. Notes of a Meeting of the Supreme War Council at Quai d'Orsay at 2:30 on January 12, 1919, WP, LC.

4. Ibid.; "Plan for Draft Resolution," January 14, 1919, and fully adopted on January 18, "Programme of Arrangements for the Opening meeting on Saturday, January 18, 1919, at 3:00 p.m.," WP, LC.

5. Lansing, Desk Diary, January 16 and 18, 1919, Lansing Papers, box 65, LC; William H. Buckler to Lansing, January 18, 1919, *PWW,* vol. 54, 136.

6. William H. Buckler to Lansing, January 18, 1919, *PWW,* vol. 54, 136; Bliss, Diary, January 19, 1919, Bliss Papers, box 65, LC.

7. Hankey's Notes of Two Meetings of the Council of Ten, January 21, 1919, 10:30 a.m., *PWW,* vol. 54, 179, 181–83.

8. Ibid., 184–87. It was exactly at this time that the Omsk government said it was doing well against the Bolsheviks even though it had vainly awaited Allied aid. See "Paraphrase of a Cable received from the Ministry of Foreign Affairs, Omsk," to Bakhmetev, January 21, 1919, f. 1770, op. 512/4, d. 115, l. 14, AVPRI.

9. Lansing, Desk Diary, January 21 and 22, 1919, Lansing Papers, box 65, LC; Kennan, *Russia and the West*, 123; Grayson, Diary, January 22, 1919, *PWW*, vol. 54, 199.

10. Text of Wilson's Statement, January 22, 1919, *PWW*, vol. 54, 205–6; check also Kennan, *Russia and the West*, 123; Wilson's Statement, January 22, 1919, *PWW*, vol. 54, 206. Hankey's Notes of a Meeting of the Council of Ten, January 22, 1919, *PWW*, vol. 54, 205–6; for Chicherin's response, see *FRUS, 1919, Russia*, 39–42 and for Buckler's conversations with Litvinov, *FRUS, 1919, Russia*, 15–17, and also check note 12 to follow.

11. G. V. Chicherin to WW, January 29, 1919, *PWW*, vol. 54, 345–46. For quotes, see Walworth, *Woodrow Wilson*, vol. 2, 266, and also Kennan, *Russia and the West*, 123.

12. J. Tschakste to President Wilson, February 10, 1919, *FRUS, 1919, Russia*, 50, for Estonian acceptance. Poole to Acting Secretary of State, January 30, 1919, *FRUS, 1919, Russia*, 36; Ernest L. Harris, American Consul at Irkutsk, to Acting Secretary of State, February 6, 1919, *FRUS, 1919, Russia*, 44; G. Sidorenko to Clemenceau, February 10, 1919, *FRUS, 1919, Russia*, 71; S. Ughet to Polk, February 19, 1919, encl. Ministry of Foreign Affairs at Omsk to the Russian Embassy at Washington, *FRUS, 1919, Russia*, 71; Sazonov and N. V. Tchaikovsky to Secretariat-General of the Paris Peace Conference, February 12, 1919, *FRUS, 1919, Russia*, 54.

13. Walworth, *Wilson*, vol. 2, 266.

14. Bullitt to House, January 30, 1919, House Papers, CtY; Poole to Amembassy, Paris, January 31, 1919, Bullitt Microfilm, CtY.

15. Poole to Amembassy, Paris, January 31, 1919, Bullitt Microfilm, CtY; Bliss to WW, February 8, 1919, Bliss Papers, box 70, LC; for the northern campaign of General Poole, see Leonid I. Strakhovsky, *Intervention at Archangel: The Story of Allied Intervention and Russian Counter-Revolution in North Russia, 1918–1920*. Bliss, Diary, February 9, 1919, Bliss Papers, box 65, LC; Naval Operations to WW, February 9, 1919, WP, LC; Bliss, Memorandum for WW, February 12, 1919, Bliss Papers, box 174, LC.

16. Bullitt, Memo for House, February 11, 1919, Bullitt Microfilm, CtY.

17. Lansing to Frank Polk, February 11, 1919, Lansing Papers, box 3, NJP.

18. P. H. Kerr to Lloyd George, February 11, 1919, F/89/2/72, Lloyd George Papers, BL; Lloyd George to Philip Kerr, February 12, 1919, F/89/2/8, Lloyd George Papers, BL.

19. War Cabinet Meeting no. 531, PRO.

20. Hankey's Notes of a Meeting of the Supreme War Council, February 14, 1919, *PWW*, vol. 55, 178–83; Kennan, *Russia and the West*, 124.

21. Hankey, *PWW*, vol. 55, 181–82.

22. Ibid., 183. Retribution was, by now, well known as in the case of the Red Terror. For instance, see Allen Wardwell to G. Chicherin, September 18, 1918, f. 129, op. 2, p. 2, d. 16, l. 58–59, AVPRF, where he complains about "wholesale execution" and "unwarranted slaughter" and Chicherin's justification of such behavior as "class terror," and a necessary battle with autocracy, calling attention to the barbarity of the other side. Chicherin to Wardwell, September 11, 1918, f. 29,

op. 2, p. 2, d. 16, l. 66–67, AVPRF. In like tone, see Poole to Chicherin, September 4, 1918, f. 129, op. 2, p. 1, d. 3, l. 76, AVPRF.

23. Churchill to Lloyd George, February 15, 1919, F/8/3/16, Lloyd George Papers, BL.

24. Churchill to P.M., February 15, 1919, F/8/3/16, Lloyd George Papers, BL.

25. W. Churchill to Prime Minister, February 16, 1919, F/8/3/17, Lloyd George Papers, BL.

26. Prime Minister to W. Churchill, February 16, 1919, f/8/3/18, Lloyd George Papers, BL; Churchill to Balfour, February 16, 1919, Balfour Papers, BM.

27. Balfour to Churchill, February 16, 1919, Balfour Papers, BM.

28. Kerr to Lloyd George, c. February 16, 1919, F/84/c/17, Lloyd George Papers, BL.

29. Bliss, Memorandum for Colonel House, February 17, 1919, Bliss Papers, box 69, LC.

30. House, Diary, February 17, 1919, House Papers, CtY; Lansing to WW, February 17, 1919, WP, LC.

31. House to WW, February 17, 1919, WP, LC.

32. House, Diary, February 17, 1919, *PWW*, vol. 55, 203–4, and note 1 on 204.

33. Auchincloss, Diary, February 16, 1919, Auchincloss Papers, CtY; Lansing, Desk Diary, February 16, 1919, Lansing Papers, box 65, LC; House, Diary, February 14, 1919, House Papers, CtY; John M. Thompson, in *Russia, Bolshevism, and the Versailles Peace*, 151, remarks that House and Wilson conferred the morning of February 14, the day of Wilson's departure for America, and "settled all the important questions." (Quote from House's Diary.) Thompson states that "Although direct evidence is lacking, it seems almost certain that at this time House asked for, and received, discretionary authority to send a fact-finding mission to Russia" (151). Thompson goes on to say that "Wilson never denied having prior knowledge of the mission" (151). Beatrice Farnsworth, *William C. Bullitt and the Soviet Union*, 35–36.

34. Meeting of the 14th Session of the Supreme War Council, February 14, 1919, *FRUS, 1919, Russia*, 57; Farnsworth, *Bullitt*, 35–36.

35. Farnsworth, *Bullitt*, 36; *PWW*, vol. 55, 541n1. See also Thompson, *Russia, Bolshevism, and the Versailles Peace*, 154, where he quotes Bullitt as saying that Kerr discussed it with Lloyd George and Balfour. On the sensitive subject of Bullitt's mission, Kennan remarks: "It was, perhaps, improper for Bullitt to make public this note, as he subsequently did; but I am not aware that its authenticity has ever been denied. It was with this document in his pocket that Bullitt set off for Moscow. One can only regard his visit, therefore, as having British as well as American sanction." Kennan, *Russia and the West*, 126–27.

36. War Cabinet Meetings no. 535 and no. 537, February 24 and 26, 1919, PRO.

37. A. J. Balfour, Memo, "The Russian Situation," February 26, 1919, Balfour Papers, BM.

38. Ibid.

39. Farnsworth, *Bullitt*, 37, 39, 40–41; Bullitt to House, March 4, 1919, Bullitt Microfilm, CtY. For Kerr's and House's discussion, see Kerr to PM, February 18, 1919, F/89/2/23, Lloyd George Papers, BL. Bullitt cabled Lansing and House on March 10, 1919, that he had just arrived in Petrograd and spoken with Chicherin and Litvinov, who were "speaking with authority" and that "the Soviet Government is most favorably disposed towards the cessation of hostilities and a peace conference." Furthermore, Bullitt was assured of the Soviets' "full confidence in

the good will of the American government." See Bullitt to Lansing and House, March 10, 1919, f. 04/4, op. 3, p. 4, d. 121, l. 11, AVPRF. Check also Chicherin to Lenin in early March, 1919, in which the former writes that Bullitt considered the withdrawal of Allied troops impossible without a clause that would guarantee that the Red Army would not become a threat to Europe; he also mentioned another proposal from Bullitt—to withdraw the Allied forces immediately with a reduction of the Red Army proportionate to the reduction in the number of troops opposing it. It is interesting that Chicherin expressed concern about the voting system, which would determine the status of disputed territories; in the socialist democracy one vote of a factory worker equaled the votes of five peasants. See Chicherin to Lenin, March 12, 1919, f. 04, op. 3, p. 7, d. 121, l. 22–23, AVPRF. Finally, see Chicherin's note to Joffe a few days later in which the final draft of the Allies' address to all Russian governments is said to be attached. According to Chicherin, Bullitt had told him he hoped to be able to get the text adopted by the Allies, and the invitation to the conference to all Russian parties would be issued in April. See Chicherin to Joffe, March 17, 1919, f. 04, op. 3, p. 7, d. 121, l. 27, AVPRF. Kennan, *Russia and the West*, 127.

40. Paper from Robert Lansing to M. Pichon at Meeting of Council of Ten, March 15, 1919, Bliss Papers, box 69, LC; as to the French, see Kennan, *Russia and the West*, 127. Lansing to Pichon at Meeting of Council of Ten, March 15, 1919, Bliss Papers, box 69, LC.

41. Text of Projected Peace Proposal by the Allied and Associated Governments, March 14, 1919, *FRUS, 1919, Russia*, 78–80 (sent by Bullitt to Wilson, Lansing, and House).

42. Bullitt to WW, March 16, 1919, *PWW*, vol. 55, 541–42.

43. Ibid., 545.

44. WW to J. P. Tumulty, July 17, 1919, *PWW*, vol. 61, 509. In note 2 the editors comment, "There is also no written evidence to contradict Wilson's statement that he knew nothing of the 'Allied terms,' and that he did not believe in the truth of the *Nation*'s statement about Kerr's memorandum" (509).

45. Memorandum for the President and the Commissioners Plenipotentiary to Negotiate Peace from William C. Bullitt, c. March 28, 1919, *PWW*, vol. 56, 389.

46. Memorandum by Mr. William C. Bullitt for the President and the Commissioners Plenipotentiary to Negotiate Peace, March 25 (?), 1919, *FRUS, 1919, Russia*, 94.

47. Thompson, *Russia, Bolshevism, and the Versailles Peace*, 237.

48. White to M. Sazonov, March 18, 1919, Henry White Papers, box 40, LC. It is useful to note that at this very time Bakhmetev formulated the Whites' policy toward the Allies: prevent Allied negotiations with Lenin, contrast Bolshevism to democracy, prepare public opinion for a direct and decisive Allied intervention, and get the Allies to declare that they would never recognize the Bolshevik government. See Bakhmetev's Note, March 17, 1919, f. 5805, d. 538, l. 1–4, GARF (hereafter State Archive of the Russian Federation).

49. Lansing, Desk Diary, March 19, 1919, Lansing Papers, box 65, LC; J. C. Grew to Alexander Kirk, March 21, 1919, Lansing Papers, vol. 42, LC; Lansing, Memorandum for the President, March 22, 1919, marked "Urgent," WP, LC; Lansing to Polk, March 22, 1919, WP, LC; Lansing to Wilson, March 24, 1919, WP, LC.

50. Hoover to WW, March 28, 1919, *PWW*, vol. 56, 378. Hoover later recounted that though the plan had faint hope of success, Wilson welcomed it to keep Allied

militarists busy debating, and, if it did succeed, it would save lives and help stabilize Europe. See Hoover, *Ordeal of Woodrow Wilson*, 119.

51. Farnsworth, *Bullitt*, 47–53, and especially note 35 on p. 195 dealing with Steed and Auchincloss; as to the breakfast, see Thompson, *Russia, Bolshevism, and the Versailles Peace*, 246.

52. House, Diary, March 25, 1919, House Papers, CtY.

53. Ibid., March 26, 1919.

54. Drummond to Balfour, March 26, 1919, FO 800/215, Balfour Papers, PRO; Auchincloss, Diary, March 26, 1919, Auchincloss Papers, CtY.

55. Lansing to Richard Crane, March 26, 1919, Lansing Papers, box 3, NJP; Bakhmetev "Aide Memoir" to Lansing, November 20, 1918, f. 170, op. 512/4, d. 41, l. 160–162, AVPRI. He implores Lansing not to decide the future of his country without Russia's "cognizance and consent." Lansing, Desk Diary, March 26, 1919, Lansing Papers, box 65, LC.

56. House, Diary, March 27, 1919, House Papers, CtY. Sergei Ughet analyzed U.S. policy as "doing nothing," feeling that Americans did not understand and that Wilson hesitated in contrast to Britain and France. See Ughet to Minister of Foreign Affairs, Omsk, April 1, 1919, f. 200, d. 538, No. 290, l. 4–5, GARF.

57. *PWW*, vol. 56, 551–52n1, concerning newspaper accounts of Bullitt's mission to Russia.

58. Ibid., 552.

59. Tumulty to WW, April 2, 1919, *PWW*, vol. 56, 551.

60. Ibid.

61. Lansing to WW, March 27, 1919, WP, LC; Bliss to WW, March 28, 1919, WP, LC.

62. House, Diary, March 29, 1919, House Papers, CtY.

63. Cecil to Prime Minister, March 29, 1919, F/6/6/20, Lloyd George Papers, BL.

64. McCormick, Diary, March 18 and 29, 1919, McCormick Papers, CtY; Cecil, Diary, March 29, 1919, Cecil Papers, BM; Lloyd George to Bonar Law, March 31, 1919, F/30/3/40, Lloyd George Papers, BL.

65. Farnsworth, *Bullitt*, 53.

66. The American Commissioners to Negotiate Peace to WW, March 31, 1919, WP, LC.

67. Thompson, *Russia, Bolshevism, and the Versailles Peace*, 242–43. Link notes that Thompson thought House had "buried the memorandum" so that Wilson never saw it (*PWW*, vol. 56, 468n1). Link points to a brief note to Lansing from Wilson of April 1, 1919: "I think the settlement suggested by you and your colleagues in this matter is the right and necessary one" (WW to Lansing, April 1, 1919, in *PWW*, vol. 56, 512). In a footnote to this letter, Link et al. survey the arguments for and against the president ever having seen this memorandum. In favor of this letter referring to the memorandum are Lansing's initials on it implying the president thought it was from him and read it. Since it is in the Wilson Papers, there is nothing else the editors can find in the papers to which the president could conceivably be responding. Oppositely, in favor of Thompson is the fact that there are no markings on the document such as Wilson often made, and Wilson did not implement it. The editors observe that "developments in Paris, abroad, and in the United States soon took control of Russian policy out of Wilson's hands" (ibid., vol. 56, 513). Finally, on April 21 Wilson wrote William G. Sharp that he went along with Sharp's views, which were to give Soviet Russia some sort of recognition (ibid., vol. 56, 513; vol.

57, 476, 559). Whatever may be the case, that is, whether or not Wilson ever read the memorandum and whether House was or was not responsible for burying it, Thompson would seem to have the better of the argument, according to Link et al. Bullitt to WW, April 18, 1919, *PWW,* vol. 57, 459, 462*n2–3.* Also see Bullitt to WW, April 18, 1919, accession no. 48247, Woodrow Wilson Papers (as collected by Arthur S. Link), NJP, where Bullitt quoted Lloyd George's speech and asked Wilson about its veracity.

68. House, Diary, April 6, 1919, House Papers, CtY; Auchincloss, Diary, April 6, 1919, Auchincloss Papers, CtY; Nansen to WW, April 3, 1919, *PWW,* vol. 56, 575–76; WW, draft of letter to Nansen, April 7, 1919, House Papers, CtY; Farnsworth, *Bullitt,* 51–53; Kennan, *Russia and the West,* 130.

Eight. The First Cold Warriors

1. Heckscher, *Woodrow Wilson,* 590–91. On May 27, 1919, Wilson and the Council of Four promised munitions, supplies, and food to Kolchak if he met the following conditions: reconstitute the Constituent Assembly of January 1918; freely elect local governments; prevent the revival of any aspect of the tsarist system; guarantee the independence of Finland and Poland; recognize autonomous territories in the Caucasus and Transcaspia; hold a peace conference on Bessarabia's future; join the League of Nations; pay the national debt. On June 4, 1919, Kolchak responded, giving assurances to all but the recall of the old Constituent Assembly (he would constitute a new one). See Hankey's Notes of a Meeting of the Council of Four, May 26, 1919, and Despatch to Admiral Koltchak, May 27, 1919, *PWW,* vol. 59, 543–46 and Kolchak to Clemenceau, June 4, 1919, *PWW,* vol. 60, 141–44.

2. For quote of Senate Resolution, Tumulty to Polk, June 30, 1919, encl. George A. Sanderson to Sir, June 28, 1919, WP, LC. N. Baker to WW, July 9, 1919, WP, LC; Polk to Tumulty, July 10, 1919, WP, LC; Polk to N. Baker, Memorandum, July 10, 1919, WP, LC.

3. Agwar to Graves, no. 292, July 1, 1919, WD, RG407, Cable Section, box 144, NA; Agwar to Graves, no. 297, July 3, 1919, Tele, WD, RG407, Cable Section, box 144, NA; Graves to Amembassy, Tokyo, July 5, 1919, Tele, Morris Papers, box 4, LC.

4. "Report of a Press Conference," July 10, 1919, *PWW,* vol. 61, 417–24; "A News Report," July 10, 1919, *PWW,* vol. 61, 424–26; An Address to the Senate, July 10, 1919, *PWW,* vol. 61, 426–36; Two News Reports, July 10, 1919, *PWW,* vol. 61, 437–39.

5. For the complicated history of the resolution, see *PWW,* vol. 61, 353–54*n2.*

6. Polk to WW, July 11, 1919, WP, LC; Polk to WW, July 11, 1919, SD, RG59, reel 99, 861.48/905, NA; Polk to Morris, July 11, 1919, Tele, Morris Papers, box 4, LC.

7. R. L. Eichelberger, Intelligence Summary, Vladivostok, July 12, 1919, WD, RG395, AEF in Siberia, Historical Files, box 9, NA; Polk to WW, July 12, 1919, WP, LC.

8. WW to Josephus Daniels, July 17, 1919, WP, LC; Polk to WW, July 14, 1919, SD, RG59, reel 22, 861.00/4042, NA.

9. Baker to WW, July 15, 1919, encl., Bliss to Baker, July 15, 1919, WP, LC; Polk to WW, July 16 and 18 (encl.), 1919, WP, LC.

10. Daniels to WW, July 23, 1919, WP, LC. The resolution is summarized at the

start of Wilson's reply, WW to President of Senate, July 22, 1919, *PWW*, vol. 61, 579.

11. For quote, see WW to President of Senate, July 22, 1919, *PWW*, vol. 61, 581. The reorganization of Siberian railways was a constant source of friction. In January 1919 the Omsk government seemed to turn the whole affair over to the Allies in anticipation of further "vast aid of the Allied powers" (paraphrase of Cable received by the Russian Embassy from the Ministry of Foreign Affairs, Omsk, January 19, 1919, f. 170, op. 512/4, d. 115, l. 23–24, AVPRI). On the actual management mechanism, there was to be a special inter-allied committee with one representative per ally with troops in Siberia and a Russian chairman and a special Allied technical commission under Stevens as director-general, but each railway was to have a Russian manager under the Omsk government. See paraphrase of Cable received by the Russian Embassy from the Ministry of Foreign Affairs, Omsk, January 22, 1919, f. 170, op. 512/4, d. 115, l. 25–26, AVPRI. These were points for negotiation, but Omsk was very sensitive as to ultimate control; for instance, "We also object to the intention of Mr. Morris to negotiate with General Horvath which is being rumored." Paraphrase of Cable received by the Russian Embassy from the Ministry of Foreign Affairs, Omsk, January 24, 1919, f. 170, op. 512/4, d. 115, l. 27, AVPRI. The emphasis was only control of technical aid and not infringement of sovereign rights. See Acting Secretary of State to Ughet, March 29, 1919, f. 170, op. 512/4, d. 115, l. 88, AVPRI. Walworth indicates that a technical error led the U.S. to land 8,500 troops rather than the 7,000 agreed upon, thus allowing Japan to take advantage of this error and justify sending tens of thousands. See Walworth, *Wilson*, vol. 2, 262*n2*.

On the actual authorship of the statement, see N. Baker to Tumulty, July 22, 1919, N. Baker Papers, box 11, LC; on July 25, 1919, the president's message was read to the Senate and ordered to be printed; see U.S. Senate Document, 66th Cong., 1st sess., Document no. 60, WD, RG 395, AEF in Siberia, Historical Files, box 1, NA.

12. Albert W. Fox, "Deny Wilson Power," July 23, 1919, *PWW*, vol. 61, 596–97.

13. Heckscher, *Wilson*, 591.

14. Lansing, Desk Diary, July 25, 1919, Lansing Papers, box 65, LC; Lansing to WW, July 25, 1919, 39588—transmitted by Caldwell of the Smith telegram to the Omsk Government, WP, LC; Stevens to Lansing, July 19, 1919, encl. in Lansing to WW, July 25, 1919, *PWW*, vol. 61, 636*n1*.

15. Morris to Acting Secretary of State, July 10, 1919, *FRUS, 1919, Russia*, 389; Polk to Morris, May 15, 1919, *FRUS, 1919, Russia*, 349; Reinsch to Acting Secretary of State, June 3, 1919, encl. Harris to Reinsch, May 31, 1919, *FRUS, 1919, Russia*, 371–72.

16. Phillips to Morris, June 30, 1919, encl. President's Statement, *FRUS, 1919, Russia*, 388; Polk to Morris, July 11, 1919, *FRUS, 1919, Russia*, 390.

17. Morris to Acting Secretary of State, July 22, 1919, *FRUS, 1919, Russia*, 394, 395, 396.

18. Morris to Secretary of State, July 24, 1919, *FRUS, 1919, Russia*, 396–98.

19. Lansing to Baker, July 25, 1919, *FRUS, 1919, Russia*, 398; Lansing to Consul General at Irkutsk (Harris), temporarily at Omsk, for Morris, July 26, 1919, *FRUS, 1919, Russia*, 398, 399.

20. Lansing, Desk Diary, July 26, 1919, Lansing Papers, box 65, LC; Kerr to Prime Minister, July 31, 1919, F/89/3/15, Lloyd George Papers, BL. (Kerr was referring to Morris's report of July 17th, *PWW*, vol. 61, 571–73.) Lansing, Private

Memo, July 31, 1919, Lansing Papers, box 67, LC. See also Tompkins, *American-Russian Relations in the Far East*, who considered it an American necessity to stop the Japanese drive for empire in the Far East.

21. Graves to N. Baker, June 21, 1919, encl. in N. Baker to Wilson, July 31, 1919, *PWW,* vol. 62, 82–90, quotes from 86, 87.

22. Ibid., 88.

23. Ibid., 89; Knox to Graves, August 27, 1919, Graves Papers, box 1, Hoover Institute (hereafter HI).

24. WW to Baker, August 2, 1919, *PWW,* vol. 62, 116.

25. Morris to Secretary of State, July 27, 1919, *FRUS, 1919, Russia,* 399–400.

26. Morris to the Secretary of State, July 27, 1919, *FRUS, 1919, Russia,* 567–68. The Railway Commission under Stevens served some fifty days in 1917. The Russian Railway Service Corps was under Colonel George Emerson, consisted of about three hundred officers and mechanics, and served on and off through 1919. An Inter-Allied Railway Committee was formed on January 9, 1919, with the stipulation that a Russian be the chair of it. However, it had a number of specialized agencies under it, most important of which was the Technical Board, whose president was John Stevens. He in reality carried out the administration of the whole railway enterprise. The guarding of the rails was much more complex. For the full story, see White, *The Siberian Intervention,* especially 145–60.

27. Morris to the Secretary of State, July 30, 1919, *FRUS, 1919, Russia,* 294.

28. Ibid., 293–94.

29. Morris to the Secretary of State, July 31, 1919, *FRUS, 1919, Russia,* 401, 402; Morris to the Secretary of State, July 31, 1919, *FRUS, 1919, Russia,* 269.

30. Morris to the Secretary of State, August 4, 1919, *FRUS, 1919, Russia,* 403.

31. Ibid., quote from 404.

32. Ibid., 404, 405.

33. Morris to the Secretary of State, August 8, 1919, *FRUS, 1919, Russia,* 407, 408. An interesting characterization of the Siberian situation can be found in "The Interview on Kolchak and Denikin with Vilenski (Sibiriakov) and Narimanov—a Siberian and a Caucasian," in mid-August 1919. These men were probably Socialist Revolutionaries or pro-Bolshevik. Both were anti-White and anti-Allies. Vilenski talks about military failures of Kolchak, the anti-Kolchak insurgency in Siberia, the fact that Kolchak's army was composed to a large extent of the officers of the old army, and the remainder being peasants who would bolt at the first opportunity. Vilenski also characterized the military situation in Siberia from the point of view of the disposition of counterrevolutionary intervention forces. Narimanov spoke about the disappointment of the British in Georgia and Azerbaijan. See f. 5, op. 1, d. 2229, l. 1–2, RTsKhIDNI.

34. Long, Memo, August 1, 1919, Long Papers, box 182, LC; Baker to WW, July 31, 1919, encl. Graves to Agwar, June 21, 1919, *PWW,* vol. 62, 85–86. Iosef Loris-Melikov reported for Kolchak in early October 1919 about his six-week visit in the United States and noted that the sentiment of the politicians he had met with, the press, and the public were definitely in favor of Omsk. He noted dissatisfaction with Wilson's Russian policy. Nevertheless, reports by Morris definitely had shaken America's confidence in Kolchak. See Loris-Melikov's telegram, October 7, 1919, f. 39499, op. 1, d. 130, l. 3, Russian State Military Archive (hereafter RGVA). Bakhmetev also wrote about his efforts to move U.S. policy toward providing military aid to Kolchak. Interestingly, he notes that his efforts ran into fierce opposition from Baker under the excuse that such aid would not be legally

justifiable. See Bakhmetev to Minister of Foreign Affairs, August 4, 1919, f. 5805, d. 555, l. 31, GARF. Bakhmetev also noted that the State Department had confidentially told him that American policy was to support the Omsk government against Bolshevism. Check Bakhmetev to Minister of Foreign Affairs, October 4, 1919, f. 5805, d. 555, l. 31, GARF.

35. Lansing to WW, August 7, 1919, Lansing Papers, box 2, NJP; Lansing, Desk Diary, August 7, 1919, *PWW*, vol. 62, 202; Lansing to WW, August 21, 1919, WP, LC.

36. WW to Lansing, August 21, 1919, *PWW*, vol. 62, 441.

37. Poole to Lansing, August 21, 1919, *PWW*, vol. 62, 441, 444, 445; Morris to the Secretary of State, August 11, 1919, *FRUS, 1919, Russia*, 409–10.

38. Morris to the Secretary of State, August 12, 1919, *FRUS, 1919, Russia*, 411, 412.

39. Commission to Negotiate Peace to the Acting Secretary of State, July 21, 1919, *FRUS, 1919, Russia*, 289, where Clemenceau's telegram is quoted. The Secretary of State to the Commission to Negotiate Peace, August 8, 1919, *FRUS, 1919, Russia*, 295; The Secretary of State to the Consul General at Irkutsk (Harris), temporarily at Omsk, for Morris, August 12, 1919, *FRUS, 1919, Russia*, 412–13.

40. Morris to the Secretary of State, September 23, 1919, *FRUS, 1919, Russia*, 433–34; Morris to the Secretary of State, October 11, 1919, *FRUS, 1919, Russia*, 440–41. Russian disappointment with the American effort was powerful, often extremely critical. For instance, see S. D. Merkulov to Ieremiia Gregorevich [?], late fall 1918, f. 129, op. 3, p. 2.a., d. 10, l. 1, 3–5, AVPRF, who charged that the U.S. contingent consisted of Jews and socialists sympathizing with the Bolsheviks and that they corrupted the morale of Russian military units, spread venereal disease, and provided a refuge for Bolshevik activists. On the other hand, he was ecstatic about the Japanese. These themes were echoed in Captain Semënov's report, April 1, 1919, f. 39507, op. 1, d. 50, l.5–12, RGVA, and he added that the railway repair plant in Vladivostok provided a shelter for Bolshevik sympathizers. One critic accused American soldiers for having fought with the Soviets. See the report of an anonymous colonel, f. 39515, op. 1, d. 197a, l. 4, RGVA. In a report by Lt. General Dutov to Kolchak, he complains that Americans did nothing but harm. See Dutov to Kolchak, n.d., f. 39515, op. 1, d. 191, l. 82, RGVA. Ughet, chargé in Washington, cabled Sukine, Kolchak's foreign minister, that the fault lay with America's lack of understanding and Wilson's oscillation. See Ughet to Sukine, April 1, 1919, f. 200, d. 538, No. 290, l. 4–5, GARF. A diplomatic official in the Far East expressed similar opinions. See Klemm to Sukine, March 25, 1919, f. 200, d. 538, No. 582, l. 6, GARF.

41. Kansas City Address, September 6, 1919, *PWW*, vol. 63, 70, 73; Des Moines Coliseum Address, September 6, 1919, *PWW*, vol. 63, 77; Grayson, Diary, September 8 and 10, 1919, *PWW*, vol. 63, 95, 152; Minneapolis Armory Address, *PWW*, vol. 63, 134; St. Paul Auditorium Address, September 9, 1919, *PWW*, vol. 63, 145; Billings Auditorium Address, September 11, 1919, *PWW*, vol. 63, 174–75; Coeur d'Alene Address, September 12, 1919, *PWW*, vol. 63, 216; Seattle Arena Address, September 13, 1919, *PWW*, vol. 63, 263.

42. Heckscher, *Wilson*, 607; Walworth, *Wilson*, vol. 2, 366; Farnsworth, *Bullitt*, 67; for Lansing's analysis, see Robert Lansing, *The Peace Negotiations: A Personal Narrative*, chap. 19, "The Bullitt Affair," where Lansing accused Bullitt of distortion. Bullitt is quoted in Farnsworth, *Bullitt*, 61, see also 62–63. Wilson is quoted by Walworth, *Wilson*, vol. 2, 366–67.

43. Lansing to WW, September 17, 1919, *PWW,* vol. 63, 337, 338–40*n1–4,* quote from p. 340.

44. San Francisco Luncheon Address, September 18, 1919, *PWW,* vol. 63, 349; Phillips to WW, September 19, 1919, *PWW,* vol. 63, 394–95; Carter Glass to WW, September 25, 1919, *PWW,* vol. 63, 518 and note 1; WW to Phillips, September 20, 1919, *PWW,* vol. 63, 421.

45. Long to Bakhmetev, September 2, 1919, Long Papers, box 41, LC; Lansing to Amembassy, Tokyo, September 3, 1919, Morris Papers, box 4, LC; Long, Memo, September 4, 1919, Long Papers, box 182, LC. Sazonov pointed out to Bakhmetev that the sudden change in the attitude of the United States with respect to assistance to Siberia had produced a most depressing effect. Withdrawal, according to him, would be perceived as yielding to Japan and would be prejudicial to America's prestige and authority in the eyes of Russians. Sazonov was probably reacting to the same note that brought Bakhmetev to Long's office. See Sazonov to Bakhmetev, September 11, 1919, f. 170, op. 512/4, d. 115, l. 292, AVPRI.

46. Note on Situation in Russia. Military Section, September 5, 1919, F/202/1/7, Lloyd George Papers, BL; Conversation with Mr. Phillips, September 8, 1919, Lansing Papers, vol. 49, LC.

47. War Cabinet Meeting no. 622, September 18, 1919, PRO; House to WW, September 20, 1919, WP, LC; War Cabinet Meeting no. 628, October 7, 1919, PRO. Yet simultaneously, Bakhmetev and Ughet implied to Omsk that the State Department pursued the goal of supporting Kolchak. See Bakhmetev and Ughet to the Minister of Foreign Affairs, Omsk, October 4, 1919, f. 5805, d. 555, No. 1021, l. 31, GARF. At the same time, Bakhmetev asked the United States to allow the Japanese mandate. See Bakhmetev to the Minister of Foreign Affairs, Omsk, October 10, 1919, f. 5805, d. 555, No. 1047, l. 38, GARF. In a second telegram of that same date he criticized the "timidity" of the State Department for allowing a Japanese mandate. Bakhmetev to Minister of Foreign Affairs, Omsk, October 10, 1919, f. 5805, d. 555, No. 1048, l. 39, GARF. And on October 21, 1919, he complained that Wilson's illness immobilized U.S. policy. See Bakhmetev to the Minister of Foreign Affairs, Omsk, October 21, 1919, f. 5805, d. 555, No. 1031, l. 51, GARF. Lloyd George to Churchill, October 10, 1919, F/9/1/31, Lloyd George Papers, BL.

48. British Cabinet Meeting, November 4, December 15, 1919, PRO.

49. Long, Diary, September 24, 1919, Long Papers, box 2, LC; Graves to Agwar, September 26, 1919, WD, RG407, (AGOffice) Central Decimal File, box 1380, NA; Agwar to Graves, September 26, 1919, no. 385, WD, RG407, Cable Section, box 144, NA.

50. Phillips to WW, September 27, 1919, WP, LC; Long, Diary, September 30, 1919, Long Papers, box 2, LC; Lansing, Desk Diary, September 30, 1919, Lansing Papers, box 65, LC.

51. Lansing to Polk, October 1, 1919, *PWW,* vol. 63, 539; Lansing, Memorandum, February 9, 1920, *PWW,* vol. 64, 385; Lansing to WW, February 9, 1920, *PWW,* vol. 64, 388, 389; WW to Lansing, February 11, 1920, *PWW,* vol. 64, 404; Lansing to WW, February 12, 1920, *PWW,* vol. 64, 408–10.

52. Lansing, Memorandum, February 13, 1920, *PWW,* vol. 64, 416; see also House, Diary, February 18, 1920, *PWW,* vol. 64, 444–45; WW to Polk, February 24, 1920, *PWW,* vol. 64, 464; House, Diary, March 2, 1920, *PWW,* vol. 65, 41.

53. Graves to Agwar, October 7, 1919, no. 493, WD, RG407, Cable Section, box 142, NA; N. Baker to Grayson, October 9, 1919, N. Baker Papers, box 9,

LC; Lansing, Desk Diary, October 9, 1919, Lansing Papers, box 65, LC; Agwar to Graves, October 14, 1919, no. 408, WD, RG407, Cable Section, box 142, NA.

54. Lansing, Private Memo, October 9, 1919, Lansing Papers, box 67, LC; Lansing, Desk Diary, October 27, 1919, Lansing Papers, box 65, LC; Julius Barnes to Lansing, Memorandum to be Read to the President, October 22, 1919, WP, LC; Tumulty to Lansing, October 28, 1919, and Lansing to Tumulty, October 25, 1919, WP, LC.

55. Arthur Bullard to Morris, November 26, 1919, Morris Papers, box 2, LC; N. Baker to Bliss, November 1, 1919, N. Baker Papers, box 9, LC; Lansing, Private Memo, November 30, 1919, Lansing Papers, box 67, LC.

56. Long, Conversation with Russian Ambassador, December 2 and 9, 1919, Long Papers, box 182, LC.

57. Lansing to WW, December 4, 1919, WP, LC; Lansing to Amembassy, Tokyo, December 5, 1919, Morris Papers, box 4, LC, reporting to Morris on Polk's conversation with Lloyd George of November 24, 1919. Nevertheless, Bakhmetev complained that the United States simply played a waiting game. See Bakhmetev to the Minister of Foreign Affairs, Omsk, December 11, 1919, f. 5805, d. 555, No. 1275, l. 74, GARF. Yet on December 20, 1919, Bakhmetev felt U.S. policy was principled in contrast to Lloyd George's policy. See Bakhmetev to the Minister of Foreign Affairs, Omsk, December 20, 1919, f. 5805, d. 555, No. 1298, l. 80, GARF.

58. Long, Diary, December 22 and 27, 1919, Long Papers, box 2, LC; Lansing, Desk Diary, December 22 and 24, 1919, Lansing Papers, box 65, LC. As to Polk's request, see Lansing, Desk Diary, December 29, 1919, Lansing Papers, box 65, LC. March to Graves, December 29, 1919, WD, RG407, Cable Section, box 142, NA.

59. Graves to Agwar, January 21, 1920, no. 663, WD, RG407, Cable Section, box 142, NA; R. L. Eichelberger, Intelligence Report, no. 4, WD, RG395, AEF in Siberia, Historical Files, box 11, NA; N. Baker to Acting Secretary of State, February 19, 1920, WD, RG407 (AG Office), Central Decimal Files, box 1381, NA.

60. Daniels to WW, June 11, 1920, WP, LC.

61. Aide-Mémoire by Russian Embassy, March 1, 1920, Long Papers, box 182, LC; N. Baker to Senator James A. Reed, February 1, 1921, WD, RG165, Chief of Staff, 1917–1921, box 173, NA.

62. Report of Operations, July 1, 1919, to March 31, 1920, WD, RG395, AEF in Siberia, Historical Files, box 13, NA; Baker to Graves, August 31, 1920, N. Baker Papers, box 12, LC.

63. Lansing to Kennan, February 2, 1920, Kennan Papers, box 4, LC.

64. Report of General T. H. Bliss on the Supreme War Council, February 6, 1920, WD, RG120 (AEF), American Section, Supreme War Council, NA.

65. Morris to Colonel William J. Donovan, February 6, 1920, Morris Papers, box 3, LC.

66. J. Van MacMurray to Morris, February 7, 1920, Morris Papers, box 3, LC.

67. Geddes to Prime Minister, June 8, 1920, Curzon Papers, box F, Geddes Folder, India Office. For a guide to the Red Scare, see Peter H. Buckingham, *America Sees Red: Anti-Communism in America, 1870s to 1980s: A Guide to Issues and References;* see especially 186–89. Geddes to Colby, June 9, 1920, Bainbridge Colby Papers, box 3A, LC; see also John Spargo, *Russia as an American Problem.*

68. Colby to Gompers, June 12, 1920, Colby Papers, box 3A, LC.

69. Hoover, *Ordeal of Woodrow Wilson,* 150.

70. Colby to WW, with encl., August 9, 1920, *PWW,* vol. 66, 20.

71. Ibid., 20–21.

72. Ibid., 22.

73. Ibid., 22–23. The anti-Bolsheviks reacted warmly to the Colby Note. The statement of the Paris group of the Russian Constitutional Democratic Party (Kadet) embraced wholeheartedly "the wise principles of statesmanship" expressed in the Colby Note, especially "the repudiation of the tyrannical domination of the Bolsheviks" and the "equally strong denunciation of the dismemberment of Russia." See P. Miliukov to the Russian Embassy to be transmitted to the Secretary of State, September 16, 1920, f. 170, op. 512/4, d. 195, l. 185, AVPRI. See also "America and Russia," an editorial published in Prague by a group of leaders of the Socialist Revolutionary Party in which the writer praised the "position assumed by the U.S. in the Russian problem." See "America and Russia," 1920, f. 170, op. 512/4, d. 195, l. 204–5, AVPRI. For samples of Soviet and pro-Bolshevik reaction to the Colby Note, see "Draft Report on Relations with the United States," 1920, where it stated that the condition of those relations did not yield itself easily to analysis. It emphasized the morbid hostility toward Soviet Russia expressed by the Colby Note and manifested in such facts as the American government's indirect assistance to the Whites and Poland. On the other hand, the report noted the drive by American business circles to establish commercial relations with Soviet Russia. It expected the Republicans, the party of big business, to be more cooperative. See "Draft Report on Relations with the United States," f. 129, op. 4, papka [folder] 3, d. 6, l. 18–19, AVPRF.

74. On the blockade, see Lansing to WW, August 1, 1919, *PWW,* vol. 62, 108, and encl. to Ammission, 108–10; on trade, see Colby to WW, with encl., June 11, 1920, *PWW,* vol. 65, 389–90; Norman Davis to WW, June 23, 1920, *PWW,* vol. 65, 445; Davis to WW, June 24, 1920, *PWW,* vol. 65, 455–56. Bakhmetev wrote that the recent events had not changed the American government's attitude toward the Soviets, which, according to him, remained intensely negative. America was by no means leaning toward a policy of the kind proposed by Lloyd George of normalizing relations with the Bolsheviks. Military failures and political instability had made America doubt the viability of the Omsk government. Yet certain industrial circles were pressing for lifting the trade embargo against the Bolsheviks. This last fact was interesting because there were references that toward the end of 1919 certain powerful business groups in the United States started to push for normalizing trade relations with the Reds; for instance, the Vanderlip syndicate's mission in 1920 was the culmination of that effort. See Bakhmetev to the Minister of Foreign Affairs, Omsk, December 11, 1919, f. 5805, d. 555, l. 74, GARF. David W. McFadden in an interesting article, "After the Colby Note: The Wilson Administration and the Bolsheviks, 1920–21," shows that Russian relations continued to trouble the last months of the Wilson administration, however clear-cut the Colby Note appeared. Then there was the question of thirty American prisoners in Russia and pro-Bolshevik Russians in the United States who wanted to return. There were informal talks, but direct contacts were avoided. Russian submarines in the Baltic ran close to the U.S. flagship, *Pittsburgh,* food and relief ideas continued, but only the Quakers continued their work until Hoover's program during the Harding administration. Finally, Litvinov carried out unofficial talks from Copenhagen with American businessmen Leo Hertz, Max Rabinoff, and John J. O'Brien. It should also be mentioned that Ludvig C. A. K. Martens, a German engineer, had been appointed the diplomatic and commercial agent of the Soviet government in

January 1919. His assistant, Santeri Nuroteva, headed Martens's Soviet Russian Information Bureau in New York. They issued a weekly, *Soviet Russia*, and handed out contracts, for instance, to Emerson P. Jennings, president of the Lehigh Machine Company, amounting to $4.5 million. Nevertheless, Martens's credentials were rejected and his affairs investigated. Secretary of Labor William B. Wilson recommended that Martens be taken into custody and deported. On January 22, 1921, Martens canceled all orders and left the United States voluntarily. See Joan Hoff Wilson, *Ideology and Economics: U.S. Relations with the Soviet Union, 1918–1933*, 52–55.

Conclusions. 1921: The First Cold War

1. For a brief discussion of this period, see Eugene P. Trani and David L. Wilson, *The Presidency of Warren G. Harding*, 1–2, 5–28, 53–54, 116–136, 177; for details on trade, see Wilson, *Ideology and Economics*. For Churchill, check his *The World Crisis*, vol. 3, 234. For an excellent article on Wilson's formidable moral and intellectual prestige, see Robert W. Tucker, "An Inner Circle of One: Woodrow Wilson and His Advisors."

2. WW, A Draft of an Essay, *PWW*, vol. 68, 323; for the published essay, see *PWW*, vol. 68, 393–95.

3. Heckscher, *Wilson*, 667.

4. See Peter Filene, *Americans and the Soviet Experiment, 1917–1933*.

5. For the quote, see William R. Keylor, "Post-mortems on the American Century;" also check Frank Ninkovich, *The Wilsonian Century: U.S. Foreign Policy since 1900* and Tony Smith, *America's Mission: The United States and the Worldwide Struggle for Democracy in the Twentieth Century*.

6. Paul Johnson, *Modern Times: The World from the Twenties to the Nineties*, 432.

7. Kennan's disdain for what we call the "inside" game is nicely stated in chap. 11, "The Long Telegram" in his *Memoirs, 1925–1950*, especially 283–84, 287–88, 290–97. For a contemporary commentary, see Johnson, *Modern Times*, chap. 13, "Peace by Terror," particularly 432–34.

8. Kennan, *Memoirs*, 560–65. One should also read Clark Clifford, "American Relations with the Soviet Union: A Report to the President by the Special Counsel to the President," September 24, 1946, Truman Papers, Naval Aide file, Harry S. Truman Library, Independence, Missouri, quotes from iv, 1, 9. A very good essay on the making of the "Clifford Report" is Carol Ann Briley, "George Elsey's White House Career, 1942–1953."

9. Kennan later agreed with Lippmann that containment was political, not military. He also agreed that certain sectors had to be defended and not carte blanche around the Soviet Union's entire periphery. See Kennan, *Memoirs*, 359–61, 547–59.

10. Kennan, "The Sources of Soviet Conduct," in his book, *American Diplomacy, 1900–1950*, 91, 93, 99, 104.

11. Walter Lippmann, *The Cold War: A Study in U.S. Foreign Policy*, 36.

12. Kennan, "Sources of Soviet Conduct," 90–95, 104.

13. See Dean Acheson, *Present at the Creation: My Years in the State Department*, particularly chap. 25 and pt. 3. For the quote, check Walter Isaacson and Evan Thomas, *The Wise Men: Six Friends and the World They Made*, 435.

14. See Foglesong, *America's Secret War*, 92–103 on money schemes, and 104–26 on the spy activities of Xenophon Kalamatiano. Furthermore, as Foglesong points

out, "[Adolf A.] Berle, [DeWitt Clinton] Poole, [William J.] Donovan, and the Dulles brothers [John Foster, Allen W.], Cold Warriors whose careers extended back to the Wilson administration, included Norman Armour, Christian Herter, and William C. Bullitt" (321).

15. For a succinct discussion of Wilson's "idealism," see John Milton Cooper, Jr., *Breaking the Heart of the World: Woodrow Wilson and the Fight for the League of Nations*, 410–11, esp. note 64. Thomas J. Knock sensitively compares "Kennan versus Wilson" in his article of that title in John Milton Cooper, Jr., and Charles E. Neu, eds., *The Wilsonian Era: Essays in Honor of Arthur S. Link*, 302–26. Knock noted that Wilson was not an impractical idealist (303), and that he "was not unmindful or heedless of the practical uses to which the concept of the balance of power could be put . . ." (312). This, Knock maintained, "served as Kennan's point of departure" for advocating realism (312). Kennan added a rejoinder: "Comments on the paper entitled 'Kennan versus Wilson' by Professor Thomas J. Knock" (327–30) and wrote: "I have to correct or modify, at this stage of my own life, many of the impressions I had about him [Wilson] at an earlier stage" (330). Likewise, Senator Daniel Patrick Moynihan quizzed Kennan in 1989 at a hearing of the Committee on Foreign Relations, where Kennan said much the same thing. See Daniel Patrick Moynihan, *On the Law of Nations*, 151.

16. Two recent articles suggest the same contention: Walter L. Hixson, "Cold War Evolution and Interpretations," in Alexander DeConde et al., eds., *Encyclopedia of American Foreign Policy*, vol. 1, 207–22, where he writes, "Ideology is a central element in coming to grips with the Cold War. In this respect, the Cold War actually began in 1917, with the triumph of the Bolshevik communist revolutionaries in Russia" (207). Similarly, Anders Stephanson in his article, "Cold War Origins," in that same volume, 223–39, posits a similar possibility, though he goes on to disagree with it: "If the Cold War is coeval with the entire relationship and simply rooted in systemic difference, then, for one thing, it would seem natural to locate the beginning in the Bolshevik Revolution. This is a coherent position but," he adds, "immediately puts into question how one is to characterize the alliance during the Second World War" (223).

An Essay on Notes and Sources

1. There were earlier studies such as those by Leonid Strakhovsky, Foster Rhea Dulles, and Thomas Bailey, but Williams set the lines of argument; see Williams, *American-Russian Relations, 1781–1947*, Kennan, *Russia Leaves the War; The Decision to Intervene,* and *Russia and the West Under Lenin and Stalin;* Unterberger, *America's Siberian Expedition, 1918–1920: A Study of National Policy, American Intervention in the Russian Civil War,* and *The United States, Revolutionary Russia, and the Rise of Czechoslovakia;* Thompson, *Russia, Bolshevism, and the Versailles Peace;* Link et al., eds., *The Papers of Woodrow Wilson.* The opening of some Russian archives has been useful, but not as revealing as anticipated because the Presidential Archive remains closed.

2. In a provocative study, John Lewis Gaddis notes that "The events of 1917–18 created a *symbolic* basis for conflict between communism and capitalism by setting the self-proclaimed objectives of the United States and Soviet Russia against one another in the most fundamental way. But this clash of ideas brought few *actual* conflicts over the next quarter-century. International rivalries aligned themselves less than one might have anticipated along the ideological polarities Wilson and

Lenin had left behind" (italics by Gaddis). See his *We Now Know: Rethinking Cold War History*, 6. On this clash of ideologies, also see Georg Schild, *Between Ideology and Realpolitik: Woodrow Wilson and the Russian Revolution, 1917–1921*, 5. In two earlier Cold War studies, D. F. Fleming, *The Cold War and Its Origins* and John Lukacs, *A New History of the Cold War*, each author indirectly alluded to an earlier Russo-American relationship fraught with difficulties. Especially, Fleming raises the problem of the Red Scare of 1919–1920. In our view, it was a parallel to the McCarthyism of the 1950s (38–41). Lukacs singles out national self-determination as the "chief Wilsonian idea" as an explanation, in our opinion, of Wilson's anti-interventionist stance (24).

Peter H. Buckingham in his book, *America Sees Red: Anticommunism in America, 1870s to 1980s* calls the 1950–1954 period the "Second Red Scare" (chaps. 2 and 3). As to our use of "quarantine," there are other applications, such as the Stimson Doctrine, that could also fall under that umbrella. We use this term in the sense of a passively aggressive posture; that is, Colby never intended using force to prevent others from relationships with Soviet Russia. His was purely a moral example. For a discussion of "quarantine," as FDR used the term, see Ninkovich, *The Wilsonian Century*, 122–23.

3. Kennan, *American Diplomacy, 1900–1950*, 82–83: "I see the most serious fault of our past policy formulation to lie in something that I might call the legalistic-moralistic approach to international problems. This approach runs like a red skein through our foreign policy of the last fifty years. It has in it something of the old emphasis on arbitration treaties, something of the Hague Conferences and schemes for universal disarmament, something of the more ambitious American concepts of the role of international law, something of the League of Nations and the United Nations, something of the Kellogg Pact, something of the idea of a universal 'Article 51' past, something of the belief in World Law and World Government." David Mayers has Kennan as a "short-lived Wilsonian," but acknowledges that although Kennan has long and correctly been called a realist, this is "despite his private discomfort with the label." See David Mayers, *George F. Kennan and the Dilemmas of U.S. Foreign Policy*, 23, 6. Walter L. Hixson points out that as late as 1958 Kennan used realism as a sound guide to diplomacy and "condemned the type of idealism that had led President Woodrow Wilson to embrace the illusion that democracy might triumph in authoritarian Russia." Check his book, *George F. Kennan: Cold War Iconoclast*, 196. John Lewis Gaddis takes a more centrist position by arguing that for Kennan a balance of power politics was not "inconsistent with moral principles." See John Lewis Gaddis, *Strategies of Containment: A Critical Appraisal of Postwar American National Security Policy*, 342.

4. Kennan, *Russia and the West under Lenin and Stalin*, 397, 388–89.

5. Woodrow Wilson, A Draft of an Essay, *PWW*, vol. 68, 323; for the published essay, see *PWW*, vol. 68, 393–95; Williams, *American-Russian Relations*, 283. McFadden rightly points out that "A striking feature of this diplomacy on the American side is the habitual absence, except at certain points, of the guiding hand of President Woodrow Wilson or Secretary of State Robert Lansing" (9). McFadden goes on to call Wilson's Russian policy laconic and spasmodic, never definitive (9). This was certainly true until the Colby Note for Wilson and "left the door open for a variety of experimental interactions," which McFadden exhaustively examines. See David W. McFadden, *Alternative Paths: Soviets and Americans, 1917–1920*. For reassessments of Williams, see an interesting roundtable discussion of him with the relevant articles: Justus D. Doenecke, "William Appleman Williams

and the Anti-Interventionist Tradition," Patricia Nelson Limerick, "Dilemmas in Forgiveness: William Appleman Williams and Western American History," Paul Buhle, "Williams for 2000: A Comment," and "What Is Still Living in the Ideas and Example of William Appleman Williams? A Comment."

6. Williams, 107. For the "X" article, see Kennan, "Sources of Soviet Conduct." See also notes 14 and 15 of the Conclusions.

7. Unterberger, "Woodrow Wilson and the Bolsheviks: The 'Acid Test' of Soviet-American Relations," 71.

8. At one end of the spectrum, Victor M. Fic, *The Collapse of American Policy in Russia and Siberia, 1918: Wilson's Decision Not to Intervene (March–October, 1918)*, maintains that Wilson was against intervention for anti-Bolshevik purposes and that this decision was a great mistake. On the other end of the spectrum, Foglesong, *America's Secret War*, argues that Wilson carried on a "secret" war against Bolshevism and took the initiative in covert actions. For more on this, see Unterberger, "Wilson vs. Bolshevism." For Foglesong's spirited defense, see "The SHAFR [Society for Historians of American Foreign Relations] Newsletter." Schild reaches a similar conclusion about Wilson's fence-leaning, which he terms contradictory or alternating between an "outright condemnation of Bolshevism and an acknowledgement of the validity of certain Soviet complaints" (4). Later, he remarks, "The Wilson who agreed to the Allied intervention in the summer of 1918 and the Wilson who sought to maintain Russian territorial unity one year later at the Paris Peace Conference almost seem like two different people" (130). Schild, in his book *Between Ideology and Realpolitik*, attributes this ambivalence to Wilson's oscillation between ideology and realpolitik. He also touches on a Wilsonian version of containment when he says, "As the best way to *contain* [italics ours] Bolshevism, Wilson recommended that the Western democratic states should eradicate its causes" (4).

9. M. I. Stishov, *Razgrom Triokh Pokhodov Antanty; Pobeda Sovetskoi Vlasti na Natsionalnikh Okrainakh i na Dal'nem Vostoke.*

10. S. F. Naida, *Sovetskaia Istoriografiia Grazhdanskoi Voiny i Inostrannoi i Voennoi Interventsii v SSSR.*

11. L. M. Spirin, *Razgrom Armii Kolchaka;* M. I. Gubelman, *Bor'ba za Sovetskii Dal'nii Vostok;* V. V. Tarasov, *Bor'ba s Interventami v Severnoi Rossii (1918–1929);* G. V. Kuz'min, *Grazhdanskaia Voina i Interventsiia v SSSR: Voenno-Politicheskii Ocherk.*

12. A. Stefankov, *Kommunisticheskaia Partiia — Organizator Razgroma Ob'edinennogo Pokhoda Antanty.*

13. V. M. Ustinov and L. I. Zharov, *Internatsional'nye Chasti Krasnoi Armii v Boiakh za Vlast' Sovetov v Gody Inostrannoi Voennoi Interventsii i Grazhdanskoi Voiny v SSSR.*

14. O. L. Stepanova, "Protiv Falsifikatsii Uchastiia SShA v Antisovetskoi Interventsii," in *Prepodavanie Istorii v Shkole;* A. D. Skaba, *Parizhskaia Mirnaia Konferentsiia i Inostrannaia Interventsiia v Strane Sovetov, Ianvar' - Iun' 1919 Goda.*

15. V. P. Naumov, *Letopis' Geroicheskoi Bor'by: Sovetskaia Istoriografiia Grazhdanskoi Voiny i Imperialisticheskoi Interventsii v SSSR (1917–1920).* (Please refer to John M. Thompson, "Lenin's Analysis of Intervention.")

16. N. N. Azovtsev et al., *Krakh Pervogo Nashestviia Imperialistov na Stranu Sovetov* (Moscow, 1973) and his monograph, *Grazhdanskaia Voina v SSSR.*

17. P. Sh. Ganelin, *Sovetsko-Amerikanskie Otnosheniia v Kontse 1917- Nachale 1918g.*

18. G. B. Kuz'min, *Razgrom Interventov i Belogvardeitsev v 1917–1922gg.*

19. S. G. Livshits, *Imperialisticheskaia Interventsiia v Sibiri v 1918–1920gg.*

20. N. I. Lebedev, *SSSR v Mirovoi Politike 1917–1980* (Moscow, 1980); I. I. Mints,

God 1918; M. I. Svetachev, *Imperialisticheskaia Interventsiia v Sibiri i na Dal'nem Vostoke (1918–1922gg).*

21. For important recent discussions of the uses of Russian archives, see "Symposium: Soviet Archives: Recent Revelations and Cold War Historiography," in *Diplomatic History* 21, no. 2 (spring 1997): 215–305. The articles especially related to the discussion above are Jonathan Haslam, "Russian Archival Revelations and Our Understanding of the Cold War," 217–28; Raymond L. Garthoff, "Some Observations on Using the Soviet Archives," 243–57; and Odd Arne Westad, "Secrets of the Second World: The Russian Archives and the Reinterpretation of the Cold War History," 259–71. Also, see the provocative article by Steven Merritt Miner, "Revelations, Secrets, Gossip and Lies: Sifting Warily through the Soviet Archives," as well as Todd Bennett, " 'My Mission to Moscow': Researching Soviet Propaganda in the Russian Archives."

Bibliography

Manuscripts

London and Oxford:

Beaverbrook Library, London (BL)
      David Lloyd George Papers
      Andrew Bonar Law Papers
Bodleian Library, Oxford (BLO)
      Herbert H. Asquith Papers
      Alfred Milner Papers
British Museum, London (BM)
      Lord Robert Cecil Papers
      Arthur Balfour Papers
India Office
      George Curzon Papers
Public Record Office, London (PRO)
      Cabinet Office, Foreign Office, and War Office Papers
      Eric Drummond Papers
      Lord Reading Papers
      Cecil Spring Rice Papers

Moscow:

Archive of the Foreign Policy of the Russian Empire (AVPRI)
Archive of the Ministry of the Foreign Policy of the Russian Federation (AVPRF)
Archive of the Russian Center for the Preservation and Study of the Documents of Contemporary History (RTsKhIDNI)
Russian State Military Archive (RGVA)
State Archive of the Russian Federation (GARF)

291

Washington:

Library of Congress (LC)
>   Newton D. Baker Papers
>   Ray Stannard Baker Papers
>   Tasker Howard Bliss Papers
>   William Jennings Bryan Papers
>   Albert S. Burleson Papers
>   Bainbridge Colby Papers
>   George Creel Papers
>   Josephus Daniels Papers
>   Hermann Hagedorn/W. B. Thompson Papers
>   George Kennan Papers
>   Robert Lansing Papers
>   Breckinridge Long Papers
>   John Bassett Moore Papers
>   Roland S. Morris Papers
>   Elihu Root Papers
>   Hugh Scott Papers
>   Oscar Straus Papers
>   Joseph P. Tumulty Papers
>   Stanley Washburn Papers
>   Woodrow Wilson Papers (see also Princeton)

National Archives (NA)
>   Record Group 59: General Records of the Department of State
>   Record Group 63: Records of the Committee on Public Information
>   Record Group 84: Records of the Foreign Service Posts of the Department of State
>   Record Group 94: Records of the Adjutant General's Office
>   Record Group 120: Records of the American Expeditionary Forces (World War I), 1917–1923—American Section, Supreme War Council
>   Record Group 151: Records of the Bureau of Foreign and Domestic Commerce
>   Record Group 165: Records of the War Department General and Specific Staffs
>   Record Group 182: Records of the War Trade Board
>   Record Group 256: Records of the American Commission to Negotiate Peace
>   Record Group 261: Records of the Former Russian Agencies—Russian Consulates in the U.S. and Canada and the Russian Sup-

ply Committee, and its Successor, the Division of Supplies of the Russian Embassy

Record Group 345: U.S. Army Overseas Operations and Commands, 1894–1942, AEF (American Expeditionary Force) in Siberia

Record Group 395: Records of U.S. Army Overseas Operations and Commands, 1898–1942, AEF in Siberia, Historical Files

Record Group 407: Adjutant General Office (War Department Cable Section)

Central Decimal Files

Russian Decimal Files: 861.00 Series

War Department Cable Section: Box 144

Microfilms of the National Archives: M-316, Records of the Department of State Relating to Internal Affairs of Russia and the Soviet Union, 1910–1929; M-333, Records of the Department of State Relating to Political Relations between the United States and Russia and the Soviet Union, 1910–1929; M-340, Records of the Department of State Relating to Political Relations between Russia and the Soviet Union and Other States, 1910–1929; and M-367, Records of the Department of State Relating to World War I and Its Termination, 1914–1929, all portions of Record Group 59; and M-820, General Records of the American Commission to Negotiate Peace, 1918–1931, from Record Group 256.

Archives of the American National Red Cross

Other:

American Jewish Archives, Hebrew Union College, Cincinnati
    Jacob H. Schiff Papers
Columbia University (CU)
    Charles Crane Papers
    DeWitt Clinton Poole Transcript (Oral History Research Office)
    Allen Wardwell Papers, Russian and East European Archive
Franklin Delano Roosevelt Library
    Thomas W. Brahany Papers
Harry S. Truman Library, Independence, Mo.
    Harry S. Truman Papers
Harvard Library (HL)
    William Phillips Papers
Hoover Institute and Library, Stanford University, Stanford (HI)
    General William S. Graves Papers

Massachusetts Historical Society (MHS)
    Curtis Guild Papers
Missouri Historical Society, St. Louis (MOSHI)
    David R. Francis Papers
Newberry Library (NL)
    William V. Judson Papers
Princeton University (NJP)
    Arthur Bullard Papers
    Raymond B. Fosdick Papers
    Robert Lansing Papers
    Woodrow Wilson Papers (as collected by Arthur S. Link)
Regenstein Library of the University of Chicago
    Samuel N. Harper Papers
State Historical Society of Wisconsin, Madison (WSHS)
    Alexander Gumberg Papers
    DeWitt C. Poole Papers
    Raymond Robins Papers
    Alexander Gumberg Papers
Yale University, New Haven (CtY)
    Gordon Auchincloss Papers
    William C. Bullitt Papers, Microfilm
    Edward M. House Papers
    Vance McCormick Papers
    Frank L. Polk Papers
    Sir William Wiseman Papers

Printed Public Documents

Great Britain:

War Office. *The Evacuation of North Russia, 1919.* London, 1919.

Russia:

Anglo-Sovetskie Otnoshenia, 1917–1927. Noty i Dokumenty (Anglo-Soviet Relations, 1917–1927. Notes and Documents). Moscow, 1927.
Dekrety Sovetskoi Vlasti (Decrees of the Soviet Power). 13 vols. Moscow, 1957–1989.
Grazhdanskaia Voina v Sibiri i Severnoi Oblasti (The Civil War in Siberia and the Northern Provinces). Moscow-Leningrad, 1927.

Gromyko, Andrei A. ed. *Dokumenty vneshnei politiki* (Documents of Foreign Policy). Vols. 1–5. Moscow, 1957–1961.

Mints, I. I. *Interventsiia na Severe-v Dokumentakh* (Intervention in the North-in Documents). Moscow, 1933.

Sovetsko-Amerikanskie Otnoshenia, 1919–1933. Sbornik Dokumentov (Soviet-American Relations, 1919–1933. A Collection of Documents). Moscow, 1934.

United States:

Bolshevik Propaganda, Hearings before a Subcommittee of the Committee on the Judiciary, United States Senate, 65th Cong., 3d sess. and thereafter Pursuant to S.Res. 439 and 469. Washington: Government Printing Press, 1919.

Congressional Record, 62d Cong., 2d sess., 1911. Washington: Government Printing Press, 1911.

The German-Bolshevik Conspiracy, War Information Series, No. 20-October, 1918 (Committee on Public Information, George Creel, Chairman). Washington: Government Printing Press, 1918.

Department of State. *Papers Relating to the Foreign Relations of the United States, 1911.* Washington: Government Printing Press, 1918.

———. *Papers Relating to the Foreign Relations of the United States, 1914, Supplement, The World War.* Washington: Government Printing Press, 1928.

———. *Papers Relating to the Foreign Relations of the United States, 1915, Supplement, The World War.* Washington: Government Printing Press, 1928.

———. *Papers Relating to the Foreign Relations of the United States, 1916, Supplement, The World War.* Washington: Government Printing Press, 1929.

———. *Papers Relating to the Foreign Relations of the United States, The Lansing Papers, 1914–1920.* 2 vols. Washington: Government Printing Press, 1939–1940.

———. *Papers Relating to the Foreign Relations of the United States, 1918, Russia.* 3 vols. Washington: Government Printing Press, 1931, 1932.

———. *Papers Relating to the Foreign Relations of the United States, 1919, Russia.* Washington: Government Printing Press, 1937.

Kesaris, Paul. ed., *Confidential U.S. Diplomatic Post Records, Part I, Russia, 1914–1918.* Frederick, Md.: Microfilm project of University Publications of America, 1982.

Link, Arthur S. et al., eds. *The Papers of Woodrow Wilson.* 69 vols. Princeton, N.J.: Princeton University Press, 1966–1993.

Malloy, William M. *Treaties, Conventions, International Acts, Protocols and Agreements between the United States of America and Other Powers.* 4 vols. Washington: Government Printing Office, 1910–1938.

Proceedings of the Brest-Litovsk Peace Conference: The Peace Negotiations between Russia and the Central Powers, 21 November, 1917–3 March, 1918. Washington: Government Printing Office, 1918.

Report of the Librarian of Congress and Report of the Superintendent of the Library Building and Grounds for the Fiscal Year Ending June 30, 1905. Washington: Government Printing Office, 1905.

United States, Army War College, Historical Section. *Order of Battle of the United States Land Forces in the World War, American Expeditionary Forces.* Vol. 1, *General Headquarters, Armies, Army Corps, Services of Supply and Separate Forces.* Washington: Government Printing Press, 1937.

United States Bureau of the Census. *Historical Statistics of the United States from Colonial Times to the Present.* New York: Basic Books, Inc., 1976.

Newspapers

Boston Globe
Boston Herald
Commercial Bulletin
London Times
New York Herald
New York Times
New York Town Topics
Washington Post

Articles, Books, Dissertations, Theses, and Typescripts

Acheson, Dean. *Present at the Creation: My Years in the State Department.* New York: W. W. Norton and Company, 1969.

Adler, Cyrus. *Jacob H. Schiff: His Life and Letters.* 2 vols. Garden City, N.Y.: Doubleday, Doran and Co., 1928.

Ambrosius, Lloyd E. *Woodrow Wilson and the American Diplomatic Tradition: The Treaty Fight in Perspective.* Cambridge: Cambridge University Press, 1987.

The American Jewish Yearbook: 5665. Philadelphia: Jewish Publication Society of America, 1904.

The American Jewish Yearbook: 5672. Philadelphia: Jewish Publication Society of America, 1911.

The American-Russian Chamber of Commerce. *The Russian Market: Its Possibilities and Problems.* New York: n.p., n.d.

Anderson, Paul B. *No East or West.* Edited by Donald E. Davis. Paris: YMCA Press, 1985.

Azovtsev, N. N., et al. *Krakh Pervogo Nashestviia Imperialistov na Stranu Sovetov* (The Failure of the First Invasion of the Imperialists in the Country of the Soviets). Moscow, 1980.

Babey, Anna. *Americans in Russia, 1776–1917: A Study of the American Travellers in Russia from the American Revolution to the Russian Revolution.* New York: Comet Press, 1938.

Baedecker, Karl. *Russia with Teheran, Port Arthur, and Peking: A Handbook for Travellers.* Leipzig: Karl Baedeker, 1914. Reprt., New York: Arno Press, 1971.

Bailey, Thomas A. *America Faces Russia: Russian-American Relations from Early Times to Our Own Day.* Ithaca, N.Y.: Cornell University Press, 1950.

Baker, Ray Stannard. *Woodrow Wilson, Life and Letters,* 8 vols. Vol. 7, *War Leader, April 6, 1917–February 28, 1918.* New York: Doubleday, Doran and Co., Inc., 1939.

———, and William E. Dodd, eds. *The Public Papers of Woodrow Wilson: War and Peace.* 2 vols. New York: Harper and Bros., 1927.

Bennett, Todd. " 'My Mission to Moscow': Researching Soviet Propaganda in Russian Archives." *SHAFR Newsletter* (December 2000): 16–30.

Berman, Myron. "The Attitude of American Jewry towards East European Jewish Immigration, 1881–1914." Ph.D. diss., Columbia University, 1963.

Boiarskii, V. A. *Vtorzhenie Imperialistov SShA v Sovetskuiu Rossiiu i Ego Proval* (The Invasion of Imperialist U.S.A. into Soviet Russia and Its Collapse). Moscow, 1961.

Botkine, Pierre. "A Voice for Russia." *Century* 45, n.s. 13 (February 1893): 611–15.

Briley, Carol Ann. "George Elsey's White House Career, 1942–1953." Master's thesis, University of Missouri, Kansas City, 1976.

Browder, Robert P., and Alexander F. Kerensky, eds. *The Russian Provisional Government, 1917: Documents.* 3 vols. Stanford, Calif.: Stanford University Press, 1961.

Bryant, Louise. *Six Red Months in Russia.* New York: George H. Doran Co., 1918.

Buchanan, George. *My Mission to Russia and Other Diplomatic Memories.* 2 vols. Boston: Little, Brown and Company, 1923.

Buckingham, Peter H., ed. *America Sees Red: Anti-Communism in America, 1870s to 1980s: A Guide to Issues and References*. Claremont, Calif.: Regina Books, 1988.

Buhle, Paul. "Williams for 2000: A Comment." *Diplomatic History* 25, no. 2 (spring 2001): 301–8.

Bunyan, James, and H. H. Fisher. *The Bolshevik Revolution, 1917–1918: Documents and Materials*. Stanford, Calif.: Stanford University Press, 1934.

Burnham, John C. "The Progressive Era Revolution in American Attitudes toward Sex." *Journal of American History* 59 (March 1973): 885–908.

Byrnes, Robert F. *Awakening American Education to the World: The Role of Archibald Cary Coolidge, 1866–1928*. Notre Dame, Ind.: University of Notre Dame Press, 1982.

Campbell, Craig W. *Reel America and World War I: A Comprehensive Filmography and History of Motion Pictures in the United States, 1914–1920*. Jefferson, N.C.: McFarland and Company, 1985.

Carley, Michael J. "The Origins of French Intervention in the Russian Civil War, January to May 1918: A Reappraisal." *Journal of Modern History* 48 (September 1976): 413–39.

———. *Revolution and Intervention: The French Intervention and the Russian Civil War, 1917–1919*. Kingston, Ontario: McGill-Queen's University Press, 1983.

Churchill, Winston S. *The World Crisis*. Vol. 3. New York: Charles Scribner's Sons, 1927.

Clifford, Clark. "American Relations with the Soviet Union: A Report to the President by the Special Counsel to the President." September 24, 1946.

Cockfield, Jamie H., ed. *Dollars and Diplomacy: Ambassador David Rowland Francis and the Fall of Tsarism, 1916–17*. Durham, N.C.: Duke University Press, 1981.

Cohen, Naomi W. "The Abrogation of the Russo-American Treaty of 1832." *Jewish Social Studies* 25, no. 1 (January 1963): 3–41.

Coletta, Paolo E. *William Jennings Bryan: Political Evangelist, 1860–1908*. Lincoln: University of Nebraska Press, 1964.

———. *William Jennings Bryan: Progressive Politician and Moral Statesman, 1909–1915*. Lincoln: University of Nebraska Press, 1969.

Collier, John. "Film Shows and Lawmakers." *Survey* (February 8, 1913): 643.

Cooper, John Milton, Jr. *Breaking the Heart of the World: Woodrow Wilson and the Fight for the League of Nations*. Cambridge: Cambridge University Press, 2001.

Cowles, Virginia. *1913: An End and a Beginning.* New York: Harper and Row, 1967.

Creel, George. *How We Advertised America.* New York: Harper and Bros., 1920.

―――. *Rebel at Large: Recollections of Fifty Crowded Years.* New York: G. P. Putnam's Sons, 1947.

Cronon, E. David, ed. *The Cabinet Diaries of Josephus Daniels, 1913–1921.* Lincoln: University of Nebraska Press, 1963.

Cumming, C. K., and Walter W. Petit, eds. *Russian-American Relations, March, 1917–March, 1920: Documents and Papers.* New York: Harcourt, Brace and Howe, 1920.

Daniels, Josephus. *The Wilson Era: Years of War and After, 1917–1923.* Chapel Hill: University of North Carolina Press, 1946.

Davis, Donald E., and Eugene P. Trani. "The American YMCA and the Russian Revolution." *Slavic Review* 33, no. 3 (September 1974): 469–91.

―――. "An American in Russia: Russell M. Story and the Bolshevik Revolution, 1917–1919." *Historian* 36, no. 4 (August 1974): 704–21.

Davis, Jerome. *The Russian Immigrant.* New York: Macmillan Co., 1922.

Deborin, G. A. *Sovetskaia Vneshnaia Politika v Pervye Gody Sushchestvovaniia Sovetskogo Gosudarstva, 1917–1920gg* (Soviet Foreign Policy in the First Years of the Soviet State's Existence, 1917–1920). Moscow, 1951.

Deutscher, Isaac. *The Prophet Armed: Trotsky, 1879–1921.* Oxford: Oxford University Press, 1954.

Dillon, E. J. *The Eclipse of Russia.* New York: George H. Doran Co., 1918.

Doenecke, Justus D. "William Appleman Williams and the Anti-Interventionist Tradition." *Diplomatic History* 25, no. 2 (spring 2001): 283–91.

Dudley, William, ed. *The Cold War: Opposing Viewpoints.* San Diego: Greenhaven Press, 1992.

Dulles, Foster Rhea. *The Road to Teheran: The Story of Russia and America, 1781–1943.* Princeton, N.J.: Princeton University Press, 1944.

Farnsworth, Beatrice. *William C. Bullitt and the Soviet Union.* Bloomington: Indiana University Press, 1967.

Ferrell, Robert H. *Woodrow Wilson and World War I, 1917–1921.* New York: Harper and Row, 1985.

Fic, Victor M. *The Collapse of American Policy in Russia and Siberia, 1918: Wilson's Decision Not to Intervene (March–October, 1918).* New York: Columbia University Press, 1995.

Figes, Orlando. *A People's Tragedy: The Russian Revolution, 1891–1924.* New York: Viking, 1997.

Fike, Claude E. "The Influence of the Creel Committee and the American Red Cross on Russian-American Relations, 1917–1919." *Journal of Modern History* 31, no. 2 (June 1959): 93–109.

Filene, Peter. *Americans and the Soviet Experiment, 1917–1933.* Cambridge, Mass.: Harvard University Press, 1967.

Fischer, Louis. *The Soviets in World Affairs.* 2 vols. London: Jonathan Cape, 1930.

Fleming, D. F. *The Cold War and Its Origins.* Garden City, N.Y.: Doubleday and Company, Inc., 1961.

Foglesong, David S. *America's Secret War against Bolshevism: U.S. Intervention in the Russian Civil War, 1917–1920.* Chapel Hill: University of North Carolina Press, 1995.

———. "Reply." *SHAFR Newsletter* (March 1997): 27–30.

Fowler, Wilton. *British-American Relations, 1917–1918: The Role of Sir William Wiseman.* Princeton, N.J.: Princeton University Press, 1969.

Francis, David R. *Russia from the American Embassy: April, 1916–November, 1918.* New York: Charles Scribner's Sons, 1921.

Gaddis, John Lewis. *Strategies of Containment: A Critical Appraisal of Postwar American National Security Policy.* New York: Oxford University Press, 1982.

———. *We Now Know: Rethinking Cold War History.* Oxford: Clarendon Press, 1997.

Ganelin, P. *Sovetsko-Amerikanskie Otnosheniia v Kontse 1917-Nachale 1918g* (Soviet-American Relations at the End of 1917–Beginning of 1918). Leningrad, 1975.

Gardner, Lloyd C. *Safe for Democracy: The Anglo-American Response to Revolution, 1913–1923.* New York: Oxford University Press, 1984.

———. *Wilson and Revolutions: 1913–1921.* Philadelphia: J. B. Lippincott Company, 1976.

Garthoff, Raymond L. "Some Observations on Using the Soviet Archives." *Diplomatic History* 21, no. 2 (spring 1997): 243–57.

Gelfand, Lawrence. *The Inquiry: American Preparations for Peace, 1917–1919.* New Haven, Conn.: Yale University Press, 1963.

George, Alexander L., and Juliette L. George. *Woodrow Wilson and Colonel House: A Personality Study.* New York: Dover Publications, Inc., 1956.

Gershov, Z. *Vudro Vil'son* (Woodrow Wilson). Moscow, 1983.

Girshfeld, A. "O Roli SShA v Organizatsii Anti-Sovetskoi Interventsii v Sibiri i na Dal'nem Vostoke" (About the Role of the USA in the Organization of Anti-Soviet Intervention in Siberia and in the Far East). *Voprosy Istorii* (Questions of History) 4, no. 8 (August 1948): 3–32.

Goldenweizer, Alexis A. "Legal Status of Jews in Russia." In Jacob Frumkin et al., eds., *Russian Jewry (1860–1917)*. New York: T. Yoseloff, 1966.

Golder, Frank A., ed. *Documents on Russian History, 1914–1917.* Reprt., Gloucester, Mass., 1964.

Gompers, Samuel. *Seventy Years of Life and Labor: An Autobiography.* New York: E. P. Dutton, 1925.

Graves, William S. *America's Siberian Adventure.* New York: Jonathan Cape and Harrison Smith, 1931. Reissued by Arno Press and the New York Times, 1971.

Grimsted, Patricia K. *Archives and Manuscript Repositories in the USSR: Moscow and Leningrad.* Princeton, N.J.: Princeton University Press, 1972.

Gromyko, A., ed. *Dokumenty Vneshnei Politiki SSSR* (Documents of the Foreign Policy of the USSR). 5 vols. Moscow, 1957–1961.

———, and B. Ponomarëva, eds. *Istoriia Vneshnei Politiki SSSR 1917–1945* (A History of the Foreign Policy of the USSR, 1917–1945). Vol. 1. Moscow, 1980.

Gubelman, M. I. *Bor'ba za Sovetskii Dal'nii Vostok* (The Struggle for the Soviet Far East). Moscow, 1958.

Guild, Curtis. "Russia and Her Emperor." *Yale Review* n.s. 4, no. 4 (July 1915): 712–22.

Guirand, Albert. "German Capital in Russia." *Twentieth Century Russia and Anglo-Russian Review* 1, no. 1 (September 1915): 39–51.

Gvishiani, L. A. *Sovetskaia Rossiia i SShA* (Soviet Russia and the United States). Moscow, 1970.

Hagedorn, Herman. *The Magnate: William Boyce Thompson and His Time, 1869–1930.* New York: John Day Co., 1935.

Hard, William. *Raymond Robins' Own Story.* New York: Harper and Bros., 1920.

Harper, Paul V., ed. *The Russia I Believe In: The Memoirs of Samuel N. Harper, 1902–1941.* Chicago: University of Chicago Press, 1945.

Hart, Robert D., and Arthur W. Thompson. *The Uncertain Tradition: America and the Revolution of 1905.* Amherst: University of Massachusetts Press, 1970.

Hasegawa, Tsuyoshi. *The February Revolution: Petrograd, 1917.* Seattle: University of Washington Press, 1981.

Haslam, Jonathan. "Russian Archival Revelations and Our Understanding of the Cold War." *Diplomatic History* 21, no. 2 (spring 1997): 217–28.

Healy, Ann E. "Tsarist Anti-Semitism and Russian-American Relations." *Slavic Review* 42, no. 3 (fall 1983): 408–25.

Heckscher, August. *Woodrow Wilson.* New York: Charles Scribner's Sons, 1991.

Heller, Mikhail, and Aleksandr Nekrich. *Utopia in Power: The History of the Soviet Union from 1917 to the Present.* New York: Summit Books, 1982.

Hicks, Granville. *John Reed: The Making of a Revolutionary.* New York: Macmillan Co., 1936.

Hixson, Walter L. "Cold War Evolution and Interpretations." In Alexander DeConde et al., eds., *Encyclopedia of American Foreign Policy,* vol. 1, 207–22. New York: Charles Scribner's Sons, 2002.

———. *George F. Kennan: Cold War Iconoclast.* New York: Columbia University Press, 1989.

Hodge, Larry G. "American Diplomacy towards Transcaucasia during the Russian Revolution, March 1917–March 1918." *New Review: A Journal of East European History* 15, nos. 1–2 (1975): 20–38.

Hogan, John V. "Russian-American Commercial Relations." *Political Science Quarterly* 27, no. 4 (December 1912): 631–47.

Hoover, Herbert. *The Memoirs of Herbert Hoover: Years of Adventure, 1874–1920.* New York: Macmillan Company, 1951.

———. *The Ordeal of Woodrow Wilson.* New York: McGraw-Hill Book Company, Inc., 1958.

Howe, Frederic C. "What to Do with the Motion-Picture Show: Shall It Be Censored?" *Outlook* (June 20, 1914): 412–13.

Huntington-Wilson, F. M. *Memoirs of an Ex-Diplomat.* Boston: Bruce Humphries, Inc., 1945.

Isaacson, Walter, and Evan Thomas. *The Wise Men: Six Friends and the World They Made.* New York: Simon and Schuster, Touchstone Books, 1988.

Jessup, Philip C. *Elihu Root.* 2 vols. New York: Dodd, Mead and Co., 1938.

Johnson, Paul. *Modern Times: The World from the Twenties to the Nineties.* New York: Harper Perennial rev. ed., 1992.

Kallen, Horace. *Culture and Democracy in the United States: Studies in the Group Psychology of the American Peoples.* New York: Boni and Liveright, 1924.

Karp, Abraham J. *Haven and Home: A History of Jews in America.* New York: Schocken Books, 1985.

Kedrov, M. S. *Za Sovetskii Sever* (For the Soviet North). Leningrad, 1927.

———, ed. *Bez Bolshevistkogo Rukovodstva (iz Istorii Interventsii na Murmane); Ocherki* (Without Bolshevik Leadership [From the History of the Intervention in Murmansk]; A Survey). Leningrad, 1930.

Kennan, George. "Alliance with 'Russian Barbarism.' " *Outlook* (January 6, 1915): 26.

————. "The Attitude of the Russian People." *Outlook* 84 (October 6, 1906): 328–32.

————. "Russian Despotism." *Outlook* 85 (March 30, 1907): 753, 755.

————. "A Voice for the People of Russia." *Century* 46, no. 3 (July 1893): 461–71.

Kennan, George F. *American Diplomacy 1900–1950.* New York: Mentor Books, 1951.

————. "Comments on the Paper Entitled 'Kennan versus Wilson' by Professor Thomas J. Knock." In John Milton Cooper, Jr., and Charles E. Neu, eds., *The Wilsonian Era: Essays in Honor of Arthur S. Link,* 327–30. Arlington Heights, Ill.: Harlan Davidson, Inc., 1991.

————. *The Decision to Intervene.* Princeton, N.J.: Princeton University Press, 1958.

————. *Memoirs, 1925–1950.* Boston: Little, Brown and Company, 1967.

————. *Russia Leaves the War.* Princeton, N.J.: Princeton University Press, 1956.

————. *Russia and the West under Lenin and Stalin.* Boston: Little, Brown and Company, 1960.

————. "The Sisson Documents." *Journal of Modern History* 27, no. 2 (June 1956): 130–54.

————. "The Sources of Soviet Conduct." *Foreign Affairs* 25, no. 4 (July 1947): 566–82.

————. "Soviet Historiography and America's Role in the Intervention." *American Historical Review* 65, no. 2 (January 1960): 302–22.

Kennedy, Paul. *The Rise and Fall of the Great Powers: Economic Change and Military Conflict from 1500 to 2000.* New York: Random House, 1987.

Kerensky, Alexander F. *The Catastrophe: Kerensky's Own Story of the Russian Revolution.* New York: D. Appleton and Co., 1927.

Keylor, William R. "Post-mortems on the American Century." *Diplomatic History* 25, no. 2 (spring 2001): 317–27.

Killen, Linda. *The Russian Bureau: A Case Study in Wilsonian Diplomacy.* Lexington: University Press of Kentucky, 1983.

————. "The Search for a Democratic Russia: Bakhmeteff and the United States." *Diplomatic History* 2, no. 3 (summer 1978): 237–56.

Knock, Thomas J. "Kennan vs. Wilson." In John Milton Cooper, Jr., and Charles E. Neu, eds., *The Wilsonian Era: Essays in Honor of Arthur S. Link,* 302–26. Arlington Heights, Ill.: Harlan Davidson, Inc., 1991.

Knox, Alfred. *With the Russian Army 1914–1917: Being Chiefly Extracts from the Diary of a Military Attache.* London: Hutchinson and Co., 1921.

Kochan, Miriam. *The Last Days of Imperial Russia.* New York: Macmillan Publishing Co., 1976.

Kuklick, Bruce. "William Appleman Williams and His Interpreters." *Diplomatic History* 21, no. 4 (October 1996): 663–66.

Kunina, A. E. "K Kollokviumu Istorikov SSSR i SShA" ("To the Colloquium of Historians of the USSR and USA"). *Novaia i Noveishaia Istoriia* (The Recent and the Latest History) 1 (1985): 212–16.

———. *Proval Amerikanskikh Planov Zavoevaniia Mirovogo Gospodstva v 1917–1920gg* (Failure of the American Plans for World Domination, 1917–1920). Moscow: Gospolizdat, 1954.

Kuz'min, G. V. *Grazhdanskaia Voina i Voennaia Interventsiia v SSSR: Voenno-Politicheskii Ocherk* (The Civil War and Military Intervention in the USSR: A Military-Political Survey). Moscow, 1958.

———. *Razgrom Interventov i Belogvardeitsev v 1917–1920gg* (The Destruction of the Interventionists and White Guards). Moscow, 1977.

Lane, Anne W., and Louise H. Wall, eds. *The Letters of Franklin K. Lane.* Boston: Houghton Mifflin, 1922.

Lansing, Robert. *The Peace Negotiations: A Personal Narrative.* Boston: Houghton Mifflin Company, 1921.

———. *War Memoirs of Robert Lansing, Secretary of State.* New York: Bobbs-Merrill Co., 1935.

Lasch, Christopher. "American Intervention in Siberia: A Reinterpretation." *Political Science Quarterly* 77, no. 2 (June 1962): 205–23.

———. *The American Liberals and the Russian Revolution.* New York: Columbia University Press, 1962.

Lebedev, N. I. *SSSR v Mirovoi Politike 1917–1980* (The USSR in World Policy, 1917–1980). Moscow, 1980.

Leffler, Melvyn P. *The Specter of Communism: The United States and the Origins of the Cold War, 1917–1953.* New York: Hill and Wang, 1994.

Lenin, Vladimir I. *Polnoe Sobranie Sochinenii* (Complete Collected Works). 55 vols. 5th ed. Moscow: Gospolizdat, 1963.

Levidov, M. *K Istorii Soiuznoi Interventsii v Rossii* (To the History of the Allied Intervention in Russia). Leningrad, 1925.

Levin, N. Gordon. *Woodrow Wilson and World Politics: America's Response to War and Revolution.* New York: Oxford University Press, 1968.

Libbey, James K. *Alexander Gumberg and Soviet-American Relations, 1917–1933.* Lexington: University Press of Kentucky, 1977.

———. *American-Russian Economic Relations, 1770's-1990's: A Survey of Issues and Literature.* Claremont, Calif.: Regina Books, 1989.

Liddell Hart, B. H. *History of the First World War.* London: Pan Books Ltd., 1972.

Limerick, Patricia Nelson. "Dilemmas in Forgiveness: William Appleman

Williams and Western History." *Diplomatic History* 25, no. 2 (spring 2001): 293–300.

Lincoln, W. Bruce. *In War's Dark Shadow: The Russians before the Great War.* New York: Dial Press, 1983.

Link, Arthur S. *The Higher Realism of Woodrow Wilson and Other Essays.* Nashville: Vanderbilt University Press, 1971.

———. *Wilson: Campaigns for Progressivism and Peace, 1916–1917.* Princeton, N.J.: Princeton University Press, 1965.

———. *Wilson: The New Freedom.* Princeton, N.J.: Princeton University Press, 1956.

———. *Wilson: The Struggle for Neutrality, 1914–1915.* Princeton, N.J.: Princeton University Press, 1960.

———. *Woodrow Wilson and the Progressive Era, 1910–1917.* New York: Harper and Row, 1963.

Lippman, Walter. *The Cold War: A Study in U.S. Foreign Policy.* New York: Harper and Row, 1972.

Lipset, Seymour Martin, and Earl Raab. *The Politics of Unreason: Right-Wing Extremism in America 1790–1970.* New York: Harper and Row, 1970.

Livshits, S. G. *Imperialisticheskaia Interventsiia v Sibiri v 1918–1920gg* (The Imperialist Intervention in Siberia in 1918 to 1920). Barnaul, 1979.

Lockhart, R. H. Bruce. *British Agent.* New York: G. P. Putnam's Sons, 1933.

Long, John W. "American Intervention in Russia: The North Russia Expedition, 1918–1919." *Diplomatic History* 6, no. 1 (winter 1982): 45–67.

———. "Civil War and Intervention in North Russia, 1918–1920." Ph.D. diss., Columbia University, 1972.

Lowe, Karl H. "American Polar Bears Defense of Vladivostok." *Military History* (October 1997): 40.

Lukacs, John. *A New History of the Cold War.* Garden City, N.Y.: Anchor Books, 1966.

MacDonald, William. "American Ideals." *Nation* 106, 2743 (January 24, 1918): 85–87.

McFadden, David W. "After the Colby Note: The Wilson Administration and the Bolsheviks, 1920–21." *Presidential Studies Quarterly* 25, no. 4 (fall 1995): 741–50.

———. *Alternative Paths: Soviets and Americans, 1917–1920.* New York: Oxford University Press, 1993.

McKeever, William A. "The Moving Picture: A Primary School for Criminals." *Good Housekeeping* (August 11, 1910): 184.

McKinzie, Richard D., and Eugene P. Trani. "The Influence of Russian Émigrés on American Policy toward Russia and the USSR, 1900–

1933, with Observations on Analogous Developments in Great Britain." *Coexistence: A Review of East-West and Development Issues* 28, no. 2 (June 1991): 215–51.

Marye, George Thomas. *From '49 to '83 in California and Nevada.* San Francisco: A. M. Robertson, 1923.

———. *Nearing the End in Imperial Russia.* Philadelphia: Dorrance and Co., 1929.

Masaryk, Thomas G. *The Making of a State: Memories and Observations, 1914–1918.* Philadelphia: Frederick A. Stokes Company, 1927.

Mayer, Arno J. *Wilson vs. Russia: Political Origins of the New Diplomacy, 1917–1918.* New York: World Publishing Company, 1964.

Mayers, David. *George F. Kennan and the Dilemmas of U.S. Foreign Policy.* New York: Oxford University Press, 1988.

Melton, Carol Willcox. *Between War and Peace: Woodrow Wilson and the American Expeditionary Force in Siberia, 1918–1921.* Macon, Ga.: Mercer University Press, 2001.

Miliukov, Paul. *Political Memoirs, 1905–1917.* Ann Arbor: University of Michigan Press, 1967.

Miner, Stephen Merritt. "Revelations, Secrets, Gossip and Lies: Sifting Warily through the Soviet Archives." *New York Times Book Review,* May 14, 1995.

Mints, I. I. *Angliiskaia Interventsiia i Severnaia Kontrrevoliutsia* (English Intervention and Northern Counterrevolution). Moscow, 1931.

———. *God 1918* (The Year 1918). Moscow, 1982.

———, comp. *Iaponskaia Interventsiia v 1918–1922gg v Dokumentakh* (Japanese Intervention in 1918–1920 in Documents). Moscow, 1934.

———, ed. *Interventsiia na Severe v Dokumentakh* (Intervention in the North in Documents). Moscow, 1933.

Morley, James William. *The Japanese Thrust into Siberia, 1918.* New York: Columbia University Press, 1957.

Moynihan, Daniel Patrick. *On the Law of Nations.* Cambridge: Harvard University Press, 1990.

Naida, S. F. *O Nekotorykh Voprosakh Istorii Grazhdanskoi Voiny v SSSR* (On Certain Questions of the Civil War in the USSR). Moscow, 1958.

———. *Sovetskaia Istoriografiia Grazhdanskoi Voiny i Inostrannoi i Voennoi Interventsii v SSSR* (Soviet Historiography of the Civil War and Foreign Military Intervention in the USSR). Moscow, 1966.

Naumov, V. P. *Letopis' Geroicheskoi Bor'by: Sovetskaia Istoriografiia Grazhdanskoi Voiny i Imperialisticheskoi Interventsii v SSSR (1917–1920)* (A Chronicle of the Heroic Struggle: Soviet Historiography of the Civil War and Imperialist Intervention in the USSR [1917–1920]). Moscow, 1972.

Newbolt, Henry. *History of the Great War Based on Official Documents by Direction of the Historical Section of the Committee of Imperial Defence, Naval Operations.* London: Longmans, 1931.

Ninkovich, Frank. *The Wilsonian Century: U.S. Foreign Policy since 1900.* Chicago: University of Chicago Press, 1999.

Notter, Harley. *The Origins of the Foreign Policy of Woodrow Wilson.* Baltimore: Johns Hopkins Press, 1937.

Owen, Gail L. "Dollar Diplomacy in Default: The Economics of Russian-American Relations, 1910–1917." *Historical Journal* 13, no. 2 (1970): 251–72.

Paléologue, Maurice. *An Ambassador's Memoirs.* 3 vols. New York: George H. Doran Company, 1925.

Parry, Albert. "Charles R. Crane, Friend of Russia." *Russian Review* 6, no. 2 (spring 1947): 20–36.

Peacock, N. *The Russian Almanac 1919.* London: Eyre and Spottiswoode, Ltd., n.d.

Pershing, John J. *My Experiences in the World War.* 2 vols. Philadelphia: Frederick A. Stokes Company, 1931.

Pidhainy, Oleh S., Loventrice A. Scales, and Alexander S. Pidhainy. "Silver and Billions: American Finances and the Bolshevik Revolution." *New Review: A Journal of East European History* 14 (1974): 1–47.

Pipes, Richard. *The Russian Revolution.* New York: Alfred A. Knopf, 1990.

Pokrovsky, M. N. *Vneshniaia Politika Rossii v XX Veke* (The Foreign Policy of Russia in the 20th Century). Moscow, 1926.

Poole, DeWitt Clinton. *The Reminiscences of DeWitt Clinton Poole.* Oral History Typescript, Columbia University, 1952.

"President Wilson: His Inauguration, Cabinet, and Problems." *Outlook* (March 15, 1913): 553–58.

Rabinowitch, Alexander. *The Bolsheviks Come to Power: The Revolution of 1917 in Petrograd.* New York: W. W. Norton and Company, 1976.

Radziwill, Ekaterina. *Behind the Veil at the Russian Court.* New York: John Lane Co., 1914.

Reed, John. *Ten Days That Shook the World.* New York: Boni and Liveright, Inc., 1919.

Reikhberg, G. *K Istorii Interventsii na Dal'nem Vostoke* (To the History of the Intervention in the Far East). Moscow, 1934.

Resek, Carl, ed. "Monsignor John Ryan Calls for a Living Wage." In *The Progressives.* Indianapolis: Bobbs-Merrill Company, Inc., 1967.

Reznikoff, Charles, ed. *Louis Marshall Champion of Liberty: Selected Papers and Addresses.* Philadelphia: Jewish Publication Society of America, 1957.

Ribuffo, Leo P. "What Is Still Living in the Ideas and Example of William Appleman Williams?" *Diplomatic History* 25, no. 2 (spring 2001): 309–16.

Richard, Carl J. " 'The Shadow of a Plan': The Rationale behind Wilson's 1918 Siberian Intervention." *Historian* 59, no. 1 (November 1986): 64–84.

Robien, Louis de. *The Diary of a Diplomat in Russia.* New York: Praeger Publishers, 1970.

Root, Elihu, et al. *America's Message to the Russian People: Addresses by the Members of the Special Diplomatic Mission of the United States to Russia in the Year 1917.* Boston: Marshall Jones Company, 1918.

Salzman, Neil V. *Reform and Revolution: The Life and Times of Raymond Robins.* Kent, Ohio: Kent State University Press, 1991.

———, ed. *Russia in War and Revolution: General William V. Judson's Accounts from Petrograd, 1917–1918.* Kent, Ohio: Kent State University Press, 1998.

Sanders, Ronald. *Shores of Refuge: A Hundred Years of Jewish Emigration.* New York: Holt and Co., 1988.

Saul, Norman E. *Distant Friends: The United States and Russia, 1763–1867.* Lawrence: University Press of Kansas, 1991.

———. *Concord and Conflict: The United States and Russia, 1867–1914.* Lawrence: University Press of Kansas, 1996.

———. *War and Revolution: The United States and Russia, 1914–1921.* Lawrence: University Press of Kansas, 2001.

Schild, Georg. *Between Ideology and Realpolitik: Woodrow Wilson and the Russian Revolution, 1917–1921.* Westport, Conn.: Greenwood Press, 1995.

Seleznëv, G. K. "Ekspansiia Amerikanskogo Imperializma v Rossiu v 1917 godu" (The Expansion of American Imperialism in Russia in 1917). *Voprosy Istorii* (Questions of History) 10, no. 3, Moscow, 1954.

———. *Krakh Zagovora Agressii SShA Protiv Sovetskogo Gosudarstva v 1917–1920* (The Failure of the Conspiracy of Aggression of the USA against the Soviet State, 1917–1920). Moscow, 1963.

Sisson, Edgar. *One Hundred Red Days: A Chronicle of the Bolshevik Revolution.* New Haven, Conn.: Yale University Press, 1931.

Skaba, A. D. *Parizhskaia Mirnaia Konferentsiia i Inostrannaia Interventsiia v Strane Sovetov, Ianvar'-Iun' 1919 Goda* (The Paris Peace Conference and Foreign Intervention in the Country of the Soviets, January–June, 1919). Kiev, 1971.

Smith, Tony. *America's Mission: The United States and the Worldwide Struggle for Democracy in the Twentieth Century.* Princeton, N.J.: Princeton University Press, 1994.

Smith, Willard H. *The Social and Religious Thought of William Jennings Bryan.* Lawrence, Kans.: Coronado Press, 1975.

Spargo, John. *Russia as an American Problem.* New York: Harper and Bros., 1920.

Spirin, L. M. *Razgrom Armii Kolchaka* (The Destruction of Kolchak's Army). Moscow, 1957.

Stalin, J. *Kratkii Kurs* (The Short Course). Moscow, 1938.

Stefankov, A. *Kommunisticheskaia Partiia-Organizator Razgroma Ob'edinennogo Pokhoda Antanty* (The Communist Party-Organizer of the Destruction of the United Campaign of the Entente). Moscow, 1960.

Stepanova, O. L. "Protiv Falsifikatsii Uchastiia SShA v Antisovetskoi Interventsii" (Against the Falsification of US Participation in the Anti-Soviet Intervention). In *Prepodavanie Istorii v Shkole* (The Teaching of History in School). Moscow, 1971.

Stephanson, Anders. "Cold War Origins." In Alexander DeConde et al., eds., *Encylopedia of American Foreign Policy,* vol. 1, 223–39. New York: Charles Scribner's Sons, 2002.

Stishov, M. I. *Razgrom Triokh Pokhodov Antanty; Pobeda Sovetskoi Vlasti na Natsionalnikh Okrainakh i na Dal'nem Vostoke* (The Failure of the Three Campaigns of the Entente: The Victory of the Soviet Power in National Border Regions and in the Far East). Moscow, 1953.

Stone, Helena M. "Another Look at the Sisson Forgeries and Their Background." *Soviet Studies* 37, no. 1 (January 1985): 90–102.

Strakhovsky, Leonid I. *American Opinion about Russia, 1917–1920.* Toronto: University of Toronto Press, 1961.

———. "The Franco-British Plot to Dismember Russia." *Current History* (March 1931): 839–42.

———. *Intervention at Archangel: The Story of Allied Intervention and Russian Counter-Revolution in North Russia, 1918–1920.* Princeton, N.J.: Princeton University Press, 1944.

———. *The Origins of American Intervention in North Russia, 1918.* Princeton, N.J.: Princeton University Press, 1937.

Svetachev, M. I. *Imperialisticheskaia Interventsiia v Sibiri i na Dal'nem Vostoke (1918–1922gg)* (Imperialist Intervention in Siberia and in the Far East [1918–1922]). Novosibirsk, 1983.

Tarasov, V. V. *Bor'ba s Interventsiiami v Severnoi Rossii (1928–1920gg)* (The Struggle with the Interventionists in Northern Russia [1918–1920]). Moscow, 1958.

Terebov, O. V. "Partii i Politicheskiia Bor'ba v Kongresse SShA po Voprosam Amerikanskoi Interventsii v Sovetskoi Rossii (1918–1920)"

(Party and Political Struggle in the U.S. Congress on the Question of American Intervention Toward Soviet Russia [1918–1920]). Moscow, 1989. Avtoreferat kandidatskoi dissertatsii (abstract of the candidate's dissertation).

Thompson, John M. "Allied and American Intervention in Russia, 1918–1921." In C. Black, ed., *Rewriting Russian History.* New York: Vintage Press, 1962.

———. "Lenin's Analysis of Intervention." *American Slavic and East European Review* 17, no. 2 (April 1958): 151–60.

———. *Russia, Bolshevism, and the Versailles Peace.* Princeton, N.J.: Princeton University Press, 1966.

Tompkins, Pauline. *American-Russian Relations in the Far East.* New York: Macmillan Company, 1949.

Trani, Eugene P. "Herbert Hoover and the Russian Revolution, 1917–1920." In Lawrence E. Gelfand, ed., *Herbert Hoover, the Great War and its Aftermath, 1914–23.* Iowa City: University of Iowa Press, 1979, 113–42.

———. "Russia in 1905: The View from the American Embassy." *Review of Politics* 31 (1969): 48–65.

———. *The Treaty of Portsmouth: An Adventure in American Diplomacy.* Lexington: University of Kentucky Press, 1969.

———. "Woodrow Wilson and the Decision to Intervene in Russia: A Reconsideration." *Journal of Modern History* 48, no. 3 (September 1976): 440–61.

———, and David L. Wilson. *The Presidency of Warren G. Harding.* Lawrence: Regents Press of Kansas, 1977.

Trask, David. *The United States in the Supreme War Council: American War Aims and Inter-Allied Strategy, 1917–1918.* Middletown, Conn.: Wesleyan University Press, 1961.

Travis, Frederick F. *George Kennan and the American-Russian Relationship, 1865–1924.* Athens: Ohio University Press, 1990.

Tucker, Robert W. "An Inner Circle of One: Woodrow Wilson and His Advisors." *National Interest* 51 (spring 1998): 3–26.

Tumulty, Joseph. *Woodrow Wilson as I Know Him.* Garden City, N.Y.: Doubleday, Page and Co., 1921.

Tuve, Jeanette E. "Changing Directions in Russian-American Economic Relations, 1912–1917." *Slavic Review* 31, no. 1 (March 1972): 52–70.

Ullman, Richard H. *The Anglo-Soviet Accord.* Princeton, N.J.: Princeton University Press, 1972.

———. *Britain and the Russian Civil War: November 1918–February 1920.* Princeton, N.J.: Princeton University Press, 1968.

———. *Intervention and the War.* Princeton, N.J.: Princeton University Press, 1961.

Unterberger, Betty Miller. *America's Siberian Adventure, 1918–1920: A Study of National Policy.* Durham, N.C.: Duke University Press, 1956.

———. "President Wilson and the Decision to Send American Troops to Siberia." *Pacific Historical Review* 24, no. 1 (February 1953): 63–74.

———. "The Russian Revolution and Wilson's Far-Eastern Policy." *Russian Review* 16, no. 2 (April 1957): 35–46.

———. *The United States, Revolutionary Russia, and the Rise of Czechoslovakia.* Chapel Hill: University of North Carolina Press, 1989.

———. "Woodrow Wilson and the Bolsheviks: The 'Acid Test' of Soviet-American Relations." *Diplomatic History* 11, no. 2 (spring 1987): 71–90.

———, ed. *American Intervention in the Russian Civil War.* Lexington, Mass.: D.C. Heath and Company, 1969.

Ustinov, V. M., and L. I. Zharov. *Internatsional'nye Chasti Krasnoi Armii v Boiakh za Vlast' Sovetov v Gody Innostrannoi Voennoi Interventsii i Grazhdanskoi Voiny v SSSR* (International Units of the Red Army in the Battle for the Power of the Soviets in the Years of Foreign Military Intervention and Civil War in the USSR). Moscow, 1964.

Veltman, M. N. *Sovetskaia Rossiia i Kapitalisticheskaia Amerika* (Soviet Russia and Capitalist America). Moscow, 1922.

Viroubova, Anna. *Memories of the Russian Court.* New York: Macmillan Company, 1923.

Waldman, Morris D. *Not by Power.* New York: International Universities Press, 1953.

Walling, William E., ed. *The Socialists and the War: A Documentary Statement of the Position of the Socialists of All Countries; with Special Reference to Their Peace Policy.* New York: Henry Holt, 1915.

Walworth, Arthur. *Woodrow Wilson.* Baltimore: Penguin Books, Inc., 1969.

Wardwell, Allen. "American Red Cross Mission to Russia, 1917–1918." Excerpt from diary and letters, typescript, Columbia University, n.d.

Warth, Robert D. *The Allies and the Russian Revolution: From the Fall of the Monarchy to the Peace of Brest-Litovsk.* Durham, N.C.: Duke University Press, 1954.

West, Rachel. *The Department of State on the Eve of the First World War.* Athens: University of Georgia Press, 1978.

Westad, Odd Arne. "Secrets of the Second World: The Russian Archives and the Reinterpretation of Cold War History." *Diplomatic History* 21, no. 2 (spring 1997): 259–71.

Weyant, Jane Gilmer. "The Life and Career of General William V. Judson, 1865–1923." Ph.D. diss., Georgia State University, 1981.

Wheeler-Bennett, John W. *Brest-Litovsk: The Forgotten Peace, March 1918.* New York: St. Martin's Press, 1966.

White, John Albert. *The Siberian Intervention.* Princeton, N.J.: Princeton University Press, 1950.

Who's Who in America. Chicago: A. N. Marquis and Co., 1929.

Williams, William Appleman. "American Intervention in Russia, 1917–1920." *Studies on the Left* 3, no. 3 (fall 1963): 24–88 and 4, no. 1 (winter 1964): 39–57.

———. *American-Russian Relations, 1781–1947.* New York: Rinehart and Co., 1952.

———. "Raymond Robins and Russian-American Relations, 1917–1938." Ph.D. diss., University of Wisconsin, 1950.

Wilson, Joan Hoff. *Ideology and Economics: U.S. Relations with the Soviet Union, 1918–1933.* Columbia: University of Missouri Press, 1974.

Wilson, Woodrow. *College and State: Educational, Literary and Political Papers (1875–1913).* Edited by Ray Stannard Baker and William E. Dodd. New York: Harper and Brothers/Kraus Reprint Co., 1970.

———. *Congressional Government: A Study in American Politics.* Boston: Houghton Mifflin and Co., 1885.

———. *A History of the American People.* 10 vols. New York: Harper and Bros., 1918.

———. *When a Man Comes to Himself.* New York: Harper and Bros., 1901.

Wish, Harvey. "Getting Along with the Romanovs." *South Atlantic Quarterly* 48, no. 3 (July 1949): 341–59.

Wixman, Ronald. *The Peoples of the USSR: An Ethnographic Handbook.* Armonk, N.Y.: M. E. Sharpe, Inc., 1984.

Index

Acheson, Dean, 205
"Acid test" of Allied goodwill, 100, 107, 109, 110, 127, 261n26
Adee, Alvey A., 4
Agriculture: development of, 97, 235n10; and resources of Russia, 117, 120, 125
Aid, 247n40; for Alekseyev, 95; and Allied occupation of Murmansk, 129; British, 94, 123–24; history of U.S., 198–99; for Japanese intervention, 127, 147; for Kaledin, 94, 95–96, 110; military, 46, 167–68, 176; for Omsk government, 176, 177, 183–84, 186–87, 274n8, 278n1,, 280n34; to Provisional Government vs. Bolsheviks, 71–72; and Root Mission, 43, 48–49; for Russia to continue war, 41–42, 44–45, 47–48, 52, 56, 62–63, 90–91, 100, 102, 113; for Russian return to democracy, 174; U.S., 46, 51, 101, 243n57, 282n45; U.S. funneling through Allies to Kaledin, 93, 151; and U.S. Russian policy, 97–98, 111, 140–41, 246n33. See also Loans; Relief
Alaska, sale of, 3
Alderman, Edwin, 22
Alekseyev, M. V., 89, 95–96
All Russia Union of Cooperative Societies, 142–43
"Allied Intervention at Archangel and Murmansk" (Supreme War Council), 132
Allies, 100; aid from, 47, 52–53, 55, 186–87, 278n1, 279n11; conference in Paris (1916), 25, 26; development of policy toward Soviet government, 77, 82, 85–86; fear of Soviet expansion, 165, 275n39; interventions against Bolsheviks, 158, 162–65, 199; isolation of Soviet government, 85, 128, 151,

191–92, 209; and peace conference, 159–60; pressuring Russia to continue war, 84, 91, 112–13, 180; and Provisional Government, 108; relations with Soviet government, 83–84, 86–87, 134–35, 165, 167–68; response to Russian/German peace, 59, 70, 79–80, 106; and Russian civil war, 159, 163–64; Russian relations to, 63, 80; and Russia's internal affairs, 78–79, 82, 154, 163–64; Russia's requirements to stay in war, 49, 100; Soviet government's willingness to cooperate with, 169, 247n41; support for Czechs in Siberia, 144–45; support for Kaledin, 93, 94, 98–99; support for Kolchak, 170, 182, 184; support for Romanian army, 94; support of All Russia Union of Cooperative Societies for, 143; Trotsky exposing early treaties of, 106, 110; Trotsky's relations with, 68–69, 75–77, 91, 131–32; war aims, 78–80, 98, 99, 100–101, 105–6; and Whites, 85, 95–96, 166–67, 276n48; in WWI, 71–72, 78, 112; WWI in Russia, 54, 102, 104, 120, 128–29. See also Britain; Interventions, in Russia; Italy; Japan
Alurievsky, L., 26
Ambassadors: of Allies, 79; Guild as, 16–17; intervening for POWs, 21–22; Marye as, 23–24, 240n33; memoirs of U.S., 211–12; Russia to U.S., 97- 98, 180, 240n35, 243n59; selecting U.S. to Russia, 2–3, 17–18, 24, 238n7; U.S. and Russian, 237n23; U.S. to Russia, 10, 19, 21–22, 238n7, 268n44; U.S. to Soviet Union, 203; Wilson appointing, 13, 208
American Association of Manufacturers, 7

313